# REBUILDING URBAN PLACES
# AFTER DISASTER

THE CITY IN THE TWENTY-FIRST CENTURY

*Eugenie L. Birch and Susan M. Wachter, Series Editors*

Published in collaboration with the Penn Institute for Urban Research

# Rebuilding Urban Places After Disaster

## Lessons from Hurricane Katrina

Edited by Eugenie L. Birch
and Susan M. Wachter

**PENN**

UNIVERSITY OF PENNSYLVANIA PRESS

Philadelphia

10  9  8  7  6  5  4  3  2  1

Published by
University of Pennsylvania Press
Philadelphia, Pennsylvania 19104-4112

A Cataloging-in-Publication Record is available from the Library of Congress
ISBN-13: 978-0-8122-1980-7
ISBN-10: 0-8122-1980-5

# CONTENTS

# PREFACE: "THE WOUND"
Amy Gutmann

Hurricane Katrina was a wound.

"Wound" is a better word than "disaster," which connotes a purely natural occurrence. "Wound" makes room for human agency. And when a wound is inflicted by human beings, so too, are women and men left with the task of its healing—or, to borrow Abraham Lincoln's phrase, "to bind up our nation's wounds."

Hurricane Katrina was most obviously inflicted by nature, not by man. But was it solely a random, natural misfortune? Or were its effects also the product of human injustice? The Lisbon earthquake of 1755, as Judith Shklar has pointed out, was the first natural disaster after which such questions rose to the fore. At 9:20 A.M. on the morning of November 1, 1755, an earthquake, now believed to have equaled 9.0 on the Richter scale, struck the Portuguese capital. A devastating tsunami and fire followed. Some 90,000 people—a third of the city's population—are estimated to have perished. Eighty-five percent of Lisbon's buildings were destroyed. The catastrophe prompted intense debate and speculation in religious and intellectual circles across Europe. Was it a random act of nature? Was it a divine punishment? Or was the failure to plan for foreseeable tragedy a human crime?

"We shall find it difficult to discover," Voltaire famously declared, "how could the laws of movement operate in such fearful disasters *in the best of all possible worlds*." Surely, this could not be the work of a just, even if incomprehensible, God, Voltaire argued, but merely a random misfortune of impersonal nature. But it was Jean-Jacques Rousseau who recognized that if nature made the wound, it was human beings themselves who had held the knife. If the population had not been concentrated in such a small area and if the homes had not been built so many stories tall, the toll in physical and human loss would have been much less. The Lisbon disaster challenged both Catholic theology and Enlightenment rationalism, and in part through the early writings of Immanuel Kant, it spurred the earliest beginnings of a truly scientific seismology.

Now, in the twenty-first century, there is no doubt that Hurricane Katrina was not just a misfortune, but also an injustice. It was not purely a natural disaster, though it may appear so on its face. What if human beings had done the right thing in advance of Katrina? How dramatically different the outcome, and its aftermath, would have been! Of course, we mortals never completely do the right thing. But rarely have we so completely done the wrong thing.

All too often, we do the wrong thing because we ignore facts; we ignore knowledge that we actually have. The tragedy—more accurately, the injustice—of Katrina and similar wounds follows directly from the fact that *we know things* that could have made a difference. We know a great many things about urban spaces. We know much about environmental threats; about civil engineering; about city planning; about regional economic development and the management of risk; about Geographic Information Systems; about economic disparity, community formation, and racial inequality; about governmental and bureaucratic inefficiency—and how to make them more efficient; about supporting and restoring displaced populations; and about ameliorating the traumas of catastrophes.

None of this knowledge, even taken alone, is easy to acquire, master, or apply. But more difficult still is putting such disparate knowledge together into an integrated and comprehensive understanding of such a multifaceted event. Integrating our knowledge to comprehend how the many aspects of the problem work together is the challenge that complex problems like Katrina present. Fortunately, there is a base of empirical knowledge, theoretical understanding, and practical professional experience on which we can draw. So while knowledge is always a great challenge, it is not really our greatest challenge. Our greatest challenge, which we learned the hard way in Katrina, is the integration and dissemination of that knowledge—and most importantly, our willingness to engage it and to use it.

H. G. Wells put this well in his 1920 book, *The Outline of History*. "Human history," he wrote, "becomes more and more a race between education and catastrophe." The mission of education is to race as successfully as we can against catastrophe. The catastrophe catches up with us when education lags behind. "Education," here, means not only what we do in universities, which is extremely important. We also need to attend to the education of civic and political leaders, of legislators, of journalists, and of ordinary citizens in advance of, and in the wake of, catastrophes. Such civic education is equally important, and it is not primarily learned in the classroom. It is rather the kind of learning that can occur only in some kind of "meeting"—some kind of "convocation"—whether it is a meeting of the state legislature, the city council, the neighborhood association, the editorial board of a newspaper, the live conversations with "experts" on CNN and MSNBC, or the kind of conference that brings together scholars, professional practitioners, political leaders, and ordinary citizens, as did the conference on which this volume is based.

Only through this kind of mutual education can we learn from and with each other, integrate what we have learned from multiple sources, and communicate our collective knowledge and understanding so as to make our learning truly useful. Albert Einstein made a similar point, half a century ago, when he noted that "the unleashed power of the atom has changed every-thing—save our modes of *thinking*, and we thus drift toward unparalleled catastrophes." The major change in our modes of thinking that is needed today is learning from and with each other—and communicating that knowledge effectively—so no one at risk is ignored. We need the kind of learning that happens when people come together—despite all their differences of background, class, race, education, and circumstance—to deliberate about their common future. And we need that kind of deliberative learning, because otherwise many people are ignored. Before Katrina struck, we had the needed knowledge to avert catastrophe. What we lacked—out of neglect rather than incapacity—were the convocations, the meetings, the communications, the effective sharing of what we know that would have enabled us to put our knowledge into practice in anticipation of the event, instead of—if we are—only after the fact.

Katrina exemplifies the problem that knowledge in isolation creates—just as does a politics that is only about power and not about putting knowledge into power. To rectify this problem, we must, very self-consciously, deliberate together—deliberation not for its own sake, but for the sake of making better decisions, decisions reflective of broader understanding and respect for the lives and well-being of all the people affected. Such self-conscious and inclusive deliberation is essential if we are to confront success-fully the causes of catastrophes that are not simply natural, but which, in whole or in part, have a human cause—a human cause often not because of what human beings do, but because of what they fail to do.

Deliberation is not always pretty or easy. In fact, effective deliberation has a good deal of controversy built into it and can be really tough. But deliberation is always important as a means to more respectful and responsible decision-making. Deliberation is all the more valuable in this regard when the human consequences are so enormous and likely to shape our cities and regions for decades to come.

There is no true deliberation without decision and no decision without something practical to deliberate about. Otherwise there is just (often seem-ingly endless) discussion. Discussion is fine—we do it all the time. But true deliberation has an end in clear sight. Deliberation is part and parcel of decision-making at its best. Hurricane Katrina has left many difficult decisions in its wake, which call for deliberation: For whom are we rebuilding? How do we provide for the needs of all the people who were displaced by this catastrophe? How do we restore? *Can* we restore? To what extent do we need to create anew?

Rebuilding, surely, is not doing everything the same, re-creating the old New Orleans and Gulf Coast. There is no going back to what existed before Katrina. So, how do we restore or create anew a sense of community, culture, and home, where far too little now exists? Some people will determine whether and how to revitalize the unique arts and culture of New Orleans. Who should those decision-makers be? Analysts often turn to cost-benefit analysis to help them make complex decisions that measure trade-offs between quality of life, risks to life, and public and private costs of benefits. Is cost-benefit analysis adequate to this task? What civic principles and moral values can we agree upon to frame and push any such analysis forward?

These are some of the major questions posed by the hard tasks that confront our nation, now that the wound has been inflicted. Our society will certainly confront questions like these again and again in the future. We now have an opportunity to make a better future out of what has been one of the worst disasters and injustices of our time. This work that we have to do together, as a society, is only barely begun—not only the work of rebuilding, but also the work of collective deliberation. The present volume is intended both to reflect and advance that deliberation and to further our understanding of the difficult choices that we collectively will have to make.

As these essays demonstrate, the tasks of rebuilding are ones for which we as a society possess expert knowledge and wide-ranging experience. The tasks of rebuilding—a city, a culture, a region, even a nation—have been accomplished many times in human history, both recent and distant. Lisbon is a good example: after the earthquake, the army was quickly mobilized to prevent chaos, looting, and mass flight. Corpses were gathered and buried at sea to prevent disease. Within a year, the city was cleaned of debris and well along in its rebuilding. The government envisioned and planned a dramatically beautiful new city, with broad thoroughfares and avenues that are still evident today. Along these thoroughfares, the first structures ever built specifically to resist seismic events were designed, tested, and constructed. Massive reconstruction—now required for rebuilding New Orleans and the Gulf Coast in some yet to be determined fashion—has been accomplished repeatedly in human history, in the wake of devastating wars, natural disasters, plagues, and social, political and economic crises.

We in the nation's universities have much to contribute to this rebuilding. This is a practical task, but it is also a moral one. It is part of the educational, practical, and moral mission of our institutions. In this spirit, Hurricane Katrina brought forth a dramatic demonstration of the University of Pennsylvania at its very best: inclusive, engaged, deliberative, and practical. Penn went into action to offer space to displaced college students, to provide medical and technical assistance, and, in the months since, to bring together experts and participants at both the theoretical and practical levels to grapple with the extremely difficult challenges Katrina left to us in its wake.

On February 3, 2006, Penn convened the second of two national conferences to examine the challenge of "Rebuilding Urban Places After Disaster" and draw lessons for the present and the future from our experience to date with the aftermath of Katrina. The second conference, under the leadership of Professors Eugenie L. Birch and Susan Wachter, codirectors of the Penn Institute for Urban Research, focused on the specific dilemmas and challenges of rebuilding New Orleans and the Gulf Coast. The essays in this volume reflect and build on the deliberations of the conference participants. The first conference, "On Risk and Disaster," convened in Washington, D.C., in early December 2005 under the leadership of Provost Ron Daniels. It focused on the problems of risk assessment and the roles of government and the private sector in preparing for catastrophes and resulted in the book *On Risk and Disaster: Lessons from Hurricane Katrina*. These books and conferences exemplify how, in responding to challenges such as Katrina, universities model the kind of deliberation that is necessary to cope with the most challenging and complex problems of our time.

From such an integrated and comprehensive perspective, the challenge of rebuilding after Katrina is far from unique, even in a strictly American context. The magnified impact of television and 24/7 cable news networks makes catastrophic events that seemed once very distant—like the Great Chicago Fire of 1871, the Galveston flood of 1900, and the San Francisco earthquake and fire of 1906—seem immediately earth-shattering, close at hand, and terrifying. The vivid impact can be so immediate and so terrifying as to distract us from the less immediately striking moral challenges of what we could have done and can do to make a difference.

Many thoughtful people have been unsettled by the rapid fading of post-Katrina issues of rebuilding from our daily digest of news, conversation, and entertainment. But this is not surprising. The immediacy of the news, that which gives it such a great impact on human emotion, is not the thoughtful analysis of what can be done or should have been done. It is rather the bombardment of the terrifying. Once that terrifying immediacy is gone, the hard questions about something that is so obviously important to our nation's future fade from our news, our conversations, our consciousness—even (save a sentence) from the President's State of the Union Address. Yet the lack of a sense of immediacy at several months remove from the event does *absolutely nothing* to diminish the scope and scale of the work we can and should, indeed must, do together.

Of course, every disaster is different—but the strategic and the moral mindset that envisions the possibility of future disasters, that prepares for them regardless of what form they may take, that responds to them comprehensively and promptly, and that understands what can be done in their wake is more critical to us today than ever before in human history. It is also more available to us today than ever before. We have the tools, if only we can figure out how to use them together. And what holds true today, in the wake of

Katrina, holds true for every other important public policy question concerning our society in our time. In this case, as in all the others, we must—practically and morally *must*—deliberate *together* and decide how best to move ahead.

Effective and inclusive deliberation can help answer some of the questions left to us in Katrina's wake. It also can help heal some of the physical wounds Katrina has inflicted, by leading us to fair and effective reconstruction policies. And it can help heal—if we do it right or if we do it at least a lot better than we have done it in the past—the too long festering wounds of racial, ethnic, and economic disparity, by creating a new and deeper sense of shared community and common purpose. Collective deliberation can do that. Morally, we *must* try to do that.

There are so many comparisons that can be made, and are made day in and day out, by some of the people who were most wounded by Katrina. We have spent over $200 billion in Iraq, and by most estimates, we will spend over a trillion dollars before we leave Iraq. Whether one favors or rejects withdrawal from Iraq, we are still forced by circumstances to ask: "How much are we willing to spend here at home in the wake of a catastrophe where the certainty of our being able to help is much greater?" This is not a hypothetical, but rather a real and inescapable, indeed urgent, comparison. How do we look our fellow citizens in the eye who have been displaced by this catastrophe and say, "we are just not willing to spend as much on *you*"? We obviously cannot look them in the eye and say *that*. Will our nation's words belie or be true to our deeds?

Clearly, we have much work to do together. The discussions that follow are intended to contribute to that work. They engage with the compelling public priorities and perspectives that characterize the rebuilding after any major disaster. They are intended to model and stimulate the kind of engaged public conversations that are sorely needed if we are to come to terms with the inevitable conflicts over reconstruction priorities and preparations for future disasters. In this spirit, then, we must collectively deliberate in order to help bind up our nation's wound in the wake of Hurricane Katrina.

# Introduction: Rebuilding Urban Places After Disaster

## Eugenie L. Birch and Susan M. Wachter

Natural disasters such as hurricanes, floods, and earthquakes or unnatural events such as a terrorist attacks have long been part of the American experience. And in the past five years, U.S. cities have experienced a full range of calamities from Category 5 hurricanes to hundred-year floods to bombings of high-density buildings. The challenges of preparing for disasters, withstanding their impact, and rebuilding communities require strategic responses by different levels of government in partnership with the private sector and public will.

Disasters have a disproportionate effect on urban places. Dense by definition, cities and their environs face major disruptions in their complex, interdependent environmental, economic and social systems. Weaknesses not readily apparent in pre-disaster times surface as longstanding structural and substantive problems become prominent: environmental abuses are exposed; the local economy falters; municipal services collapse; social and political rifts widen; and cultural resources that give identity to such places disappear. The post-Katrina plight of New Orleans and several smaller cities on the Gulf Coast exemplifies this phenomenon.

Experts often measure the costs of disasters in loss of life and property. But they can put no dollar amount on the toll that a catastrophe has on the individuals who have experienced the event and then struggle to restore their homes, their families, their senses of self and community. The dilemmas and challenges of rebuilding take place against a backdrop of personal testimonies, ones that the rash of recently published newspapers, magazines and books with their searing photographs and reportorial narratives of the victims and wreckage do not express.

Rebuilding entails making choices, shaped by government regulations, economic, political, geologic, cultural, and other considerations tempered by the survivors' hopes and aspirations. The young, middle-aged, and older have diverse views about the places that they hope to reconstruct. The three short essays below, drawn from New Orleans residents, trace the course of imagining a rebuilt city, moving from the sadness and despair caused by the event through the painful steps to recovery laced with the recognition that their city has changed forever to the optimism and steely determination to envision a post-Katrina city. Collectively, the new city of their imaginations embodies their values and ideals.

The first essay, by New Orleans native Martha Carr, reflects on her multiple roles as a citizen, a mother, and a *Times-Picayune* reporter. She highlights the meanings of urban places and the role of civic journalism in rebuilding. The second, by Thomas Bonner, Jr., Kellogg Professor of English at Xavier University of Louisiana, emphasizes the importance of New Orleans's African American universities in recovery efforts. The third, "Postcards from Five Xavier University Freshmen," a writing assignment given by Professor Bonner to his students upon their return to Xavier in January, shows the disaster and rebuilding through youthful eyes. Together these writings represent the voices of the people who will rebuild New Orleans; their courage, strength, spirit and energy will shape its future.

## Martha Carr, *Times-Picayune*

[I want you] to remember, as viscerally as I remember, the faces of a community that died on August 29, the face of a major American city that was brought to its knees in one chaotic, unimaginable week. That city was my home. It was the place where my great-grandparents, both immigrants from France, met and fell in love. The place where my grandmother, who spoke only French, lived her entire life on a single street. The place where my mother, as a little girl, played on the narrow, brick-lined streets of the French Quarter. Then, as a young woman, married in the St. Louis Cathedral, and went on to migrate to the suburbs to raise seven children.

It's the place where I lived until, at age twenty-five, I finally left its insular embrace to venture to Chicago for my master's degree. And it's the city that, with its indescribable lure, yanked me back home after only three short years, when I was pregnant with my first child and longing to be in the comfortable cocoon of this tight-knit, inexplicable community we call New Orleans.

So when I sat in a hotel room the week of August 29—having evacuated the city to care for my infant daughter—and I watched as my beloved city was taken first by floods, then by looters, then by the government's failure to send help, I cried for days. And when I finally clawed my way back to the shambles of a news operation we had spread across makeshift newsrooms from New Orleans to Baton Rouge, I still cried.

Imagine your high school, your college, the parks where you played as a child—in ruins. Imagine your childhood home, the home you had built for your children, your kids' school, flooded and contaminated by mold. Imagine your husband's job gone, your parents' jobs gone, your siblings too afraid to raise their children in the city anymore.

Then imagine equally tragic versions of that same story happening to pretty much everyone you work with, all of your friends and neighbors, every member of your family, everyone you meet in the street, and you'll know what my experience has been in the last six months.

Now, imagine it is your job to tell the story of this community, to help choose the stories that will fill the pages of the newspaper every day. The best word to describe it: surreal. In the early 1970s, the *Washington Post*'s Watergate story spawned an era of gotcha journalism where the mark of an excellent journalist came in what sins you uncovered, which crook you nailed. I believe that Katrina—the most devastating natural disaster this nation has ever seen—has marked a sudden return to civic journalism at the *Times-Picayune*, where reporters—and the newspaper, for the that matter—believe that journalism has an obligation to public life—an obligation that goes beyond just telling the news or unloading facts. Each of us, more passionately than ever before, want to see the community take positive steps toward recovery. After all, our very survival depends on it.

Interestingly, in the early days of the storm, those of us at the *Times-Picayune* found ourselves in the best position to cover the chaos and mass human tragedy that was occurring. The paper, which prides itself on its extensive local news coverage, was entrenched in the city's and state's institutions, knew the city's streets (street signs or not), and had longtime sources who were immersed in the action.

But we were also in the worst position. We had to evacuate our building because of impending flood waters, we lost nearly all communications, we had no contingency plan on where we publish, and if it were not for a small crew of heroic reporters who insisted on returning to the city in the midst of the flooding, we might have missed some of the most important stories due to our failure to have a catastrophe plan.

Those reporters, by the way, literally scratched out stories on notepads and lived in houses without running water or electricity for weeks, all the while witnessing the death of their community, and dealing with the shock of losing all of their worldly possessions. Our reporters and photographers were faced with gut-wrenching decisions: do I shoot the picture, or help pull victims out of the floodwaters? Do I share my water and food, or just watch the masses of starving people suffer in the sweltering heat? Do I leave to file my story, or stay at the Convention Center for just a few more minutes, so these people, desperate to tell their story to anyone in the outside world who would listen, might experience some comfort? Daily ethical challenges still exist. All of us are stakeholders in the stories that now fill our pages, and we are called upon to use our skills to keep our news coverage balanced.

But there is a clear agenda that has surfaced out of this experience, held by most in the community. I suppose it's not unlike the way Americans galvanized around a common enemy after 9/11, or coalesced around a common grief, as during the Depression.

In New Orleans, we want an end to corruption, we want stronger levees, we want justice for those who lost everything in the storm. We want stronger institutions, a chance for both the poor and the rich to return, we want our culture preserved, and we want our suffering acknowledged by the American people and the nation's leaders.

So how is this new journalistic reality affecting our coverage? Our editorials are more strongly worded than before, and the paper has even published a rare front page editorial urging the president to make the city a top priority. More reporters and editors are writing guest editorials, as a way of giving voice to the shared experiences of those of us who have returned. They talk about what it's like to wait for months for a FEMA trailer, what it feels like to have your flooded home invaded by looters—twice—and they talk about the persistent guilt they feel for not being able to help the desperate evacuees who sat waiting for help outside the Convention Center. In addition, our newsroom debates are much more lively, and emotion-laced conversations fill our days. It's quite amazing, actually. As my dear friend Frank Donze tells me on a regular basis, this isn't a story of a lifetime, this is a story of three lifetimes. The way I see it, this is what journalists train their whole careers to do. To give a voice to those who have no voice; to provide tools to a community so it can chart its own destiny; and to hold government leaders accountable for what they do, or fail to do for the humblest of this nation's citizens.

We are not alone in our devotion to this place; town hall meetings in New Orleans are attracting thousands; citizens are organizing and demanding reform; and more than 900,000 of our metro area's 1.3 million residents have returned to try to rebuild their lives. I pray that all of you remember the faces of our people, and their deep suffering, and in your own way, contribute to our collective fight to save an important American city. I also extend to you our deep gratitude for all you have done to directly aid our community, the place I call home. I'll leave you with this one request: don't forget our city. And don't let your leaders forget us either.

## Thomas Bonner, Jr., Xavier University of Louisiana

Education has been important to New Orleanians of African American descent since early in the nineteenth century. Prior to the Civil War they produced *Les Cenelles,* the first anthology of poetry by their race in the United States, most of the contributors having been taught at small private academies and religious schools. In the aftermath of that conflict, three universities were established for their education in the city: Southern University, Dillard University, and Xavier University. Their philosophies were closer to the academic views of W. E. B. Du Bois than to those of Booker T. Washington. My own institution, Xavier University, was established by Philadelphian St. Katharine Drexel and her order, the Sisters of the Blessed Sacrament.

These institutions originally had campuses on the outer borders of the city, but as it has grown, they now occupy areas well within it, but in areas considered less desirable by the upper middle class. Every one of the campuses flooded after Hurricane Katrina passed. Water levels ranged from 5 to 10 feet, and Dillard University had two buildings destroyed by fire. Before the storm these campuses provided stable green environments amid encroaching concrete and commercial interests. Xavier University lies between an elevated highway and a drainage canal, next to which is a now largely abandoned poor African American neighborhood. The University is trying to maintain its art department and social service operations there, part of a long term effort to bring an improved architectural presence and more planted spaces amid the hip-to-hip, run down cottages.

On the western side of the campus lies a commercial and retail district, for example, tire stores, bakery, food stores, cleaners, low end clothing stores, and fast food outlets. Prior to the flood, the 4,500 members of the Xavier community were active patrons of these businesses. Sadly, many of these are still shuttered, but the 3,100 students who have returned are inspiring more openings. Of course, the recovery needs of the University have brought contractors and their employees into the neighborhood. Beyond that the faculty and staff are investing in the city with their taxes, especially important in the loss of taxes from three destroyed middle class neighborhoods.

The aftermath of the flood has emphasized the importance of the University in assisting the displaced. Like the instructions for oxygen masks received on aircraft, the institution must place the mask on itself before placing it on its less able companions. As a result trailers for staff, contractors, and workers fill parking lots, and the convent on campus is housing faculty and staff. From her Virginia exile and now from the campus, Sr. Donna Gould has been organizing students to work with Habitat for Humanity. Graduate education courses are now online to reach the teachers who are away from the city.

What does it mean to New Orleans that Xavier is back? It is a signal to families that higher education is returning in force to the beleaguered city. As important is the symbolic value that a major part of the city's African American culture has not disappeared: Michael White is playing his clarinet; *Xavier Review* is in press with a flood-themed issue; our President Norman Francis is chairing the state's recovery committee; our students are once again part of the milieu who walk on Royal Street in the French Quarter and on Magazine Street uptown. The other HBCUs are also making their marks—Southern University in New Orleans is assisting the recovery of the historic black, middle-class neighborhood near its campus and Dillard University, having its classes in the riverfront Hilton Hotel, is reminding downtown visitors and office workers that African Americans are at the center of life and culture in New Orleans. These three universities, like the green insinuating itself through the dried and matted brown grass and muck are offering hope in the face of devastation.

Now more than ever the epic hero Aeneas's words to his crew who had experienced great difficulties in the voyage to found Rome ring true: *Forsan et haec olim meminisse juvabit*—perhaps it will help to remember even these days. I would add, especially these days.

## Postcards from Five Xavier University Freshmen

Dear Nala,

I made it, I'm finally back to New Orleans. Although my family insisted on my not returning, I've realized that I'm an adult now and I have to make a choice for myself. Even though upon return the view from the airplane looked like a picture from World War II, and there wasn't a green leaf in sight, it wasn't that bad. It actually puts you in the mind frame of a new beginning, which is a plus. . . . I'm fine. Hope to hear from you soon.

Sean

Dear Sharee,

New Orleans has changed since I was here in August before the storm. The trees and grass were a bright shade of green and now they are almost brown. The campus is dull and there is a gate separating it from the surrounding housing community. Most of the houses are boarded up with cars in the yard victimized by the tragedy. Very few stores are open near or around the school, so if you go to Wal-Mart or Target you better make the best of it because there is no telling when or how your next time will be. Though, there is a bright side to the situation, there are many job availabilities. Some jobs such as Popeye's and Mc-Donalds are paying very well. Nine and up, I thought it was a joke. But soon the city will come to and be as it was again, if not better.

Bonita

Dear Ma,

When we first came to New Orleans it was so full of life & energy. The trees and grass were somewhat blue. Now ever since the hurricane New Orleans is dull. I remember being stuck in what is called the worst hurricane in American history. We were stuck in St. Joseph's Hall while the first floor was flooded. There was no air whatsoever. We traveled through the filthy water twice & were left on a highway for ten hours with now homeless people. Late that night we finally got a bus that was being shot at by angry and desperate people from the Superdome. All of this left a physical aftermath of brown trees & grass, & a gray sky & water. But it has been said, after every storm there is a rainbow. It's taking a while but New Orleans will see its rainbow & go back to its "infamous" life & energy.

Jacqueline

Dear James,

Hello! As you know, it was time for me to go back to school in New Orleans. It's so difficult to adjust back to life as it was in August. Everything is so different since the hurricane hit New Orleans. There were so many things I could do and places I could go. Now that has changed because most of all those places have closed down. Riding down the streets there are sights of trees broken and cars that look as if they haven't been touched since before the storm. Nevertheless I'm ready for the rebuilding to take place and hopefully the finishings can be better than they were before!

Britney

Dear Erin,

When I first got back to New Orleans, everything was different as expected. The city is very deserted; you can't spot as many people as you could in August. To be able to see a nice size crowd I have to go on Canal Street or walk down Bourbon Street. But even walking down those streets, there aren't as many people as you would expect. The school looks very different, even if I was here during the storm to see most of these changes. With the water that was on the campus no longer here, it has seemed to have taken the grass with it all around the campus—there's only a few patches of grass. But there seems to be a whole lot of mud around to replace the grass. Even though I saw how high the water got, I will never be able to forget because there are still visible water lines around the city and the school. Remember I told you about the many stores that were open right across the street from the school; well they're not open anymore, but there are a few down the street that have re-opened but not many. To shop I have to go to Canal Street from the school, when before all I had to do was walk across the street. I believe that it's just a matter of time before New Orleans bounces back from hurricane Katrina.

LaTisa

Taking a cue from these testimonials, *Rebuilding Urban Places After Disaster* illuminates the dilemmas and challenges of rebuilding after disaster by assembling a variety of approaches In so doing, this work may offer contradictory advice about what choices are available to those working on the new urban places that are emerging. While these places will recall the former cities, they will be different. How different remains to be seen.

The second of a two-book series, of which the first, *On Risk and Disaster: Lessons from Hurricane Katrina*, addresses issues of how to think conceptually about risk and natural catastrophes, *Rebuilding Urban Places After Disaster* extends this work into several other disciplines that contribute to city-building.[1] It elucidates why urban places and their rebuilding matter to the overall economy and to the nation. It argues that the issues of rebuilding are fundamentally place-based, involving questions of what, where, and how to rebuild, and person-based, involving questions of whose homes and whose neighborhoods will be brought back. This collection looks at the identification of the locus of responsibility for rebuilding, displaying its multiple layers: public and private sectors joined with not-for-profit and individual action. Most important, it maintains that rebuilding requires integrated knowledge drawn from several disciplines.

Rebuilding urban places involves many disciplines because these areas are complex, dynamic, and layered. They encompass symbiotic physical, engineered and socioeconomic subsystems, each shaped by centuries of decisions and investment and understood through expert knowledge and professional practice (Comfort 2006). Unifying or coordinating these subsystems to form resilient urban places is the central challenge of rebuilding. The natural sciences, social sciences, and humanities, the practice of planning, architecture, landscape architecture, and urban design, the social work, public health, education, and criminology all contribute to the process.

While a multidisciplinary approach is essential, it is also difficult, yielding different, sometimes contradictory solutions. Where a geologist would recommend rebuilding in an entirely different locale because of flooding risks, a cultural historian would call for the preservation of buildings, street patterns, and other remnants of a city's past. Today's spatial techniques map hazards, but at the same time contemporary participatory political practices encourage their being ignored. Social justice concerns and rational planning efforts collide with efficiency and utility in thinking about the speed and location of redevelopment.

The trick is not only to lay out the range of choices as drawn from the disciplines, but also to develop modes of thinking and tools that foster integrative approaches tailored to the specific needs of individual places. This book moves beyond merely calling attention to different domains to uniting multidisciplinary knowledge to inform public policy and practice. In some cases, analysts literally place this information "on a map" through developing and statistically analyzing physical, economic, and political data to identify the geography of risk, allowing for the implementation of preventive as well as post-disaster responses. In others, they look to the interplay among different factors—environmental, cultural, social—to distinguish a place's essential qualities to be melded into rebuilding approaches. Finally, they recognize race and class, account for the needs of the disadvantaged and disabled, and understand and appreciate demographic diversity in reconstruction.

The absence of an integrated approach has resulted in the pattern of ever increasing disasters as we as a society draw development to environmentally sensitive and hazardous areas, which undermines the environment, which worsens the risk and increases the likelihood of disaster as well as increasing the exposure of vulnerable populations to risk, inevitably exacerbating the impacts of natural disasters over time.

But getting the decision making right of what, where, and how to rebuild is not simply a matter of knowledge. It is also a matter of structural shifts and policy reformulation to align incentives so that decisions are made cooperatively on multiple levels to respond to the challenges. Here, too, the book presents policy responses to this critical need and past failures. For example, many authors discuss various incentives that use new knowledge to develop specific solutions such as those related to managed growth, relocation away from environmentally vulnerable land and others.

The need to address the collective action problem and the need for cooperation across multiple levels of government and by individual actors as well as private and not for profit sectors (because the impact is in fact dispersed throughout the region and involves public as well as private goods) is key. In particular, the needed scope of the spatial decisions goes from the parcel to the regional level. The relevant region goes beyond state borders and involves the cooperation of multiple jurisdictions. This is compellingly demonstrated by the description of the regional impacts of the disaster—and specifically the implications of the newly evolving pattern in the United States of major regional entities, the eleven megapolitan areas, one of which is the Gulf Region (Regional Plan Association 2006).

Working at the local level is necessary as well. Megapolitan regions are the sum of many parts. The smallest unit is the home, then the block and neighborhood. Strengthening these elements through providing decent housing, improving social welfare, educational, economic development, and community planning all come into play here. While these products are tangible, caring for the intangible is equally important. Disasters disrupt the social networks that hold urban places together; their repair is as urgent as the restoration of physical facilities.

The hurricane damage of 2005 affected an area the size of the United Kingdom. It literally wiped out several urban places ranging in size from almost half a million people to a few thousand. It disrupted crucial and interdependent systems—physical, engineered and socioeconomic—that frame modern urban life.

This tragedy is attracting billions of federal, private, and nonprofit dollars. The process of repairing and rebuilding will take years and it will test the ingenuity and endurance of the participants. Yet the events offer unparalleled opportunities for the creation of new metropolitan areas through knowledge-informed practices that have the potential to serve as models for responses to future disasters. With its multidisciplinary approach, this book provides a map containing several routes for collective action. It shows how to forge incentives and other methods to fashion resilient cities. Finally, this book offers choices, not answers. Informed by debate and discussion, answers must come from deliberative and democratic planning. This is the only way to live and rebuild in our democratic society.

## Note

1. These volumes resulted from separate conferences sponsored by the Office of the Provost and the Penn Institute for Urban Research. The first, held in Washington, D.C., in December 2005, explored the means to remedy the failures in the existing institutional, legal and policy landscape to respond to the challenges of risk management of natural disasters in America. The second, following in February 2006, assembled national experts, Louisiana and Mississippi representatives and Penn scholars in Philadelphia to consider environmental, economic, social welfare, and cultural/physical concerns related to post-Katrina reconstruction.

The essays and letters in this chapter are used by permission of the writers.

# Part I

# MAKING PLACES
# LESS VULNERABLE

# CHAPTER 1

# Physical Constraints on Reconstructing New Orleans

## Robert Giegengack and Kenneth R. Foster

The public discussion about rebuilding New Orleans has not been well informed about the physical constraints imposed on the long-term safety of the region by the geologic and hydrologic conditions that now prevail. To a large extent, those conditions are the result of a 250-year history of human attempts to engineer the Mississippi River and its watershed. Those efforts have led, ultimately, to an environmental decline that directly threatens New Orleans.

In this essay, we outline the physical processes that build and maintain river floodplains and their deltas; we describe the well-intended efforts of generations of river-dwellers to protect their homes and livelihoods from frequent floods on the Mississippi; and we conclude that instabilities now engineered into the system preclude the possibility that modern engineering can prevent future disasters in the city. Yet, although the long-term prospects for maintaining the city in its present configuration are poor, we believe that, in the short term, measures can be taken to improve the acceptability of Gulf Coast risks.

In this essay we summarize the geologic and hydrologic conditions in the Mississippi Watershed that have led us to the conclusion that New Orleans cannot be protected from a repetition of Hurricane Katrina, from the effects of a major flood on the Mississippi system that originates higher in the watershed, or from the consequences of the inevitable diversion of the Mississippi into a new distributary, the Atchafalaya River. To support this assertion, we offer herein an extended technical discussion of the geologic and hydrologic conditions that now prevail in the Mississippi Watershed. In the second part of this essay, "Can New Orleans Be Made Safe?" we explore strategies to reduce the risks that New Orleans and its citizens will face in the short term, while recognizing that long-term risks cannot be reduced to an acceptable level.

## OLD MUDDY

The Mississippi River today drains 41% of the area of the continental United States, including the east slope of the Rocky Mountains, the western slope of the Appalachians, and the vast mid-continent in between. The Mississippi watershed is the third largest in the world, after only the Amazon and the Congo, and typically carries more water, about 550,000 million cubic meters per year (Mcm/yr), than all other streams except the Amazon, Congo, Yangtse, Ganges, Brahmaputra, and Yenisei (Leopold 1962).

The Mississippi watershed has expanded to its current size via a process of systematic capture of streams that, before the last series of glacial episodes, drained to Hudson's Bay from both the northern Rocky Mountains and the northern Appalachians. Those north-flowing streams were dammed against the ice barrier that advanced south across North America repeatedly in Pleistocene time (the last 3 million years or so), and overflowed into the valley of what is today the lower Mississippi. At times of maximum glacial extent, the water that constituted continental ice sheets was withdrawn from the global ocean, depressing global sea level by at least 125 m. Thus, the Mississippi River that captured so much of the drainage of the interior U.S. carried its water and sediment load across the continental shelf that was exposed in glacial times, and delivered that water and sediment farther out to sea than the position represented by the present shoreline of the Gulf Coast. In flowing across the continental shelf to the open ocean, the Mississippi excavated its bed to the base level represented by lowered sea level.

As sea level rose after each glacial period, the Mississippi filled its eroded canyon with river-borne sediment, and removed that sediment again when sea level fell in the ensuing glacial period. Today, sea level is rising at the rate of approximately 1.8 mm/yr, the consequence of the return of water to the world ocean as continental ice sheets continue to melt, and of thermal expansion of the surface layers of the ocean in the present warming trend.

In addition to about 550,000 Mcm/yr of water, the Mississippi normally carries about 300 million tons/yr of suspended sediment, derived from erosion in the headwaters of the Mississippi. This sediment is held in suspension by upward vectors of turbulent flow that exceed the settling velocity of individual sediment grains. That settling velocity is directly proportional to grain size, and the turbulence of flow is directly proportional to flow velocity. Thus, when flow velocity increases, as it does in time of flood when the increased volume of flow loses less energy to friction with the bed and banks of the river, the river carries in suspension not only more sediment, but sediment of larger grain size. When and where velocity of flow diminishes, the larger grain sizes settle to the bed of the river first, followed, in time and often in space, by deposition of the finer grain sizes. Therefore, when and where the Mississippi escapes from its channel in time of flood, the coarsest sediment is deposited immediately adjacent to the river, forming a "natural levee," a low linear mound that lies along both banks of the river. The finer sediment settles out of the water after it is distributed over the floodplain beyond the natural levee.

When the river reaches sea level at the Gulf of Mexico, the velocity of flow is abruptly reduced to zero, and sediment settles out of suspension. This process is accelerated by dissolved salt in the sea water, which provides adsorption nuclei on which tiny charged particles of suspended clay accumulate to increase the grain size of the sediment, a process known as flocculation. Once delivered to the Gulf, this sediment is moved along the shore by waves and near-shore currents, and it accumulates in places that may be far from the mouth of the river.

The last glacial episode ended about 18,000 years ago, and water that had been sequestered in ice sheets on land began to flow back into the world ocean, raising global sea level at a rate that must have averaged 6 mm/yr for the last 18,000 years. In the last several thousand years, that rate has slowed to about 1.8 mm/yr. During those 18,000 years, the Mississippi has deposited sediment on its bed to keep pace with rising sea level, overflowed its channel repeatedly to deposit sediment on its natural levees and across its floodplain, and continued to deliver enough sediment to the Gulf of Mexico to maintain its delta along a broad front and to push that landform out into a rising ocean.

## GEOMETRY OF DISTRIBUTARIES IN THE DELTA

Another process, the abandonment of one distributary and the occupation of another, also changes the configuration of the delta dramatically from time to time.

Where sediment is carried to tidewater by the river, that sediment falls to the bed of the river and forms a streambed barrier to continued flow. The river then deposits sediment in the slack water behind the barrier until the gradient is adjusted enough to enable the river to surmount the barrier and carry its sediment farther seaward. When sediment is provided in abundance, the river both extends its length and raises its bed to continue to transport its water and sediment to the ocean. As this process continues, the channel that carries the river grows both longer and higher, increasing the height of floods, which results in additional sediment being deposited on the rising natural levees and on the adjacent surface of the floodplain. As long as the river is more or less confined within its channel, it grows both longer (in proportion to the mass of sediment it carries and deposits at the ocean margin) and higher (in proportion both to its increase in length and to rising sea level). When a given channel grows so long that its height above its floodplain can no longer be sustained, it is abandoned in a flood event as the natural levee is breached. The water falls down a steep slope to its floodplain, and flows to the sea via a shorter, and hence steeper, route, establishing a new distributary. In some cases, this distributary becomes established progressively in many successive flood events over many years, during which the river may be able to maintain more than a single active distributary.

Reconstruction of the recent geologic history of the Mississippi Delta provides abundant evidence for changes in the geometry of Mississippi distributaries, at approximately thousand-year intervals. It is clear from the column of sediment under the delta, probed at many thousands of locations by water-well drillers, that at least four other distributaries have been occupied by the river in the last 5,000 years (Fischetti 2001; Fisk 1955; Frazier 1967; Coleman and Gagliano 1964). The sediment that lies under the Delta even as far away as the border between Louisiana and Texas has been delivered there by one or another Mississippi distributary. Averaged over thousands of years, the leading edge of the Mississippi Delta will advance on the Gulf of Mexico along a symmetrical arc. It now presents a very asymmetrical face to the waves and currents of the Gulf. Another sudden change in the course of the river is imminent.

Adjustment of a river system to even subtle changes in environmental variables has been described by many observers throughout history. When Herodotus visited the Nile Delta in the fifth century B.C.E., he described five active distributaries; later travelers described as many as seven. Today the Nile flows to the Mediterranean via two main distributaries, the Rosetta and the Damietta. When Herodotus first visited the Nile, he probably was unaware that the sea level was rising, but he was aware of the mechanisms whereby the Nile Delta was being maintained. He also recognized that the landmass of the Delta was advancing into the Mediterranean. In the years since Herodotus, many generations of students of river and delta dynamics have improved our understanding of the processes of stream flow and stream manipulation of sediment. The summary description offered above is widely understood, and can be reviewed in any introductory text on sedimentary geology (Pettijohn 1957; Friedman and Sanders 1978; Blatt et al. 1980; Boggs 2001).

## IMPENDING CAPTURE OF THE MISSISSIPPI BY THE ATCHAFALAYA

The process described above is about to happen on the Mississippi Delta. The Mississippi will soon occupy the Atchafalaya River, a stream that drains much of the Delta west of the current Mississippi channel, as its new distributary, via a sequential process that began early in the nineteenth century.

The southernmost principal tributary to the Mississippi is the Red River, a major stream that rises in eastern Texas, drains the High Plains south of the watershed of the Arkansas River, and, until 1831, entered the Mississippi River at Simmesport, Louisiana (see Figure 1a, b, c and Louisiana University Center 2005). At times when the main stem of the Mississippi has been in flood, Mississippi water has advanced far up the lower Red River and, joined by flood water from the Red, has overflowed or breached natural levees along the

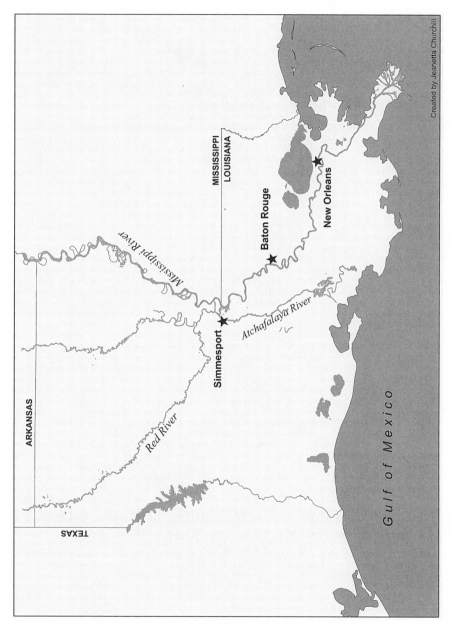

FIGURE 1a.　The lower Mississippi Valley and Delta. LUCEC, USACE, created by Jeanetta Churchill.

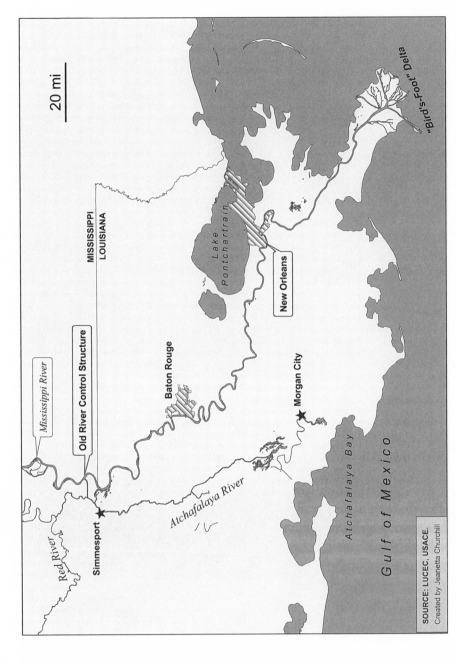

FIGURE 1b.  Detail of the eastern Mississippi Delta downstream of the Old River Control Structure. LUCEC, USACE, created by Jeanetta Churchill.

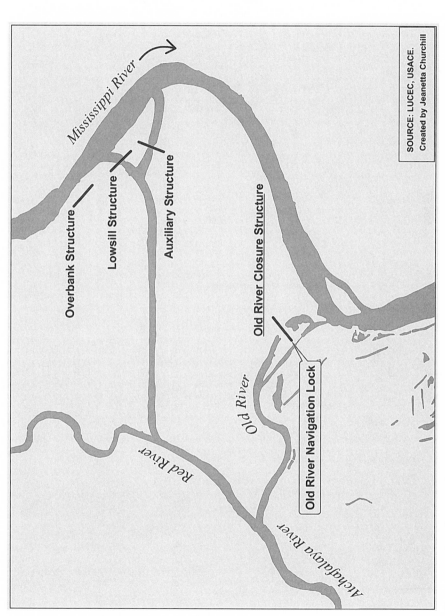

Within the figure:

Mississippi River

Overbank Structure

Lowsill Structure

Auxiliary Structure

Old River Closure Structure

Old River

Red River

Old River Navigation Lock

Atchafalaya River

SOURCE: LUCEC, USACE.
Created by Jeanetta Churchill

FIGURE 1C.   Detail of installations at the Old River Control Structure. LUCEC, USACE, created by Jeanetta Churchill.

lower Red River and flowed across the floodplain to join the Atchafalaya. Once in the Atchafalaya, water from the Mississippi and the Red flowed to the Gulf via a route that was shorter, and hence steeper, than the main stem of the Mississippi. Since that route was steeper, water flowed along it at higher velocity and maintained a higher capacity to carry sediment in suspension; the result has been that the upper Atchafalaya eroded sediment from its bed, increasing the gradient between the Red and the Atchafalaya.

In the fifteenth century, the Red River entered the Mississippi at the north end of a large meander loop of the Mississippi, later known as Turnbull's Bend (Figure 1). At times of flood, the Mississippi overflowed at the southern end of Turnbull's Bend and entered the Atchafalaya directly, supplementing flow that had reached the Atchafalaya via overflow of the lower Red River. To facilitate steamboat travel around the long meander loop of Turnbull's Bend, Henry Shreve in 1831 cut a new channel through the neck of the meander. This new channel greatly shortened the route that steamboats would take, and it set the stage for the full capture of the Red by the Atchafalaya, which occurred by 1850. In times of Mississippi flood, excess Mississippi water was diverted into the Atchafalaya by flowing *up* the lower stretch of the meander loop abandoned after 1831. That short channel came to be known locally as Old River; at times of high water, steamboats traveled freely between the Mississippi and Atchafalaya watersheds via the Old River. It was apparent as early as 1890 that the Mississippi would soon be fully diverted into the Atchafalaya.

The Mississippi is not unique among major rivers. There are today about seventy major deltas distributed around the world's coasts. Most carry water and sediment into a rising ocean (at high northern latitudes, continental masses are still rebounding from having been relieved of the weight of masses of glacier ice that began to return to the sea as liquid water some 18,000 years ago; at those locations, apparent sea level is falling, since the rate of rebound exceeds the rate of global sea-level rise); most maintain two or more distributaries. Many of these delta regions are recognized as unsuitable for human exploitation and remain undeveloped, or, in some cases, have been set aside as wildlife refuges; some few have been intensively developed, as the Nile, Ganges, Indus, and Mississippi for agriculture, or the Niger for hydrocarbon extraction. Few major cities have been built on active deltas.

Thus, the Mississippi River is a complex natural system, constantly changing in three dimensions of space and the fourth dimension of time. The changes are driven by alterations in the environment, most notably the rise in sea level, oscillations of climate, and tectonic movements of portions of the land that make up the Mississippi Watershed. The river exercises no control over changes in sea level, nor can it directly influence changes in global climate, but it does exert a long-term influence on the size and shape of its watershed by systematic capture of drainage elements, primarily in its headwaters, and by depositing sediment in its delta at a rate fast enough to depress the underlying crust at a measurable rate. And, by redistributing sediment on its floodplain and delta, the river rapidly accommodates itself even to very subtle short-term changes in its immediate environment. That natural system, as complex as it is, has been substantially modified by human intervention, which has introduced into the natural system substantial instabilities that would not have been sustained without that intervention.

## MANAGEMENT OF THE LOWER MISSISSIPPI NEAR NEW ORLEANS

The city of New Orleans was settled in 1718 as a French river port. The first residences and commercial establishments in New Orleans were constructed on the natural levees, which were higher than the surrounding floodplain and, thus, offered a small margin of safety from floods on the river. As the value of riverfront structures grew, residents of New Orleans, and then an early version of a municipal authority, began to add sediment to the natural levees to increase that margin of safety. In time, levees were constructed to enclose fully the most valuable sections of the city to keep flood waters out entirely. By that mechanism, managers of the Mississippi system set in motion the strategy that would quite successfully deny the entire Mississippi floodplain the more or less annual increment of flood-borne sediment that would enable its surface to keep pace with sea-level rise, and with the subsidence of the delta under the weight of sediment delivered to the continental shelf.

The entire Mississippi Watershed became part of the United States via the Louisiana Purchase of 1803, and soon thereafter engineers of the U.S. Army assumed responsibility to maintain navigation on the river and to protect riverfront property from floods. The work of the Army Engineers facilitated river travel through the War of 1812. In the years after the War of 1812, the Army Engineers erected massive flood-protection structures along the lower Mississippi; by 1850 the river was lined with flood walls built on the crests of natural levees as far north as Baton Rouge on the east bank and Simmesport (the head of the Atchafalaya) on the west.

Barry (1997) writes in some detail about the technical disagreements within the community of hydraulic engineers who undertook management of the river, both for navigation and for flood protection. A principal issue was the relative merits of (a) allowing the river to escape to its floodplain at selected localities in time of flood, thus lowering the flood crest and providing a margin of safety for riverfront residents downstream, versus (b) confining the river to a narrow channel, thus concentrating its flow and ensuring that the entire volume of water and suspended sediment would be carried out to the Gulf of Mexico. The value of the latter strategy was dramatically illus-trated by the success of James Buchanan Eads, who in 1876 constructed a complex of massive jetties along both sides of the Mississippi far below New Orleans to concentrate river flow and flush out of the bed of the river the barrier of flocculated sediment that limited river travel to shallow-draft ships. Eads's strategy worked—the bar was flushed away, and deep-draft vessels were able to sail up the Mississippi to the port of New Orleans.

The real cost of Eads's jetties, of course, was the loss of the entire sedi-ment supply of the river to the continental slope, far beyond the reach of coastal waves and currents. Thus, not only was the floodplain denied the annual increment of sediment it needed to keep pace with sea-level rise and delta subsidence, but also the coastal zone was denied the sediment that pre-viously had been distributed along the face of the delta. With the construction of Eads's jetties, the process of accelerated erosion of the seaward edge of the delta, a process not recognized to be important in 1876, began, and continues to this day. Delivery of the water and sediment confined between Eads's jetties to the deep ocean further required the course of the Mississippi to grow longer, which has resulted in deposition of sediment in the bed of the river, in excess of that required to keep pace with sea-level rise, which lifts the river a finite increment each year, even as the land adjacent to the river continues to subside, denied its compensating annual layer of sediment.

Thus, the Mississippi rises higher as the land around it subsides. Today, 80% of the City of New Orleans lies below sea level, some of it as much as 12 feet. Depending on the stage of flood, water in the Mississippi within the city limits of New Orleans now lies 15–30 feet higher than the lowest land behind the levees. John McPhee, in his celebrated book *The Control of Nature* (1989), points out that the keels of ocean-going ships tied up in the port of New Orleans are higher than the Astroturf on the floor of the New Orleans Super-dome. Residents of New Orleans don't stroll down to the river in the cool of the evening; if they want to look out on the Mississippi, they must climb *up* the levee to see it.

These efforts over the years have also attracted skeptical and bemused comments from Mark Twain and others. In *Life on the Mississippi* (1883), Twain wrote with some disdain of the futile efforts of the Army Engineers to manage the Mississippi:

> for the West Point engineers have not their superiors anywhere; they know all there is to know of their abstruse science; and so, since they conceive that they can fetter and handcuff that river and boss him, it is but wisdom for the unscien-tific man to keep still, lie low, and wait until they do it. . . . Otherwise one would pipe out and say that the Commission might as well bully the comets in

their courses and undertake to make them behave, as try to bully the Mississippi into right and reasonable conduct.

In the years since capture of the Red River by the Atchafalaya, the engineers of the U.S. Army have focused attention on the site at which the Mississippi must soon enter the Atchafalaya as its next distributary. Since 1850, it has become clear that a larger share of Mississippi water flows to the Gulf via the Atchafalaya each year. In 1950 the Army Engineers, by then well established as the U.S. Army Corps of Engineers (USACE), reported to Congress that, at rates of flood diversion then measured, the Mississippi could be expected to be fully captured by the Atchafalaya by 1975. In 1953 Congress apportioned the funds required to build the Old River Control Structure (ORCS), a massive facility designed to control the volume of flow from the Mississippi into the Atchafalaya and to facilitate passage of river traffic from one watershed to the other via the Old River Navigation Lock. The ORCS was completed in 1963, and a decade later was almost lost in the Mississippi flood of 1973 (McPhee 1989).

## Has Climate Change Enhanced the Hurricane Risk?

Many recent observers of the contemporary global warming trend, both from the popular media and from the scientific community, have suggested that an apparent recent increase in the number and intensity of tropical hurricanes can be attributed to global warming, in particular to the rise in Earth-surface temperatures over the last 150 years. Projection of that trend into an uncertain future introduces the alarming possibility that the number and intensity of tropical storms will increase.

Given the fact that we know that ocean-surface temperature is a controlling factor in the growth of tropical storms and their eventual development into hurricanes, the fear that global warming is responsible for the severity of the last two hurricane seasons in the Atlantic has gained wide currency. Recent observations clearly show that surface temperatures in the southern North Atlantic and the Gulf of Mexico have risen in the last few years (Earth Scan Lab 2006). For example, the mean surface temperature of the North Atlantic has risen by approximately 0.8° C since the 1930s, with the major part of this increase occurring since 1990. There is thus empirical support for the prediction of an increase in the number and destructiveness of hurricanes as a result of global warming.

In the past few months, several investigators have maintained that the intensity (if not the frequency) of hurricanes has increased in recent years, in synchrony with changes in the surface temperature of the sea in different parts of the world. Emanuel (2005) concluded that the destructiveness of hurricanes, as measured by the amount of power that they represent, has increased markedly since the 1990s, in close association with the rise in sea temperature of the North Atlantic. His results "suggest that future warming may lead to an upward trend in tropical cyclone destructive potential, and—taking into account an increasing coastal population—a substantial increase in hurricane-related losses in the twenty-first century." Emanuel acknowledged, however, that studies have failed to detect an increase in the frequency of hurricanes, apart from short-term fluctuations, including those associated with El Niño episodes (2005). Emanuel's work was supported by another paper published shortly afterward by Webster et al. (2005), who found that, while there was "no global trend" in the number of hurricanes, there has been an increase in the number that reached categories 4 and 5.

Other investigators remain unconvinced that these effects, if present, will have major social impact, given other changes that are occurring. Pielke (2005) found no long-term trend in "normalized hurricane damage" over the twentieth century (that is, estimates of dollar value of damage, corrected for changes in population and other factors) along coastal areas. "It is exceedingly unlikely," Pielke concluded, "that scientists will identify large changes in historical storm behavior that have significant societal implications. Looking to the future, Emanuel provides no evidence to alter the conclusion that changes in society will continue to have a much larger effect than changes in climate on the escalating damage resulting from tropical cyclones."

Another important effect, not directly related to global warming, is the operation of short-term cycles in weather, such as the El Niño/La Niña cycle. Students of the effects of short-term weather cycles on hurricane dynamics seem disinclined to attribute the severity of the 2004 and 2005 hurricane seasons to global warming (Goldenberg et al. 2001; *NOAA Magazine* 2005). They draw attention, instead, to patterns of atmospheric and oceanic circulation in the world's oceans that drive tropical storms to landfall against different stretches of the North American coastline in different periods: a *tropical multidecadal cycle*. By that analysis, the pattern of atmospheric and oceanic dynamics of the last ten years is similar to the pattern that directed hurricanes to the Gulf Coast of the U.S. in the period 1961 to 1980, and is quite different from the pattern that drove hurricanes up the Atlantic coast in 1951–1960, and from the pattern that drove hurricanes ashore in Florida in 1941–1950.

Thus, we conclude that no link has yet been firmly established between global warming and the frequency and/or destructiveness of hurricanes in the Gulf of Mexico, although the existence of a link between rise in ocean-water temperature and destructiveness of hurricanes (if not with their frequency) is strongly defended by some scientists. Few scientists, however, would argue that Katrina developed into a Category 5 storm (instead of remaining a lesser storm) exclusively because of global warming.

NOAA meteorologists expect a continuing high frequency of hurricanes in the Gulf of Mexico in coming years, a consequence of short-term variation in environmental conditions in the ocean as expressed by the tropical multi-decadal cycle.

Factors other than global warming are crucial in predicting the future destructiveness of hurricanes in the Gulf. These include the social factors that Pielke described—for example, human population growth in high-risk coastal areas, and the amount and value of construction in those areas. And, as we describe here, human intervention in the Mississippi Watershed has brought about environmental changes in the Delta that greatly increase the risk of hurricane damage along the Gulf coast and of floods from the river itself. The accumulated instabilities in the Mississippi System represent an escalation of hurricane risk for New Orleans and the Delta far in excess of any increased risk from climate change.

## CAN NEW ORLEANS BE MADE SAFE?

A number of factors contribute to the growing vulnerability of New Orleans, both to coastal storms and to loss of its river.

1. Sea level is rising at the rate of approximately 1.8 mm/yr, a consequence both of the melting of continental glaciers worldwide and the expansion of surface layers of ocean water in the present warming trend.

2. Land in the Mississippi Delta is subsiding, a consequence of:

a. Depression of the Earth's crust under the Delta by the accumulated mass of Delta sediment and by tectonic movements in response to that load (Shinkle and Dokka 2004; Dokka 2006). The spatial resolution of this process is not precise enough to allow those portions of the Delta that do not now receive sediment to escape subsidence; the interior of the Earth interprets the load of Delta sediment as a regional load, and responds with regional subsidence.

b. Compaction of the column of Delta sediment as oil, gas, and associated fluids are pumped out of rock reservoirs underlying the Delta.

c. Compaction of surface soils as a consequence of artificial dewatering to keep homes and businesses dry.

Subsidence of the ground beneath New Orleans proceeds today at a rate of 5–10 mm/year, depending on the location at which the measurement is made, and apparently is accelerating (Burkett et al. 2003; Shinkle and Dokka 2004). Burkett et al. remark: "Landfall of a Category 5 hurricane in New Orleans would place [an intersection in the city] at least 9 m below storm-surge level today and, based on the same sea-level rise and land-subsidence trends discussed above, at 10.5 m or more below storm-surge level by the end of the 21st century."

3. Subsidence is not being compensated by accumulation of flood-plain sediment, since that sediment is now contained within the system of levees, floodwalls, and jetties, and carried to deep water in the Gulf of Mexico. This is accelerating the erosion of wetlands in the coastal region, which otherwise would provide a buffer to New Orleans against the effects of storm surges approaching from the Gulf.

4. The Mississippi is rising, even as land adjacent to it subsides, a direct consequence of the rise in sea level and the extension of the length of the river to carry its confined burden of water and sediment to the Gulf.

5. The seaward margin of the Delta, denied its annual allocation of river-borne sediment, is being eroded by waves and coastal currents at an unprecedented and alarming rate. Modern estimates (Louisiana Department of Natural Resources 1998; Fischetti 2001; Bourke 2004; Shinkle and Dokka 2004; Dokka 2006; Kolbert 2006) include such figures as 50 km²/yr, one acre every 35 minutes, a football field every 38 minutes, 2000 mi² since 1850, and so on. One consequence of this erosion has been the loss of the buffer zone of coastal wetlands that has served to absorb the energy of approaching tropical storms and damp the storm surge that typically accompanies such storms. The margin of the Mississippi Delta is being lost to erosion at a rate faster than any "beach erosion" monitored in the world today.

The net effect of these changes has been a steady increase in the vulnerability of the city to two imminent risks: flooding under the storm surge driven ashore by a tropical storm advancing across the Gulf of Mexico and flooding from the Mississippi in response to unusually heavy rainfall in the heartland of America.

New Orleans faces a third risk as well: the loss of the Mississippi by its diversion into its Atchafalaya distributary. That event, which is fully predictable, would relegate New Orleans, Baton Rouge, and other settlements along the lower Mississippi to the role of back-country bayou towns. It would cause immense damage to bridges and other infrastructure located along the Atchafalaya, and devastate Morgan City. The damage to New Orleans would be more economic than physical. The city would lose its fresh water supply as salt water occupied the abandoned Mississippi channel, the port facilities would no longer connect river traffic with the Gulf of Mexico, and industries located on the river would lose their source of process and cooling water.

The media rings with calls for government to make New Orleans "safe" by improving the flood-control system. Safety is, however, a complex issue. We separately consider the risks that the city faces, and the much more elusive concept of safety.

The city faces risks that are immense compared to those for which policy

TABLE I. Saffir-Simpson Scale, Associated Storm Surge, and Return Period of Hurricanes of a Given Magnitude in the New Orleans Region (NOAA)

| Category | Wind speed, mph | Storm surge "generally greater than," ft[a] | Return period, New Orleans area, years[b] |
|---|---|---|---|
| 1 | 74–95 | 4–5 | 8 |
| 2 | 96–110 | 6–8 | 18 |
| 3 | 111–130 | 9–12 | 31 |
| 4 | 131–155 | 13–18 | 65 |
| 5 | greater than 155 mph | greater than 18 | 170 |

[a]http://www.nhc.noaa.gov/aboutsshs.shtml; [b]http://www.nhc.noaa.gov/HAW2/english/basics/return.shtml

makers routinely plan. Some idea of the magnitude of the risks can be seen from previous plans to safeguard the city. The U.S. Army Corps of Engineers designed the lakeside floodwalls to withstand a "standard project hurricane," which is equivalent to a fast-moving Category 3 hurricane (with a storm surge assumed to be 11.5 ft above sea level), as such a storm was characterized in 1960. The floodwalls on the river side were designed to handle water levels 18 ft above sea level (4 ft above the average annual high-water level in the river).

The likelihood of a hurricane of a given magnitude impacting a region is described in terms of its "return period," which is the mean of intervals between passages of a hurricane of a given intensity within 75 miles of a given point. A return period of 31 years for a Category 3 hurricane means that, during the previous 100 years, a Category 3 hurricane passed within 75 miles of that location about three times. If all things were equal, in the next 100 years there would be an additional three Category 3 hurricanes at that location. The return period does not, of course, predict when a storm will actually hit, but rather describes the probability that a storm of a given magnitude will hit during any given season. For Categories 3 and 5, this corresponds to a probability of occurrence in any given year that ranges from a few tenths of a percent (Category 5), to a few percent (Category 3).

Table 1 summarizes the Saffir-Simpson scale, together with the storm surge that is typically associated with hurricanes of each magnitude, and the return period for the New Orleans region.

Thus, the flood-control system in New Orleans was designed (in the 1960s) to be able to withstand a storm that would, statistically, be expected to land within 75 miles of New Orleans three times a century (in fact, the system failed to live up to its design strength, but that is a separate matter that we discuss later in this essay). Increasing the design strength of the city's flood-control system to withstand Category 5 hurricanes would fortify the city, in theory, against storms with a return period of 170 years.

For several reasons, however, the chances of a storm of a given intensity hitting New Orleans in a given season cannot be calculated with any accuracy. First, the return period is itself uncertain; the numbers in Table 1 were based on observations during the twentieth century, which included a small number of severe hurricanes in the New Orleans area. The period of record is far too short to inspire great confidence in the statistical projection. Second, the frequency of hurricanes in the Gulf varies considerably from decade to decade due to changing short-term weather conditions, and consequently the probability of landfall of a large storm will also vary.

Moreover, the extent of damage that a storm will produce cannot be predicted from its Saffir-Simpson category. The magnitude of storm damage depends on factors that are not considered in the Saffir-Simpson category: storm speed (not only wind speed), storm diameter, amount and distribution of contained moisture, tidal amplitude, synchrony of landfall with the tidal cycle, geography of the target shoreline, and distribution of cultural infrastructure. Consequently, the Saffir-Simpson scale is not a good predictor of the total potential damage resulting from landfall of a hurricane. Second, due to the deteriorating environment in the Mississippi Delta, in particular the loss of wetlands due to erosion, the city will become increasingly vulnerable to damage from a storm of a given category as that erosional loss of the wetlands buffer continues.

The shockingly low level of protection (given the high statistical risk of severe storms) is clear by comparison with the flood-control systems in the Netherlands. In that country, the flood-control systems are designed to limit the occurrence of floods to 1 in 10,000 years for provinces with high economic value, and 1 in 4,000 years for provinces with lower economic value (Jonkman et al. 2005). The corresponding figure for New Orleans, based on the return period given in Table 1 and assuming that the system would fail in a Category 4 storm, is one in 65 years.

## Reducing Risks to the City

The risks of catastrophic flooding in New Orleans can certainly be reduced, but there are limits. The city presently relies on levees and floodwalls for protection against floods from the Mississippi and from hurricane-induced storm surges. However, the engineering already pushes the limits of conventional practices. Thus, for example, the 2000 edition of the Corps of Engineers manual *Design and Construction of Levees* says that the height of flood walls built on levees, like those used in New Orleans, "rarely exceed" seven feet (2000). But in numerous places the floodwalls that protect New Orleans from the deluge are far higher than this, for example, rising to 11 feet above the dirt berms along the Seventeenth Street and London Avenue canals—and these were designed to protect against a Category 3 hurricane.

The efforts that would be needed to design and construct systems to prevent flooding in more severe storms would be truly heroic. There are presently calls to improve the flood-control system to withstand a Category 5 hurricane (this is not, strictly speaking, a well-defined goal, because a Category 5 hurricane has no defined upper limit to its wind speed and storm surge). For example, one proposal is to construct a gate across the Rigolets strait, which connects Lake Pontchartrain to Lake Borgne. This would supposedly prevent a storm surge from entering Lake Pontchartrain. The gate would have to span a long distance of water (nearly two-thirds of a mile), and would be a very expensive undertaking (Schwartz 2005). The costs presently being discussed in the news media for upgrading the flood-control system of the city to withstand a Category 5 storm exceed $30 billion, and there is no way to tell how effective that expenditure would prove to be.

Apart from any construction deficiencies in the system, gradual environmental changes over the years would erode the safety factors originally designed into the system. As time progresses, the river will grow longer, its bed will rise, and land under the city will continue to subside. In practice, this means that a steadily increasing level of investment would be needed to maintain a given level of protection.

The Netherlands has undertaken massive engineering works to address a similar problem. After a devastating flood in 1953 in which nearly 2,000 people died, the Netherlands erected a massive flood-control system, called the Delta Works, at a cost of $8 billion over a quarter century, which probably exceeds, but not by orders of magnitude, the proposed investment of $30 billion in today's dollars in New Orleans. The (current) annual maintenance costs for the Dutch system are $500 million per year. Given the small size of the country (with a population of 15.5.million), this is a remarkable commitment.

While the magnitudes of investment in the Delta Works project in the Netherlands and in a proposed project to protect New Orleans against a Category 5 storm might be comparable, there are very large differences. One is in the level of protection. The Dutch system was designed to offer a 10,000 year protection level, while a Category 5 storm in the vicinity of New Orleans would be roughly a 1 in 200 year event. In important respects, the Dutch have a simpler task: Amsterdam does not lie on a coast subject to the kinds of storm surges routinely associated with tropical storms, and Amsterdam faces a potential enemy at only one front: it does not have one of the world's largest rivers carrying 550,000 Mcm/yr through the heart of the city on an elevated trackway.

There is also a huge difference in the economic value of the assets protected—in the case of the Netherlands, the whole country is at risk, while in the case of New Orleans a similar investment would be required to protect a single city.

The Dutch have also realized that the flood-control system creates its own environmental problems. "When we constructed the Delta Works we really closed ourselves off from the sea, so the deposition process of sea sediment onto the land came to an end. This in combination with the drainage of all the agricultural land caused an enormous subsidence of the land in the polders," Toine Smits, an expert in sustainable water management at Erasmus University in Rotterdam was quoted (de Bakker 2004). "So we are now facing a quite awkward situation that we are living way below sea level." That parallel with the situation in the Mississippi Delta is striking.

Ultimately, the level of protection that is achievable for New Orleans depends, in part, on the resources that could be spent on the project. Clearly, New Orleans has been victimized by the same underinvestment in infrastructure that has plagued many other American cities, and the safety of the city could be greatly increased by further investment. The question, however, is how much safety can be provided, at what costs.

A recent cost-benefit analysis by von Winterfeldt (2006) concluded that "keeping all other parameters at their base level, the 1,000 year protection level decision [from rebuilding stronger flood control systems] has lower expected costs than the decision to rebuild to pre-Katrina levels." A detailed discussion of cost-benefit analysis in reconstructing New Orleans after Katrina is beyond the scope of this essay. However, we offer two comments about von Winterfeldt's analysis:

1. The analysis discusses a "1,000-year protection" scheme. This scheme would not keep the city alive for 1,000 years but, more accurately, would reduce yearly risks of catastrophic flooding to less than roughly 0.1%—for the present. A very different analysis would be needed to estimate the costs of maintaining this level of protection in the future, taking into account the steady deterioration in the environment. Indeed, in a hundred years or so, New Orleans might well be under water.

2. An important factor in this analysis is the monetized value of lives lost due to the failure of the flood-control system with Katrina. We believe that it would be morally unacceptable to rely on flood walls and levees alone to prevent loss of life. Whatever measures are taken to prevent future floods in the city, a reliable plan is needed to prevent loss of life should the floodwalls fail again during a future major storm. This is an urgent need, because of the patchwork nature of the flood-control system in New Orleans, the "serial" nature of the system (in which the failure of one section of the levees or flood walls would produce a major flood in the city), the lack of a backup flood-control system that would protect residents after the levees have failed, and

the experience after Katrina. A fundamental ethical requirement of engineering design is to prevent loss of life if the system should fail—"safe exits" in the words of one standard text on engineering ethics (Martin and Schinzinger 2005). Unlike earthquakes, floods from major storms come with advance warning, and populations can be evacuated from areas of danger. Perhaps that is the reason why the Dutch did not consider it feasible to include the economic cost of loss of lives when calculating the costs and benefits of their flood-control system (Jonkman 2005).

Our point is not that the risks of future catastrophes cannot be reduced (they surely can, at least for the short term). However, no technological fix will save the city from destruction in the long term (unless the deterioration in the environment is reversed, at unimaginable expense), and any conceivable reconstruction of the flood-protection system will nevertheless result in risks that will still be far greater than those that many people would find acceptable. We cannot rely on technology to make New Orleans "safe"; social factors must be considered as well.

Equally, or perhaps more, important is to implement a strategy to improve the safety of the city by social measures, as opposed to technological fixes. "Safety," as used by engineering and other professionals, refers to the acceptability of risk and not to the absence of hazard. For example, one standard text on engineering ethics defines safety as a condition in which the "risks about a technology, were they fully known, would be judged acceptable by a reasonable person in light of their settled value principles" (Martin and Schinzinger 2005).

Factors that would increase the safety of the city, considered as acceptability of risk, include

- Transparency on the part of government about the level of protection that it offers to residents of the city in its reconstruction efforts. An ad hoc rebuilding of the flood walls, for example, without public discussion of the level of protection that they will be expected to offer, is hardly sufficient. Assertions that are now surfacing, that the floodwalls are being rebuilt improperly, with inadequate materials and following substandard construction practices, are truly frightening.
- Transparency and effectiveness in monitoring the performance of the flood-control system, with effective public participation. That was supposedly a function of the levee boards, which have been widely criticized as being ineffective. Recent strategies to unify the levee boards are a promising step, but care must be taken to ensure that those boards will remain effective.
- An effective plan for evacuating the city. According to news reports, the city of New Orleans did not have any workable plan before Katrina to

evacuate residents who did not have cars or who were otherwise unable to transport themselves out of the city. It does not appear that a workable evacuation plan will be in place before the 2006 hurricane season begins.

- Other infrastructure to provide safe exits from a flood. These might include floodwall structures to protect selected regions of the city, to compartmentalize the city in case of flood. An example of such an approach is the "Community Havens" project, developed by Joseph Suhayda, formerly Director of the Louisiana Water Resources Research Institute at Louisiana State University (Suhayda and Korevic 2000). The plan would involve erecting massive concrete walls down the middle of New Orleans, to prevent flooding of large parts of the city in the event of another Katrina, to safeguard vital infrastructure such as hospitals, and to provide a haven for residents and tourists trapped by the storm.
- Relocating residents to safer areas of the city, typically in higher-lying regions and away from the immediate proximity of flood walls.

These steps will increase the safety of the city (considered in terms of acceptable risk) for the short term. But the hard fact remains: New Orleans will remain vulnerable to future Katrina-like events, and the risk of such events will gradually increase (other factors being the same) in the future, due to systematic deterioration of the natural environment of the Mississippi Delta. The long-term fate of the city is hardly in question.

Transparency and effectiveness are needed for managing other catastrophic risks in the region. Does Morgan City have an effective plan to evacuate its residents in the event that the Old River Control Structure near Simmesport (which keeps the Mississippi in its present channel) fails and the entire Mississippi River comes down the Atchafalaya toward Morgan City?

## CONCLUDING DISCUSSION

Many people were harmed by the Katrina tragedy. To a large extent, this resulted from government incompetence, and public discussion properly focuses on the need of those who lost homes and livelihoods for some form of compensation and an opportunity to put their lives back in order. This need is particularly urgent because the Katrina disaster has disproportionately affected the old, the poor, ethnic and racial minorities, and the otherwise disenfranchised and vulnerable. Why these people remained in the path of the storm and were denied the help they needed in its aftermath carries deeply troubling implications for our society. Our skepticism about the feasibility of a technological fix for New Orleans should not be mistaken for lack of concern about the welfare of these many people.

Many plans thus far presented for the reconstruction of the Gulf Coast (and most specifically downtown New Orleans) offer as a primary first premise that "flood control" will be achieved, at whatever cost (Schwartz 2005). It is now clear that American technology can reduce the chances of a repetition of Katrina, at least in the short term, but cannot forestall such catastrophes in the future. American technology can forestall, but probably not prevent, the loss of New Orleans's legendary river. Yet there is a powerful urge on the part of many former residents of the city to return home, and this urge is daily reinforced by impassioned pleas from city and state officials. Somehow, government needs to balance the understandable need of these many people to return home with a sensible accommodation of the serious risks that the deteriorating environment of the city imposes.

Our sentiment is accurately conveyed in a recent article in the *New Yorker* (Kolbert 2006) that quotes Judith Curry, chair of Georgia Tech's School of Earth and Atmospheric Sciences:

> speaking from the climate and the environmental-science perspective, a hundred years from now there's just no way there's going to be a city there. You just know that isn't going to happen. We can fight it. We can rebuild it and wait until it gets wiped out again. If you look at the geological record, these coastal areas come and go. Sometimes they're under water and sometimes they're not. Maybe a colossal engineering effort can do something, but at some point that is going to fail. This is just the way geology and climate work. You can't fight it forever.

Or, to paraphrase the Rev. Jesse Jackson: you can fight City Hall if you choose, but you might lose. You can fight gravity if you choose, but you're sure to lose.

# CHAPTER 2

# Negotiating a Fluid Terrain

## Anuradha Mathur and Dilip da Cunha

We need to expand our perception of the Lower Mississippi landscape, particularly below Simmesport, Louisiana, from a terrain of hard distinctions of land and water, river and settlement, channel and floodplain, to one that accommodates ambiguity and relative flows. This view opens fresh possibilities for inhabiting a place that a traveler in the eighteenth century described as undecided between land and sea, part of both, belonging to none. This perspective also affords a new look at interventions of control, particularly levees, as enforcers of a clarity that resides more in the eye of settlers than it does in the delta. It is an eye that has singled out the Mississippi to be a river defined by two lines on a map, lines that are manifested on the ground in levees that have grown and strengthened over the years even as they have extended out along "spillways" in a complex system the purpose of which is ultimately the separation of water and land. Katrina in this expanded view is not just a Category X hurricane that wrought havoc on New Orleans and probed the depths of political and social injustice in the United States, it is also a material flow—one of many in the fluid terrain of the Mississippi Delta—that blurred this separation that has been both a driving force and an objective for settlers in this landscape.

In the light of this separation of land and water, the tragedy that struck New Orleans in the wake of Katrina was only immediately caused by a failure to keep Lake Pontchartrain out of the city; its deeper cause lies in a success at keeping the Mississippi within levees. It is a success that has come at the cost of a natural land-building process that the Mississippi once conducted through the agency of its meanders and overflows. The loss of this process may have resulted in adjacent areas falling relative to a river that has risen, areas that have been made into vulnerable bowls by the extensions of levees in a flood control system that has consumed the entire delta; but it has more seriously resulted in the absence of any appreciation among residents in this terrain for the intrinsically dynamic condition of a delta landscape (Figures 1 and 2).

There is little doubt that levees and their urban counterpart, the floodwall that crevassed in the wake of Katrina, were built primarily to control and manage the Mississippi River. Three centuries after these structures began in low mounds and short runs to keep the high waters of a river out of adjacent

FIGURE 1. "Map of the Father of Waters," from Captain Willard Glazier, *Down the Great River: An Account of the True Source of the Mississippi* (Philadelphia: Hubbard Bros., 1888). The Mississippi was perceived by European settlers as a river defined as a flow between two lines.

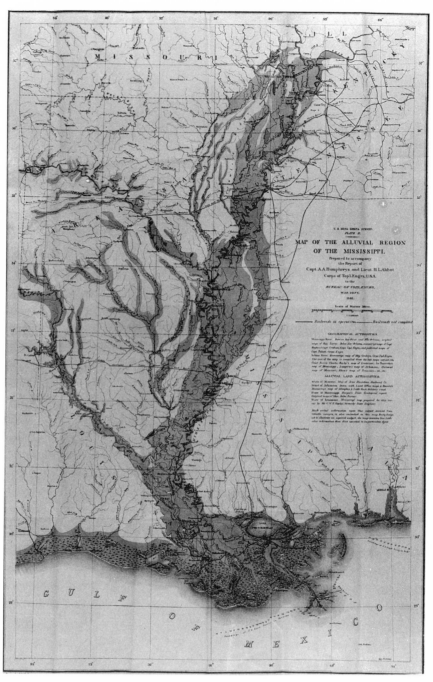

FIGURE 2.    "Map of the Alluvial Region," from U.S. Mississippi Delta Survey
report by A. A. Humphreys and H. L. Abbot (1861). The map situates New Orleans
in the alluvial valley of the Lower Mississippi, which begins near Cairo, Illinois. More
specifically, it situates New Orleans in the Mississippi Delta, an even more restless
terrain below Simmesport, Louisiana, where distributaries vie with each other for the
material flows coming off the continent. Courtesy U.S. Army Corps of Engineers.

property, they have acquired the status of a meta-infrastructure, a taken-for-granted and everyday datum against which the infrastructure of the city operates. Only occasionally do they come into public focus, and only to question their strength and efficacy, not their existence. To question their existence one must be able to conceive a mode of settlement with their absence, and this is difficult to do in a land where levees have facilitated the idea of property as much as they have protected property from a potentially anarchic river.

It is not an alternative to the levee that is required, however; rather, we need the recognition and accommodation of the temporal nature of the levee's natural predecessor—the "high grounds" formed by the spilling over and settling of sediments carried by speedier flows through this fluid terrain. This process of building "natural levees" situates New Orleans on a river but also in a world of constant change that is always yet to be mapped, needing ongoing engagement and negotiation. As designers, our question is not *whether* or not we settle this place, but *how* we settle it with an eye for both a river and the flux from which this river has been abstracted as a fixed entity. What is called for is a dual vision in conceiving the infrastructure of New Orleans, one beginning with the firm ground of a river, the other with the shifting ground of a fluid terrain.

In order to situate where we are today and the urgency for a dual vision, we need to review the settlement of the Mississippi Delta. This settlement, in our view, is not merely the occupation of the mouth of a river which La Salle claimed in the name of Louis XIV in 1682 together with "all rivers that enter it and all the country watered by them," a possession that has since evolved into a unique cultural and ecological region of the United States (Goetzmann and Williams 1985). It is, more fundamentally, the occupation of a terrain of relative flows that took imagination and considerable design initiative on the part of settlers to divide between land and river and to single out a dominant flow—the Mississippi. Thereafter it has taken engineering skill, innovation, and increasing control over an increasingly wider area to maintain this divide and dominance. To situate New Orleans in this landscape is to see its devastation by Katrina not as a natural disaster but as the result of human effort at work to create in the face of considerable adversity a hard distinction between water and land, perhaps unnecessarily.

## DEPOSITION TO PROTECTION

The Lower Mississippi begins near Cairo, Illinois, where Willard Price observes, "the modest river hiding within its walls becomes a brazen exhibitionist riding on top of the world. . . . You look down upon the upper river from the precipices that contain it. You look up to the lower river from lands that have to be protected from it by levees" (Price 1962). There is a shift in the agency of the river at this point: if the upper river has cut its way into the ground, the lower river has deposited alluvium in a vast trough through which it pushes and winds down to the Gulf of Mexico. Much of this deposition that has gradually extended south over millennia happens in the act of meandering as the river, forcing its way across a relatively flat terrain, deposits on the inner side of bends while eroding the outer, engineering its own roaming across the surface of the trough. Deposition, however, also occurred in surges when the river overflowed. The larger and heavier sediments settled nearby raising the ground in its immediate vicinity, while the finer and lighter sediments traveled farther away. It was only a matter of time before a surge was more than could be held by these "natural levees" and the Mississippi "jumped" to begin a new flow and a new land-building operation.

Below Simmesport, Louisiana, where the delta of the Mississippi begins, the trough of alluvium is much younger and more fluid and the river is much more restless and divided. While there is a dominant flow here that has long been called the Mississippi River, it is only one among many flows. But it was on one of the natural levees of this dominant flow in this fluid terrain that Jean-Baptiste Le Moyne, sieur de Bienville, initiated the settlement of New Orleans in 1718. It was not long before this settlement and others like it in the delta found the need to construct a firm edge to the high ground that they occupied in order to protect from overflows and the potentially transformative surges that now constituted potentially devastating "floods." These edges or artificial levees revealed a clear choice of protection over deposition, stability over fluidity; but they also sowed the seed of absolute difference between land and water in a terrain where the two were inseparable within the fluvial processes of the delta. As shaky as this distinction was initially for settlements like New Orleans, which by all accounts braved considerable odds to hold onto its high ground, the divide took root. It separated a river from its natural levee but it also began the isolation of the Mississippi within the trough. The other flows within this trough were increasingly seen not as part of a terrain that once accommodated a roaming Mississippi but as bayous of a "backswamp" (Figure 3).

## PROTECTION TO CHANNEL

The firm edge extended and connected "as cities rose along the Mississippi River, as farms were developed and forests cleared" and, it may be added, lesser flows in the backswamps drained. The continuity was articulating a river and with it the need for an authority that reached beyond the delta. It called into play the engineers of the United States government, the Army Corps of Engineers. Their vision of the levee was more than a protector of land from river; it defined a channel for navigating and draining a continent. The delta

PLATE 22
SHEET 9

FIGURE 3. Map of the ancient courses of the Mississippi River meander belt, from Harold N. Fisk, *Geological Investigation of the Alluvial Valley of the Lower Mississippi River* (Vicksburg: Mississippi River Commission, 1944). Levees are formed by depositions during period of overflow. Larger sediments fall faster while smaller ones move farther, raising the ground immediately adjacent to a flow faster than ground farther away. This build-up is curtailed when the flow changes course all together and levees begin elsewhere.

was to them "land's end," which the river passed through on its way to the Gulf. Indeed, this exit and entry of the river was so important to them that for many years around the turn of the twentieth century they saw levees as not merely edges but constrictors of the river. Pinching the Mississippi, they believed, would hasten its flow to the sea. Furthermore it would scour its own bed, not only preventing sediment from settling but also deepening the river, self-maintaining as it were a shipping channel. Some engineers speculated that the deepening would occur to such an extent that it would eventually render the levee as protector redundant. On the one hand, this "levees-only policy" homogenized the Lower Mississippi, treating the delta in much the same way as the lower river above Simmesport. On the other hand, it made a world of flows and hard-to-distinguish separations in a fluid terrain even more difficult to perceive than before (Plate 1) (Elliot 1932; Barry 1997).

## CHANNEL TO BASIN

In flood, however, one momentarily glimpses a primordial condition, a land-scape without firm distinctions. The 1927 Flood offered such a moment (Plate 2). The immense pressure of water and sediment within a confined channel was more than the edges could take. While levees gave way in many places on the lower river, New Orleans was spared inundation by the controversial dynamiting of the levee at Caernarvon, fourteen miles below the city. The resulting crevasse took the pressure off the city's riverfront even as it destroyed local communities. Levees thereafter were situated within a more complex system of controls of a Mississippi that was expanded in definition from chan-nel to basin. This basin included the vast surface that drained into the main channel as well as the spillways that drained the excess out of this channel. These flows in and out came, on the one hand, with extensive studies and predictions and, on the other hand, with an array of control structures the efficacies of which could be calculated or demonstrated. It was called Project Flood (Plate 3). The subject of Project Flood was most dramatically visualized in the Mississippi Basin Model in Clinton, Mississippi.

The Basin Model was built in the 1940s by the Army Corps of Engineers to monitor water in the river basin, particularly in times of flood, and to test structures of control. It was a scaled representation of the basin that covers 41% of the continental United States and parts of two Canadian provinces—comprising a massive 1,250,000 square miles. One horizontal step on the model was a mile, a vertical foot was one hundred feet, and 5.4 minutes was a working day. The model reveals the fierce clarity with which engineers per-ceived the distinction between land and water. Land in the model was cast in concrete and water was made to flow over it, its speed and volume gauged from the vantage of the firmness of land. Ultimately this working model, which lies abandoned today not because it is rejected but because it has moved into cyberspace, did not represent the real landscape as much as present possible scenarios. Hurricanes featured in these scenarios as did other variables across a basin with calculably different conditions (Figures 4, 5, and 6) (U.S. Army Corps of Engineers n.d.; Mathur and da Cunha 2001).

Levees in the delta work today within this complex system of predictable consequences, operating in response to multiple conditions across the basin. They also extend out from the main channel of the Mississippi to border outlets like Bonnet Carré Spillway, which was designated by Project Flood to carry the excesses of the Mississippi into Lake Pontchartrain. Levees were evidently en route to becoming more than edges of a river. In the delta they were becoming enclosures of land, enclosures of vulnerable bowls, many of them maintained at heights below even sea level.

## Basin to Delta

There have been no major floods in the Mississippi Delta since 1927. But there has been the aftermath of Katrina, which could be viewed as the waters of the Mississippi basin entering New Orleans through the back door. It has exposed the vulnerability of Project Flood as much as it has that the bowls of human settlement that have been created in the delta. Katrina in this regard can be seen as a factor that has tested the limits of and provided feedback for the management of the Mississippi basin. Indeed, this is how it appears to be viewed by engineers and the public at large. At the same time, however, Katrina can be seen as another flow in a terrain that is more primordial than has been granted by a mode of settlement that has sought clarity in distinguishing water from land. It reminds us that in this terrain levees are not firm dividers as much as fluid grounds that exist within the processes of deposition.

These two readings of Katrina—as management factor and material flow—are reflected in two perceptions of New Orleans. The first is New Orleans on the Mississippi River, a city separated from a river by levees that in a delta and in the wake of Project Flood are not restricted to a "riverfront" but extend along numerous edges of land and water that run in continuity and by coordinated levels. The second perception is New Orleans as a settlement in a field of flows. In this case the Mississippi is not a river that runs by a city; it is the fluid terrain that permeates it. This New Orleans could be what was drawn in maps of the nineteenth century when the settlement resided on Orleans Island (Figure 7). Although the Mississippi was singled out as a dominant flow in these maps, it was still part of a terrain of flows. The "other" flows, though they tended to be reduced to backswamps and bayous by comparison, appeared open to accommodating overflows as well as changes in the course of the river. It offers a dynamic if ruptured configuration of levees, a configuration that was evidently adopted by Native Americans who treated high grounds in this fluid

FIGURES 4, 5, and 6.    The Mississippi Basin Model in operation during the 1973 flood and abandoned thereafter. The MBM tested flood control structures against the simulated flows of the Mississippi across a terrain of articulated concrete. Its hard distinctions were eventually absorbed into digital simulations. Courtesy U.S. Army Corps of Engineers.

terrain not as continuities but as islands. They even built these high grounds as such—features called Indian mounds. In the process they granted the entire terrain to a rising and falling Mississippi rather than confining it to a channel in order to carve out "land." The difference is between a settlement on a river and a settlement in an open terrain (Figures 8 and 9).

These two articulations of New Orleans do not offer a choice: they suggest the need for a dual vision. There is too much invested in the firmness and continuities of 2000-odd miles of levees, locks, and gates to grant an open terrain, an investment that is fortified in no small measure by the notion of property; and there is too little invested materially and conceptually in the openness of the terrain below Simmesport, Louisiana. However, there is also too much at stake not to consider the fluidity of levees, particularly with the increased dangers and uncertainties facing systems like the Mississippi basin today, uncertainties that stem not necessarily from comprehensible and probable events but from incomprehensible and improbable ones.

For three centuries the vulnerabilities inherent in the pursuit of clarity—levees as protectors against high waters, edges of a navigational and drainage channel, and a system of flood control—have been exposed only in times of

tragedy when their continuities have been ruptured by flood. At these times anger and frustration at the loss of control of the distinction of water and land afford little room for considering another mode of settlement. As a result levees as firm dividers remain the driving force of settlement until, that is, the next flood. There is little to suggest that things will be different in the after-

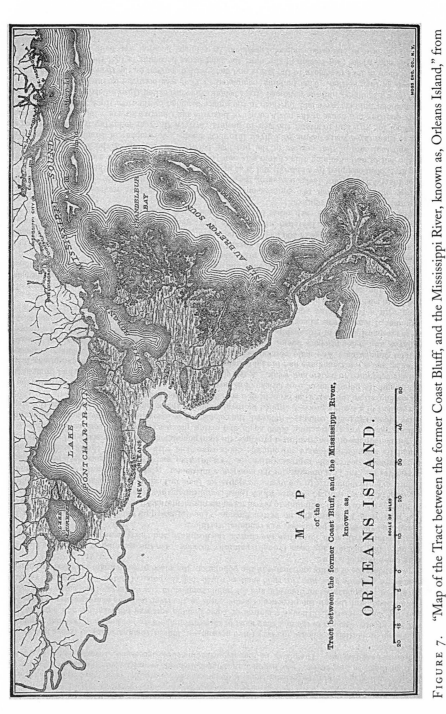

FIGURE 7. "Map of the Tract between the former Coast Bluff, and the Mississippi River, known as, Orleans Island," from George E. Waring, Jr., *Report on the Social Statistics of Cities* (Washington, D.C.: U.S. Census Office, 1887).

FIGURES 8 and 9.   Two high grounds in the Lower Mississippi were revealed by the flood of 1927. They suggest two different attitudes to settlement as well as two perceptions of the Mississippi. The continuity of levees confines the Mississippi to a river while making a place for settlement on a "riverfront," settlement open to the appropriation of "backswamps." The autonomy of the Indian mound, on the other hand, appreciates the Mississippi as an open terrain, rising and falling, breathing and living. Settlement extended and receded by the rhythms of this Mississippi. Courtesy U.S. Army Corps of Engineers.

FIGURE 10. The edge of the Mississippi delta reveals a terrain of temporal fluidity rather than spatial clarity, a landscape profoundly in process. Courtesy U.S. Army Corps of Engineers.

math of Katrina. But while engineers, planners, and a majority of the public call for strengthening the levees, this may be a useful moment to seed an appreciation for a world of flows, an appreciation that does not subvert the river model of settlement as much as initiates a parallel course, developing arts and practices needed to settle a fluid terrain. A beginning could be made by looking beyond maps, texts, and images that have reinforced divisions of river and settlement, water and land, channel and floodplain to actively cultivate new imaginings among the public and those who "manage" this terrain. A beginning could also be made through projects that do not take the levee for granted but demonstrate an appreciation for the intrinsic dynamism of the delta, incrementally seeding a new infrastructure that (like the Indian mounds) respond to a fluid, perhaps living, terrain rather than assume the strength and security of enclosures (Figure 10).

It has taken centuries and many floods for the pursuit of a river and riverfront to reveal its limitations in the delta of the Mississippi. It will likewise take many years to develop a mode of habitation that relies less on spatial clarity and more on temporal fluidity. But we could begin now.

# CHAPTER 3

# The Problems of Containment and the Promise of Planning

Raymond J. Burby, Arthur C. Nelson, and
Thomas W. Sanchez

When the expansion of cities is constrained either by natural barriers, such as New Orleans, or by policy efforts to limit urban sprawl, development pressures in hazardous areas can markedly increase. As floodplains, steep slopes, earthquake fault zones, and other hazardous locations are converted to urban uses, the locality's vulnerability to hazard events increases as does the potential for serious losses of lives and property in natural disasters. The devastation of New Orleans from Hurricane Katrina is an extreme example of the phenomenon. But this threat can be neutralized if hazards are recognized in advance of exposure and appropriate counter-measures are adopted. The difficulty is that in the absence of state planning and hazard mitigation requirements, many localities ignore hazards in planning for and regulating urban development, as shown most recently by Steinberg and Burby (2002).

New Orleans and Miami, Florida, provide excellent examples to evaluate the effects of adequate planning and preparation for cities in hazardous areas. New Orleans provides an example of what can occur in a city with severe constraints on buildable land and a lack of adequate public concern for hazards or urban development planning. In contrast, decisions made by policy makers in the State of Florida and by the Miami-Dade County Government illustrate how concern for hazard avoidance and resource protection can lead to policies that sharply limit development in flood-prone areas. To see if lessons revealed by these two cases could be replicated nationwide, we examine natural disasters and associated property damages in samples of metropolitan counties with varying degrees of containment brought about by policy decisions or natural conditions and with varying degrees of planning. And our findings are extremely telling. Metropolitan counties with either natural or policy containment experienced higher property losses in disasters when states left planning and development decisions wholly to local government discretion. Where states intervened and demanded that localities plan and manage development with hazard mitigation in mind, property losses are strikingly lower.

These findings are significant for several reasons. Urban containment programs are proliferating throughout the United States as governments attempt to counter various adverse effects of urban sprawl (Nelson and Dawkins 2004). Yet with the exception of our earlier work on containment and hazards (Burby et al. 2001), planning literature makes virtually no mention of the potential for containment programs to foster unsafe development patterns. In fact, a recent paper published by the Brookings Institution (Pendall et al. 2002) enumerates a number of issues related to containment that the authors believe require the attention of planning scholars, but they make no mention of the potential for larger losses in disasters. This is a serious oversight. Natural hazards on average result in economic losses of approximately $26 billion per year in the United States (Mileti 1999), and, rather than decreasing, losses are increasing as urban development continues unabated in areas at risk (Cohn et al. 2001; Cutter 2001; Mileti 1999).

Beginning with a description of urban containment programs and noting their increasing use in urban areas of the United States, this essay then explains the rationale for our hypotheses that containment, either by natural features or by sprawl-busting public policy, may accelerate development in hazardous areas and why state planning mandates may provide an antidote to this peril. This is followed by a discussion of the methods we employed to test these propositions and their limitations. The research findings follow in two stages. An examination of the experience of New Orleans shows that as the growth of the city came face to face with natural constraints, it chose to allow development in its very hazardous backswamps. The result, obviously, was quite poor. We contrast this with the growth of Miami and Dade County, where policy makers in the 1970s decided to limit the expansion of the city into low-lying hazardous areas by enacting an urban growth boundary. Following these case studies, we examine the magnitude of property losses in natural disasters in U.S. counties that have various degrees of natural containment and that have and have not adopted urban containment policies. This essay concludes with a discussion of the implications of our findings for state and local efforts to manage urban growth, and for federal disaster policy.

## URBAN CONTAINMENT

Unbounded urban growth is constrained in many places by various natural features that limit or channel urban development. Typically, urban development in these cities occurs at fairly high densities, reflecting limits on the land supply. For example, urban expansion in Los Angeles, considered by some to be an exemplar of urban sprawl, is constrained by the Pacific Ocean to the west and mountains to the east. Surprising to some, at more than 7,000 people per square mile, densities in Los Angeles are higher than in most U.S. metropolitan areas. Other U.S. cities with a high degree of natural containment and relatively high densities include Miami, New Orleans, New York City, San Diego, and San Francisco.

Community efforts to contain urban development within legislatively prescribed boundaries trace their roots to the origins of urbanization, as human settlements used walls to provide protection from hostile neighbors and gates to control entry and exit. Medieval walled cities continued this practice, and it persisted even after the creation of modern nation states. In England in 1580, Queen Elizabeth I forbade building within three miles of London to limit the spread of plague and protect farmland from urban encroachment (Easley 1992). European efforts to contain urban sprawl have continued ever since.

The idea of containing urban expansion originated in the United States in the early years of the twentieth century (Scott 1969), and it was vigorously argued for by Lewis Mumford and other urbanists in the years before World War II (Daniels 1999). The first formal urban growth boundary in the U.S., however, was not adopted until 1958, when Lexington, Kentucky, put in place policies to limit urban development to a core area of 67 square miles. The goal was to protect blue grass farms and horse breeding operations from urban intrusions (Porter 1997). Outside the boundary, residential density was limited to one dwelling unit per ten acres. Three years later, in 1961, the State of Hawaii created the Hawaii State Land Use Commission to zone all land in the state into three classifications: urban, agricultural, and conservation (Healy 1976). The state's primary goals were to curb urban sprawl and protect land for agricultural production (De Grove 1983).

During the 1970s, other states and cities began to initiate urban containment programs. Oregon's Land Conservation and Development Act (1973) requires urban growth boundaries for incorporated cities and urban areas of counties and restricts the use of land outside the boundaries to rural activities (Leonard 1983). In 1975, Dade County, Florida, implemented a containment program by enacting a growth boundary (Freilich 1999). That same year, Sarasota County, Florida, adopted a boundary plan with three tiers for development: urban, semi-rural, and rural (Freilich 1999).[1]

## Urban Containment and Exposure to Hazards

As urban containment programs limit land available for development, one of their first effects is usually an increase in land values (Hall et al. 1973; Whitelaw 1980). This initially leads developers to use land more efficiently, building housing and other projects at higher densities than before (Landis 1986; Howe 1993; Nelson 2000). Another potential effect is pressure to develop land exposed to natural hazards that prior to the containment program developers avoided when looking for sites for residential and nonresidential projects. This occurs for several reasons. First, as vacant land for development begins to become scarce, hazardous land may be some of the only vacant property readily available. Second, because development constraints such as hazards should have been capitalized into land values, hazardous land may be the lowest price land available, all other factors being equal. If developers invest in measures to reduce the risk of hazards, such as elevation of roads in flood-plains, construction and maintenance of flood control works, installation of slope-stabilization measures on hillsides, and strengthening of infrastructure system components, vulnerability to damage from natural hazards may remain relatively constant. However, if local governments have inadequate development and infrastructure design regulations in place or regulations are inade-quately enforced, which is not uncommon, losses in hazard events should escalate.

There are a number of steps local governments can take to counter the potential effects of containment programs on the vulnerability of development to damage in disasters: (1) *preventive* policies and actions, such as conservation zoning, to limit the exposure of new development to losses from hazards; (2) *property protection* policies and actions, such as building standards and assis-tance to property owners to retrofit buildings to increase their resilience to hazards; (3) *structural protection* policies and actions such as flood control works to provide areawide protection from hazards; (4) *emergency services* poli-cies and actions to lessen the impact of a hazard after its onset; and (5) *infor-mation* programs to build awareness of hazards and knowledge of actions that can be taken to reduce the risk of loss (Burby et al. 2001). The problem is hazard mitigation tends to be a very low priority for local governments as revealed by numerous studies (Rossi et al. 1982; Burby and May 1998; and Burby 2006). In fact, Burby et al. (1997) found that local governments are not likely to pursue such measures vigorously without being forced to do so through mandates imposed by state governments.

Containment of urban growth, in sum, either by natural topographic and hydrologic features or through conscious public policy, will lead to increased development of hazardous areas and increased losses in natural disasters. This effect can be countered if states require that local governments pay attention to hazard mitigation in planning for and managing urban growth. These ex-pectations are illustrated in Table 1.

## INVESTIGATING THE EFFECTS OF CONTAINMENT

Increased vulnerability to natural hazards should manifest itself first through changes in the value of land in hazardous areas and then in the likelihood and intensity of development of those areas. In the face of a hazard event, this should in turn result in higher losses in the contained jurisdiction than would

TABLE 1.   Predicted Losses with Varying Degrees of Urban Containment and State-Mandated Local Government Hazard Mitigation

| Local hazard mitigation mandated by state | Containment of urban growth | |
|---|---|---|
| | **Low** | **High** |
| Yes | Lower losses | Intermediate losses |
| No | Intermediate losses | Higher losses |

have occurred if urban expansion had not been contained by natural features or by policy makers through enactment of an urban containment program. In the research undertaken for this essay, we focus on the association of containment programs and property damages experienced in natural disasters.

Our case studies of Miami/Dade County and New Orleans are based on secondary data sources that include, among others, historical treatments of the development of New Orleans and Miami, government documents detailing efforts to plan for and manage urban development and mitigate flood and hurricane threats, insurance claims data assembled by the National Flood Insurance Program and the Institute for Business and Home Safety, and newspaper accounts of various events related to the vulnerability of the cities to disasters. Our accounts of development and hazard mitigation decision making were shared with various experts to help avoid errors in our descriptions of events and in our interpretations of them.

Our national cross-sectional data come from a number of sources as well. The Institute for Business and Home Safety (IBHS) provided data on property losses in natural disasters. The data were developed by IBHS from loss claims data provided by member insurance companies for claims stemming from natural disasters during the period January 1, 1994, through December 31, 2000. Member company claims data represent a significant portion, but not all, of the losses by insurance companies that paid claims for disaster events during this period. IBHS expanded these losses to develop estimates of *total* insured losses paid (in constant 2000 dollars) using data on the market share of the member insurance companies. The loss data exclude two significant sources of losses: earthquake losses to residential and commercial property and flood losses to residential property. We excluded earthquake losses because they are concentrated narrowly in a few states (principally California due to the Northridge earthquake in 1994). Flood losses to residential property are excluded because for the most part these are handled by the National Flood Insurance Program rather than private insurers.

The degree of natural containment was measured for a random sample of metropolitan counties as the sum of the lengths of the natural containment boundaries of each county divided by this sum plus the length of the county boundaries less the length of any of the county boundaries that are coincident with natural containment boundaries. The natural containment boundaries we measured include lakes, rivers, mountains, and ocean and Great Lakes coastlines. The degree of policy containment was measured using data obtained from surveys of local government growth management policies conducted by Nelson and Dawkins (1999) and Pendall et al. (2001). Based on the enumeration of places with containment policies from those sources, Nelson and Dawkins (2004) collected 100 local plans to verify that, in fact, the jurisdictions had developed policies to contain urban growth. They found that the most widely used approaches to containment were the adoption of formal boundaries to physically constrain urban expansion, followed by use of urban service extension boundaries and various growth phasing policies. Because it takes some time for growth management policies to translate into significant effects on urban development patterns, we limited our study to the sixty-eight counties in which containment policies were adopted in 1990 or earlier. Counties were counted as having containment policies in effect if containment programs were adopted at the regional level (such as Portland and Twin Cities metropolitan areas), county level (such as Dade County), or by one or more cities within the county (such as Eau Claire, Wisconsin). In many cases, city and county governments jointly pursued containment programs (such as San Diego and San Diego County). Because of the small number of places with policy containment, we adopted a simple 1 (containment exists) / (containment does not exist) coding scheme, although we recognize that there are a number of ways in which containment manifests itself that may influence the effects of these programs on urban development patterns.

Data on state planning mandates and state hazard mitigation policy were provided to us by the Institute for Business and Home Safety, which contracted in 2002 with the American Planning Association (APA) to survey state planning legislation related to local planning and hazard mitigation. These data include information on whether the state requires cities and counties to develop comprehensive plans and whether the state requires that local plans include hazard mitigation elements. The data developed by APA revealed that twenty-four states require all or some counties to prepare comprehensive plans and ten states require that these plans attend to hazards. We used a simple coding scheme to reflect the existence of these state mandates, coding these variables 1 in counties in states with the mandates and 0 for counties in states without the mandates.[2]

## CONTRASTING CHOICES MADE BY NEW ORLEANS AND MIAMI/DADE COUNTY

New Orleans and Miami provide a sharp contrast in how urban areas with similar degrees of natural containment confront natural hazards and plan for and manage development. Historically, urban expansion in New Orleans has been constrained by wetlands and Lake Pontchartrain to the north of the initially settled area along the Mississippi River, the Mississippi River to the south and beyond that additional wetlands, Jefferson Parish to the west, and wetlands and Lake Borgne to the east. Historically, urban expansion in Miami has been constrained by Biscayne Bay to the east and the Everglades to the west and south; in fact, 45% of the county is designated as wetland and 56% is located in regulatory floodplains. Because of their coastal locations and extensive areas of low-lying wetlands, both areas are highly vulnerable to natural hazards. Over the past 135 years, New Orleans experienced 36 hurricanes that struck or came with sixty miles of the city (a recurrence interval of 1 every 3.8 years); Miami experienced 50 hurricanes over the same period (a recurrence interval of 1 every 2.7 years).[3]

Prior to 1965 the development history of both of these areas was also similar in many respects. Faced with hostile natural environments, state officials, city leaders, and developers strove to create urban development opportunities by draining and filling wetlands, which resulted in severe vulnerability to flooding as the drained land subsided, often to levels well below sea level.

After 1965, their paths diverged. Urban growth in New Orleans exploded into the swamps of eastern New Orleans to take advantage of development opportunities created by the construction of Interstate Highway 10 and the concurrent efforts of the U.S. Army Corps of Engineers to enhance hurricane storm surge protection by extending levees to the east of the Industrial Canal. In doing this, it continued a century-long process of accommodating population pressures by draining wetlands. In contrast, after 1965, the Florida state government intervened with a series of laws that sought to strengthen local governments' ability to plan for and manage urban development and to protect wetlands and other flood hazard areas.

The effect of natural containment on development in New Orleans began to be felt toward the end of the nineteenth century. Lewis (2003, 20) notes that the city was "shoehorned into a very constricted site," but nevertheless initially capitalized on the natural levees of the Mississippi River and two abandoned distributaries of the river (Bayou Metairie and Bayou Gentilly) as sites for urban expansion. "The hideous alternative," he notes, "was to build in the backswamp: the low, perennially flooded area back from the river a mile or two—during most of the city's history a pestilential morass . . . the soil being a black slimy material that varies in consistency between thin soup and dense glue" (Lewis 2003, 27). By the turn of the century, however, land on the relatively flood-free natural levees had been built out, and the city began to expand into the backswamps. This became feasible with the invention of the Wood pump by New Orleans city engineer A. Baldwin Wood. Wood's invention made it possible to remove large amounts of swamp water very quickly, so that the backswamps could be drained effectively and provide sites for new housing. In rapid order, New Orleans developed steadily to the north toward Lake Pontchartrain through a succession of wetland drainage projects, pumping and storm water drainage improvements to remove runoff from periodic rainstorms, and levee building to keep out storm surges from lakes Pontchartrain and Borgne. These efforts were capped in the 1920s, when the Louisiana legislature authorized the Orleans Levy Board to create a 5.5 mile stepped levee, not along the shoreline of Lake Pontchartrain but 3,000 feet out into the lake, and to reclaim the land between the new levee and old lake shoreline for a series of new residential subdivisions (and later a branch of the state university and modern airport).

By the 1950s, urban development occupied most of the land between the new lakefront levees and older parts of the city. Suburban sprawl was well underway in adjoining Jefferson Parish to the west. To compete with its neighbor, New Orleans looked to the swamps and already drained swamps of eastern New Orleans as the next site for urban expansion.

Three developments, each aided by the federal government, made this financially feasible. First, the passage of the Interstate Highway Act in 1957 promised federal aid (interstate highways are built with 90% federal funding and 10% state and local funding) for the highway improvements that would be needed to provide access. In short order, Interstate 10 was under construction from the Rigolets through the heart of eastern New Orleans to the city's downtown to the southwest. Second, Hurricane Betsy in 1965 (America's first billion-dollar hurricane) revealed the highly hazardous nature of the area chosen for urban growth when it flooded the already developed Lower Ninth ward and most of eastern New Orleans, which at that time was largely undeveloped. The Army Corps of Engineers was ready with a solution to the problem with its plan for Lake Pontchartrain hurricane protection. The Lake Pontchartrain and Vicinity Hurricane Protection Project, authorized by Congress in 1965 (see U.S. House 1965), directed the Corps to assume responsibility for building levees to protect the undeveloped eastern part of Orleans Parish (79% of the benefits that justified the project were to come from new development that would be made possible by the project) (U.S. GAO 1976). The Orleans Levee Board (a state agency) was to strengthen levees to protect older parts of the city to avoid flooding by storms similar to Hurricane Betsy. The Corps assumed major responsibility for this as well, when the Lake Pontchartrain project was reformulated in the mid-1980s (U.S. Army Corps of Engineers 1984). Third, in 1968 Congress enacted the National Flood Insurance Act, which would provide federally subsidized insurance to cover flood risk to older development in the city and would cover, at actuarially sound rates, the residual risk of flood damage to new homes protected by the new

Corps levees and new drainage works constructed in the developing eastern part of the city by the city's sewerage and water board.

The New Orleans City Planning Commission facilitated the urbanization of the eastern part of the city with plans endorsing this site for urban expansion enacted in 1966 and 1970. With the planning commission's blessing, Lewis notes,

> By the 1970s suburban construction was already under way on a grand scale. . . . The largest was called "New Orleans East," fifty square miles (32,000 acres) owned by a single corporation. . . . According to promotional literature, it will be a "totally planned community where 250,000 people will eventually live, work, and play." (Lewis 2003, 76)

The bust in the oil industry in the 1980s deflated the New Orleans economy and quashed these dreams. Nevertheless, by the year 2000 some 22,000 new housing units had been built in the former swamps of the eastern part of the city, and the city planning commission wanted more. In its 1999 New Century New Orleans Land Use Plan, the city planning commission argued,

> Moreover, there are extensive opportunities for future development of the vacant parcels that range from single vacant lots to multi-thousand acre tracts. Long term, these development opportunities represent not only population increases but also significant potential employment for the city. (City of New Orleans 1999, 201)

Ironically, in the New Century plan the commission made absolutely no mention of the extreme flood hazard facing the city, ways of mitigating the hazard through land use or building regulations, or how the city might recover from an event such as Hurricane Katrina. Equally ironically, just six years later, the entire area of urban growth in the newly drained swamps of the eastern part of the city was under water.

In contrast to the recent urban development history of New Orleans, in Miami the past thirty-five years have seen a concerted effort by the State of Florida and the Miami-Dade County Government to limit urban development in hazardous areas similar to eastern New Orleans. This was not always the case. In earlier years and with an economy based on tourism and land speculation, in 1906 the State of Florida embarked on an ambitious program to drain the Everglades. George (2006), notes,

> Everglades reclamation (or drainage) led to the birth of a feverish real estate industry for Miami and much of southeast Florida as large speculators purchased millions of acres of reclaimed land from the State of Florida, then marketed it

aggressively in many parts of the nation. The unsavory sales tactics of promoters who sold unwitting investors land that was underwater earned for Miami an enduring reputation for marketing "land by the gallon."

The consequences for Miami of building on unsafe land, like those experienced by New Orleans, were grave. The hurricane of 1926 left 373 killed, 811 missing, and 40,000 homeless, and hurricanes in 1935, 1945, 1947, 1948, 1950, 1964, and 1965 caused considerable damage.

With the advent of the environmental movement in the 1960s and mounting population pressures on available resources, the state dramatically changed course. In 1972, the legislature enacted laws to protect the Everglades from exploitation and required the state government to develop a plan for sound future growth. In 1975, additional legislation was passed to require local governments to prepare comprehensive plans. This requirement was strengthened by the State and Regional Planning Act of 1984 and the 1985 Omnibus Growth Management Act. These laws put in place a top to bottom planning system in which the state formulates broad policy objectives that are then implemented through multicounty regional plans and local government comprehensive plans. The state directed that the coastal management provisions of local comprehensive plans must: (1) limit public expenditures that subsidize development in high-hazard areas unless the expenditures are related to the restoration or enhancement of natural resources; (2) direct population concentrations away from known or predicted high-hazard areas; (3) maintain or reduce hurricane evacuation times; and (4) include post-disaster redevelopment plans to reduce exposure of human life and property to natural hazards (Burby et al. 1997, 52–65). In Dade County, in addition to complying with the state's planning and resource protection requirements, the Miami-Dade County Government in 1975 adopted a regulatory urban growth boundary to concentrate future land development in core areas of the county and to prevent further urban expansion into the wetlands in the western portions of the county. This act stands in sharp contrast to the New Orleans city government's wholesale exploitation of the flood-prone wetlands of eastern New Orleans from the mid-1960s onward.

The benefits in terms of reduced exposure to property losses in natural disasters of Florida's and Miami-Dade County's proactive approach are striking. Our data on claims paid by property insurance companies for disaster losses between 1994 and 2000 indicate that they are much lower in Dade County ($33 per capita for residential claims; $6 per capita for commercial claims) than in Orleans Parish ($287 per capita for residential claims and $101 per capita for commercial claims). National Flood Insurance Program claims payments over the twenty-five-year period between 1978 and 2002 are equally revealing: $72 per capita in Dade County versus $708 per capita in Orleans

Parish. In sum, this brief comparative case study of two places with natural containment suggests that with adequate planning and attention to hazards, losses from natural hazards can be sharply curtailed. Without such planning, catastrophes of the dimensions of Hurricane Katrina can result.

## CONTAINMENT AND DISASTER LOSSES NATIONWIDE

The experiences of New Orleans and Miami-Dade County have been repeated in metropolitan counties across the U.S. In comparison to counties without containment programs, contained counties experienced greater total insured losses to residential property between January 1, 1994 and December 31, 2000 (an average of $37.3 million per county for contained counties versus $30.7 million for uncontained counties) and greater losses per housing unit ($293 versus $291). Although they are in the direction predicted, none of these differences are statistically significant. This anomaly, however, is due to the effect of state planning and hazard mitigation mandates that limit the impact of containment on losses in a portion of the counties with containment programs.

Commercial losses present a similar picture. Average losses to commercial property are higher in counties with containment ($9 million versus $7.8 million), but losses per capita are somewhat lower in contained counties ($24 versus $31). Again the differences are not statistically significant.

State hazard mitigation mandates have a strong effect in reducing insured losses, as shown in Table 2. Average losses per county over the study period were $40 million in states that do not require attention to hazards in local comprehensive plans but only $16 million per county in states with hazard mitigation mandates. Average losses per housing unit were also more than twice as high in states without hazard mitigation mandates. Commercial losses present a similar picture.

The combined effects of containment and state planning mandates are shown in Table 3, which is constructed to mirror the table of hypothesized effects presented earlier. In the top panel for residential losses and bottom panel for commercial losses, we see that, as predicted, losses are highest in jurisdictions that have enacted containment programs and are located in states that do not require attention to hazards in local planning programs. Contrary to our expectations, losses are lowest in counties *with* containment programs in states that require attention to hazard mitigation in local planning. The differences between the two groups of contained counties are striking.

Average per county residential losses per housing unit are $491 in contained counties without state hazard mitigation mandates versus only $95 in contained counties with a mandate. Differences in commercial losses are equally striking, with average losses per capita of $41 in contained counties

TABLE 2.   State Hazard Mitigation Mandates and Insured Losses (2000 dollars) to Residential and Commercial Property in Natural Disasters, January 1, 1994–December 31, 2000[a]

| State hazard mitigation requirements[a] | Residential losses | | Commercial losses | |
|---|---|---|---|---|
| | Total insured losses | Insured losses per housing unit[b] | Total insured losses | Insured losses per capita |
| Counties in states that *do not* mandate local hazard mitigation (*n* = 115) | Mean: $40,288,000 Median: 9,700,000 | Mean: $360 Median 176 | Mean: $9,531,000 Median: 2,115,000 | Mean: $32 Median: 11 |
| Counties in states that do mandate local hazard mitigation (*n* = 45) | Mean: $16,180,000** Median: 8,475,000 | Mean: $118*** Median: 87 | Mean: $5,116,000* Median: 895,000 | Mean: $18* Median: 4 |

* p = .10   ** p = .05   *** p = .01 (one tailed, difference of means test)

[a]Sample consists of metropolitan counties with containment programs established 1990 and earlier and a random comparison sample of metropolitan counties without containment programs. Counties that did not experience losses in a natural disaster between January 1, 1994 and December 31, 2000 are not included in the analysis.

[b]Calculated by dividing total insured losses by the total number of housing units in a county. Since all housing units are included rather than just those that carried insurance for property losses, the losses per insured housing unit shown are smaller than those per housing unit carrying insurance (i.e., insurance companies experience higher losses per insured household than shown here).

not subject to state hazard mitigation mandates versus $7 in contained counties with state mandates.

Comparing counties across state hazard mitigation mandates (rows) also illustrates the importance of state hazard mitigation mandates. Average losses in contained counties in states without hazard mitigation mandates are $491 per housing unit versus average losses of $306 per housing unit in counties without containment. Where the states mandate attention to hazards the picture is reversed. Contained counties actually have lower losses per housing unit than those without containment, providing strong vindication for the containment and hazard mitigation policies pursued by states such as Florida, Maryland, and Oregon that vigorously champion both containment and hazard mitigation in state planning policy.

Our findings for natural containment mirror those for containment policy, except that both states with and without state hazard mitigation mandates contained counties experienced higher losses than uncontained counties. As shown in the top panel of Table 4, in states with hazard mitigation mandates, losses per housing unit are considerably higher in counties with an above average degree of natural containment (72%) than in counties with a below average degree of containment. In counties subject to state hazard mitigation

TABLE 3. Joint Effects of Urban Containment programs and State Hazard Mitigation Planning Mandates on Insured Losses (2000 dollars) to Residential and Commercial Property in Natural Disasters, January 1, 1994–December 31, 2000[a]

a. Residential property losses per housing unit (average for sample: $292)

| Local hazard mitigation mandated by state | Mean losses per housing unit[b] by containment of urban growth* | |
| --- | --- | --- |
| | Containment program exists | Containment does not exist |
| No | $491 ($n = 34$) | $306 ($n = 81$) |
| Yes | $95 ($n = 34$) | $190 ($n = 11$) |

*p = .001 (one tailed, difference of means test; p = .000 for square root transformation to adjust for skewed distribution of losses)

[a]Sample consists of metropolitan counties with containment programs established 1990 and earlier and a random comparison sample of metropolitan counties without containment programs. Counties that did not experience losses in a natural disaster between January 1, 1994 and December 31, 2000 are not included in the analysis.

[b]Calculated by dividing total insured losses by the total number of housing units in a county. Since all housing units are included rather than just those that carried insurance for property losses, the losses per insured housing unit shown are smaller than those per housing unit carrying insurance (insurance companies experience higher losses per insured household than shown here).

b. Commercial property losses per capita (average for sample $28)

| Local hazard mitigation mandated by state | Mean losses by containment of urban growth* | |
| --- | --- | --- |
| | Containment exists | Containment does not exist |
| No | $41 ($n = 34$) | $28 ($n = 81$) |
| Yes | $7 ($n = 34$) | $52 ($n = 11$) |

*p = .03 (one tailed, difference of means test; p = .003 for square root transformation to adjust for skewed distribution of losses)

[a]Sample consists of metropolitan counties with containment programs established 1990 and earlier and a random comparison sample of metropolitan counties without containment programs. Counties that did not experience losses in a natural disaster between January 1, 1994 and December 31, 2000 are not included in the analysis.

mandates, losses are 40% higher in the counties with a higher degree of natural containment. The results for losses to commercial property shown in the bottom panel of Table 4 are similar, with losses per capita notably higher in counties with a high degree of natural containment. As with residential losses, counties in states with hazard mitigation mandates suffered much lower commercial losses per capita, in both areas with a high degree of natural containment and also areas with a low degree of natural containment.

To this point, our analyses do not control for other factors that can affect the magnitude of losses in natural disasters. Multiple OLS regression provides a way to isolate the effects of public policies such as containment and state

TABLE 4.   Joint Effects of Natural Containment of Urban Growth and State Hazard Mitigation Planning Mandates on Insured Losses (2000 Dollars) to Residential and Commercial Property in Natural Disasters, January 1, 1994–December 31, 2000[a]

a. Residential property losses per housing unit (average for sample: $293)

| Local hazard mitigation mandated by state | Mean losses per housing unit[b] by containment of urban growth* | |
| --- | --- | --- |
| | High natural containment[d] | Low natural containment[c] |
| No | $479 ($n$ = 42) | $278 ($n$ = 64) |
| Yes | $123 ($n$ = 31) | $88 ($n$ = 8) |

*p = .001 (one tailed, difference of means test; p = .000 for square root transformation to adjust for skewed distribution of losses)

[a]Sample consists of metropolitan counties with containment programs established 1990 and earlier and a random comparison sample of metropolitan counties without containment programs. Counties that did not experience losses in a natural disaster between January 1, 1994, and December 31, 2000, are not included in the analysis.

[b]Calculated by dividing total insured losses by the total number of housing units in a county. Since all housing units are included rather than just those that carried insurance for property losses, the losses per insured housing unit shown are smaller than those per housing unit carrying insurance (i.e., insurance companies experience higher losses per insured household than shown here).

[c]Low natural containment includes counties with natural containment below the median level for the sample; high natural containment includes counties with natural containment at or above the median level for the sample.

b. Commercial property losses per capita (average for sample $28)

| Local hazard mitigation mandated by state | Mean losses by containment of urban growth* | |
| --- | --- | --- |
| | High natural containment[b] | Low natural containment[c] |
| No | $51 (n = 42) | $19 (n = 64) |
| Yes | $22 (n = 31) | $6 (n = 8) |

*p = .03 (one tailed, difference of means test; p = .003 for square root transformation to adjust for skewed distribution of losses)

[a]Sample consists of metropolitan counties with containment programs established 1990 and earlier and a random comparison sample of metropolitan counties without containment programs. Counties that did not experience losses in a natural disaster between January 1, 1994 and December 31, 2000 are not included in the analysis.

[b]Low natural containment includes counties with natural containment below the median level for the sample; high natural containment includes counties with natural containment at or above the median level for the sample.

TABLE 5. Multivariate Analysis of Urban Containment and Insured Losses (2000 Dollars) to Residential and Commercial Property in Natural Disasters, U.S. Counties, January 1, 1994–December 31, 2000

| Variable | Standardized regression coefficients | |
| --- | --- | --- |
| | Losses to residential property[a] | Losses to commercial property[a] |
| *Containment* | | |
| Containment program adopted 1990 or earlier | .07 | .03 |
| Degree of natural containment | .15** | .24*** |
| *State planning policy* | | |
| State mandated local comprehensive planning | −.14* | −.08 |
| State mandated hazard element in plans | −.19** | −.20*** |
| *Socioeconomic factors* | | |
| Median household income, 1992 | .10* | −.08 |
| Total number of housing units, 1990 | .51*** | ——— |
| Value of manufacturing shipments, 1992 | ——— | 25** |
| Number of retail establishments, 1992 | ——— | .23** |
| *Model statistics* | | |
| Adjusted $R^2$ | .33 | .28 |
| *F*-value | 12.94 | 10.41 |
| Significance | .000 | .000 |
| Number of cases | 145 | 145 |

*p = .10   **p = .05   ***p = .01 (one-tailed test)
[a]Total losses with square root transformation to adjust for skewed distributions.

planning mandates while simultaneously taking into account other factors that can affect losses in disasters. The results of these analyses are summarized in Table 5, which shows that containment programs do not have a statistically significant effect on losses, while state planning mandates have negative and statistically significant effects. These findings parallel the results reported above. That is, containment policy has a very moderate effect in magnifying losses while state hazard mitigation mandates reduce losses.

The regression results show that natural containment has a much stronger (and statistically significant) effect in increasing losses in disasters than legislated containment policy. This is not unexpected, for two reasons. First, we would expect that places with high degrees of natural containment (versus high degrees of policy containment) to face higher risks of loss when containment is caused by hazardous conditions, such as lake or ocean shorelines susceptible to hurricane-driven storm surges or steep mountain slopes susceptible to landslides. Second, natural containment by wetlands, rivers, lakes, ocean shoreline, and mountains has been present, where it exists, since urbanization began in naturally contained counties. In contrast and as noted earlier, legislated containment programs are for the most part of relatively recent origin. Over a longer period of time, we would expect to see stronger effects of containment, although probably not as strong as those found for natural containment.

The effects of the other control variables are what we would expect. Counties with more housing units and wealthier people experience more losses to residential property than counties with fewer housing units and poorer people. The reasons may be that wealthier people are better able to afford and purchase insurance, more likely to live in more expensive housing, and possibly more likely to choose housing locations near hazardous areas to gain exclusive enjoyment of views, privacy, and related amenities. In the case of losses to commercial property, variables representing the magnitude of retail and manufacturing property at risk are associated with losses, while household income has little effect.

## Some Policy Implications

When the path of urban expansion is blocked by natural features or legislatively by growth boundaries put in place to combat urban sprawl, pressures to develop land exposed to natural hazards can increase. This inevitably leads to higher property damages in natural disasters than would have otherwise occurred. Our findings indicate that the tendency for urban containment to increase vulnerability to natural disasters can be limited (and even reversed) if states enact policies that require local governments to prepare comprehensive plans and attend to hazard mitigation in these plans and in related growth management efforts. Thus, cities such as New Orleans that have limited opportunities for urban expansion outside of hazardous areas and cities with smart growth programs designed to control urban sprawl need not suffer extraordinary property losses in disasters. Smart, safe growth is possible, but only if states simultaneously adopt policies to combat sprawl and reduce vulnerability to losses from natural hazards. States such as Florida, Maryland, and Oregon have been path breakers in this regard and can serve as models for other states that want to be proactive in dealing with urban sprawl and natural hazards.

Prior to Hurricane Katrina, the federal government paid little attention to requirements for attention to natural hazards in local government comprehensive plans. Its hazard mitigation efforts focus primarily on measures to facilitate development in hazardous areas (such as building elevation requirements of the National Flood Insurance Program and flood control programs of the Corps of Engineers) and measures to reduce the adverse consequences to households and businesses when this development is destroyed in disasters (such as flood insurance, disaster relief, and subsidized loans and tax deductions for reconstruction). Incentives for local government hazard mitigation planning are limited and focus narrowly on hazard mitigation, primarily to unwise developments at risk, rather than on planning for and managing the location, as well as the character, of urban development and redevelopment.

At the time of this writing, however, legislation is pending in Congress to help local governments plan effectively for land exposed to various hazards. The Safe Communities Act of 2005 (HR 3524) was introduced in the House of Representatives on July 28, 2005, just a month before Hurricane Katrina struck the Gulf Coast. The safe communities bill authorizes grants of up to $1.25 million per jurisdiction to help states update their comprehensive planning statutes and to help localities to assess their vulnerability to hazards, prepare comprehensive plans, integrate hazards considerations into comprehensive plans and transportation plans, and to update building codes and zoning and other land use regulations so that they give adequate attention to hazard mitigation. If passed, this legislation should go far in realizing the promise of comprehensive plans to counter the potential for natural containment and smart growth containment policies to exacerbate exposure to losses in disasters.

Financial support for this research was provided by a grant from the National Science Foundation (Research Grant CMS-0100012), for which the authors are grateful. We are also indebted to the Institute for Business and Home Safety, which provided data on claims paid by insurance companies for losses in natural disasters and data on state planning and hazard mitigation laws. Our data on natural containment were provided by Professor Laura Steinberg of the Department of Civil and Environmental Engineering at Tulane University; Dade County wetland and flood hazard data were developed by Professor Samuel Brody of the Texas A&M Environmental Planning & Sustainability Research Unit. We wish to also acknowledge the assistance with this research provided by Anna Davis and Mary Margaret Shaw of the University of North Carolina. Of course, the findings reported here are not necessarily endorsed by the National Science Foundation or those who provided assistance with the research.

## Notes

1. There are many other examples. The 1978 comprehensive plan for Boulder, Colorado, also implemented a three-tiered, phased development system, in this case reinforced by a publicly owned greenbelt (Freilich 1999). Based on state enabling legislation enacted in 1976, Minneapolis-St. Paul established a regional urban service boundary in 1980 (Orfield 1997). Since 1980, urban containment policies have been encouraged or mandated by the states of Florida, Maryland, New Jersey, and Washington (Weitz 1999), and have been adopted by cities in over 100 metropolitan regions (Nelson and Dawkins 2004).

2. Our research design uses OLS regression analysis to control for other factors that can affect the magnitude of losses from natural disasters. These factors include the size of the building stock that could be damaged and a measure of income as a proxy for the value of the building stock. Data to measure the magnitude of the housing stock, number of retail establishments, industrial activity, and median household income come from *USA Counties 1998*, a publication of the U.S. Department of Commerce Economics and Statistics Administration, U.S. Census Bureau.

Before proceeding to the research findings, several limitations of the data should be noted. First, our data on losses in disasters are very narrow, since they are limited to claims payments for damage to buildings. They do not include uninsured property losses, losses to public infrastructure, losses from business interruptions, and losses to residential property from flooding or earthquakes. We assume that our insured loss data reflect other types of losses, but we do not have data to verify that assumption. Second, we found it impossible to measure and control for the severity of the hazards experienced by the samples of counties with varying degrees of containment, since records on rainfall and other hazards are not available for every county in the United States. We do not view this as a serious limitation, because in a companion study to this in which we looked at coastal flood losses and controlled for the frequency of flood events, we found that the effects of state planning requirements were similar to those we report here (see Burby 2006). Third, although every effort to be exhaustive has been made in identifying places with urban containment programs, there is some possibility that some containment programs have been missed so that the sample of places without containment may have a few places that, in fact, have containment programs of one sort or another. Also, the containment programs studied vary considerably in stringency, which should affect their impacts on land markets and development pressures in hazardous areas. For example, the programs vary in the amount of land included within growth boundaries, but it was beyond the resources available for this study to physically measure the detailed characteristics of each program. Finally, half the containment programs we studied were adopted between 1980 and 1990, so that not much time had elapsed for them to affect development patterns that could have contributed to losses experienced in disasters between 1994 and 2000. The various limitations of our containment data make it more difficult to detect the effects of containment programs on exposure to hazards and losses in natural disasters. Thus, to the extent we find such effects, readers can have some confidence that the effects are real; to the extent we do not find effects, however, one explanation (in addition to a real lack of effect) could be the crude nature of our measures and the need for more time for the effects of containment to manifest themselves.

3. Notable hurricanes causing catastrophic losses in New Orleans include storms in 1915 (25,000 buildings flooded), 1947, 1965 (Hurricane Betsy), 1969 (Hurricane Camille), 1995 (unnamed rainstorm flooded 20,000 homes), and 2005 (Hurricane Katrina); severe hurricanes striking Miami include the storms of 1926 (which killed 373 and literally destroyed the entire city), 1981 (tropical storm Dennis flooded the entire area), 1992 (Hurricane Andrew), 1999 (Hurricane Irene), and 2005 (Hurricanes Katrina and Wilma) (data from Hurricane City 2006a, b).

# CHAPTER 4

# Mapping for Sustainable Resilience

Frederick Steiner, Barbara Faga, James Sipes, and Robert Yaro

The Gulf Coast has been battered by major hurricanes in recent years and the results have been devastating. On August 29, 2005, Hurricane Katrina slammed into the Gulf of Mexico. At landfall, it had winds of 140 miles per hour and a storm surge of more than 30 feet and impacted a 108,000-square-mile area (Figure 1). It left 527,000 people homeless, resulted in 1,299 casualties, and caused well over $250 billion in property damage. A few weeks later, hurricanes Rita and Wilma also ripped through the area. By late December, FEMA had taken 2,530,657 registrations from the hurricane victims. Figure 2 provides a typical example of the hurricane destruction in Holly Beach, Louisiana where more than 500 structures were leveled by Hurricane Rita's tidal surge and winds.

The hurricanes wreaked havoc on the region's natural resources, sweeping away more than thirty square miles of Louisiana wetlands and 25% of Mississippi marshes. These losses contributed to a longstanding environmental problem. Since the 1930s the Louisiana coast has lost about 1,900 square miles of marsh and swamp, making it increasingly vulnerable to hurricane and storm surges. Furthermore, as is well known, New Orleans reaped the results of this ecological damage when its levees and floodwalls failed, inundating the city with water as deep as 20 feet in many places (Plate 4).

Hurricane Katrina caused such costly damage because several million people currently live in coastal communities along the Gulf of Mexico, a 350% increase since the 1950s (Plate 5). The combination of the waterfront amenity and a lull in severe storms along the Gulf Coast over the last decades has lent a false sense of security to government officials, the development community, and buyers who are driving this growth. This folly is apparent in Plate 6, an illustration of the paths of all severe storms hitting the Gulf Coast from 1851 to 2000. These historical data underscore the danger of current settlement patterns.

Past trends of natural disasters are expected to continue in the future. A major hurricane has hit the Gulf Coast every year since 1994, and in 2005 the area experienced 26 named storms and 14 hurricanes, 7 of them major. In

FIGURE 1. On August 29, 2005, Hurricane Katrina slammed into the Gulf of Mexico. At landfall it had winds of 140 miles per hour, a storm surge of more than 30 feet, and impacted an area of 108,000 square miles. Image courtesy of National Hurricane Center.

2006, even before the start of the hurricane season, experts predicted that warm water temperatures in the North Atlantic would make it worse and estimated an 81% chance of a major hurricane hitting the Gulf Coast.

Being able to determine which areas are most likely to be impacted by hurricanes, storm surges, flooding, and other natural disasters would assist decision makers in preparing for and minimizing their impacts. This paper presents the beta version of a developmental sustainability analysis tool, a set of nested maps, for such purposes. The tool provides guidance for today's rebuilding and tomorrow's land development. It aims to help enhance the region's resilience—a word rooted in the Latin verb *resilire*, resilience, meaning to spring back or rebound—and its sustainability.

We have many examples of how places have planned their own sustainable resilience. Dayton, Ohio, is one. After a flood destroyed the city in March 1913, its leaders pursued new protective arrangements, namely, the creation of the nation's first watershed district, a concept invented by a consulting engineer, Arthur Morgan. Now known as the Miami Conservancy District (MCD), this district encompasses approximately 4,000 square miles (www .miamiconservancy.org.). It has five flood control gates and a series of protective levees along the river corridors of the Dayton metropolitan region (Morgan 1951). Authorized by the state legislature and withstanding a Su-

FIGURE 2.   Millions of people in Louisiana and Mississippi were displaced by Hurricanes Katrina and Rita. As of December 20, 2005, FEMA had taken 2,530,657 registrations from victims. In this neighborhood of Holly Beach, Louisiana, more than 500 structures were leveled by Hurricane Rita's tidal surge and winds. There is much debate on where, and if, housing should be reconstructed. In some areas, safe drinking water may not be available for years to come. Should we rebuild in the same places, or do we need to rethink how and where we build along the Gulf Coast? Image courtesy of MARVIN NAUMAN/FEMA.

preme Court challenge (*Orr v. Allen*, 248. U.S. 35, 1918), the MCD has purchased 4,500 acres outright as a result of its original plan and now owns and controls 7,200 acres and controls an additional 54,000 acres through flood easements. Subsequent to the creation of the MCD, the Dayton metropolitan region leadership developed a greenway system based on a series of plans and designs by Olmsted Brothers for various projects that began before the flood and continued through the 1920s and 1930s. This approximately 12,000-acre system links to the MCD, which owns or maintains thirty miles of recreational trials.

In non-flood times, the MCD-controlled land is in agricultural, recreational, and conservation use. During storms, the flood gates close, allowing for the capture, storage, and gradual release of excess water after the storms subside. The Miami Conservancy District was the model for a much larger flood control project, the Tennessee Valley Authority, another example of sustainable resilience.

## Toward a Resilient and Sustainable Region: Disaster or Not

In the post-9/11 world we tend to associate resilience with disasters. Recently, Lawrence Vale and Thomas Campanella, editors of *The Resilient City: How Modern Cities Recover from Disaster* (2005b), examined how societies have recovered after natural and human-made disasters, concluding, "Many disasters may follow a predictable pattern of rescue, restoration, rebuilding, and remembrance, yet we can only truly evaluate a recovery based on special circumstances" (2005b, B6). Lawrence Vale applied this observation to New Orleans for this book.

While Vale and Campanella link urban resilience to the specific qualities of the place where it occurs, they also present twelve axioms that generally characterize resilience after disaster. Four seem especially important for the Gulf Coast region: (1) disasters reveal the resilience of governments; (2) local resilience is linked to national renewal; (3) resilience, like disaster, is site-specific; and (4) resilience entails more than rebuilding. In a recent speech, former New Orleans Mayor Marc Morial expanded the latter notion, noting that today's challenge "is not only about rebuilding New Orleans and the Gulf Coast, it is about rebuilding a culture, a human system." The mapping tool, explained later in this chapter, provides spatial criteria to address the four axioms, especially the third, listed above.

Thinking about resilience unassociated with disaster is also helpful for guiding Gulf Coast rebuilding. Concepts from planning, ecology, and design provide direction. For example, they include restoration economy, that is, an economy based on rebuilding ecosystems, cultural heritage, buildings, watersheds, fisheries, and infrastructure (Cunningham 2002; Schach 2005); ecological literacy, the realization that all human activities have consequences for ecosystems (Orr 1994, 2002, 2005); root shock, where communities are ruptured and people dispersed, resulting in the destruction of human relationships (Fullilove 1996, 2004); sustainable regional industries, the development of green regional clusters around energy, manufacturing, agriculture, building materials, health, media, and/or education (Hess 2005); regional alternative futures, scenarios that suggest possibilities based on landscape analysis (Steinitz et al. 2003); attention to leftover places, the act of filling the gaps and reweaving the fabric of underdeveloped urban areas (Forsyth and Nicholls 2005), and civic ecology, which encourages citizen participation and deliberative decision making (Shutkin 2000; Fischer 2005). Recently, understanding the ecological resilience of urban places has advanced through the work of the National Science Foundation-funded long-term ecological research (LTER) projects in Phoenix and Baltimore (http://www.caplter.asu.edu and http://

www.beslter.org). The National Science Foundation supports 24 LTERs. Most are far removed from large cities, but the Phoenix and Baltimore LTERs focus on studying the ecology of urban systems (Grimm and Redman 2004; Pickett et al. 2005).

Finally, knowledge of history supplements recent urban resilience literature. When the French sited New Orleans in the early eighteenth century, they respected the Mississippi Delta's ecological constraints as they settled on the highest ground behind the area's natural levees (Lewis 2003; Barry 1997). New Orleans thrived as a result of that wisdom. Later, outside forces, often at odds with natural systems, altered the developmental patterns of the region and the city (Lewis 2003). Taken together, contemporary and historical teachings could begin to light the path towards the creation of truly resilient and sustainable cities and regions.

## MAPPING ENVIRONMENTALLY SENSITIVE AREAS: A BEGINNING

Today's challenge is to apply this and other knowledge to rebuild the Gulf Coast region. An important first step is gaining a better and more systematic understanding of the area's natural constraints. After Hurricane Katrina, people and groups, locally and globally, offered help based on their particular expertise. New York City had experienced a similar outpouring of interest after the 9/11 attacks, and in fall 2001 the Regional Plan Association (RPA) organized the Civic Alliance, a consortium of more than eighty-five civic, business, environmental, and community associations. Its collective work in participatory decision making, highlighted by the successful "Listening to the City" meetings capturing widespread citizen input, shaped the World Trade Center rebuilding efforts.

In 2005, amid myriad public and private post-Katrina recovery efforts, RPA identified another need, a vacuum related to understanding large-scale environmental issues in the extended Gulf Coast region. It convened representatives from several national design and planning organizations, universities, and corporations to address this concern. Included are several professional associations—the American Institute of Architects (AIA), American Planning Association (APA), American Society of Landscape Architects (ASLA), Urban Land Institute (ULI), several universities (Harvard, University of Washington, Louisiana State, Tulane, Clemson, University of Pennsylvania, University of Texas at Austin, and Arizona State University), and two corporations (ESRI, the computer mapping software pioneer, and EDAW, the environmental consulting company). They formed the National Consortium to Map Gulf Coast Ecological Constraints. The authors of this essay are founding members of the Consortium. The narrative below outlines the Consortium's work.

## Mapping Environmentally Sensitive Areas: The Approach

We chose to give attention to an *extended* Gulf Coast region, running from the coast of Texas to the edge of the Florida panhandle, an area united by its environmental cohesion and economic importance (Lang, Zandi, et al., this volume). One of ten to twelve very large, rapidly growing "megapolitan areas," in the United States, the Gulf Coast megapolitan area has more than 10 million residents, including more than 5 million in the region's most important city, Houston (University of Pennsylvania School of Design 2004; Lang and Dhavale 2005a). Due to its geography, the entire area is susceptible to hurricanes and flooding.

The Gulf Coast megalopolis plays an important role in the national economy especially in the energy and trade sectors. For example, the Port of South Louisiana is the largest (in tonnage) U.S. port and fifth in the world. It has annual exports of fifty-two million tons (corn, soybeans, and wheat) and imports of fifty-seven million tons (crude oil, chemicals, fertilizers, coal, and concrete). Geopolitical analyst George Friedman offers a succinct summary: "a simple way to think about the New Orleans port complex is that it is where the bulk commodities of agriculture go out to the world and the bulk commodities of industrialism come in" (Friedman 2005).

We did not attempt to produce a Gulf Coast or New Orleans plan or even specific designs; many others are engaged in those efforts.[1] Instead, we aimed at organizing public and proprietary information for service in rebuilding with sustainable resilience. We had observed that, while a profuse amount of data was available for the Gulf Coast, it lacked coordinated organization and maintenance. Additionally, due to its rapid Internet dissemination, it had little or no explanatory metadata with regard to its generation and use. These data, encompassing hurricanes, high winds, storm surges, flooding, land loss, development patterns, and the impacts of hurricanes Katrina, Rita, and Wilma, are overwhelming even for the skilled analyst, much less the ordinary decision maker.

Flowing from public and private entities, the data are at once confusing and remarkable for their breadth and depth. Several groups supply a wide array of information in many formats—GIS, remote sensing, aerial imagery, and others. Some data are freely available, other are open to selected users. Five cabinet-level departments and several independent federal agencies provide information. They include the U.S. Department of Homeland Security (DHS) through the Federal Emergency Management Agency (FEMA); the U.S. Department of Interior through the U.S. Geological Survey (USGS) with its Earth Resources Observation and Science (EROS) data management system, Mapping Division, National Wetlands Research Center (USGS-

NWRC), and other centers; the U.S. Department of Commerce with its National Oceanic and Atmospheric Agency (NOAA) housing the U.S. Weather Service National Hurricane Center and the National Centers for Environmental Prediction (NCEP) and Tropical Prediction Center (TPC) and the Satellite Services Division of the National Environmental Satellite, Data and Information Service (NESDIS); the U.S. Department of Defense (DOD) with the National Geospatial-Intelligence Agency (NGA), the U.S. Department of Health and Human Services with its National Institute of Environmental and Health Science (NIEHS); and the National Aeronautics and Space Administration (NASA).

A number of private groups actively disseminate data. They are ESRI with its Hurricane Resources site; Stewart Information Services Corporation through GlobeXplorer with satellite images of the disaster area; Geodecision's IRRIS portal that has U.S. infrastructure information; ORBIT GIS Technologies that offers a free, downloadable software for reading its before and after imagery of parts of the Gulf Coast; and *USA Today* Storm Center that has historic and current data. Additionally, several collaborative data systems related to Katrina exist. Among them are "GIS for the Gulf," jointly sponsored by USGS, DHS, and NGA, and an EROS clearinghouse dedicated to Katrina data sponsored by the USGS and FEMA. It has aerial, satellite, and ground information as submitted by commercial, federal, and international sources available to relief groups via FTP.

In the past year, we have also seen an incredible increase in the number of web-based map servers that provide imagery for such significant events as hurricanes or other natural disasters. For Katrina alone, GeoFusion, Ka-Map!, PrimaGIS, Telescience, NIEHS, Google Earth, and NASA WorldWind have downloadable data. Imagery from NOAA and DigitalGlobe was available on Google Earth a day or so after Hurricane Katrina hit. Google Earth has an option to log into a server that directly accesses data about specific hurricanes.

We are using these resources in our two-part project to design and implement a mapping tool for rebuilding with sustainable resilience. Our goal is not to create science, but to employ data-driven environmental analysis to minimize future loss of life and property and protect public health, safety, and welfare. The first phase is to create a GIS-based "development suitability analysis" tool that takes into account natural, social, and economic factors to prioritize developable land and places. The second phase is to apply the tool through a participatory process to evaluate design and planning options at the local level. Figure 3 illustrates the project flow. EDAW and ESRI are leading the endeavor, supported by a voluntary national advisory committee of geologists, landscape ecologists, transportation planners, urban designers, architects, landscape architects, water resource specialists, demographers, and

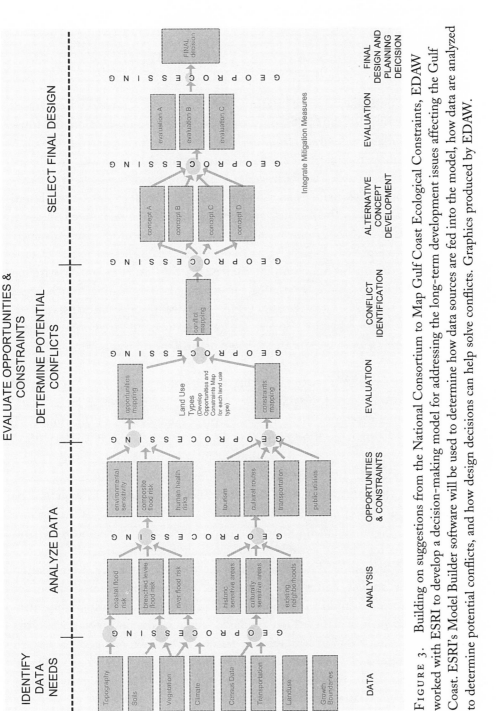

FIGURE 3. Building on suggestions from the National Consortium to Map Gulf Coast Ecological Constraints, EDAW worked with ESRI to develop a decision-making model for addressing the long-term development issues affecting the Gulf Coast. ESRI's Model Builder software will be used to determine how data sources are fed into the model, how data are analyzed to determine potential conflicts, and how design decisions can help solve conflicts. Graphics produced by EDAW.

regional planners.[2] We completed the first phase in March 2006 and anticipate starting the second in June 2006.

## MAPPING ENVIRONMENTALLY SENSITIVE AREAS: THE FIRST PRODUCTS

The "developmental suitability analysis" tool consists of a set of environmental
assessment maps for the Gulf Coast region from Pensacola, Florida, to Houston, Texas. Plate 7 illustrates the key map, an overview of a part of the Texas
coast. The map summarizes the composite potential risk for the area based
upon data from the Coastal Risk Atlas. This map ranks development suitability according to five risk levels, ranging from "no build" to "build" indicated
in shades of red with the darkest representing the highest risk. The first zone,
"Highest Risk," indicates places not to build under almost any circumstance.
The second zone, "High Risk," and the third zone, "Medium Risk," outline
places that should be built only at the risk of the property owner with no
public subsidy, insurance guarantee, or emergency relief. The fourth zone,
"Low Risk," displays places where building can occur under special state and/
or local regulatory disaster control measures. The fifth zone, "Minimal Risk,"
encompasses places that can be developed according to local norms and regulations.

We can replicate Plate 7 for other localities along the coast. Additionally
we can adapt specific information to show a single environmental factor. Plate
8, for example, illustrates the potential storm surge areas near Houston.

Geospatial data and prediction models drawn from the 18 sources listed
in Table 1 provide the base information for these maps. These data types were
combined to create a composite map that indicates the areas of greatest concern. Future research is needed to determine how these factors should be
weighted. For this effort, all factors were weighted the same. These maps are
intended to complement ongoing mapping efforts and to expand upon this
existing work by adding sensitivity and vulnerability information.

This developmental suitability analysis tool has additional application
for planning and implementing sustainable resilience. For example, we can
represent environmental assumptions about the future spatially. We undertook such an exercise with sea rise predictions to see how they would affect the
floodplain calculations in Lacombe, Louisiana. First, we mapped Lacombe's
existing floodplain levels (Plate 9). Next, we applied the scientists' anticipated
21″ to 44″ rise in sea elevation over the next 50 to 100 years, using the median
number, 35″, to determine the new high tide mark (Plate 10). Finally, we
calculated the new floodplain after a 35″ rise in sea elevation (Plate 11). This
quick study indicates that even if there are no hurricanes or severe storms
along the Gulf Coast, many areas are still in danger because of sea rise. In

TABLE I. Modeling Processes Combined to Determine Vulnerability

Societal risk (Coastal Risk Atlas)
Flood risks (FEMA)
High wind risk areas (MEOW)
Storm surge (Coastal Risk Atlas)
Population density (U.S. Census Bureau)
Population growth projections (local county governments)
Economic impacts (HAZUS)
Impact on natural resources (HAZUS)
Displaced households
Sea rise vulnerability (CVI)
Historic hurricane patterns—Allen, Andrew, Aubrey, Betsy, Camille, Opal, unnamed 1915,
     unnamed 1928, unnamed 1935) (National Hurricane Center)
HAZUS-MH—FEMA Software Program for Estimating Potential Losses from Disasters
Coastal Risk Atlas (CRA)—developed by NOAA, NCDDC and CSC.
Inland Wind Model and the Maximum Envelope of Winds (MEOW)—developed by NHC.
SLOSH (Sea, Lake and Overland Surges from Hurricanes)—model run by the NHC to
     estimate storm surge heights and winds.

Lacombe, much of the existing town will be in the new floodplain that will result from a rise in sea elevation.

We can also show the relationships between natural systems and demographic factors. Plate 12, for example, shows that that the elderly poor, those with no automobile, and those living in public housing, rental housing, or structures built before 1970 were more vulnerable to Katrina than others. This type of map emphasizes the importance of including social and economic factors in planning for sustainable resilience.

We anticipate developing more diagnostic maps for the Gulf megapolitan region. Included are ones that go back in time, show current conditions, and develop environmental scenarios for the future, 2030 or 2050. They will incorporate hurricane patterns, climate change, flooding, land subsidence, land use, and associated social and economic costs.

## CONCLUSION

Katrina flooded the media, breaking through the levees of our inattention. Environmental neglect collided with social inequity on the evening news before the local shooting of the day. Images from the streets of New Orleans, along the coasts of Mississippi, and across the interstate highways of the Gulf region challenged how we think about our nation, and our leaders.

Interest, like oil supplies, peaks. Interest, like the tides, subsides. We move on. Natural disasters come and go: from Hurricane Andrew in 1992, through the Mississippi floods of 1993, on to the Indian Ocean tsunami of December 2004.

Might Katrina be different? Might it present an opportunity for learning? For rethinking urbanism and regionalism? For rethinking humanity in this first urban century? As the media flood recedes, might Katrina challenge us for a bit longer?

Katrina left many wounds in its wake and revealed many more that had festered before the storm. These wounds are clear to even those without an ecological education. The residents of the Gulf Coast region need not live alone with those wounds. Ecological understanding can be advanced through mapping exercises, but such mapping should be viewed as part of a larger network of thinking about how people interrelate with land and water.

Advanced ecological planning theory asserts that the "insight relevant to linking ecology with planning and design is that *human perception, learning, and resultant actions are a part of the human ecosystem*" (Pickett 2004, 378). Mapping environmentally sensitive areas thus becomes a vital part of the "learning loop" initiated by Katrina. Universities, private firms, and nonprofit organizations can contribute to this learning loop, as illustrated by the National Consortium to Map Gulf Coast Constraints. If we can learn from disasters such as Katrina, the promise is we can reduce the loss of life and of property and can minimize the disruptions to lives. Floods will continue to inundate the lands along the Mississippi River. Hurricanes will continue to create surges along the Gulf Coasts. We can map the lands prone to flooding and storm surges with relative accuracy. Let us learn from those maps and plan our future settlements with that knowledge.

We appreciate data derived from a variety of sources, including

1989 Congress Report on Climate Change: http://www.usgcrp.gov/usgcrp/nacc/default.htm

Coastal Classification Map: shttp://coastal.er.usgs.gov/coastal-classification/

FEMA Mapping and Analysis Center: http://www.gismaps.fema.gov/rs storms.shtm

GIS for the Gulf: http://gos2.geodata.gov

GlobeXplorer: http://www.globexplorer.com/disasterimages

High Wind Risk Areas: http://www.nhc.noaa.gov/HAW2/english/wind/risk_areas.shtml

Historical Hurricane Tracks: http://www.nhc.noaa.gov/pastall.shtml

Hurricane Katrina Flood Recovery Maps: http://www.fema.gov/hazards/floods/recoverydata/katrina_index.shtm

"Maps of Lands Vulnerable to Sea Level Rise—On the Gulf Coast": http://yosemite.epa.gov/oar/globalwarming.nsf/content/ResourceCenterPublicationsSLRMapsGulf.html

MODIS Rapid Response System: http://rapidfire.sci.gsfc.nasa.gov

Multihazard Mapping: http://www.hazardmaps.gov/atlas.php

NASA Earth Observatory: http://earthobservatory.nasa.gov

National Assessment of Coastal Vulnerability to Sea-Level Rise: http://woodshole.er.usgs.gov/project-pages/cvi/

National Hurricane Center: http://www.nhc.noaa.gov

NESDIS: http://www.gis.ssd.nesdis.noaa.gov

NOAA Historical Hurricane Tracks: http://hurricane.csc.noaa.gov/hurricanes/viewer.html

SLAMM: http://www.oceanservice.noaa.gov/programs/nccos/nos_science/SeaLevelRisePark.pdf

National Map Hazards Data Distribution System: http://www.gisdata.usgs.gov/website/disaster_response

USGS EROS: http://eros.usgs.gov/katrina

We appreciate the involvement of our generous National Consortium to Map Gulf Coast Ecological Constraints, which includes Eugenie L. Birch, University of Pennsylvania; Peter Black, Environmental Defense; Kent Butler, University of Texas at Austin; Jonathan Fink, Arizona State University; Michael Fishman, Halcrow; Hank Garie, U.S. Geological Survey; Gary Hack, University of Pennsylvania; Kristina Hill, University of Washington; Robert Lang, Virginia Tech; Bill Miller, ESRI; Elizabeth Mossop, Louisiana State University; Bob Paterson, University of Texas at Austin; Robert Pierce, USGS; Catherine Ross, Georgia Institute of Technology; Janice Cervelli Schach, Clemson University; Nancy Somerville, American Society of Landscape Architects; Carl Steinitz, Harvard University; Petra Todorovich, Regional Plan Association; Dana Tomlin, University of Pennsylvania; and Steve Verderber, Tulane University.

## Notes

1. Our group gathered at ASLA headquarters in Washington, D.C., for our kick-off meeting on December 19, 2005. Senior representatives from EDAW and USGS explained the wide range of data available for New Orleans and the Gulf Coast region. We quickly concluded that we were not facing a data shortage challenge. Rather, the challenge was to assess that data and, then, clearly communicate it to decision makers, professionals involved in the recovery and restoration efforts, and citizens both locally and nationally.

2. See, for example, the work of WRT and the Urban Land Institute in New Orleans (Barnett 2006; Taylor 2006), Fregonese Calthorpe for Louisiana, and Andres Duany and the Congress for the New Urbanism in Mississippi (www.mississippirenewal.com).

# CHAPTER 5

# Natural Hazards Science—A Matter of Public Safety

## P. Patrick Leahy

Nature has given us several tragic reminders in the past few years of the importance of increasing our resiliency to natural hazards. More than twenty-seven major disasters were declared in the United States between March 2004 and 2005, including earthquakes, landslides, fires, floods, and hurricanes. Every year, natural hazards that occur in the United States result in hundreds of lives lost and in billions of dollars of destroyed public and private properties and disrupted commerce.

New Orleans is vulnerable to flooding because most of its area is below sea level and the city is located near the mouth of the Mississippi River, where it flows into the Gulf of Mexico. These are geological realities that are well understood. Science will play a critical role in the decisions made by the state of Louisiana and the city of New Orleans and others about how and where the city will be rebuilt; however, science will not be enough. The scientific community needs to develop new tools to bridge the gap between science and policy and to improve linkages between the physical processes associated with severe storms and other natural hazards and society's vulnerability and risk. While science will inform the decisions made about rebuilding the city after Katrina and Rita, factors such as economics, transportation, tourism, and preservation of historical buildings and neighborhoods, in addition to storm and flood susceptibility, will be important to the community. Our role at the U.S. Geological Survey (USGS) is to provide unbiased scientific information to minimize loss of life and property, and we will continue to develop more effective approaches to link our science with information about the vulnerability and risk faced by our coastal cities, such as New Orleans.

## NATURAL HAZARDS AND THE FEDERAL ROLE

Within the federal government, the National Oceanic and Atmospheric Administration (NOAA) is responsible for forecasting, tracking, predicting the landfall of, and issuing warnings for hurricanes and tropical storms in the United States and its territories to the public, the media, and other government agencies and authorities. Science to forecast hurricane impacts is a collaborative effort among the USGS, NOAA, the National Aeronautics and

Space Administration (NASA), the U.S. Army Corps of Engineers, and others.

The USGS has the lead federal responsibility under the Disaster Relief Act (P.L. 93–288, popularly known as the Stafford Act) to provide notification for earthquakes, volcanoes, and landslides, to enhance public safety, and to reduce losses through effective forecasts and warnings based on the best possible scientific information. It is our goal to provide scientific research and analysis that help the public, the emergency management community, and policy makers make informed decisions on how to react to each hazard and how to safeguard society. We produce coastal-change vulnerability products to provide pre-hurricane forecasts of impacts to infrastructure, essential for evacuation and post-storm recovery efforts. In the case of wildfires, USGS with federal partners monitor seasonal fire danger conditions and provide firefighters with maps of current fire locations, perimeters, and potential spread.

## USGS and Natural Hazards

One of the objectives of the USGS is to improve our capability to predict coastal change that results from severe tropical and extratropical storms. Such a capability may facilitate locating buildings and infrastructure away from coastal change hazards. New technology in the form of airborne laser surveys and imagery enables us to more accurately portray coastal change. Hurricanes Katrina, Wilma, Rita, and the ones we have yet to face highlight the increasing need for scientific knowledge.

With USGS science and technology, we are striving to prevent natural hazards from becoming disasters. We must improve our understanding of natural processes, alleviate risks, and develop tools and technology for assessment, and for predictive and prescriptive strategies. Our science can help save lives, minimize property damage, and reduce risks that may result from natural hazards. USGS research on natural hazards is no longer just a scientific endeavor—it is a matter of public safety.

Before a hurricane makes landfall, the USGS ensures that equipment along the Gulf and Atlantic coasts is ready to monitor coastal change. A USGS network of streamgages also reports real-time stream flow to officials issuing flood warnings. USGS geospatial databases and maps assist pre-storm evacuation planning and post-storm rescue and recovery. Before and after major storms, scientists survey habitats and document erosion on coasts and barrier islands by using airborne and satellite imagery. The USGS deploys amphibious aircraft to conduct environmental assessments and to aid emergency response. Immediately after Hurricane Katrina, the USGS used satellite and aerial imagery to create maps linking 911 calls to locations where people needed to be rescued. USGS scientists also assisted federal and state agencies by conducting water quality and sediment testing to indicate the safety of water for human contact. Scientists also conducted ground surveys to help land managers with habitat and wildlife impact assessments, and to secure scientific equipment in remote field sites. The USGS provides scientific research and analyses that help the public, policy makers, and emergency management communities make informed decisions on how to prepare for and react to hurricane hazards and reduce losses from future hurricanes.

One of the most damaging aspects of hurricanes is the storm surge. Storm surge, a dome of ocean water, can exceed twenty feet in height and extend alongshore for hundreds of miles. As Katrina demonstrated, hurricanes can affect the nation's energy supply; more than one-fourth of U.S. crude oil production is from the Gulf of Mexico. Often, hurricanes leave an area more vulnerable to subsequent storms.

Specifically, the USGS science priorities for addressing hurricane impacts are to develop an ability to make near real-time maps for emergency planning and response and increase our ability to record hurricane impact and recovery of natural systems. We use airborne and other remote sensing techniques with hurricane response models to improve coastal mapping and to predict where barrier islands and evacuation routes will likely be severed or washed over in an approaching hurricane. Also, we are expanding the network of near real-time streamgages for flood forecasting and developing an ecological alert system based on a hurricane's potential to spread wildlife diseases and invasive species and destroy critical habitat.

## HURRICANES

Hurricanes bring destructive winds, storm surge, torrential rain, flooding, and tornadoes. A single storm can wreak havoc on coastal and inland communities and natural areas over thousands of square miles. In 2005, Hurricanes Katrina, Rita, and Wilma demonstrated the devastation that hurricanes can inflict and the importance of hurricane hazard research and preparedness. More than half of the U.S. population live within 50 miles of a coast, and these numbers are increasing. Many of these areas, especially the Atlantic and Gulf Coasts, will be in the direct path of future hurricanes. Hawaii is also vulnerable to hurricanes.

As seaside populations and development escalate, so does property damage from hurricanes. Recent Atlantic hurricane seasons have been the costliest on record, with losses of $42 billion in 2004[1] and in the hundreds of billions in 2005. Research suggests that Americans should brace for more of the same, because the Atlantic basin is in an active period that might persist for decades.

Hurricanes and coastal storms can devastate great swaths of the coast and inland structures. They not only destroy structures but cause extreme coastal erosion, overwash, barrier island loss, flooding, wetland loss, and sometimes landslides as they move inland.

Barrier islands and coastal wetlands are the first line of defense for many Atlantic and Gulf Coast communities, and many are rapidly eroding. Wetlands reduce storm surge and buffer hurricane impacts. However, since the 1930s, Louisiana has lost about 1,900 square miles of coastal land from subsidence, inundation, and erosion during hurricanes. Hurricane Katrina eliminated more than 100 square miles of wetlands protecting New Orleans. In 2004, Hurricane Ivan eroded Alabama's coast an average of forty feet.

Hurricane Katrina caused significant damage in New Orleans with much of the city being inundated by flood waters. The challenge of rebuilding New Orleans is complex, requiring multiple skills and capabilities, as well as diverse opinions and perspectives from federal and state government agencies, the local government and the citizens of New Orleans.

## USGS RESPONSE TO HURRICANES KATRINA AND WILMA

Hurricane Katrina made landfall as a Category 4 storm in Plaquemines Parish, Louisiana, on August 29, 2005. Immediately, the USGS began collecting satellite imagery to assess the impact on wetlands, coasts, and changes in elevation, collecting water samples to determine the water quality in areas where there had been significant salt-water intrusion, marking and flagging high-water marks to document flooding and storm surge, and repairing and replacing damaged streamgages to restore flood warning capabilities.

Aerial video, still photography, and laser altimetry surveys of post-storm beach conditions were collected August 31 and September 1, 2005, for comparison with pre-storm data. The comparisons show the nature, magnitude, and spatial variability of coastal changes such as beach erosion, overwash deposition, and island breaching. These data are being used to further refine predictive models of coastal impacts from severe storms. The data are available to local, state, and federal agencies for purposes of disaster recovery and erosion mitigation via the internet.

Hurricane Wilma made landfall in the U.S. as a Category 3 storm at approximately 6:30 a.m. EDT on October 24, 2005 at Cape Romano, Florida, approximately 20 miles south of Naples, Florida. The long, thin barrier islands that comprise the Gulf of Mexico coast of West Florida have been particularly vulnerable to inundation during hurricanes because of their low elevation. In a cooperative research program between the USGS, NASA, and Corps of Engineers, these islands have been surveyed using airborne laser mapping (lidar) providing detailed elevation maps of the island's "first line of defense," essentially the Gulf-front dune (or in the absence of dunes, the crest of the beach berm or seawall).

Pre-landfall vulnerability estimates were made available by the USGS online for west Florida's barrier islands falling within the October 21 cone of uncertainty for Wilma's predicted path. These predictions extended south from Anclote Key to Ft. Myers Beach, but did not include the Marco Island-Cape Romano area where Wilma made landfall. Nonetheless, these maps highlighted the extreme vulnerability of the west Florida coastline to a direct hit from the waves and surge accompanying a storm of Wilma's magnitude. The beaches north of Cape Romano were very lucky to have Wilma's powerful right-front quadrant pass to their south, sparing them from a major wave and surge event.

## TRANSLATING SCIENCE INTO USEFUL INFORMATION: SCIENCE IMPACT

Despite significant advances in understanding the processes of natural hazards, the scientific community has been less successful in bridging the gap between science and policy. Science information is not always used as effectively as it could be. Decisions are sometimes made without benefit of the best available scientific information. In some cases, institutions have not been established to react effectively to scientific information. To some extent, this was the case in December 2004 with the Indian Ocean tsunami. In other situations, scientific information is presented in forms that are not especially useful or easy to use by decision makers who are not scientists.

The scientific community has a proactive responsibility to ensure that scientific information informs public policy decisions as effectively as possible. This means taking steps to translate that information into forms that are meaningful to decision makers. It also means working with professionals in other disciplines to develop methods and tools for using scientific information more effectively sometimes in combination with other information important to decision makers such as socioeconomic information.

With regard to natural hazards, the scientific community needs to focus on the fundamental issues relating to understanding hazards processes and the spatial and temporal likelihood of hazard events occurring. In this endeavor, we need to keep our focus on the key societal goals of reducing our nation's risk from natural hazards and of increasing our resiliency in responding to hazard events. Increasing our scientific knowledge and information relating to natural hazards is important to our ability to achieve these goals. However, this by itself will not result in reduced risk and in increased resiliency. The science is a necessary condition to achieving these goals, but it is by no means sufficient.

In discussing natural hazards, three terms are commonly used to describe natural events and their relationship with society: (1) hazards, (2) vulnerability, and (3) risk. "Hazards" relates to the physical processes and the spatial and temporal likelihood of an event occurring. This is the area that physical science addresses. To achieve our societal goals of reducing risk and increasing resiliency, we need to improve our physical understanding of hazard processes and the likelihood of an event occurring.

However, the societal impact of a hazard depends in large part on population and property exposure to the hazard and on society's ability to respond. Certainly, a natural hazard in a deserted part of the world will have less significance than that same hazard in a population center. "Vulnerability" addresses the population and property exposure to the hazard, the sensitivity of these assets to a hazard, and society's resilience in responding and adapting to an extreme event if it occurs. Even if the likelihood of a hazard is similar throughout a region, local variations in land use, demography, economies, and cultural settings can create different levels of community vulnerability.

"Risk" relates to the likelihood of life or property loss to a natural hazard. It combines information on the likelihood of the hazard with information on societal vulnerability. As a society, we need to understand risk to make informed decisions on land use as well as on where, when, and at what level mitigation efforts should be implemented.

The usefulness and value of our knowledge about natural hazards depend in part on our ability to combine physical understanding of the hazard with knowledge and information about our societal vulnerability to the hazard and the resulting risk. Understanding only one part of this process will not allow us as a society to make the most informed and effective decisions. It should be emphasized that these decisions are based on both information and values. Information on the hazard as well as on vulnerability and risk informs decision makers, but is used in combination with societal values to develop public decisions.

We need to remember that societal decisions can affect vulnerability and risk, but for the most part, have little impact on the hazard itself. For instance, we can take steps to reduce risk and increase resiliency to earthquakes if we understand earthquake processes and their likelihood, as well as population and property vulnerability. However, there is little that we can do to reduce the hazard of the earthquake itself.

To bridge the gap between science and policy for natural hazards, the scientific community needs to improve linkages between the physical processes associated with hazards and society's vulnerability and risk. This means in some cases extending research efforts to combine and integrate physical and socioeconomic investigations. It also means developing tools and methods for more effectively using physical science information in combination with information on vulnerability and risk.

The need for these efforts is compounded by the fact that vulnerability and risk are not static. As society changes, so do our vulnerability and risk. Population is growing and is expected to continue to do so in areas with significant natural hazards. For instance, the Gulf Coast and coastal Florida are expected to sustain significant increases in population over the next twenty-five to fifty years, which means that exposure to hurricane hazards will grow even if the physical hazard does not change. Areas along the west coast with significant hazard for earthquakes and landslides are also experiencing rapid population growth. Our vulnerability and risk from natural hazards will increase if we as a society do not act proactively to address these issues, even if the physical hazard itself does not change.

The USGS is taking explicit steps to narrow the gap between science and policy so that science can be used more effectively to reduce risk and increase resiliency. We are developing an integrated multi-hazards initiative that responds to the need for improved information on natural hazards processes and the associated spatial and temporal likelihood. The initiative addresses the need to fill key information gaps in our understanding of natural hazards such as earthquakes, volcanoes, landslides, and floods. The initiative also focuses on the development of methods and tools for more effectively using hazards information in combination with vulnerability and risk information.

As part of the hazards initiative, the USGS in the fall of 2006 will initiate a Multi-Hazards Demonstration Project to show that integrating information and products about multiple hazards can reduce loss of life and property from natural hazards. The Demonstration Project will bring the unique research and systems capabilities of the USGS to bear on the complex issues surrounding natural hazards events, especially interrelated hazards, such as fire, floods, and debris flows, or earthquakes and tsunamis.

The Demonstration Project will be conducted in southern California, which has one of the nation's highest potentials for extreme, catastrophic losses from a number of natural hazards. Estimates of expected losses from natural hazards in the eight counties of southern California exceed \$3 billion per year[2] and are expected to increase as the present population of 20 million grows at more than 10% per year. The project will focus on those natural hazards posing a significant threat to life and property in southern California—earthquakes, floods, landslides, tsunamis, and wildfires—and will build on work already underway in the study area.

The project will have three principal components. Modernizing earth observation hazard networks will include adding 18 streamgages and raingages to the streamgaging network and developing a prototype flash-flood and debris-flow warning system for burned areas in Southern California. Targeted research on hazard processes and prediction will focus on assessment of the southern San Andreas Fault, the role of fire suppression and fuel accumulation in chaparral ecosystems and the wildland-urban interface, tsunami and inundation mapping and modeling, and developing models for predicting landslides and debris flows. To improve communication of USGS science to communities at risk, the USGS will work with local planners, emergency managers, and first responders to develop products and tools such as integrated hazard maps, tools to assess coastal vulnerability to extreme storm events, rainfall intensity-duration thresholds, and planning scenarios and decision tools.

The USGS is also developing a Science Impact program (SI), a focused research effort to increase the use and value of USGS science information in informing societal decisions. SI encompasses developing methods and tools to combine USGS natural science with socioeconomic information to enhance linkages between science and decision making. For natural hazards, this means combining our understanding of the hazard with vulnerability and risk analyses. The methods and tools developed as part of the Science Impact program will be applied to the multi-hazards initiative described above.

USGS efforts to bridge the gap between science, policy, and the public requires expertise in disciplines beyond those that are traditional to the USGS. Combining vulnerability and risk analysis with an understanding of the physical hazard requires an understanding of the decision sciences, economics, and social sciences, as well as the physical sciences. To promote external innovation and gain access to these skills, the USGS is developing partnerships with universities such as the University of Pennsylvania. These partnerships are an important component of our Science Impact program and are critical to our ability to combine understanding of natural hazards with information that will help make important decisions to increase resiliency and to reduce risk.

## Conclusion

Natural hazards will always be with us. They are unpredictable and can have tragic consequences. We are doing our part to reduce risk and increase society's resiliency to natural hazards. If we can use our science to help save lives and minimize the damage caused by natural hazards, we will have achieved an enormous goal—helping to prevent natural hazards from becoming disasters.

Additional USGS Web Resources:
USGS Homepage: http://www.usgs.gov
USGS Responds to Hurricanes: http://www.usgs.gov/hazards/hurricanes/kat_rit_wil
USGS and Natural Hazard Research: http://www.usgs.gov/science/science.php?term = 53
USGS Science Impact Program: http://www.usgs.gov/science_impact

*Notes*

1. Figure taken from NOAA website: www.nhc.noaa.gov/archive/2004/tws/ MIATWSAT_nov.shtml

2. This is an estimate based on 2000 FEMA366 report numbers for earthquakes alone, updated for inflation and rounded up to include all the other hazards. That report gave expected 8-county losses at $2.4 billion. At 3%/yr inflation, that yields $2.95 billion in 2006 dollars. HAZUS®99 Estimated Annualized Earthquake Losses for the United States. Federal Emergency Management Agency Report 366, Washington, D.C., September 2000.

Part II

# Returning Urban Places to Economic Viability

# CHAPTER 6

# Measuring Katrina's Impact on the Gulf Megapolitan Area

## Robert E. Lang

"Houston, too close to New Orleans," sang the Grateful Dead in their popular song "Truckin" back in the 1970s. Although written decades ago, these lyrics nicely capture the relationship between the two big cities of the Gulf Coast. While Houston and New Orleans may not be close enough to form a Dallas/ Fort Worth-style "metroplex," they nonetheless anchor an extended Gulf Coast "megapolitan corridor" that stretches from Pensacola, Florida, in the east, to greater Houston in the west.[1] Houston, it turns out, is very close to New Orleans. The region played a key role in the Crescent City's immediate recovery from Hurricane Katrina, taking on the shipping traffic and energy business from its neighbor and providing a safe haven for the displaced.

The nation's southernmost transcontinental Interstate, I-10, serves as the Gulf Coast's "Main Street." Every major city in the megapolitan area lies along its path. Katrina, and to a lesser extent Hurricane Rita, sliced through the heart of the I-10 urban corridor. The hurricanes tore up ports, disabled refineries, and flooded large sections of the coast including much of New Orleans. The immediate national impact was an energy spike that demonstrated the Gulf Coast's critical role in oil and gas production.

This essay looks at the impact that Hurricanes Katrina had on New Orleans and the Gulf Coast Megapolitan Area. It addresses the nature of how this region is economically and environmentally integrated. It also explores how resilient the Gulf Coast will prove in the coming years. The fact that New Orleans links to a megapolitan urban network has already helped to manage the disaster. The larger Gulf Coast absorbed most of the city's displaced. The Houston and Baton Rouge metropolitan areas in particular gained both people and commerce due to Katrina. Fortunately, Hurricane Rita missed metropolitan Houston. Had it struck the region with the same intensity as Katrina did New Orleans, the Gulf Coast's two anchor metros would have been damaged at the same moment, rendering both unable to assist the other.

## WHAT IS A MEGAPOLITAN?

Megapolitan Areas are integrated networks of metropolitan and micropolitan areas. The name Megapolitan plays off Jean Gottmann's (1961) "megalopolis" label by using the same prefix—"mega." According to an analysis by the Metropolitan Institute at Virginia Tech (Lang, Nelson, and Dhavale 2006), the U.S. has eleven "Megas" (see Figure 1), with six in the eastern half of the U.S. and five in the west. Megapolitan Areas extend into thirty-seven states, including every one east of the Mississippi River except Vermont. As of 2004, Megapolitan Areas contained about a fifth of all land area in the lower forty-eight states, but captured almost 70% of the total U.S. population with more than 210 million people. The sixteen most populous U.S. metropolitan areas are also found in Megas.

By 2040, Megapolitan Areas are projected to gain over eighty-five million residents, or about three-quarters of national growth (Lang, Nelson, and Dhavale 2006). To put this in perspective, consider that this area, which is smaller than northwest Europe, is about to add a population exceeding that of Germany by mid-century. The costs of building the residential dwellings and commercial facilities to accommodate this growth could run over $35 trillion by some estimates (Nelson 2004).

A direct functional relationship as indicated by commuting only tenuously exists at the megapolitan scale. The area is simply too big to make many daily trips possible between distant sections. However, data showing "stretch commutes" of 50 and 100 miles each way indicate a growing number of people who journey for work between megapolitan metros (Lang, Nelson, and Dhavale 2006).

The changing nature of work is also feeding this transformation. In many fields workers simply need not be present in the office five days per week. The practice of "hoteling," where employees "visit" work infrequently and mostly work at home or on the road is common in high tech firms and will soon spread to other sectors. This allows people the flexibility to live at great distance to work in remote exurbs or even a neighboring metropolitan area.

But commuting is just one—albeit a key—way to show regional cohesion. Other integrating forces exist such as goods movement, business linkages, cultural commonality, and physical environment. A Megapolitan Area could represent a sales district for a branch office. Or, in the case of the Northeast Megalopolis or the Florida Peninsula, it can be a zone of fully integrated toll roads where an "E-Z Pass" or "SunPass" works across multiple metropolitan areas.

Lang and Dhavale (2005a) define Megapolitan Areas with the following list of characteristics:

- Combine at least two, but may include dozens of existing metropolitan areas;
- Total at least 10,000,000 projected residents by mid century;
- Derive from contiguous metropolitan and micropolitan areas;

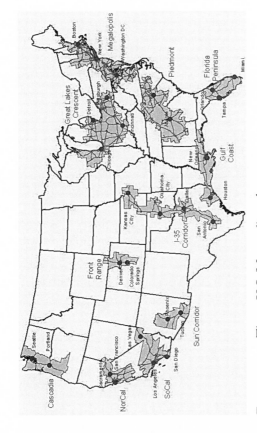

FIGURE 1.   The 11 U.S. Megapolitan Areas.

TABLE 1. Hierarchy of U.S. Urban Complexes

| Type | Description | Examples |
|------|-------------|----------|
| Twin City | Two principal cities that physically connect to form a binary core to a metropolitan area | Minneapolis/St. Paul, Tampa/St. Petersburg |
| Metroplex | Two or more metropolitan areas that share overlapping suburbs but the main principal cities do not touch | Dallas/Ft. Worth, Washington/Baltimore |
| Extended Metroplex | Two or more metropolitan areas with anchor principal cities over 75 miles apart that maintain at least 5 percent of commuting spillover between metros | New Orleans/Baton Rouge, Tampa/Orlando |
| Megapolitan Area | Three or more metropolitan areas with main principal cities over 75 miles apart that form an urban web over a broad area but do not maintain commuting linkages | Gulf Coast, Great Lakes Crescent |
| Megapolitan Pair | Two megapolitan areas that are proximate and occupy common cultural and physical environments and maintain dense business linkages | Gulf Coast and I-35 Corridor, Sun Corridor and SoCal |

Source: Metropolitan Institute at Virginia Tech.

• Constitute an "organic" region with a distinct history and identity;
• Occupy a roughly similar physical environment;
• Link large centers through major transportation infrastructure;
• Form a functional urban network via goods and service flows;
• Create a geography that is suitable for large-scale regional planning;
• Lie within the United States;
• Consist of counties as the most basic unit.

In Figure 1, the eleven Megas are depicted by the bold outline. The map also shows Interstates and "urbanized" places.

There are several distinct levels of the urban hierarchy at which New Orleans connects to the larger network of regional metropolitan areas. Table 1 shows these relationships. While New Orleans and Baton Rouge do not form a tight metroplex in the way that Dallas and Fort Worth do, they do combine into what I define as an "extended metroplex." For example, the centers of New Orleans and Baton Rouge lie at about double the distance as the gap between Dallas and Fort Worth. An extended metroplex maintains high degrees of connectivity by even such standard census measures as commuting, although its numbers in this measure fall just below what the census uses to define a "combined statistical area."[2]

At the megapolitan level, the New Orleans area links to Houston as part of the Gulf Coast. Connections at this tier in the hierarchy include stretch commuting, transportation linkages, similar environment, and business networks. Finally, at the top of the urban system, are Megapolitan Pairs. The Gulf Coast forms a pair with the I-35 Corridor area, especially in Texas.

The degree of regional cohesion drops with each level in the urban hierarchy. Space within a metropolitan area is significantly integrated and is recognized by the census as such. The partners in an extended metroplex—such as New Orleans and Baton Rouge—fall just below a metropolitan designation and level of connectivity. The links are still present, but less intense at the megapolitan scale, and are more tenuous at the pair level.

The dispersal of people and commerce due to Katrina reveals the degree of integration in the urban hierarchy. As predicted, Baton Rouge, the metropolitan area that with New Orleans forms an extended metroplex, was most impacted by the dislocation of people from Katrina. The city of Baton Rouge almost overnight became the largest in Louisiana in the wake of the storm. Traffic snarled and house prices shot up as evacuees jammed the region. *Business Week* observed:

> And the influx of displaced persons [from New Orleans] has helped boost tax revenues in the state capital of Baton Rouge, where property prices (and by extension property tax assessments) have risen, while federal aid is expected to help offset the costs of dealing with evacuees from metro New Orleans. (McNatt and Benassi 2006, 41)

Houston was the next most affected metropolis after Baton Rouge. Houston is the Gulf Coast's leading metropolitan area, with about half the region's population, and as predicted in the megapolitan model it has played a significant role in aiding New Orleans. In fact, so many former residents of New Orleans now live in Houston that the Crescent City's current mayoral candidates make regular campaign stops in the city. That is because Houston is home to "150,000 evacuees, or almost as many New Orleanians as New Orleans" (Franks 2006, A1).

Evacuees from Katrina also affected Dallas, but not nearly to the extent they did Baton Rouge and Houston. Still, the city was affected enough to ask for and receive federal aid to offset its costs due to aiding displaced people. Dallas, along with other I-35 Corridor metros such as San Antonio and Austin, form a Megapolitan pair with the Gulf Coast. The New Orleans Saints—the professional football team—moved from its home in the Superdome to the San Antonio Alamodome for the 2005 season.[3] Austin had enough Katrina evacuees to set up a resource guide website and schedule community events for hurricane victims. Thus even mid-sized metropolitan areas—500 miles from New Orleans—played a role in its recovery.

## NEW ORLEANS AND THE GULF COAST MEGAPOLITAN AREA

New Orleans is not the Gulf Coast's premier "world city." That role is played by neighboring Houston, according to analyses by Taylor and Lang (2005, 2006). Their studies looked at business connectivity between world cities, based on the network of headquarters and branch offices in producer services such as banking, finance, law, insurance, media, accounting, advertising, and management consulting. The two leading world cities were found to be New York and London. Houston was the tenth most connected U.S. world city, while New Orleans ranked thirty-seventh—below Las Vegas and ahead of Sacramento. New Orleans ranked well below such other non-Gulf Southern U.S. metro rivals as Miami (fifth), Atlanta (sixth), and Dallas (ninth).

That Houston ranks higher as a world city than New Orleans should not surprise those familiar with the Gulf Coast. For instance, airline connections to New Orleans often run through Houston. Taylor and Lang's data showed that New Orleans was heavily connected (and subordinate) to Houston in terms of producer services. Houston typically has the headquarters, and New Orleans the branch office. While Taylor and Lang did not focus on shipping and energy, it is likely that Houston maintains the same command position with respect to New Orleans in these sectors.[4] In general, Houston is the key gateway in and out of the Gulf Coast, while New Orleans constitutes an important secondary regional hub.

The New Orleans metropolitan area, with 1.36 million residents (in 2004), lies near the middle of Gulf Coast Megapolitan Area that stretches from Pensacola to Houston (see Figure 2). The Gulf Coast region features an unbroken string of nine census-defined metropolitan areas (and six surrounding rural counties) that together contain almost 10.4 million people (see Table 2).

Metros along the Gulf Coast share many environmental and economic attributes (Lang and Dhavale 2005a). First and foremost, the entire region is vulnerable to hurricanes. Most urbanized growth is near the Gulf of Mexico, and lies between wetlands and estuaries. New Orleans is famous for being mostly below sea level, but the Gulf Coast's other major metropolitan area— Houston—is also quite low, having been built over and around a series of bayous. New Orleans is not the only city along the Gulf Coast to rely on pumping systems and levees to stay dry—only the most notable one.

The Gulf Coast region contains large tourist, energy, fishing, and port-related economies. The energy sector is quite diverse and includes oil and natural gas extraction, refining, and financing. Metropolitan Houston and New Orleans have producer service firms that specialize in multiple energy sectors from finding new energy sources to extinguishing oil well fires. Houston is also home to energy futures markets, the best-known example of which was run by the now defunct and scandal ridden firm Enron.

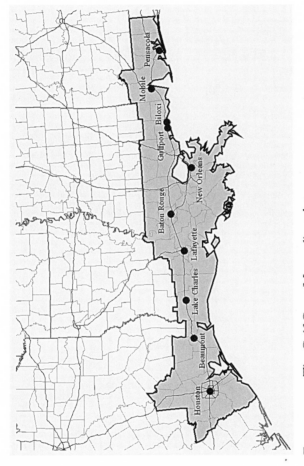

FIGURE 2. The Gulf Coast Megapolitan Area.

TABLE 2.   Gulf Coast Metropolitan Population, 2004

| Metropolitan Area | 2004 population (est.) | Number of counties/ parishes |
|---|---|---|
| Baton Rouge-Pierre Part, LA CSA | 751,965 | 10 |
| Beaumont-Port Arthur, TX MSA | 383,443 | 3 |
| Gulfport-Biloxi-Pascagoula, MS CSA | 409,045 | 5 |
| Houston-Baytown-Huntsville, TX CSA | 5,280,752 | 12 |
| Lafayette-Acadiana, LA CSA | 524,163 | 6 |
| Lake Charles-Jennings, LA CSA | 225,877 | 3 |
| Mobile-Daphne-Fairhope, AL CSA | 557,227 | 2 |
| New Orleans-Metairie-Bogalusa, LA CSA | 1,363,750 | 8 |
| Pensacola-Ferry Pass-Brent, FL MSA | 437,135 | 2 |
| Imbedded Rural Counties in LA and MS | 429,008 | 6 |
| Gulf Coast Megapolitan Area Total | 10,362,365 | 57 |

CSA = Combined Statistical Area; MSA = Metropolitan Statistical Area.

The biggest impact from the two Gulf Coast 2005 hurricanes Katrina and Rita were felt in the New Orleans, Gulfport, Lake Charles, and Beaumont metropolitan areas, or places that are home to nearly 2.4 million residents (see Table 2). This is a big impact, but represents less than a quarter of the total population of the Gulf Coast Megapolitan Area.[5]

## WHERE DID NEW ORLEANS GO AND WHO WILL RETURN?

Hurricane Katrina's impact on New Orleans is still not fully understood, but the preliminary data show that it may be the most devastated American city since the destruction of Atlanta during the Civil War. The best evidence available on the human dimensions of Katrina in the immediate aftermath of the storm was gathered by the news organizations, especially *USA Today*. *USA Today* obtained information about the dispersal of population from the city. It used two sources: the Federal Emergency Management Agency (FEMA) and the United States Postal Service (USPS). The FEMA data came from the 1.3 million people who requested aid following Katrina. FEMA kept information about where the request originated and thus produced an immediate geography of New Orleans evacuees. USPS tracked change of addresses (COA) forms for displaced households. Both sources showed where evacuees relocated after Katrina. *USA Today* mapped and reported these data (El Nasser and Overberg 2005).

The most interesting finding from the *USA Today* analysis is that most people affected by Katrina chose to stay in the Gulf Coast region. While significant numbers of evacuees located as far off as Seattle and Boston, it was much more likely to find them in Houston and Baton Rouge. The USPS service information is especially important, because it represents a longer-term relocation to a new address compared to the FEMA data.

In October 2005, the USPS found that Katrina affected 1,570,308 households. As of that date, just fewer than 300,000 COA forms had been filed. *USA Today* mapped these data using three-digit zip codes. The zip code analysis shows that about 70% of the people filing COA forms stayed in the Gulf Coast Megapolitan Area. The places receiving the most New Orleans evacuees based on the COA data are metro New Orleans (outside the affected areas), Baton Rouge, and Houston. More than half of all New Orleans evacuees have relocated to just these three metropolitan areas. The next biggest share is found in the rest of the Gulf Coast Megapolitan Area: next are the Dallas and Atlanta metropolitan areas, which lie just outside the Gulf Coast. In total, nine in ten New Orleans evacuees are still in the South, according to the COA data as of late October 2005.

*USA Today* also analyzed the COA data filed from late October to December 31, 2005 (El Nasser and Overberg 2006).[6] This second analysis included nearly a half million households and shows a somewhat different pattern from the October COA data. It found a net movement away from far-flung safe haven places along the East Coast and toward an arc of staging places around the disaster zone extending from Houston to New Orleans. Thus, the Gulf Coast Megapolitan Area is now consolidating the population displaced by Katrina, which may foreshadow a longer-range reshuffling of people to Houston and Baton Rouge.

The fact that so many people displaced by Katrina stayed in the Gulf Coast Megapolitan Area represents both a challenge and an opportunity. The opportunity lies in the fact that so many former New Orleans residents remain in the area and can potentially help rebuild and repopulate the city. Yet, the larger Gulf Coast—acting like a giant shock absorber—has taken on the bulk of Katrina's victims. Places such as Baton Rouge are especially overburdened. Katrina, particularly the movements of people it displaced, shows that the Gulf Coast is a distinct region. Perhaps future hurricane preparedness can anticipate the likely flow of evacuees to nearby places and plan at the megapolitan level.

Finally, the issue of how many people will return to their former homes in New Orleans remains an open question. *USA Today* polled evacuees on their likelihood of coming home (Page 2005). Polling evacuees presents tremendous methods challenges given that so many people have simply fallen out of contact. But working with the Gallup Organization, and using information provided by the Red Cross and FEMA, a random sample of the evacuees was possible. The *USA Today* found that 39% of people did not anticipate that they would return home. But this does not mean that they are unlikely to come back to the city of New Orleans or the region. At this point, it is hard to interpret such data. As would be expected, people are highly anxious and perhaps even pessimistic after being dislocated. Yet the numbers do hint that New Orleans may be a smaller place after Katrina, it almost will certainly be a very changed place.

John Logan (Logan et al. 2006) at Brown University reached a similar conclusion. He speculates that New Orleans is at risk for losing perhaps four in five of its pre-Katrina African American residents. He bases this assessment on a neighborhood-level analysis of damaged property, which shows a disproportionate share of minority dwellings were impacted by Katrina. Were none of these places to be rebuilt—a highly unlikely outcome—New Orleans would be a far smaller and much less diverse city. Reports such as Logan's may become a self-fulfilling prophecy if minority residents become discouraged from returning home based on starkly negative numbers. Therefore, they should be greeted with some level of both skepticism and concern.

A more recent study of New Orleans population trends conducted by the RAND Corporation estimated current (March 2006) residents at 155,000 (McCarthy et al. 2006). According to RAND, the city was almost completely abandoned just after Katrina, dropping to just a few thousand people. RAND estimates that one year after the storm (September 2006), just over half the city's pre-Katrina population will have returned. But following this date, the gains are smaller. RAND projects that by September 2008, large sections of the city including Lakeview, Gentilly, and New Orleans's East neighborhoods will have significantly fewer residents than before Katrina.

The RAND study found that the availability of housing was a key element in predicting the future population and composition of New Orleans. It concluded, "Damage to housing currently appears to be the most significant obstacle to repopulation [of New Orleans]" (McCarthy et al. 2006, 11). There is also the issue of where the people who lost their homes are now sheltered. The Brookings Institution analyzed temporary housing conditions of people displaced by Katrina (Katz et al. 2005). Brookings determined that at least half a million families found some form of federally provided transition or quasipermanent housing. The units included cruise ships hotels, shelters, trailers, mobile homes, and more rental housing. According to Brookings, the federal government has set aside over 7 billion dollars to house Katrina victims temporarily and longer-term.

Almost $3 billion will go for trailer and mobile home parks. FEMA has provided such units in past storms, including Hurricane Andrew in 1992, which did extensive damage to housing in south Florida. This housing solution is viewed as a longer-term solution and is often used by those who rebuild their nearby homes. Yet some people remain for the long term, as evidenced by the fact that there are still residents living in the FEMA trailers they received in the wake of Andrew.

Shorter-term housing options are already terminating. FEMA required that those living in hotels find rental housing by February 15, 2006. Depending on one's circumstances, FEMA will provide up to three months rental assistance. In some cases, FEMA will provide up to 18 months of assistance through its Individual and Households Program (Katz et al. 2005).

While it is desirable to find housing for most evacuees in existing permanent rental units, so many apartments and homes were lost to Katrina that some temporary dwellings are needed. This is especially true for those living in and around New Orleans. Those who rebuild the city will also need such housing. New Orleans has simply lost so many dwellings that it cannot fully accommodate in permanent facilities those workers needed to build new housing.

While placing trailers inside the city for essential workers is necessary, there is a concern that FEMA will over-house people outside the city—in suburbs and exurbs—with temporary structures. The fear is that big FEMA trailer parks will become essentially permanent housing that will cut people off from jobs and community (Katz et al. 2005). The rise of "Katrinavilles," a new kind of poverty zone, would both undermine rebuilding efforts and cheat the people who seek real housing in their former neighborhood.

The bottom line for New Orleans is this: the amount and quality of rebuilt housing will substantially shape its recovery. But a major hold up is where to build this housing. The simple reconstruction of the city in its old form is an invitation to future disaster. Thus, the governments directing the recovery have been hesitant to approve projects in places that had major flooding. Yet if quick decisions are not made, the city's population will simply leak away to other parts of the Gulf Coast and beyond.

## How Resilient a City and Region?

Can New Orleans and the larger Gulf Coast Megapolitan Area quickly recover from Katrina? The issue has been taken up by numerous publications and forums since the storm.[7] This essay is a product of one such meeting. The verdict on recovery varies but in general it is assumed that many areas lost to the hurricane will be rebuilt. How they will be restored and for whom appears to be the larger debate.

Also, the pace of the restoration now seems grudgingly slow. The Brookings Institution Metropolitan Policy Program has developed an index to track New Orleans's and the Gulf Coast's recovery and concluded there had been "little progress" by February 2006 (Katz, Fellowes, and Mabanta 2006). The early verdict, especially on the city's resiliency, seems somewhat negative.

The question of New Orleans's capacity to recover from Katrina was the subject of a roundtable organized by the *Journal of the American Planning Association* (*JAPA*) in October 2005 (Lang and Danielsen 2006). It included the authors Lawrence Vale and Thomas Campanella, whose book *The Resilient City* (2005b), deals directly with the challenges facing the city. Vale and Campanella are interested in "why" cities recover as much as how this process occurs. They found that recovery is determined in large part by how the city functioned socially and economically prior to the disaster. Cities on the rise at the time of the disaster, such as San Francisco just before the 1906 earthquake, have a surer path to a quick rebuilding than places that were stagnating. In that sense, New Orleans is at a disadvantage.

The *JAPA* panel offered a preliminary conclusion that recovery for New Orleans would be a mixed bag: the city would most likely be more like it was than different and probably more Hispanic than it used to be, which partly reflects the demographics of construction trades. The conclusion was based on a read of New Orleans's positive and negative qualities including: its notoriously corrupt politics, insular culture and impenetrable elite, slow growth and lack of immigrants, and fragile environment on the minus side. On the plus side, New Orleans has multigenerational social ties (and thus deep roots) and an iconic status among U.S. cities. Another bottom line seems apparent: New Orleans may be dysfunctional but it is too special a place not to be rebuilt in some form.

Historian Kenneth Jackson, in an October 2005 talk on the rebuilding of New Orleans before the Forum for Urban Design in New York, gave an even more sober appraisal of the city's resilience because of its diminished standing compared to other cities in the South.[8] Jackson noted that New Orleans was the most important city in the South as recently as the early twentieth century. But by mid-century it was already falling behind places such as Houston and Atlanta. A big problem according to Jackson is the city's entrenched elite that affords little upward mobility to entrepreneurial outsiders. This helps explain why the city has so few domestic migrants and a tiny foreign-born population despite its location near Latin America. In fact, New Orleans is among the slowest growing coastal metropolitan areas in the U.S., and is certainly among the least dynamic Sunbelt regions. This is in contrast with most other places along the Gulf Coast, especially Houston.

The bigger question of the Gulf Coast's recovery seems less uncertain. The region will absorb the damage to its second "anchor" metropolitan area and the large sections of coastal Texas, Louisiana, and Mississippi. But a reordering of urban hierarchy is possible. Baton Rouge seems likely to gain from Katrina. It is now the third largest metropolitan area in the Gulf Coast region and is poised to grab the number two spot in the wake of the disaster. New Orleans will remain the cultural heart of the state—and certainly the more popular tourist destination. But some of the city's economy and population will diffuse to the rest of the Gulf Coast, with Houston and particularly Baton Rouge the most probable destination.

New Orleans—born as a port city—will also retain the strategic advantage of maintaining its shipping trade. So much of the nation's agricultural heartland ships product through the port of New Orleans that it remains one of the most active in the nation. But even a bustling port does not provide the economic boost that it did in the past. Much of the change is due to automation and containerization, which has dramatically cut the number of workers needed to load and unload ships. The shipping industry generates jobs in related sectors such as insurance, law, and logistics, yet much of this work can be done remote from the port—even as far away as Baton Rouge.

In the short term, New Orleans should regain much of the trade that it lost due to damage by the hurricane. However, in the not-too-distant future, even the Mississippi will desert the city. As John McPhee (1990) noted in his classic work *The Control of Nature*, it may be only a matter of time before the Mississippi changes its current course and finds a new outlet to the sea via the Atchafalaya River. Despite the best efforts of the U.S. Army Corps of Engineers, New Orleans could lose its port. This blow would be large in terms of both commerce and identity. But no matter where the Mississippi enters the sea, the Gulf Coast as a whole will remain the nation's leading transshipment point for agriculture and energy.

By any measure, Katrina was one of the largest and costliest calamities in U.S. history. The storm inflicted considerable damage to the Gulf Coast and national economies. New Orleans, the city that took the largest blow, will take years to recover and may never regain its pre-Katrina size. The storm also demonstrated the interconnected nature of New Orleans to other metropolitan areas in the Gulf Coast. This connectivity challenges us to rethink the nature of resiliency. In any future urban disaster, neighboring cities that share business and social ties to the affected city can play a key role in helping with recovery and rebuilding.

The megapolitan scale should be part of disaster planning, which includes an assessment of what displaced assets and population may be housed in a nearby region. In the case of Katrina, this process occurred in an ad hoc manner. But we can do better. Imagine that Tampa were struck by a category 4 hurricane this summer. A good bet is that Orlando would play the same role in such a disaster that Baton Rouge played in Katrina. Planning for emergencies at the megapolitan scale starts with the assumption that the key to Tampa's recovery is a coordinated response with Orlando. The same relationship should be determined for all major U.S. cities using the megapolitan model. Katrina showed that Houston is too close to New Orleans—and that is just the way it should be.

## Notes

1. For a full definition and methods analysis for how these megapolitan areas were determined see Lang and Dhavale (2005a, b); Lang, Nelson, and Dhavale (2006).

2. To qualify as a combined statistical area, two metros must share at least 15 percent of commuters in a linking county. For more details, see Frey et al. (2004).

3. This coming season, the Saints will split their home games between the Alamodome and Louisiana State University college stadium in Baton Rouge.

4. Historian Carl Abbott (1993) describes how Houston emerged as the world's leading energy city, which included an aggressive outreach to all energy producing regions of the globe.

5. According to reporting by the *New York Times*, "smaller towns bore the brunt of Rita's force" (Steinhauer 2005). This included some of Louisiana's rural counties that are surrounded by the Gulf Coast's metropolitan area.

6. The staff of *USA Today* also forwarded Robert Lang unpublished maps and data that provided more detail than the news accounts.

7. An example of a publication is the January 2006 issue of *Urban Land*, which runs several articles on the topic. The cover runs the headline "Build or Bury?" Despite the challenges, the consensus seems to be the former will occur. A good summary of the challenges the city faces in rebuilding is provided by Muro and Katz (2006).

8. This forum, titled New Orleans Rebuilds, was held on October 26, 2005 at the Century Club in New York. The meeting gathered leaders from New Orleans to discuss their views on rebuilding. There was also an expert "response panel" of people from outside the region that included Kenneth Jackson from Columbia University and Robert Lang from Virginia Tech.

# CHAPTER 7

# Restarting the Economy

## Mark Zandi, Steven Cochrane, Fillip Ksiazkiewicz, and Ryan Sweet

This essay provides a policy-makers' roadmap for restarting a regional economy in the wake of a natural or manmade disaster. The roadmap has six main instructions: (1) supplying short-term income and other financial assistance to distressed households; (2) reviving the regional economy's disrupted export-oriented businesses; (3) providing financial, legal, and regulatory forbearance; (4) reconstructing public infrastructure and institutions; (5) implementing tax incentives for housing and business development; and (6) facilitating a well-functioning insurance market.

It has become the norm that regional economies beset by a disaster are made financially whole. That is, the economic aid received by an impacted regional economy, including private insurance and government support, is approximately equal to the economic cost of the disaster, including the physical damage to the region and the output lost by the disrupted economy. This is not by policy design, but more likely reflects the political realities that have developed in recent years. The nation seemingly feels that it is only equitable that hard-hit communities are supported in such a way. Of course, given budgetary considerations, it also appears that disaster-stricken regions should not expect to receive any more than that. Given the ample yet limited funds available to rebuild disaster-stricken regional economies, it is thus vital that these funds be used as effectively as possible.

The economic policy response to Hurricane Katrina offers a dramatic illustration of the importance of the policy roadmap and need for the rapid and effective use of government aid. The essay begins by putting the economic damage wrought by Katrina and the economic response in the wake of the storm into a broader historical context. The rest of the essay considers the steps policy makers have taken in the case of Katrina relative to each of the instructions in the roadmap. To date, the economic policy response to the hurricane, while very large, has been relatively unorganized and ineffectual. This suggests that the much of the impacted region's economy will not return to its pre-storm condition for many years to come.

## HISTORICAL PERSPECTIVE

Hurricane Katrina is the nation's costliest natural disaster. The human loss was overwhelming and the economic cost unprecedented. Magnifying the

TABLE 1.   Economy of Impacted Region, 2004

|  | GDP ($ billion) | Payroll employment (000) | Median household income ($ 000) |
|---|---|---|---|
| *Impacted region* | 129.1 | 1660.72 | 37,823 |
| Share of U.S. (%) | 1.1 | 1.5 | 84.1 |
| *Louisiana* | 104.94 | 1322.78 | 37,897 |
| New Orleans | 49.85 | 615.66 | 37,971 |
| Baton Rouge | 25.56 | 344.05 | 37,883 |
| Lafayette | 11.72 | 133.12 | 36,709 |
| Lake Charles | 7.19 | 87.86 | 37,340 |
| Houma-Bayou | 6.43 | 81.95 | 37,909 |
| Alexandria | 4.19 | 60.14 | 31,287 |
| *Mississippi* | 11.64 | 167.16 | 37,637 |
| Gulfport-Biloxi | 8.0 | 5113.56 | 36,942 |
| Pascagoula | 3.59 | 53.6 | 40,167 |
| *Alabama* | 12.52 | 170.78 | 33,523 |
| Mobile | 12.52 | 170.78 | 33,523 |

economic cost of the storm was the large geography and population affected. The affected region, which extends from Lake Charles, Louisiana, in the west to Mobile, Alabama, in the east, employed some 1.7 million individuals who produced $130 billion in annual output just prior to the storm (Table 1). It is important to note that the economy of this region was struggling long before the storm hit, as employment in the region has been largely unchanged since the turn of the decade.

The hurricane's economic cost includes both the physical damage and the output lost due to the disruption to the economy. Total physical damage totaled an estimated $105 billion (Table 2). One-half the estimated damage was to the region's homes (some 275,000 were completely destroyed or severely damaged), one-fourth to business structures, and the remaining one-fourth to public infrastructure, ranging from roads, bridges, and levees to the telecommunications grid and water and sewage systems.

The economic disruptions created by the hurricane cost the Gulf region and the rest of the nation an estimated $25 billion. The New Orleans and Gulfport-Biloxi, Mississippi, metropolitan area economies were far and away the most severely disrupted. Prior to the storm, some 615,000 worked in New Orleans, producing $50 billion of goods and services annually (Table 2). The Gulfport metropolitan area economy, which employed 110,000, produced $8 billion in annual output. By the end of 2005, New Orleans employment was

TABLE 2. The Economics of Disasters ($ billion)

| Disaster | Region | Date | Economic Loss | | | Economic aid | | | Economic aid as share of economic loss (%) |
| | | | Destruction | Lost output | Total loss | Insurance | Government aid | Total aid | |
|---|---|---|---|---|---|---|---|---|---|
| Hurricane Katrina | Gulf of Mexico | August 2005 | 105.4 | 24.8[a] | 130.2 | 40.2 | 90.0 | 130.2 | 100.0 |
| Hurricane Ivan | Gulf of Mexico | September 2004 | 7.2 | 6.5 | 13.7 | 7.3 | 6.3 | 13.6 | 99.3 |
| 9/11 | Entire Nation | September 2001 | 25.7 | 61.8 | 87.5 | 20.2[b] | 67.3 | 87.4 | 99.9 |
| Los Angeles Northridge Quake | Los Angeles | January 1994 | 23.6 | 12.5 | 36.1 | 16.1 | 15.5 | 31.6 | 87.5 |
| Midwest floods | Minn. to Mo. | Summer 1993 | 6.1 | 9.4[d] | 15.5 | 1.3 | 7.0 | 8.4 | 53.9 |
| Hurricane Andrew | Miami, Fl. | August 1992 | 36.7 | 11.6 | 48.4 | 21.3 | 10.8 | 32.1 | 66.3 |
| Loma Prieta quake | Bay Area, Calif.[c] | October 1989 | 10.6 | 5.4 | 16.0 | 1.6 | 7.6 | 9.2 | 57.3 |
| Hurricane Hugo | Charleston, S.C. | September 1989 | 14.5 | 4.7 | 19.2 | 6.6 | 3.1 | 9.7 | 50.4 |

Sources: ISO, Insurance Information Institute, Economy.com

[a] Lost output due to Katrina does not include the impact of higher energy prices.
[b] 9/11 insurance includes only property coverage.
[c] The Bay Area includes the metro areas of San Francisco, Oakland, San Jose, and Santa Cruz.
[d] Lost output associated with the Midwest floods includes $5 billion in crop losses.

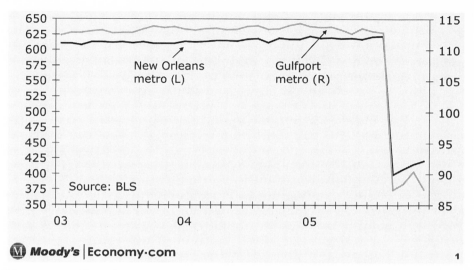

FIGURE 1.    Payroll employment (thousands) for the New Orleans and Gulfport metropolitan areas, 2003–2005, showing the massive economic shock of Katrina. Moody's Economy.com, from BLS data.

one-third of what it was prior to the storm, and Gulfport employment had been cut by more than one-fifth (Figure 1).

Unlike past natural disasters, which only affected the economy of the region stricken by the disaster, Katrina had broad and significant national macroeconomic consequences. Amplifying the national economic fallout from the storm are the disruption to the Gulf's vital seaports and damage to the region's large energy infrastructure. Even in early 2006, the ports are still not operating at full capacity and oil and natural gas production in the Gulf is only approximately 80% of normal.

The total economic cost of Katrina thus amounts to an estimated $130 billion, making by far the costliest disaster in the nation's history. Even 9/11's economic costs, equal to some $88 billion in today's dollars, were dwarfed by Katrina. Hurricane Andrew, which struck Miami in 1992, was the next costliest natural disaster, costing almost $50 billion.

Disaster-stricken regional economies are the beneficiaries of substantial economic aid, including monies from private insurers and government. In the case of Katrina, private insurers are expected to pay out some $40 billion in claims for households and businesses, and total government help will eventually total an anticipated $90 billion (see Table 2). While this is much less than some $200 billion in government aid that was being discussed in the political firestorm in the hurricane's wake, it is the largest federal government aid package to a disaster-stricken regional economy in the nation's history.

As has become the norm in recent disasters, the economic aid received by an impacted regional economy is approximately equal to the economic cost of the disaster. This is roughly the case with 9/11 and with Hurricane Ivan in 2004. In disasters prior to 9/11, insurance monies and government aid were substantial, but did not quite make up for the total economic cost. Only about two-thirds of the economic costs of Hurricane Hugo and the Loma Prieta earthquake in the Bay Area, both in the late 1980s, were eventually covered by insurance and government largesse.

It is not by policy design that the direct regional economic costs of disasters are now being fully covered; it more likely reflects the political realities that have developed in the wake of 9/11. The nation seemingly feels that it is only fair that hard-hit communities are made financially whole. Of course, given budgetary considerations, it also appears that disaster-stricken regions should not expect to receive any more than that. Indeed, very soon after talk of a $200 billion price tag for Katrina rebuilding hit a crescendo, so too did the open debate over the budgetary implications of the costs.

Given the ample, yet limited, funds available to rebuild disaster-stricken regional economies, it is important that these funds be used as effectively as possible. Increased spending, tax incentives, and regulatory and legal patience can be very helpful policy instruments, particularly if used in the appropriate way and time.

## INCOME ASSISTANCE

The most immediate government aid to a disaster-stricken regional economy, aside from the rescue and clean-up effort, is income and other financial support to the afflicted residents. This includes, but is not limited to, unemployment insurance, housing assistance, health and medical support, disease prevention, and the provision of various goods, services, and equipment. Such support is vital to establishing the confidence of hard-pressed households and businesses. If such support is not quickly forthcoming, then confidence rapidly flags, businesses are not reopened, and residents leave the region. The region's economic recovery is all but short-circuited.

There is some understandable reticence by policy makers to quickly authorize such spending, given the threat of fraud and other corruption. Indeed, in the wake of nearly all disasters there are numerous cases of bribery and insurance fraud. Policy makers should err on the side of making such mistakes, however, to ensure that money flows quickly to the afflicted area. The aggressive and public prosecution of such activity after the fact will mitigate these transgressions, at least in part, after future disasters.

Income support to Katrina victims has been substantial, but the aid has been slow in coming. To date, FEMA has allocated nearly $24 billion in support to the afflicted Gulf Coast. This includes $6 billion for rescue operations, material and equipment, and salaries, $5 billion for the purchase of manufactured housing for displaced residents, $4.5 billion for technical expertise and goods and services provided to the states, nearly $4 billion for housing assistance, $3 billion for infrastructure repair, $1.5 billion for medical, dental, and funeral expenses, and the rest for a wide range of activities from unemployment insurance to crisis counseling.

While substantial, the income support provided to Katrina victims was, at least initially, very slowly disbursed. This was due in part to the scale of the disaster and also to the lack of coordination among the various government entities charged with providing such support. Even nearly six months after Katrina struck, the number of operational manufactured homes and travel trailers, for example, is still only about one-half the total number that have been ordered by FEMA. Without shelter, families have left the region and are increasingly unlikely to return. The region's economy suffers both because of the resulting reduction in demand for goods and services, and because of the loss of labor needed to rebuild and work in those businesses that are operating in the region.

## EXPORT-ORIENTED INDUSTRIES

Government aid must also be deployed quickly to restart the economy's export-based industries. Policy makers must identify the regional economy's export industries, assess which will provide the largest and most rapid stimulus to the rest of the economy, and quickly provide substantial financial and technical aid.

It is generally not difficult to identify which industries or even businesses that are driving the rest of the regional economy. These export-oriented industries sell their goods and services to the rest of the nation and world. The generated income and profits in turn drive spending and growth throughout the rest of the regional economy. If these industries or businesses are struggling due to a disaster, then the entire regional economy will in turn struggle.

The health of some export-oriented industries or businesses is more vital to restarting a regional economy than that of others. Policy makers should give priority to industries that are large employers, particularly of more highly compensated workers, that buy goods and services from other businesses in the region, and that are active community leaders. These industries will provide a greater boost to an economy if they are able to quickly restart their own activities.

Katrina's economic devastation was exacerbated as it struck hard at the Gulf Coast's vital export industries, including energy, tourism, and the seaports. The region is vital in terms of oil and natural gas production, refining,

TABLE 3.   Gulf of Mexico Energy Production, 2005

| | Gulf of Mexico | Total U.S. | % from Gulf of Mexico |
|---|---|---|---|
| *Oil (million barrels per day)* | | | |
| Federal offshore crude oil production | 1.56 | 5.49 | 28.5 |
| Total Gulf Coast region refinery capacity | 8.07 | 17.01 | 47.4 |
| Total Gulf Coast region crude oil Imports | 6.49 | 10.75 | 60.4 |
| —of which into ports in La., Miss., Ala. | 2.52 | 10.75 | 23.5 |
| —of which into LOOP | 0.91 | 10.75 | 8.5 |
| *Natural gas (billion cubic feet per day)* | | | |
| Federal offshore marketed production (3/05) | 10.4 | 54.1 | 19.2 |

Source: Energy Information Administration.

and the importation of oil and natural gas. Pipelines from the Gulf also provide a large share of the gasoline to the Midwest and Southeast. Close to one-third of the nation's oil production and one-fifth of the natural gas production occur in the Gulf (see Table 3). One-half of the nation's refining capacity is along the Gulf Coast and nearly two-thirds of all oil imports flow through the region. Louisiana is also home to two of the four major storage areas in the nation's Strategic Petroleum Reserve.

Oil and natural gas extraction and refining activity in the Gulf are still operating below capacity. Some 20% of crude oil production and 15% of the natural gas production remain off-line. If Hurricane Ivan's impact on Gulf energy production in the summer of 2004 is any guide, then it will not be until the summer of 2006 before production is back to near capacity.

The region's tourism industry is only a shadow of its former self. Employment in the New Orleans and Gulfport leisure and hospitality industries is about one-half of what it was prior to the storm. Many of the lost jobs were in the casinos, most of which experienced substantial damage as they were located either on or next to the Mississippi and the Gulf.

While the casinos are slowly reopening, and New Orleans held Mardi Gras this year, tourism will not return to its former vigor anytime soon. Business travel will also remain depressed despite efforts by New Orleans to reopen the convention center in stages. The travel industry's recovery is being stymied in part by the large number of hotel rooms and cruise ship cabins still being used by the government's recovery efforts. Many cultural attractions, such as museums, historical sites, and science and education centers, important to supporting the travel industry, remain shuttered. Indeed, only about one-third of such attractions are now open.

The region's major seaports have yet to fully recover. Impacted Gulf ports accounted for some $75 billion in annual waterborne trade, accounting for nearly one-tenth of such trade nationwide. The principal exports that move through the ports include grains such as corn, wheat, and soybeans, and various chemical products. Indeed, nearly two-thirds of the nation's grain exports flow through the ports. The principal imports include steel, lumber products, coffee, cocoa, zinc, and aluminum.

As long as the Gulf Coast's export-oriented industries and businesses remain hobbled, the entire regional economy will continue to struggle. While it is difficult for policy makers to target any set of industries or businesses for targeted help, they can orient their clean-up, infrastructure repair, and housing redevelopment efforts to ensure these activities resume first. It is the income and profits earned in these industries that will jump-start activity in the rest of the disaster-stricken regional economy.

## FORBEARANCE

Financial and regulatory forbearance are also necessary for restarting a disaster-stricken regional economy. Households and businesses hurt by disaster quickly lose confidence in their ability to renew their economic lives, if encumbered by the economic obligations that prevailed prior to the disaster. Although this forbearance should be temporary, policy makers need to provide it quickly and transparently.

Gulf Coast households are particularly hard-pressed to meet their financial obligations due to the loss of jobs and, for many, the homes, vehicles, and other property that secured their debts. Prior to Katrina, New Orleans's households owed some $31 billion in mortgage, credit card, and other debt, totaling $76,000 per household. This is approximately double what households owed at the start of the decade. Gulfport households owed just over $5 billion, $53,000 per household. This too is nearly double the debt load at the start of the decade.

Lenders, with guidance from federal banking regulators, have provided borrowers with some time to regain their financial footing. There remains substantial confusion, however, among borrowers regarding their obligations. Moreover, lenders are very reluctant to extend new credit to the region's households and businesses, which is vital to any reconstruction effort.

State and local governments throughout the Gulf Coast are also grappling with the difficulty of paying on maturing liabilities at the same time their tax base has been sharply reduced. Twenty-nine of the fifty-one state and local government bond issues rated by Moody's Investors Service for various Gulf Coast public entities from the state of Louisiana to Tulane University were downgraded in the wake of the storm. Many of these issues are now below investment grade. The ability of state and local governments in the region to borrow in capital markets is thus now significantly more expensive, and in some cases all but impossible. Without this financial capacity, economic reconstruction in the region will be significantly impaired.

## Infrastructure and Institutions

Policy makers must also ensure that the region's economic infrastructure and institutions are quickly repaired and functioning well. This includes everything from public infrastructure, such as the transportation network and hospitals, to private institutions, such as universities and nonprofits. These institutions are committed to enhancing the region's economic well being and will be catalysts for broader economic growth if provided the opportunity.

Nearly all the Gulf Coast's infrastructure and institutions were damaged or destroyed by Katrina. Economic infrastructure on the Gulf Coast also includes the levee system and wetlands that are necessary to protecting the region's economy from future hurricanes.

Reconstruction of the Gulf Coast's infrastructure has begun, but is going slowly. Travel on the region's major throughways and through its airports is picking up, but remains impeded. The number of operational public transportation routes, for example, has only recently risen to just over one-half of the total number of routes in place prior to the storm. Of the 38 hospitals in operation before Katrina, only 20 are now up and running. Students are returning to New Orleans's universities, but Tulane has only 90% of its students back, Loyola 80%, and Xavier 75%.

The Army Corps of Engineers is spending some $3.5 billion to bring New Orleans's levee system back to its pre-Katrina standards. Whether to upgrade the system to withstand larger force hurricanes is still being debated. Whatever is decided, a hardened levee system will not be in place for the upcoming hurricane season. Discussions over how to shore up the Gulf Coast's wetlands is still very nascent.

## Tax Incentives

Economic recovery from a disaster is only complete when businesses return to serve the local population with daily needs for goods and services, ranging from groceries and clothing, to medical and dental care. It is this network of local goods and services that provides the basis for neighborhood renewal.

Business owners, however, also need housing, for themselves and for the labor pool they will need to draw from to staff their businesses. Thus, redevelopment of housing and businesses go hand in hand. One without the other will fail. Residents will not rebuild housing or return without a job or business to go to. Businesses will not thrive without a local labor pool and a local market.

The normal risks and costs associated with business development are exaggerated by the uncertainty of the post-disaster environment. These extra costs include cleanup and environmental mitigation not covered by insurance, the slow speed of government and private services that may still be in disarray, the inadequacy of public infrastructure, or the high cost of labor in a labor-short environment. Risks include the uncertainty of local markets, the uncertainty of timing of infrastructure improvements, and the quality and adequacy of available labor.

The additional costs of housing redevelopment will include high costs of materials and skilled labor when demand for both is high and added costs arise to meet new building regulations put in place to reduce the risk of a future disaster. The risks to rebuilding also are great. Managing the rebuilding of careers and personal finances at the same time as rebuilding a house can be more than a household can manage. Building in a neighborhood still in a shambles makes it hard to assess current and future land values and thus the appropriateness of rebuilding. This is particularly difficult for investors rebuilding rental housing. Furthermore, households that have evacuated to other cities must weigh the risks of remaining in their new location and starting lives over again versus returning and rebuilding anew.

Public policy needs to focus on two factors to ease and facilitate rebuilding. The first is a set of tax breaks to rebuild houses and to replace destroyed and damaged property. Given the heightened risk and uncertainty in a disaster-impacted area, tax incentives are likely to be critical to the initiation of the rebuilding process. Tax incentives to promote housing development are discussed in more detail in Chapter 11.

The second is a clear set of public rebuilding guidelines that establish zoning rules for new construction. Zoning or land-use plans must outline areas no longer eligible for development based on revised assessment of disaster risks. And they must indicate changes in projected land use that are deemed necessary to facilitate the broad redevelopment plans of the area. These would include new transportation or evacuation corridors, new drainage corridors, or other kinds of protective barriers needed to minimize future risk. These maps and regulations are necessary to ensure that investors and homeowners will have clear legal right to their property once again and that it is fully insurable against all types of losses.

In the wake of Hurricane Katrina, policy makers have been slow in responding to provide incentives for rebuilding. The local and state government response has been stymied by a lack of funding, particularly in Louisiana, where the tax base has been significantly reduced. State policy makers are formulating additional homeowner assistance programs with the promise of additional federal assistance. Louisiana is shifting away from plans to buy out homeowners and create large redevelopment programs and towards grants of up to $150,000 combined with low-cost loans to cover other costs. The emphasis is on bringing homeowners back to New Orleans to rebuild. Mississippi policy makers have made similar proposals, although they appear to be limited to lump sum checks, without additional loan assistance. The federal government response has been limited to providing emergency help to homeowners via loans, rental assistance, flood insurance, rural housing, and low-income tax credits.

Missing from current proposals are programs to offset the higher cost of building required for raising homes off the ground in the lower sections of New Orleans and for accommodating upgrades required by revisions to the building code. There also appears to be little effort at creating long-term tax incentives to offset the uncertainty of long-term costs.

There has also been little effort to provide tax incentives to businesses. Nearly all public policy is focused on attracting homeowners back to rebuild on their property. Homeowners are likely to be saddled with substantial debt from rebuilding, even after receiving government grants and private insurance payments. But there must be similar programs to generate the businesses and jobs that will support households returning to damaged areas.

Incentives to attract investors to build low, moderate, or indeed market-based rental housing are also missing. This is particularly important in New Orleans, where the homeownership rate was among the lowest in the nation prior to the hurricanes. It is clear that the policy of the City of New Orleans is to attract as many former residents as possible back to the city, but without the provision for adequate rental housing, this policy will fail a large share of the population.

Finally, the state and federal governments have been slow in generating the guidelines for land-use planning and zoning, due in part to conflict between local, state, and federal government efforts. For example, the mayor of New Orleans has put out a call for all residents to return and rebuild as soon as possible, although there is no comprehensive set of maps yet that guides where rebuilding can take place. FEMA is expected to soon provide maps which will designate those areas insurable for flooding. But even with these maps, local and state government will have to update land-use plans within the insurable areas to account for the loss of other non-insurable areas.

Mississippi officials have responded more quickly regarding land-use changes in the post-disaster environment, although their policy has focused more on business rather than residential land use, particularly relating to the Gulf Coast casinos in the state. Following Katrina, the state legislature passed revisions to its gaming law that allowed casinos to build on land rather than over the water. It is this legislation that is encouraging Mississippi's casinos to immediately construct temporary facilities to get business going again, and to begin planning new permanent land-based casinos nearby. The positive effect of this legislation is a good example of the need for speed in public policy relating to land-use planning and development incentives.

## INSURANCE

A post-disaster regional economy will only regain its long-term footing if the economic risk posed by future disasters can be mitigated or insured against. It is incumbent on policy makers to facilitate this. This requires the restoration of a private insurance market, which may require support from policy makers through the provision of a publicly-financed catastrophic backstop.

This policy was effectively used in the wake of 9/11 and the passage of the Terrorism Reinsurance Act (TRIA). The law created a federal program that backs up private insurance companies and guarantees that certain very large terrorist-related claims will be paid. The legislation was effective in reducing private insurance rates for property and casualty insurance that soared in the immediate wake of 9/11 and was weighing heavily on construction and development plans. Insurance rates have since come down and the need for TRIA appears to be fading.

Policy makers can also shape the direction of economic development through the government or private insurance markets. If development is occurring in areas that are deemed unsafe by FEMA or other government agencies, which is arguably occurring in those areas of New Orleans that are well below sea level, then they may not provide financial support to insurers originating policies in those areas. Private insurers may ultimately decide to provide insurance in these areas, but the cost will be higher, and there are other economic reasons for the development to occur.

The revival of the Gulf Coast economy has at the very least been delayed by the inadequate insurance of the region's households and businesses. Ongoing legal and regulatory disputes over insurance coverage are also curtailing insurance payouts and will likely result in less future insurance coverage. All of this stands in contrast to the rapid reconstruction that has occurred in other disaster-stricken regional economies where most of the residents had insurance.

## CONCLUSIONS

While the national economy has quickly recovered from Hurricane Katrina, the Gulf Coast economy continues to reel. Employment and incomes are still measurably below their pre-storm levels and have yet to significantly rise. The region's population has declined sharply. It is increasingly clear that the region's economic troubles are in no small part due to the slow and disjointed economic policy response to the disaster.

To mitigate the economic fallout from a disaster and to facilitate its quick recovery, policy makers must be prepared to provide immediate economic aid to distressed regional economies. Broadly, policy makers have four tools at their disposal to help afflicted economies, including increased spending, regulatory and legal forbearance, tax incentives, and risk mitigation. Government spending can be used most quickly to support confidence and the regional economies key industries and businesses. Outlays should be substantial and visible to reassure distressed households and businesses and induce them to stay and rebuild. Policy makers must also work in partnership with financial institutions to provide at least temporary forbearance to indebted households, businesses, and government. Various regulatory and legal requirements may also be waved until the economy is restarted. Tax incentives for business expansion and housing redevelopment work more slowly, but can provide substantial economic benefits if transparent. Finally, for rebuilding to occur, residents must feel that the risks posed by future disasters are reduced by government action or can be mitigated by insurance and other financial tools.

Policy makers are now working to implement these policy tools in the Gulf Coast. The aid appropriated is massive and commensurate with the scope of the disaster and the funds provided after past disasters. Unfortunately, much of the aid flowing to the Gulf was very slow in coming. Residents and businesses lost confidence and many have left, with little prospect for their quick return. Moreover, debate over just how to rebuild New Orleans, its levees and homes, is still unresolved, as is what kinds of risk residents will face during the next hurricane season.

The New Orleans and Gulfport economies are thus not expected to return to their pre-hurricane levels for some time. New Orleans in particular will struggle to entice its previous residents back home. Metro-wide population before the storm stood at 1.3 million; a number that may take more than a generation to reach again (Figure 2). Gulfport's economic recovery will be slow, but the metro area's population is expected to fully recover by early in the next decade. Gulfport does not the face the same uncertainty as New Orleans in its ability to weather future hurricanes; development will assuredly occur away from the vulnerable coast.

Katrina's most important economic policy lesson is that policy makers must provide a rapid and appropriate policy response to a disaster in order to ensure that a disaster-stricken regional economy is simply detoured and not derailed.

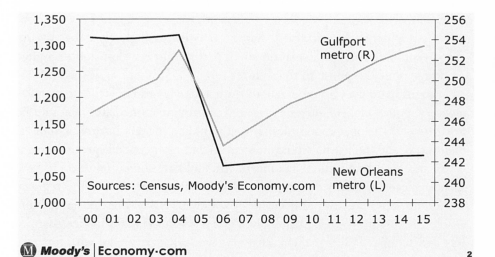

FIGURE 2.   Population and projections for New Orleans and Gulfport metropolitan areas, 2000–2015, showing the difficult economic road ahead. Moody's Economy.com, from U.S. Census data.

# CHAPTER 8

# Rebuilding Transportation

## Rachel Weinberger

Cities are organic entities, and their transportation infrastructure serves as both nervous and circulatory system. Without it the organism will die. After a disaster, restoring and rebuilding transportation is thus among the most critical activities. Because the relationship between transportation and the life of the city is temporally and spatially complex, the manner of its restoration has immediate dimensions and long-term implications that are fully interdependent. Restoration must be accomplished in a way that reestablishes order and the rhythms of life while not precluding desirable future economic and social outcomes that best serve the local people and the regional and global populations with which they must interact.

The disaster recovery response takes place within three primary time/ activity frames: immediate/permanent, immediate/temporary, and long term. Each frame has a different set of issues and actions associated with it. Actions associated with the first two frames are well established in concept and in practice, while the third is less established. Our instinctive reflection, evaluation, and collective response to disaster in general, and to Katrina in particular, will help bring this third frame into more reflexive practice. The lessons learned in the process will be of some help in rebuilding after Katrina, but will be of greater help in our responses to future disasters.

Prescribing transportation's restoration may seem complex, but from a strategic and social responsibility perspective the prescription is quite simple: the opportunities that will permit appropriate long-term outcomes must be seized right now.

## TRANSPORTATION AS LIFE SUPPORT

Cities exist to a large degree due to their economic histories and to the mutual benefit to their inhabitants of their evolution and persistence. They form because there is some advantage to be had by bringing many people and businesses together in a relatively small area. The derivative benefits of this high concentration of people have undeniable social and cultural dimensions: cities can continue to provide benefits to their inhabitants long after their economic lives have peaked.

Transportation systems are integral to our economies and to our social and cultural lives. To have a strong economy, a city must be connected with the larger economy, exchanging goods and services, providing entertainment, and engaging with the nation and world in order to create local jobs. We use transportation systems unselfconsciously to drive to work, ride our bikes to the park, walk to the grocery store, and, in some cities, ride the subway or streetcar downtown. We rely on transportation systems to deliver our mail and small packages, to bring products to our stores, and to haul away our trash. Ultimately, we rely on transportation systems for every conceivable movement of people and goods beyond the boundary of a particular building. These systems come into play in three key ways: (1) transportation systems facilitate regional and national trade and commerce by connecting places to regions, the nation, and the world; (2) transportation systems facilitate the lives and livelihoods of the individuals that make up local and national economies by providing for movement within cities, from homes to and from work, for errands and social and cultural activities; and (3) transportation systems, depending on their design and orientation, affect the distribution of activities, thus forming and being informed by the character of a place.

An adequate transportation system is perhaps the most essential element in establishing and maintaining a city's economy. Following a disaster, restoration of the transportation system is therefore one among many critical priorities. The transportation system, however necessary, is a support element to the people of the city. How well the transportation system serves the people affects the competitive advantage a place may have, but it cannot dictate a successful economy. The lack of an adequate transportation system can bring disastrous results for a growing economy but the presence of a good system will not guarantee success.

## To Build or Not to Build?

The New Orleans economy, once quite robust, has been in decline for many years. Attention to transportation systems will be important to rebuilding the economy, but rebuilding the economy will require other public interventions as well. Indeed, several questions lie logically prior to the question of whether or not to rebuild in the face of catastrophic damage. Those questions revolve around the extent of the damage, risk of recurrence, the meaning of "place," in terms of economic, social, cultural life, and the cost in both physical and human terms of relocating the economic, social, and cultural activities displaced. Here the word "place" encompasses the human dimension as distinct from geographic location. The content of the discussion on transportation rebuilding must be framed in the context of these broader questions.

Once that decision is made, however, there are many ways to proceed. Planning problems have been called wicked problems because it is difficult, if not impossible, to know at the start of a process which approach is the right one for the place in question (Rittel and Weber 1973). The solutions to rebuilding are very contextual, and so we must draw our knowledge of disaster rebuilding from previous experience and case study. Each time we react it is in part to the current disaster but primarily to all the disasters that have preceded it. The lessons we learn from Katrina will be invaluable in our responses to future disasters.

Models of reconstruction range from the powerbroker, as was seen, for example, in the actions of the Marquês de Pombal, whom we credit with rebuilding Lisbon after the earthquake of 1755, to the politically mediated market, which itself can range widely, taking many degrees of mediation from, say, the rebuilding of Chicago after the Great Chicago Fire in 1871 (lesser mediation) to the rebuilding of lower Manhattan after the events of September 11, 2001 (greater mediation). The power broker model is very unlikely to be seen in a modern democracy, leaving the question: to what extent will government interventions set the context in which private citizens will make their own investment decisions? A big question for New Orleanians is what level of public support there will be to reconstruct and reinforce the levee system and the rest of the local infrastructure. When those questions are settled, private citizens will be more comfortable making decisions about whether to reinvest in the city or to make investments elsewhere.

The questions of what to do, in terms of bricks and mortar, are value laden and themselves overshadowed by the far more complex questions of how to proceed. It is the latter that will be the greater challenge as there are many tensions that must be resolved. An example is the tension between product and process, which requires us to grapple with the question of for whom do we rebuild. Is it for the displaced community of people or is it for the damaged place? Or is it always, necessarily, for both? Questions that seem as concrete as how to rebuild transportation infrastructure become quickly complicated by the need to bring disparate perspectives of the displaced into focus.

## A Framework for Action

Faced with rebuilding after disaster, cities must take into account the results of immediate response interventions to reconnect the local economy, the efforts required to reconnect to the larger regional, national, and global context, all within a context that is consistent with and sensitive to the city's distinctive local character.

As shown in Table 1, immediate/permanent, immediate/temporary, and long-term functions are integrated, but they are also distinct. The actions required in each frame depend on the circumstances of the local context,

TABLE 1.  Time/Activity Frames for Rebuilding Transportation Infrastructure

|  | Immediate/ permanent | Immediate/ temporary | Long-term |
| --- | --- | --- | --- |
| Connect to national economy | X | X |  |
| Local mobility | X | X | X |
| Shape and character |  |  | X |

which break neither into distinct time regimes, nor into distinct function regimes.

1. *Immediate/permanent.* It is critical to prioritize the linkages that connect the local economy to the regional, national, and global economies. By and large, for New Orleans, this step has been completed, as will be shown in the sections outlining existing infrastructure and current conditions.

2. *Immediate/temporary.* Attention must be turned to the immediate needs for transportation; connecting the labor force to their places of employment, facilitating goods movement within the region, and ensuring that people have access to each other and the activities in which they must partake to make their lives meaningful. This period is characterized by stopgap measures and can imply a re-creation of what has existed immediately prior.

3. *Long-term.* It is necessary to focus on the long-term opportunities. Highway and street alignments that were sensible fifty, one hundred, even two hundred years ago, but given the changes in the structure of our economy, given our new sensibilities to resource conservation, and given the technological advances that have been made over time, may not be what we would build if starting out today.

Understanding and exercising the long-term opportunities is by far the hardest task. We adapt our lives to our existing environments, and then form strong attachments to the systems we have developed. It is a rare opportunity, and one for which we are generally ill equipped, that allows us to reimagine our cities or regions from the ground up.

## Context

New Orleans came to exist in its particular geographical location due to the excellent access feature that was the Mississippi River. The Mississippi River was an important water route, connecting to the interior of the United States, and so the Port of New Orleans grew up there. The concentration and diversity of workers required to operate the port led to the evolution of a unique culture that has not been replicated elsewhere in the country. The uniqueness of that culture, which has spawned an important tourist industry, is a national treasure. The culture has been experienced and added to by many residents and visitors to the Crescent City. It is widely recognized as one of many driving causes for rebuilding the city.

New Orleans was a key transportation facility by the early 1700s. Described by Peirce Lewis in 1977 as the "inevitable city on an impossible site," the port, established at the mouth of the Mississippi River, represented an ideal logistic center and the city's commerce and culture grew around it. Of course the location has a fatal flaw: extremely limited high ground. But the importance of controlling the access to the interior trade route trumped the danger, or lack of permanence, associated with settling the swampland.

Over time, modifications to the Mississippi River that facilitated shipping and improved conditions for the oil industry increased the threat of river floods. Efforts to guard against river floods worsened storm impacts from the ocean side (see Giegengack and Foster, this volume). While there is a complex hydrologic, economic, industrial, and cultural history that led to swamp drainage and development, as plots on the limited high ground were taken, development spread into the swamp. The development of these areas, which relied on human transformation of the wetlands, was blessed and facilitated by the government at the local and national levels. Development of the wetlands was justified in terms of economic development opportunities: a viable economy is typically justification for building infrastructure. Infrastructure, which is typically built by the state, is necessary to support the economy, even if it is not a sufficient condition. So, following this dynamic, economic development at the "many moments" of the evolving city and region was deemed more important than possible damage in the future, and to free ourselves from the psychological harm of living with the threat of harm, we assume the 100-year flood will occur 100 years from now, not once every 100 years.

The time/activity frames introduced above will be discussed below as distinct steps that must be taken to rebuild the city of New Orleans.

## STEP 1: IMMEDIATE/PERMANENT: (RE)CONNECT TO THE REGIONAL/NATIONAL/GLOBAL ECONOMIES

Rebuilding transportation in order to reestablish critical economic connections means rehabilitating the highway, rail, water, and aviation infrastructure so that primary economic functions are supported.

### Existing Infrastructure

The pre-Katrina inventory of New Orleans's transportation infrastructure is quite robust. The Port of New Orleans was the fifth busiest shipping port in the United States. It is served by six class 1 railroads representing more rail service than any other U.S. port.[1] There are two proximate airport facilities and many other airports in the Gulf region. The Louis Armstrong International Airport is located approximately fifteen miles to the west of New Orleans, in Kenner, Louisiana. This is the primary commercial aviation facility serving the city. Lakefront, on the banks of Lake Pontchartrain, is a general aviation facility in New Orleans proper. There are three passenger rail routes operated by Amtrak: the Sunset Limited, which connects Orlando, Florida, with Los Angeles, California; the Crescent, originating in New Orleans and terminating in New York City; and the City of New Orleans, which also originates in New Orleans but terminates in Chicago. The passenger rail service provides nearby regional connections to Hammond, Slidell, Shriver, and Lafayette in Louisiana and to McComb, Brookhaven, Picayune, Bay St. Louis, Gulfport, Biloxi, and Pascagoula in Mississippi. Passenger rail connections to more distant regional cities include Houston and San Antonio, Texas, Memphis, Tennessee, Mobile, Alabama, and Atlanta, Georgia. There is no existing passenger rail service connecting to Baton Rouge, the current home of many displaced New Orleans residents, but three freight rail tracks connect the two cities. Following a model such as New Jersey Transit's River Line, which operates over a freight right-of-way, rail passenger service between Baton Rouge and New Orleans, could be implemented with a relatively low capital expenditure.[2]

The principal interstate highway that connects New Orleans to the country is east-west route I-10; Interstates I-610, I-310, and the I-510 spur provide local circulation. I-10 connects to I-12 (another east-west route running along the northern border of Lake Pontchartrain) and to I-49, I-55, and I-59, all of which head north, reaching Shreveport, Louisiana, Jackson, Mississippi, and Birmingham, Alabama, respectively. Local state highways include U.S. 90, which is known locally as Chef Menteur Highway and in Mississippi as the Coast Highway (where it has been badly damaged), and U.S. 61, which primarily serves points west of New Orleans. U.S. 11 approximately parallels I-10 between New Orleans and Slidell and then follows I-59 north. The Lake Pontchartrain Causeway, which connects Metarie at the southern end with Mandeville on the north side of the lake, was not damaged.

### Current Conditions and Plans

New Orleans, which has been greatly impacted by flood damage, did not suffer much of the more severe storm damage that destroyed Highway 90, the Biloxi Bay Bridge, and the Bay St. Louis Bridge along the coast of Mississippi. Most of the highway, rail, water, and aviation infrastructure in the New Orleans region is thus already operating at relatively normal conditions. U.S. 51 (the southern extension of I-55) between route I-10 and I-12 is restricted, as are state routes 3235 and 1 between New Orleans and the Gulf. The other major roads forming a circumference around New Orleans are open but traffic is restricted. The twin span of I-10, crossing Lake Pontchartrain between New Orleans and Slidell, was badly damaged in the storm but temporary repairs are now complete. The Federal Emergency Management Agency (FEMA) has committed to funding a replacement bridge that will add 50% more capacity to that part of I-10.

The port is not yet fully operational. One of the largest impediments to its resuming full operations appears to be the shortage of trucks and drivers to meet the demand for non-rail surface hauling. Five of the six freight railroads have resumed normal operations; the sixth will, in short order. Passenger rail is almost fully restored. The City of New Orleans and Crescent routes have both resumed normal operations. The Sunset Limited is not currently serving the Gulf region, operating only between Los Angeles, California, and San Antonio, Texas. Greyhound service to New Orleans has been substantially restored.

The Gulf region's airports, including Louis Armstrong, are operating at their pre-storm levels with one exception: Lakefront is only in service 10 hours per day as daylight only, visual flight rules are in effect.

While plans are very fluid at this moment, as noted above there has been a commitment by FEMA to replace and expand the I-10 bridge over Lake Pontchartrain. The Metropolitan Planning Organization, New Orleans Regional Planning Commission, has standing plans to upgrade the transit system, most notably introducing commuter rail lines throughout the region. The Bring Back New Orleans Commission has floated plans for additional light rail lines as well.

## STEP 2: IMMEDIATE/TEMPORARY: TEND TO THE IMMEDIATE MOBILITY NEEDS

As Robert Lang points out, the vast majority of (former) New Orleans residents who have not been able to return to the city have relocated, temporarily or permanently, within the Gulf region (Lang 2006). While this bodes well for the regional economy and the labor force needed to maintain it, it means little, if anything, to the task of recovering New Orleans proper. For New Orleans a labor force is required to rebuild the infrastructure and to re-create the unique place that New Orleans is, but the infrastructure, including schools, utilities, government, and other institutions, has to be in place to support that labor force. At this writing, there is enough rudimentary infrastructure in place in New Orleans that about a fifth of the population has been able to return, but to rebuild both the cultural and human "place" and the geographic place more critical mass is required.

The main issue in this activity/time frame is housing and the lack of it. But the solution is transportation. Transportation is tasked with overcoming the obstacle of distance—in this case, a great distance—as many people who would be in New Orleans have been forced to find housing far from the city. Prescriptions imply working in a reactive mode in order to get the economy moving. It means supporting those components of the preexisting economy (limited as they are) that are still able to function and catering to the transport needs of clean up and rebuilding.

The LA Swift service being operated by the Louisiana Department of Transportation and Development is an excellent example. The LA Swift service is a free bus running almost twenty times per weekday, in each direction, between Baton Rouge, where many displaced New Orleans residents have sought temporary shelter, and New Orleans, where they are trying to rebuild. At a distance of eighty-four miles the hour and-a-half commute is a stopgap measure. It is not a viable or desirable long-term solution, but it is precisely the kind of transportation service needed to fill mobility needs during the period of rebuilding.

## STEP 3: LONG-TERM OPPORTUNITIES

Different economies require different arrangements of transportation infra-structure. But ultimately, the transportation system should be as robust and flexible as possible. A principal component of a robust system is redundancy. Indeed, redundancy in the system is what allowed New York City to achieve an incredibly high level of mobility in the immediate aftermath of 9/11. Redundancy should exist across modal systems as well as within. When one part of the system is compromised, mobility needs can still be met.

For New Orleans the way forward may be to look a bit "back to the future." The new New Orleans must be predicated on the old New Orleans. The birth of the city was in trade and in particular in port commerce; its adolescence and adulthood are based on a unique culture and the strong community ties that bind its residents together. The French Quarter, New Orleans's first residential community, is located just east of the port, New Orleans's first economic driver. The Quarter remains the epicenter of New Orleans. As the port commerce grew, the region grew, as extractive industries, and then tourism joined the mix of economic drivers. While accommodation and food services is frequently thought to be the key economy and accounted for 18% of the city's 2003 employment, this industry is not a great employer, accounting for only 5% of the city's payroll. Education, health, and social services was the bigger employer. Any attempt to preserve the tourist industry without preserving the city will result in an inauthentic and hollow experience. What was attractive about New Orleans was its authenticity.

TABLE 2. Parish to Parish Commute Patterns (percent)

| Residence parish | Same parish as residence | Workplace | | Total |
|---|---|---|---|---|
| | | Next most frequent destination | | |
| Orleans | 78 | 17 | Jefferson | 95 |
| Jefferson | 65 | 27 | Orleans | 92 |
| Plaquemines | 64 | 18 | Jefferson | 82 |
| St. Bernard | 41 | 39 | Orleans | 80 |
| St. Charles | 45 | 34 | Jefferson | 79 |
| St. John the Baptist | 41 | 25 | Jefferson | 66 |
| St. Tammany | 60 | 19 | Orleans | 79 |

## Past Trip Patterns

To assess long-term opportunities requires an understanding of past trip patterns and preferences. The New Orleans Metropolitan Statistical Area (MSA) is comprised of seven parishes. The two largest in population are Orleans Parish and Jefferson Parish, with 2004 estimated populations of 460,000 and 450,000 respectively. Saint Tammany Parish is third with an estimated population of 210,000.[3] The combined population of the remaining four parishes is about 190,000, for a total of about 1.3 million. Almost 80% of the MSA's jobs are located in Orleans and Jefferson Parishes (42% and 35% respectively) with an additional 10% in Saint Tammany Parish. Just over 70% of the labor force resides in Orleans and Jefferson. The pre-Katrina commuting pattern is illustrated in Table 2 and Plate 13. The first column of Table 2 shows the New Orleans MSA labor force by residence parish, the second column indicates the percent of the labor force working in their parish of residence, and the next column shows the next most frequent destination parish. Thus 78% of the New Orleans labor force also worked in Orleans Parish, and an additional 17% in neighboring Jefferson Parish. Likewise, 65% of the employed Jefferson Parish residents worked in Jefferson Parish, and 27% worked in New Orleans.

Plate 13 shows parish to parish commuting by job location rather than by residence of the worker. The bars represent the number of jobs in each parish. Reading from the left, the first bar shows how many of the jobs are filled by residents of the same parish; the next two bars show commuters into the parish. The arrows in the diagram indicate the parish of origin for the largest group of commuters who come from outside. For example, of the 248,500 people who work in New Orleans, 148,000 (60%) also live in New Orleans. Almost 58,000 (23%) live in Jefferson Parish; the remainder live in disparate locations including outside the MSA and even in Mississippi. Likewise, of the 205,300 jobs in Jefferson Parish, 135,800 or 66% were filled by residents of the parish. The next largest group of workers in Jefferson Parish, about 32,000 or 16%, lived in New Orleans.

To understand more fully the meaning of the job concentration, it is worth noting that the land area of New Orleans is considerably smaller than the land areas of the other parishes, about half as much land. At 181 square miles, Orleans Parish occupies 6% of the land of the MSA; it hosted 35% of the residents and 42% of the jobs. The way it could achieve this density (New Orleans's residential density was ten times greater than the average for the remainder of the MSA) was by having a public transit system to serve the local circulation. Indeed, the census indicates that mode choice for journey to work was nearly 14% transit in New Orleans but only 2.6% in Jefferson Parish, and fewer than 1% of residents in the neighboring parishes traveled to work by transit.

## Transportation Design Impacts on Urban Form

Consider transportation's effect on the shape and character of a pre-Katrina New Orleans by comparing New Orleans East, characterized by wide roads and large spaces between land uses, with older neighborhoods like the Marigny and the French Quarter. The New Orleans East style of development caters to automobile use, requiring use of a car for local mobility. The wider roads and ample parking areas permit residents to drive from activity to activity. The area is built at an automobile scale. The denser French Quarter and Marigny provide a pleasant walking environment. Residents and visitors are able to reach a wide variety of businesses within a short distance. These neighborhoods were built at a pedestrian or human scale.

New Orleans is both lauded and condemned as a city with low levels of auto ownership. The reason for this low level of auto ownership, many say, is poverty. While there is no disputing the strong correlation between poverty and carlessness, New Orleans ranked only eighth in the country, tied with Miami, far behind New York, Washington, D.C., Chicago, and San Francisco, for the most households without cars. Even with high rates of poverty, New Orleans had no monopoly on low car ownership. Contributing factors to the low level of car ownership are that (a) many neighborhoods in New Orleans are walkable and (b) the public transit system is adequate (though not great). These two things make it possible to participate in daily activities without owning a car—a feature that does not exist in many U.S. cities. Personal transportation in the United States now ranks as the second largest household expenditure after shelter, consuming on average 20% of a household's income. For a minimum wage earner owning and maintaining a car could cost a third to a half of an annual income. To be poor in a city where you do not "need" a car is a huge advantage over being poor in a city where you do need a car. Not having a car where one is needed precludes you from participating in the job market and in many ways from participating in society. Having a car because you need it rather than choose it is a heavy burden indeed.

## Density Matters

It is hard to know what the future holds, but a smaller, denser New Orleans is a logical way to accommodate the displaced citizens, return some of the wetlands to nature, and maintain both the economy and the authenticity of New Orleans. In the old New Orleans transit was just for poor people. If there is a new New Orleans, the transit system must serve everyone. Transit for local mobility needs will be an essential part of the rebuilt city. The ability to exist without a car is an asset that must be preserved. For any urban place that is putting itself back together, in the core, in the center city, it should be relatively difficult to be with a car and very easy to be without one. As many trips as are practical should be served by transit, leaving the road network to serve trips that are not well served by transit.

As a practical matter, certain areas of the wetlands should be demapped. To rebuild all of New Orleans would be a failure on the part of the government to protect the public health and welfare. Current plans noted in the section on regional connections should be reconsidered. There is a proposal for a light rail connection to Louis Armstrong International Airport and three proposed light rail or commuter rail links to the east. A classic tension in public transit planning is the tradeoff of resources between area coverage and productivity. Simply put, with a limited number of vehicles and drivers the resources can be expended to have thin coverage over a large area or dense coverage in a smaller area. Typically, transit dollars would be better spent by providing a dense transit network in the densest parts of the city and relying on the automobile for mobility in the parts of the region that are not densely settled or where there are not large commuting movements. With the major movements having been between Jefferson Parish and Orleans Parish it would make more sense to orient rail extensions to the west.

One of the effects of Katrina is likely to be that the ties between New Orleans and Baton Rouge will be strengthened. A rail line to Louis Armstrong International Airport that is incorporated into a Baton Rouge to New Orleans link and that serves the Jefferson Parish to New Orleans demand may be justified.

Traditionally highway spending has been a way to create local jobs. When President George H. W. Bush signed the Intermodal Surface Transportation Efficiency Act in 1991 he joked that he didn't know what was in the bill but he knew it meant jobs, jobs, jobs. Highway spending has also been a politically popular way to address congestion, if not necessarily practical. We have a certain inertia about the highway spending mindset, but we are learning that highway alignments are legacy alignments. They stem from times when our needs and values were different from what they are today. We think differently about our waterfronts; we have learned that urban highways can deeply divide cities and spread development in a sometimes sprawling and haphazard way. We have an opportunity to rethink these alignments. It is a mistake to let the highway departments have the only say on this. They are in the business of building highways and have a potential conflict of interest in the decision of whether or not to build highways.

A classic example of taking advantage of this opportunity is removal of the Embarcadero Freeway in San Francisco and the Cyprus Freeway in Oakland, both badly damaged in the Loma Prieta earthquake. In New York after 9/11 there were several proposals for redressing the ills of the Westside Highway; ultimately the more human scaled proposal carried the day, as the local and business community both shunned the alternative that most catered to moving traffic. Widening I-10 from New Orleans to Slidell may not be a good move, particularly if New Orleans is going to be smaller, as many predict, or denser, as I am advocating. From a rebuilding perspective, even though there is federal money promised, highway-widening decisions should be made in the context of local accessibility decisions.

The Coast Highway, U.S. 90, in Mississippi is the best example of an extended stretch of road that could be rethought and reconstructed accordingly. There will be a strong pull toward replacing that which was lost, but there may be better development uses for that stretch of coast, and the urge should be resisted until alternatives are carefully thought through. To make a pedestrian scale promenade or boulevard that serves both pedestrians and vehicular traffic would create stronger connections between the communities and the waterfront and very likely result in a positive amenity for business and residents alike.

## EVACUATION PLANS AND AUTOMOBILE OWNERSHIP

Naturally, there is a great deal of attention focused of late on evacuations. It is not my intention to create or critique an evacuation plan for New Orleans, but given the context it would be remiss to overlook this issue, in particular as I am advocating a New Orleans that works for people who do not own cars. This recommendation stands in stark contrast to the "conventional wisdom" offered by people from all walks of the political spectrum, who have floated the notion that the human toll from the flooding of New Orleans would have been considerably less had there been more individual automobile ownership, and therefore more automobility. Perhaps, they suggest, a policy of increasing auto ownership, particularly among the poor, would mitigate future disasters.

At a minimum, they argue, the death toll would have been lower as more people would have evacuated. But the conventional wisdom is wrong.

It could be the subject of several volumes to discuss automobile dependency and the structuring of our activity space around automobility. Indeed, owning an automobile is thought by many to be a prerequisite to participating fully in American society. For most of the country I would agree with that assessment. But there are some cities in which a resident or visitor can participate fully without owning an automobile. Apparently, for the residents of New Orleans it was a requirement for participating in the evacuation plan.

While the correlations between poverty and lack of auto ownership are glaring, the problems with the evacuation were not due to carlessness. Any correlation between an inability to evacuate and lack of auto ownership is spurious. In the first place, many people who owned automobiles chose not to evacuate. Second, there are many possible evacuation plans that would have been much more effective that do not rely on individuals using private vehicles. In fact, as we learned in the Hurricane Rita evacuation just a few weeks after the Katrina disaster, whatever were the successes of the Katrina evacuation would have been completely wiped out by the additional gridlock caused by thousands more private vehicles trying to use the road.

A study of New Orleans that predated Katrina made it clear that auto evacuation would neither suffice nor work well. Brian Wolshon, a professor of civil engineering at Louisiana State University, in his article "Planning for the Evacuation of New Orleans" (Wolshon 2002) identified 200,000 to 300,000 people who would not be able to evacuate due to their lack of owning a reliable personal automobile. He estimated an additional 100,000 people who would not evacuate because they would be unwilling to leave their homes and property. Noting the limited outbound road capacity as an impediment to evacuating the region, he analyzed the contra-flow evacuation plan designed to maximize available outbound capacity. The plan, which implicitly relied on the estimate that a full 40% of the population would not evacuate either by choice or by transit dependence, still produced extreme gridlock for extended periods and average travel speeds about one fifth of normal speeds.

A mass transit evacuation is the only viable plan for dense urban areas. It has been estimated that 25,000 people sought refuge in the New Orleans Superdome. An eight-car Amtrak train, as is typically run in the Northeast Corridor, can accommodate about 480 people seated. With a few people standing per car, it would have taken fifty trains to carry all the Superdome refugees to safety. With three possible alignments on which to depart, the entire evacuation could have been completed more quickly and efficiently than the helicopter and bus evacuations that were ultimately employed. The Amtrak station is three blocks from the Superdome.

As early as 1924 Sidney Walden, an executive of Packard Motor Company, observed that the popularity of the automobile was rendering it useless as an efficient means of "individual rapid transit." We see this observation starkly and dangerously revalidated during an evacuation. When each of us acts in what we believe is our own self-interest, the system performs at a level below its optimum. It is imperative that all the resources be deployed. While the use of private automobiles will be the most efficient evacuation in some areas, we would be wise to discourage the use of private automobiles in many evacuation plans.

## CONCLUSION

There are many decisions to be made with respect to rebuilding cities after disaster. There are many conflicts to resolve. I have tried with this articulation of my thoughts to give practical direction on the role and importance of transportation to revitalizing the economy while keeping in mind the philosophical questions that must be addressed simultaneously.

The refection implicit in exchanging ideas and writing about rebuilding represents tremendous opportunity. Using these opportunities to good advantage will pave the way to rebuilding stronger more viable economies and places.

Before acting on the transportation rebuilding efforts, it is imperative to address the question regarding the viability and the meaning of "places" in general, and the "place" that is New Orleans in particular. What is the meaning of bringing back New Orleans? What is to be brought back? Is it the commercial contributions of this city to the rest of the country? Is it the cultural and human interactions? Is it important to restore the economy so the displaced community can return? Or so that those determined to return will have something to return to? As participants in rebuilding we must ask ourselves: does this community merit a special effort, special support in reconstructing its institutions, because it represents a uniqueness that we value? Would every community deserve the same thought and consideration? Is the effort directed toward a vulnerable segment of society? If that is the case, are we able to ensure that those for whom our rebuilding efforts are directed are in fact the beneficiaries? If we recommend approaches that reestablish the city but the individuals who had been displaced remain displaced, then we have lost an opportunity indeed. It is questionable whether the strategy of rebuilding in the same vulnerable locations, additional fortifications notwithstanding, is wise. Communities are fluid, people come and go, but to rebuild without restoring those displaced could be an extremely poor use of resources. If it is just a geographic location, then it can be moved or absorbed into other existing places.

It is the economy that drives the cultural, social, and human aspects of the city, and gives meaning to a city, and because it is a cultural, social, and human place, these decisions take on much more importance. To restore economic viability, the basic economy has to be connected to the larger economies. If money does not come in, there will be none to circulate locally, to fuel the secondary economy. The shortage of housing must be overcome in the short term by transportation solutions that are not necessarily viable or desirable in the longer term. It is easier to move 1,000 people back and forth every day to a nearby city than it is to build 1,000 houses. The former can be organized in a matter of days, the latter would take months and require the presence of builders to accomplish the task. There are opportunities to explore new directions and ways of organizing human activities in space. We can use transportation resources to improve life quality by focusing on ways to give people greater access to activities rather than attempting to provide the means by which to traverse great distances.

Many thanks to Gretchen Ostheimer, Penelope Weinberger, Elizabeth Deakin, Karen Chapple, Amy Hillier, Randall Mason, Saskia Levy, Mical Moser, Lonnie Coplen, and the editors of this volume for their thoughtful comments on an early draft, to Michael Smart for his research assistance, and to Michael Smart and Thomas Pederson for their assistance with Plate 13.

## Notes

1. As of 2004, class 1 railroads are defined as freight railroads with annual operating revenues in excess of $277.7 million. There are seven railroads with that designation operating in the United States; six of them operate at the Port of New Orleans.

2. To do this would require a low frequency of freight trains using the tracks, a detail that would have to be thoroughly investigated.

3. St. Tammany's development was driven by the two key linkages to New Orleans: I-10 to Slidell and the Lake Pontchartrain Causeway to Mandeville.

# CHAPTER 9

# Learning from Past Disasters

Eugenie L. Birch

Over time, U.S. cities have endured major disasters including fires, hurricanes, floods, and earthquakes. Notable are the Chicago Fire (1871), hurricanes in Galveston (1900), Miami (1930), and Charleston (1989), the Johnstown Flood (1889), the Mississippi floods first affecting southern cities including Nashville and New Orleans (1927) and then later unsettling Midwestern cities including St. Louis and Des Moines (1993), and the San Francisco earthquakes (1906, 1989). Each caused massive physical damage and large numbers of fatalities and left tens of thousands homeless (Rybczynski 2006; Barry 1997; Vale and Campanella 2005).

Their stories provide many lessons for today's rebuilding and for future occurrences. Emblematic is San Francisco and its recovery from two earthquakes that bracketed an eighty-year period between 1906 and 1989. Each produced significant human and property losses; while the first was closer in scale to the calamities that struck New Orleans and the Gulf Coast, the second took place after the creation of a federal system for disaster response. Both are instructive but in different ways. The 1906 story shows how emergency solutions melded into rapid reconstruction efforts. The 1989 tale illuminates a slower recovery where the city's leadership seized opportunities to reinvent the city.

Almost one hundred years before Hurricane Katrina and its aftermath destroyed New Orleans and eleven other urban places, a massive earthquake and subsequent fire leveled San Francisco. With a population of almost 350,000, one-third of them foreign-born, San Francisco not only ranked as the nation's ninth most populous city but also was an important port of entry for Asian and European immigrants. With its natural harbor and easy river and coastal access, San Francisco was the center of Pacific Coast trade specializing in the export of agricultural (wheat) and natural (timber and minerals) resources. It had strong commercial ties with the Far East and England.

At dawn, April 18, 1906, as the city's elite were sleeping off the previous evening's festivities featuring famed tenor Enrico Caruso and its hardworking laborers were just setting off to work, an earthquake, measuring an estimated 8.3 magnitude on the Richter scale, shook San Francisco and its surrounds. Affecting a 375,000-square-mile area extending from Los Angeles to Coos Bay, Oregon, to Las Vegas, the quake ripped a gash 270 miles long and 21 feet

FIGURE I.   In 1906 an earthquake and subsequent fire destroyed San Francisco.
Courtesy of SFMUSEUM.org.

deep along the San Andreas Fault. In San Francisco, the damage was extensive, buckling streets, opening up sink holes into which whole buildings slid,
and weakening walls of the city's major commercial and civic structures (see
Figure 1).

The earthquake's aftermath was worse. The seismic activity ruptured the
city's gas and water mains; one system spewed flammable fumes and the other
depleted the water supply. A three-day conflagration ensued, incinerating a
fifth of the 25-square-mile city, destroying its business district including major
skyscrapers and City Hall, nearby Chinatown, and several other residential
neighborhoods. It killed 3,000 and displaced a quarter of a million residents.
It left property damage amounting to $350,000 to $500,000 (1906 dollars), a
sum representing almost 2% of the nation's gross national product and whose
insurance collections would later contribute to the Panic of 1907 (Odell and
Wedidenmier 2001).

San Francisco in 1906 faced many of the same issues as New Orleans in
2005 (U.S. House 2006). A large portion of the city was in ruins, thousands
of properties were damaged beyond repair, and its lifeline services (water,
lighting, sewer, gas) were devastated. Needed were basic necessities (shelter,
food, water, health care), urban functions (transportation, communications),
and a speedy rebuilding program. Additionally, the disaster exposed the city's
environmental vulnerability, corrupt municipal leadership, and rampant racism. In rebuilding, San Francisco dealt with some of these issues expeditiously
and ignored others.

FIGURE 2.   A quarter of a million San Franciscans had no homes or public services. Courtesy of SFMUSEUM.org.

In contrast to what happened in New Orleans, San Francisco's mayor had his finest hour early in the crisis. He quickly and decisively called upon the military and the private sector to meet immediate needs. The military instantly took charge of firefighting and restoring civil order. Within days, it had provided emergency services, distributing 3,000 tents, requisitioning bedrooms in undamaged houses, and serving millions of meals (the city had forbidden all home cooking for fear of fire). It organized twenty-eight refuge camps locating many in the city's parks, set up field hospitals and dispensaries, organized trainloads of food and clothing, created and maintained telegraph and other communication lines inside and outside the city, and enforced a curfew. In performing these duties, the military divided the city into seven districts, each headed by a regular Army officer and assisted by a physician. It eventually added Red Cross officials to these leadership teams and transferred power to the civilians so that within six weeks it could terminate its emergency duties.

Within hours of the earthquake, the civilians formed a Committee of Fifty to work alongside the military. Led by former mayor and banker James D. Phelan, this group took charge of the substantial private relief funds pouring into the city—eventually reaching $9 million (1906 dollars)—liaised with the Red Cross Association, and stabilized the city's banking system. It soon formalized its activities into a charitable entity, the San Francisco Relief and Red Cross Funds Relief Corporation. The Corporation, as it came to be known, had twenty committees covering all aspects of recovery, including finance, housing, transportation, and employment. It served about 300,000 people for a number of months. Within a year it had reduced its client rolls to fewer than 1,000 (Oliver 2001).

In the absence of a formal federal or state disaster relief structure, elected leaders outside the city also responded quickly. On April 19, President Theodore Roosevelt called an emergency session of Congress to appropriate $2.5 million (1906 dollars) for San Francisco. Appointing key personnel to assist the city, he sent his Secretary of Commerce and Labor, Victor H. Metcalfe, as his personal onsite representative, authorized Secretary of War William H. Taft to dispatch men and material—eventually 10% of the nation's armed forces would be deployed in the city—and charged Edward T. Devine, Director of the Red Cross Association, to act as coordinator of national relief. On April 20, Congress appropriated $22 million (1906 dollars) for rebuilding federal buildings in order to provide immediate employment for the disaster victims. At the state level, the governor activated the National Guard to assist the federal troops, appointed a geological investigating commission, initiated state acts to smooth legal entanglements emanating from the loss of property records and, as a preventive measure, moved enabling legislation to allow Los Angeles to acquire Owens Valley water for fire protection (Hansen 2006b).

Various private entities also rushed aid. For example, the Southern Pacific and Union Pacific railroads under the personal supervision of the president, Edward Harriman, transported goods and refuges free of charge for weeks. In the first month after the crisis, 1,400 rail cars arrived with water, food, clothing, and other sundries (*San Francisco Chronicle* May 7, 1906).

By May, San Francisco began to rebuild, confronting problems in the environmental, housing, social, political, and economic realms. In the environmental area, it acted expeditiously and opportunistically, but in the end unwisely. San Francisco had (and still has) a precarious geography whose limited building sites are on steep hillsides, sand dunes, and land-filled marshes. The rebuilders knew that the land-filled areas were most unstable. (Here, under extreme seismic conditions soil liquefaction occurs and spreads laterally, disrupting all on top and within.) Nonetheless, in clearing the damaged buildings, they pushed the debris into the bay, creating more, but highly vulnerable, land that with city growth would become building sites. Furthermore, the city's topography created land scarcity that helped contribute to the city's dense development. A boomtown, it was filled with shoddy, wood-frame, non-fire-retardant structures. Only a few buildings withstood the heat and flames. After the earthquake, the municipality altered its building code to reduce some of the worst fire and seismic risks, but it did not apply them comprehensively. Fire would continue to be a hazard through the twentieth century.

Current indications regarding rebuilding in New Orleans and the Gulf region are exhibiting tendencies similar to those that occurred in San Fran-

FIGURE 3.   The Earthquake Cottage employed in San Francisco in 1906 as
temporary shelter first located on public land could later be moved to a resident's site
once services were restored. Courtesy of SFMUSEUM.org.

cisco. Notable are the rush to reconstruct on environmentally vulnerable land
and resistance to incorporating FEMA-recommended higher base flood elevations in local building codes. While the urge to return to normalcy after a
catastrophe is a universal theme in history, the San Francisco story shows that
risky rebuilding has important effects. In the Loma Prieta earthquake, the
majority of damage occurred on land-filled areas, those that extended beyond
the 1906 waterfront boundary (Bardet and Kapuskar 1993, 559).

As in New Orleans and the Gulf, providing permanent workforce housing became a major concern. Here, San Francisco offers replicable examples.
First, the Corporation quickly used its relief donations for grants and loans to
middle-income homeowners to facilitate their rebuilding efforts (Stohr 2005).
Second, with the city clearing sites and rebuilding infrastructure, the Corporation, army, and city parks department collaborated on the design and construction of 5,610 earthquake cottages, using these durable, low-rent, one-
room redwood dwellings to replace the tents in the refuge camps. And as
home sites became available, the tenants purchased the cottages and moved
them to permanent locations. By 1909, the last camp closed. Over time, the
cottage owners incorporated the structures into larger dwellings or used them
for garages or other outbuildings (National Park Service 2006). The Katrina
Cottage, put forward a hundred years later to accommodate the displaced in
Louisiana and Mississippi, echoes this concept (Figure 3).

Similar to New Orleans, San Francisco's disaster emphasized the city's rampant racism, particularly against the Chinese. Here the leaders' behavior was shameful. An estimated quarter of the city's population, the Chinese concentrated in a centrally located "Chinatown," adjacent to the business district. While the majority of the area's residents evacuated to Oakland and nearby cities, the remainder encountered difficulties finding emergency shelter. They fled to one refugee camp only to be forcibly relocated two more times by the military in response to other citizen complaints. Moreover, as the rebuilding schemes emerged, the Corporation proposed relocating the entire community to an "Oriental City," five miles distant from Chinatown. The Corporation quickly backed down when the government of China stated its intention of rebuilding its consulate on its original site and threatened a trade embargo if the plan went through (Hansen 2006a).

In the economic realm, the civic leadership worked feverishly to restore national investor confidence in San Francisco. Most notable was the two-year campaign to rid the municipal government of corruption that, by 1907, resulted in the indictment of the mayor, sixteen of the eighteen members of the city Board of Supervisors, and the party boss. By 1908, the city had elected a reform slate, including an incorruptible mayor (who would be reelected five times), thus assuring political stability, an important feature in assuring the repayment of the various bond issues it floated for recovery projects.

Like today's New Orleans, San Francisco leaders turned to tourism to provide another demonstration of their city's post-disaster resilience. They executed two fairs in rapid succession. The 1909 Portola Festival (commemorating the city's founder) brought in 300,000 visitors, and the 1915 Panama-Pacific International Exposition (to celebrate the opening of the Canal), built on 625 acres including a landfilled lagoon (which after the fair became the notorious Marina district, damaged in the 1989 Loma Prieta earthquake) attracted 18 million attendees in its ten-month duration.

Finally, the private sector leaders fanned out to mount a media blitz testifying to the city's fiscal strength. For example, in summer 1907, prominent banker James D. Phelan visited Eastern cities, giving speeches that insisted that business was thriving after being temporarily "unhoused," celebrated the municipal government clean-up, outlined the strength of the city's tax base and consequent bond repayment capacities, and argued that San Francisco was a low-wage city, attractive to investors (Phelan 1907a, b).

As would occur in New Orleans and the Gulf Region, the San Francisco private sector undertook most rebuilding, securing $250 million (1906 dollars) in insurance payments. Local agreement to characterize the disaster as a great fire, not an earthquake, and high-level political pressure assured these payments despite some initial attempts on the part of the insurers to renege, claiming that the earthquake (uninsured), not the fire, caused the damage. In those pre-FEMA days, the national government jumpstarted the reconstruction through its early commitment to rebuild federal structures and its deposit of large sums in San Francisco banks, in effect making no-interest loans for rebuilding.

Guiding the rebuilding efforts was a Committee on Reconstruction, similar in form and function to the Bring Back New Orleans Commission. Charged with providing a reconstruction plan for Board of Supervisors approval, this group of forty business, professional, and labor leaders were initially optimistic about reconstructing the city according to a comprehensive plan. They had one on hand, completed in 1905 by famed designer Daniel Burnham. It envisioned San Francisco as a splendid city along the monumental lines of Washington, D.C. The only problem was that it called for a dramatic restructuring of the city's street system and a massive new civic center. Cash-strapped businessmen, anxious to get back to work—they had published a street directory for the displaced enterprises in early May—would have nothing to do with it. They insisted on being given permission to rebuild as before (Blackford 1993). Reconstruction efforts on the Gulf Coast exhibit similar trends. Biloxi, Mississippi, for example, has focused its entire effort on restoring its highly lucrative casino industry in its original form, rejecting the alternative suggestions offered by the Mississippi Renewal Forum (Speed 2006; Newsom 2006).

The Committee succumbed to the intense pressure recommending the replication of the former patterns. Given the city's residents' urgency to rebuild quickly, pursuing a plan that required extensive and costly land acquisition was unfeasible. However, the Committee did recommend strategically-important capital improvements. Key was an auxiliary water system to guarantee a supply for firefighting, thus assuring security in the event of another conflagration. In 1989, the city put this system to use after the Loma Prieta earthquake (San Francisco Fire Department 1989). The Committee also floated an idea for a new city hall/civic center, one of the Burnham recommendations. Bond issues to support these projects met with differing results. In 1908, voters enthusiastically approved the water system, but a year later turned down the city hall complex.

Within three years of the disaster, San Francisco had rebounded. It had 25,000 new buildings and a burgeoning economy (Bernasek 2005). By 1910, its population passed 400,000. And in 1911, its voters agreed to build the Burnham-recommended civic center when the popular reform mayor, James "Sunny Jim" Rolph, convinced them that constructing a grand city hall to replace the one destroyed in the earthquake would signal San Francisco's recovery (King 2004). A year later, in anticipation of Canal-induced economic growth and associated population expansion, the municipal government also funded a major construction project, the Twin Peaks Tunnel (completed in 1917), to open up new areas for suburban-style residential development in the growing city (Blackford 1993).

Judged by today's rebuilding standards, many of San Francisco's decisions were untenable. But others merit study. The treatment of the Chinese, unsound methods of debris disposal, and failure to pass strong building codes fall into the former category. Among the more notable responses were the rapid activation of the military and civilian leadership and their service delivery to well-ordered administrative units, the construction of the moveable cottages, the pressure on the insurance companies for payment, the rapid influx of federal funds, the overthrow of the corrupt government, the focus on tourism to mend the economic and psychological wounds of the fire, and the decisions to use municipal bonds to improve safety. These measures framed the city's rebuilding efforts and twentieth-century growth. By 1989, San Francisco had doubled in population (724,000) and geographic size (46 square miles).

On October 18, 1989, just as an unprecedented World Series featuring two local rivals, the Oakland Athletics and San Francisco Giants, was about to begin its third game, an earthquake shook the Bay Area. Smaller (7.1 on the Richter scale), of shorter duration, and upsetting less of the San Andreas fault than the 1906 occurrence, it nonetheless was the largest earthquake to affect the city and its surrounds since the earlier disaster. Fatalities (67), injuries (3,757), property damage ($11 billion, 1989 dollars) were lower. Although spread over 400,000 square miles, the severely damaged areas were considerably smaller. In San Francisco, the Marina district and parts of the Mission and South of Market neighborhoods were afflicted with some 23,000 housing units damaged or burned. Nearby Oakland and Santa Cruz also suffered substantial damages with Oakland losing 1,500 low income rental units and Santa Cruz its entire downtown (King 2004; Comerio 1998). Many of the area's highways and bridges were ruptured, notably the Bay Bridge, the Embarcadero Freeway, Central Skyway, and the Cypress Express viaduct (National Research Council 1994). In San Francisco, though more densely settled than in 1906, the auxiliary water system constructed in 1908 functioned properly, restricting fire damage. Ultimately, the total losses (damage plus lost output) were $16 billion offset by $9.2 billion in aid ($1.6 billion in insurance payments and $7.6 billion in government assistance). While these numbers fall far short of those associated with Hurricane Katrina (estimated total losses $125–150 billion) and total aid expected (estimated $140–160 billion), the rebuilding process, particularly the role played by FEMA is instructive (Frame et al. 2005, 9).

In the years between the 1906 and 1989 earthquakes, a national disaster emergency system had evolved. Up to the 1930s, the national government had responded to disasters with special legislation for individual events as was seen in 1906. In the 1930s, it began to distribute the response programs according to function. For example, in 1932 Congress formed the Reconstruction Finance Corporation empowering it to offer loans to rebuild public buildings after a catastrophe, by 1934 the Bureau of Public Roads had charge of rebuilding disaster-torn streets and highways, and in 1944 the Flood Control Act gave the Army Corps of Engineers responsibility for dealing with floods.

Passage of the Disaster Relief Act (1950) and ensuing legislation in 1970 and 1974 expanded the federal role, crafted a more sophisticated and defined response system, and added proactive programs for hazard mitigation and preparedness. Overall, the U.S. Department of Defense supervised civil defense while the Department of Housing and Urban Development (founded in 1965) had charge of natural disasters. In addition, other separately administered programs had emerged, the Flood Insurance Act (1968) and the National Earthquake Hazard Reduction Act (1977).

With various functions distributed through the relevant agencies, the states' governors found the system increasingly inefficient as they maneuvered through hurricanes, floods, and other catastrophes. In 1979, in an attempt to reduce the confusion, President Jimmy Carter consolidated all federal disaster and civil defense activities into a single, sub-cabinet unit, the Federal Emergency Management Agency (FEMA). Important reforms followed, culminating in the Robert T. Stafford Disaster Relief and Emergency Act (1988, amended 2000) that governs today's procedures. In general, it defines processes for presidential declaration of disasters that trigger various types of federal assistance. The Loma Prieta earthquake as well as Hurricane Hugo that preceded it by a month would be the first test of the Stafford Act.

To bring the FEMA story up to date, the twin disasters (Hugo and Loma Prieta) stressed the agency so severely that in 1993 President William J. Clinton, seeking to make FEMA more effective, raised the agency to cabinet level and appointed veteran disaster manager James Witt director. Witt proceeded to professionalize and modernize the agency (Daniels and Clarke-Daniels 2000). In 2002, Congress passed the Homeland Security Act, placing FEMA in a new cabinet-level agency, the Department of Homeland Security (DHS). The following year, President George W. Bush mandated DHS to create a comprehensive disaster program, resulting in its issuing the National Response Plan (NRP) and an associated National Incident Management System (NIMS) in December 2004. Hurricane Katrina was the first test of the NRP and NIMS.

The implementing regulations of the NRP, detailed in an appendix outlining the functions and responsible agencies, encompass fifteen support functions ranging from transportation to mass care and others. Included is a rebuilding element, Emergency Support Function 14, "Long Term Community Recovery, Mitigation and Economic Stabilization Annex," focused on infrastructure, housing, and the local economy, whose purpose is "to provide a framework for federal support to enable recovery from the long-term consequences of an incident of National Significance." Many current planning activities in Louisiana, Mississippi, and the other hurricane-ravaged places occurring in winter and spring 2006 are in compliance with ESF 14.

The evolution of national disaster response activities since 1979 represents reactive attempts to correct flaws emerging during various disasters. The Loma Prieta earthquake revealed serious shortcomings similar to many of those now surfacing in New Orleans and the Gulf region. While President George H. W. Bush acting under the Stafford Act declared a national disaster, pushed Congress to authorize an immediate $3.5 billion for emergency efforts (rising to $7.6 billion), and sent Vice President Dan Quayle as his emissary to San Francisco, FEMA was clearly not up to the job. Widespread allegations of mistreatment of the poor, homeless, or non-English-speaking, massive red tape and confusion in determining responsibility for repair and reconstruction of public facilities, major disputes regarding payments associated with historic preservation or seismic improvements, and poor staff performance proved true (National Research Council 1994, 220–25; U.S. GAO 1991; Frame et al. 2005, 9).

As the General Accounting Office detailed these flaws in several reports (U.S. GAO 1990, 1991, 1992, 1996) the primary weakness was staffing. FEMA had too few and too poorly trained employees. For example, the five permanent FEMA staff members assigned to the Bay Area were also responsible for 36 other declared disasters occurring before and after Loma Prieta (U.S. GAO 1991). While FEMA along with local authorities performed emergency response duties adequately, its record on immediate rebuilding was dismal. Before releasing recovery funds, FEMA rules demanded individual damage survey reports (DSRs). With more than 9,000 such reports required, the FEMA staff was swamped. When it hired a variety of subcontractors the DSRs were slow in coming, inconsistent, and often offered confused recommendations (U.S. GAO, 1991, 1992).

FEMA was at a particular loss in dealing with urban housing problems, especially those related to affordable shelter in central cities. Loma Prieta decimated low-cost multifamily rental and single-room occupancy (SRO) units—San Francisco lost 4,500 rentals and Oakland 1,300 SROs. Most were in buildings whose low rent reflected their overcrowded and substandard conditions (Comerio 1993). FEMA/Small Business Administration officials incorrectly assumed that the private sector would rebuild these units; the combination of increased safety requirements, high construction costs, and low tenant incomes made this impossible. Only after a Legal Aid Society suit did the government agree to a $23 million settlement to subsidize low cost housing, a one-time fix, not a permanent solution (U.S. GAO 1992; Comerio 1993; Greene and Schulz 1993).

New public facilities compensation rules in the Stafford Act also exacerbated the rebuilding problems. The act had expanded funding eligibility to "those facilities that provide essential services of a governmental nature to the general public," a much broader definition than the previous aid programs restricted to federal-, state-, or city-owned buildings. FEMA's public assistance program paid a substantial proportion of costs incurred for debris removal, emergency protective measures, and permanent restoration. This legislative change resulted in an unprecedented 391 applications from nonprofit groups like museums, zoos, libraries, and senior citizen centers. While FEMA would eventually pay out $59 million to 283 nonprofits, every settlement required intensive, time-consuming negotiations (U.S. GAO 1992).

Other issues arose in conjunction with the level of compensation for public facilities. While FEMA ostensibly favored rebuilding to mitigate further hazards, it had no way of accounting for the increased costs of safety improvements. Therefore, it rejected seismic corrections for a building when its price tag was 63% higher than reconstruction at the pre-earthquake standard (U.S. GAO 1992).

With regard to replacement versus rebuilding-to-historic-preservation standards, an issue arose around landmark buildings. For example, FEMA refused to pay $53 million for restoration of the historic Oakland City Hall when estimates for building a completely new structure came in at $46 million. During the five years of negotiations around this issue, FEMA paid $31 million for temporary relocation payments, a sum far greater than the disputed amount for rebuilding (U.S. GAO 1996, 39).

Finally, other compensation practices created difficult precedents. For example, FEMA approved a $9 million payment to the Port of San Francisco for a damaged pier, a facility not used for any public purpose but leased to a private fish-processing concern that used the grant to modernize the facility. While an argument might be made that the grant enhanced economic recovery, this expenditure further confused future interpretations regarding public facilities (U.S. GAO 1996, 39).

At the local level, San Francisco acted as it had in the past. It made few regulatory changes in its planning, building, and rent control ordinances in response to the earthquake. Anxious to encourage rebuilding, it wrote in a required upgrade for seismic safety when a certain proportion of an existing building was damaged but enforced it leniently, provided favorable treatment for rebuilding non-seismic-proof nonconforming structures, and allowed condominium conversions in rental buildings without requiring affordable units or any guarantee for previous renters to return to the converted building at prior rents as would ordinarily occur (Gladstone 2006).

Despite these problems, San Francisco leaders made important decisions about strategic, city-improving investments in its post-earthquake rebuilding. They leveraged several billion dollars in public facilities restoration funds from FEMA and other agencies to stimulate high levels of private investment that is still occurring more than fifteen years after the disaster.

Most notable are highway demolition projects that have opened up new development and renewal areas. Examples are the removal of two 1959-vintage expressways, the Embarcadero Freeway and the Central Skyway. After a two-year political fight, the San Francisco government agreed to the removal of the Embarcadero, the partially completed mile-long, 70-foot-high, 52-foot-wide stretch. Its destruction stimulated renewal along 2.5 miles of centrally located waterfront featuring new commercial, recreational, tourist, and open space facilities. Adjacent residential neighborhoods are also emerging with the city government attempting to address affordable housing needs through requiring minimum numbers of units in new construction (City and County of San Francisco Department of City Planning 2005; San Francisco Redevelopment Agency 2006). The less publicized, but equally dramatic, conversion of a nine-block section of the Central Skyway into a low-speed boulevard is also stimulating neighborhood renewal in a formerly undeveloped part of the city. Years of citizen discussion regarding rebuilding plans resulted in the recent issuance of development regulations for these new residential areas (San Francisco Department of City Planning 2005).

The demolitions are affecting a large multi-neighborhood area south of Market Street and adjacent to the city's major cultural/civic spaces, the Yerba Buena Gardens and the Civic Center, both of which host institutions or buildings that were beneficiaries of FEMA rebuilding payments. For example, the entirely renovated Civic Center has seven upgraded buildings including a restored City Hall, new main library, adaptively reused Asian Art Museum, and renovated opera house and civic auditorium, none of which would have received their upgrades without the stimulus of the earthquake. Finally, the city's cultural institutions collectively have spent about $1 billion in upgrades, renovation, and expansion, given impetus by disaster-induced damage (King 2004).

San Francisco's rebuilding has been a lengthy and expensive process. While federal recovery payments and insurance premiums have helped cover costs, the city and state governments also contributed large sums. For example, in 1989 the state instituted additional taxes to help defray its contributions, while San Francisco floated several bond issues amounting to about three-quarters of a billion dollars to pay for public safety improvements and capital expenses related to the city hall, the Asian Art Museum, and other city facilities upgrades (City and County of San Francisco 2005). In addition, private philanthropy, corporate investments, and other private sector contributions have had a substantial role in the recovery. The result is the emergence of a twenty-first-century city well equipped to meet modern economic challenges (King 2004).

The primary lesson resulting from rebuilding after the Loma Prieta earthquake is an understanding of the complexities of recovery under today's rules. These include assessing the benefits and limits of government assistance, leveraging federal payments with local funds in conjunction with a broad vision for redeveloping a modern city, and appreciating the length of time needed to formulate and execute a rebuilding program inclusive of citizen participation and political processes. The most obvious negative lesson is the inability of the federal officials in FEMA and other agencies to deal with specifically urban issues. Examples were the difficulties with assisting with affordable housing and gauging the value of heritage restoration, issues that are surfacing in New Orleans and the Gulf region today. The most positive lesson is the strength of local officials and citizens in reinventing their city.

As New Orleans and the Gulf region rebuild, the public, private, and nonprofit sectors have an enormous job. The losses from Hurricane Katrina overshadow any natural disaster experienced in the nation. For example, it destroyed an estimated 210,000 homes—50,000 in New Orleans alone—caused the loss of 280,000 to 400,000 jobs, and affected 70% of the area's banks (Brown 2006). The rebuilding environment is testing new federal disaster agencies, procedures, and local intergovernmental relationships. Figure 4, an example of how the Gulfport Mississippi mayor's office tried to understand FEMA regulations for housing compensation, is but a tiny illustration of the complexities with which local officials struggle in their efforts to balance federal requirements with constituents' demands to rebuild. In residential, institutional, and commercial reconstruction, a major stumbling block is the absence of FEMA's final base flood elevation maps that set the height for buildings in the 100-year floodplain (in which a large part of New Orleans and Gulf coastal cities lie), qualifying structures for flood insurance required by federal or federally regulated mortgage agencies as a condition of lending. While FEMA has issued advisory maps, it will not finalize them for at least 18 months (Nossiter 2006b; Schwartz 2006a). Tensions are rife regarding environmental vulnerability, economic development, social justice, and preserving the sense of place. In New Orleans, anchor institutions including universities and hospitals are playing a leading role in rebuilding the economy, as are knowledge-related services associated with oil, shipping, and cultural tourism (Pearce 2006). Yet in April 2006 the city's economic development director reported that only 2,000 of the city's 22,000 businesses had reopened (Rivlin

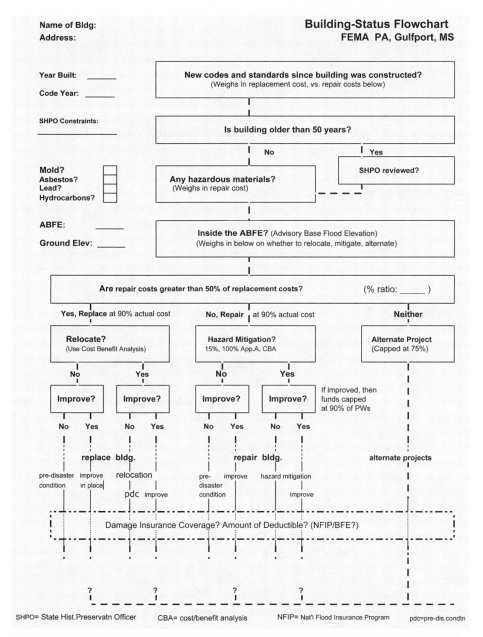

FIGURE 4. FEMA building status flowchart, Gulfport, Mississippi. Courtesy of Ron Smith, Sandy Smith, Jackson Yench, and the City of Gulfport.

2006). In the Gulf Coast, economic drivers such as the multi-billion-dollar casino industry are shaping recovery. In Biloxi alone, with only one third of the facilities open, gambling revenues returned to 75% of their pre-disaster levels by winter 2006 (Newsom 2006). In all places, however, housing shortages hindered recovery (Rivlin 2006; Smith 2006).

The federal government authorized the highest level of compensation for a natural disaster in history, responding with direct budget allocations and tax relief programs. As of spring, 2006, it has allocated $88 billion for relief and recovery activities for hurricanes Katrina, Rita, and Wilma in five states (Alabama, Florida, Louisiana, Mississippi, and Texas) and authorized $8 billion in tax relief. On the budget allocation side, the actual division of the funds between relief and rebuilding activities, its distribution to the involved states, and the amount actually spent is difficult to discern. While some experts estimate the expenditure of $30 billion of national budget allocations, others believe that the funding levels seem to reflect federal intentions or priorities (Fellowes and Liu 2006; Brown 2006).

Tracking government priorities through the budget reveals housing as the major focus. Generally, 50% of the funds are for housing (including flood insurance premium payouts, 21%; community development block grants, 13%; trailers and mobile homes, 6%; rental assistance and grants for home repair, 6%). Emergency response and restoration of federal facilities follow at 26% while infrastructure rebuilding (including 2% for levee repair, 3% for coastal restoration, and 13% for transportation and water/sewer reconstruction) account for 18% of the total.

The primary tax relief program includes incentives outlined in the Gulf Opportunity Zone (Go-Zone) legislation passed in December 2005. It dramatically expands low-income housing tax credit allocations, allows accelerated depreciation on rebuilt property, extends commercial net operating loss carrybacks, offers higher tax credits for rehabilitation of historic commercial buildings, and offers other write-offs. The Go-Zone encompasses 37 parishes in Louisiana and 50 counties in Mississippi, offering no special advantages to disaster-afflicted urban places. Early reports indicate that this broad geography is encouraging the use of the benefits outside the problematic and most damaged areas.

The states, not the localities, will determine the internal distribution of federal funds, supplemented by their own budget allocations for rebuilding. Both Louisiana and Mississippi are acting proactively to develop comprehensive redevelopment plans. In each case, private philanthropy is financing these efforts. The Knight Foundation and Netscape founder James Barksdale sponsored the Mississippi Renewal Forum, encompassing 11 Gulf Coast cities and led by Miami designer Andres Duany, while the Baton Rouge Area Foundation has spun off the LRA Fund to cover the tri-partite Louisiana Speaks program. This latter effort includes a 25-year regional vision for southeast Louisiana overseen by the California-based firm Calthorpe Associates, execution of several neighborhood design exercises run by Duany, and development of a toolkit for residential and commercial architecture undertaken by Urban Design Associates of Pittsburgh. In all cases, the lead professionals are prominent proponents of New Urbanism, a design philosophy that supports dense, compact development.

The planning efforts have differing timetables. For example, the Mississippi Renewal Forum submitted its final report in December 2005. Localities such as Gulfport and Pass Christian have had additional planning sessions to refine their rebuilding programs (Sorlien and Speed, this volume). Louisiana Speaks expects completion of the regional vision in December 2006 with the other elements coming on line earlier. Local Louisiana efforts, notably the Bring Back New Orleans Commission plan, stalled until the conclusion of the city's mayoral election (see Barnett, this volume).

While these planning activities were going forward, important project-based rebuilding decisions were occurring simultaneously. Under FEMA's Emergency Support Function 14, localities (parishes in Louisiana, counties and municipalities in Mississippi) are assembling Long Term Recovery Plans, preconditions for receiving federal funds under the Stafford Act. Basically prioritized lists of desired rebuilding tasks submitted to the state, they are time-driven and pinpoint individual projects because certain federal agencies have deadlines for disaster-grant expenditures. Under U.S. Department of Housing and Urban Development (HUD) guidance, states are formulating programs to spend the extra community block grant allocations. In April 2006, Louisiana's Road Home program with $7.5 billion for homeownership rebuilding and $1.75 billion for rental housing replacement or reconstruction was in the public comment stage while Mississippi's Homeownership Assistance Plan allocating $3.2 billion for homeowners had already secured HUD (Mississippi Development Authority 2006; Louisiana Recovery Authority 2006).

In conjunction with launching these activities, state- and local-level Louisiana reformers attempted good-government improvements with mixed results. In February 2006 the state legislature acted to consolidate the multiple levee boards in seven parishes, including New Orleans. Failing to achieve one, it compromised on two boards, one for each side of the Mississippi. At the same time its attempt to streamline the New Orleans municipal government by reducing redundant officials (that is, two sheriffs, seven tax assessors, when most places have one of each) failed entirely.

At the local level, in New Orleans, as in many of the afflicted cities, chronic fiscal distress has risen to critical levels—the city anticipates half the pre-disaster tax revenue—and is hard pressed to restore municipal services. Additionally, its dysfunctional public housing authority and educational system are in receivership (Walsh 2006). With the firing of 3,000 municipal employees, the city has been forced to improvise and change, installing a modern, computer-based building permit system, for example (Tedeschi 2006). In other areas, the disaster has created other new solutions to service delivery, including the creation of charter schools, but has left others unreformed, especially public housing, which in spring 2006 had 7,000 shuttered units on its hands (Walsh 2006).

However, several months after Hurricane Katrina, the afflicted regions were still struggling with debris removal, demolition of damaged properties, providing shelter for displaced populations, and patching up basic infrastructure—41% of New Orleans zip codes had no sewers in April 2006—while simultaneously undertaking the short- and long-term recovery planning discussed above (Nossiter 2006; City of New Orleans 2006). While some urban places are attempting to use the disaster as an opportunity to reinvent their cities with regard to the environment, urban design, and social justice, others are eager to return as they were (Newsom 2006). The public sector, especially the federal and state levels, and the citizens have opportunities to reinforce change leveraging budget and allocation of tax incentives but seizing these chances will demand political will, savvy, and vision. What is clear at this time is that existing forces, now in delicate tension, will reshape the disaster-torn urban places of Louisiana and Mississippi. But the question is, how?

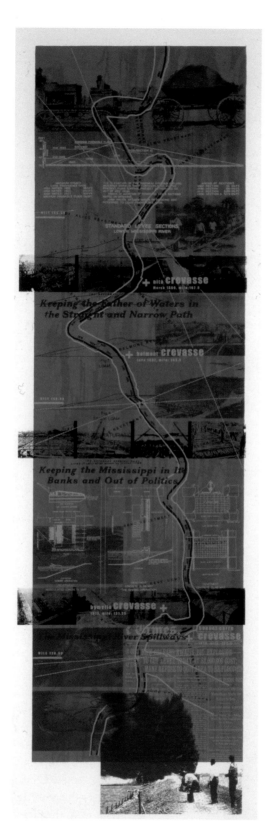

PLATE 1. "Crevassing Levees" (screen print on paper, 20" x 60"), from Anuradha Mathur and Dilip da Cunha, *Mississippi Floods, Designing a Shifting Landscape* (New Haven, Conn.: Yale University Press, 2001). Reprinted by permission.

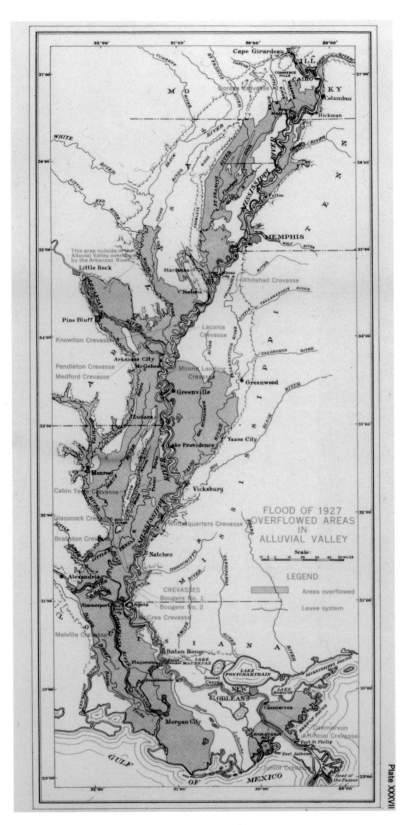

PLATE 2. "Map of the flood of 1927," from D. O. Elliot, *The Improvement of the Lower Mississippi River for Flood Control and Navigation* (Vicksburg: Waterways Experiment Station, 1932). The flood of 1927 could be seen as the Mississippi laying claim to a terrain far beyond its "channel." New Orleans resisted this claim by dynamiting the levee downriver from the city.

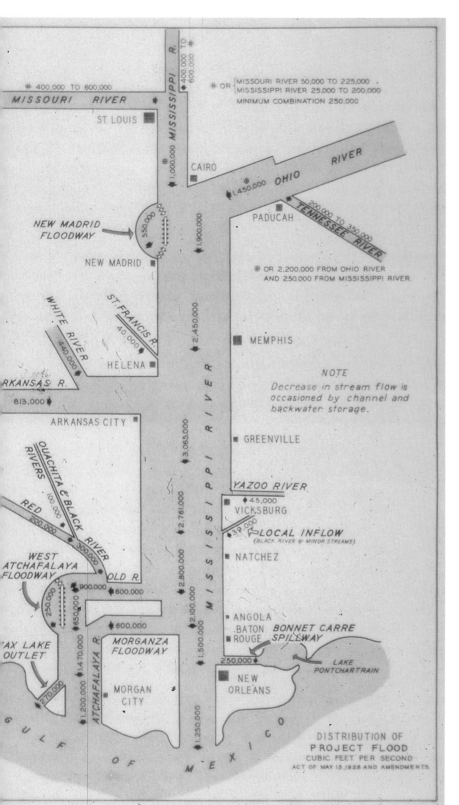

PLATE 3. "Distribution of Project Flood," from P. A. Feringa and Charles W. Schweizer, *One Hundred Years of Improvement on the Lower Mississippi River* (Vicksburg: Mississippi River Commission, 1952). Following the 1927 flood, the working image of the Mississippi was extended from a flow within a channel to a systemic volume of flows that gathered in a probable flood.

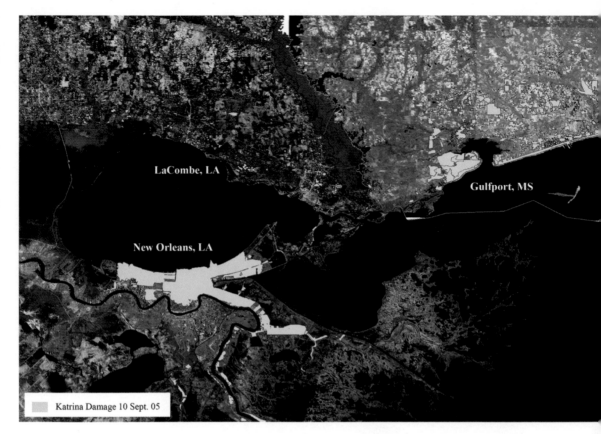

LaCombe, LA

Gulfport, MS

New Orleans, LA

Katrina Damage 10 Sept. 05

PLATE 4. Map of New Orleans, Louisiana, to Gulfport, Mississippi, showing damage from Hurricane Katrina. Map produced by EDAW from FEMA data.

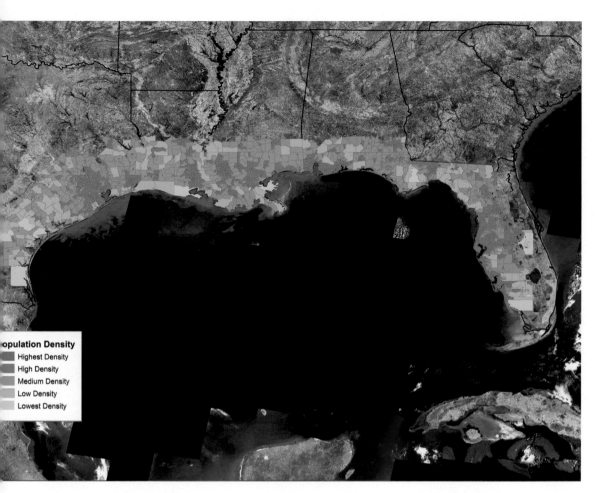

PLATE 5. One reason Hurricane Katrina caused so much damage is that more than 10 million people currently live in coastal counties along the Gulf of Mexico. This is 3.5 times the population that lived here in the 1950s. Much of that growth has occurred because of a lull in severe storms along the Gulf Coast over the last couple of decades. Map produced by EDAW from U.S. Census Bureau data.

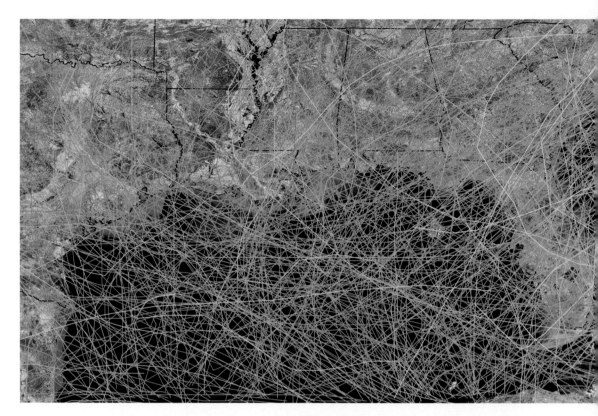

PLATE 6. Major Hurricanes, 1851–2000. This map, showing all the severe storms that hit the Gulf of Mexico from 1851 to 2000, helps illustrate the seriousness of the problem. Previous hurricane paths and resulting damages are two factors considered when determining the potential risks of an area. Map produced by EDAW from NHC data.

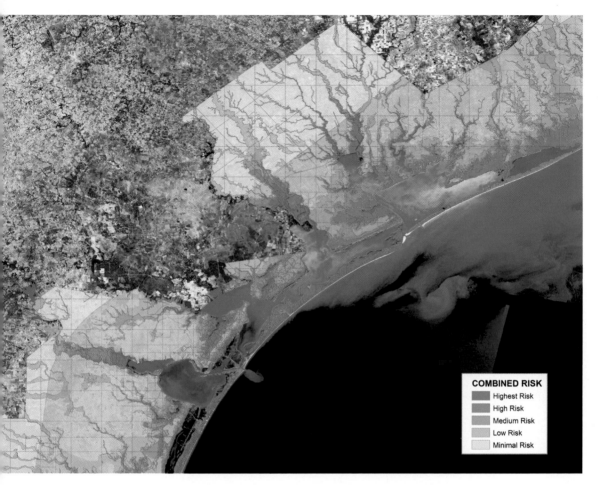

COMBINED RISK
Highest Risk
High Risk
Medium Risk
Low Risk
Minimal Risk

PLATE 7. Potential Combined Risk Areas for the Victoria, Texas, area. This map is generated by creating a composite that includes storm surge risks, wind risks, social risks, and economic risks. Map produced by EDAW from Coastal Risk Atlas data.

**STORM SURGE RISK**

Highest Risk
High Risk
Medium Risk
Low Risk
Minimal Risk

PLATE 8. Potential Storm Surge Risk Areas. This map shows the potential impacts of storm surges near Houston, Texas. Storm surge is one factor considered when determining the potential risk of an area. Map produced by EDAW from Coastal Risk Atlas data.

PLATE 9. Map of Lacombe, Louisiana, showing existing flood plain levels. Map produced by EDAW.

Existing High Tide
Projected High Tide w/ 35" Sea Rise

PLATE 10. Map of Lacombe, Louisiana, showing what the new high tide level would be after a 35" rise in sea elevation. This is based on a 21" to 44" rise in sea elevation predicted by scientists over the next 50 to 100 years. Sea rise is one factor considered when determining the potential risks of an area. Map produced by EDAW.

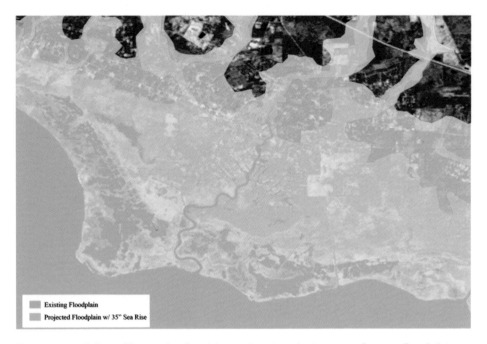

PLATE 11. Map of Lacombe, Louisiana, showing the impact of a new floodplain after 35" rise in sea elevation. This is based on a 21" to 44" rise in sea elevation predicted by scientists over the next 50 to 100 years. Sea rise and flooding potential are two factors considered when determining the potential risks of an area. Map produced by EDAW.

**Societal Risk**
- Highest Risk
- High Risk
- Medium Risk
- Low Risk
- Minimal Risk

PLATE 12. Some members of society are more vulnerable than others. High-risk populations include a high percentage of: people over age 65, single parents with children, people living in poverty or on public assistance, having no vehicle, living in rental units, or living in older structures built before 1970. These factors are combined to create a societal risk map using data from the Coastal Risk Atlas (CRA). CRA is a project operated by the NOAA Coastal Data Development Center (NCDDC) in collaboration with the NOAA Coastal Services Center (CSC). The CRA can be used to identify high-risk demographic areas, as well as those that are vulnerable to storm surge, flooding, and high winds. Map produced by EDAW from Coastal Risk Atlas data.

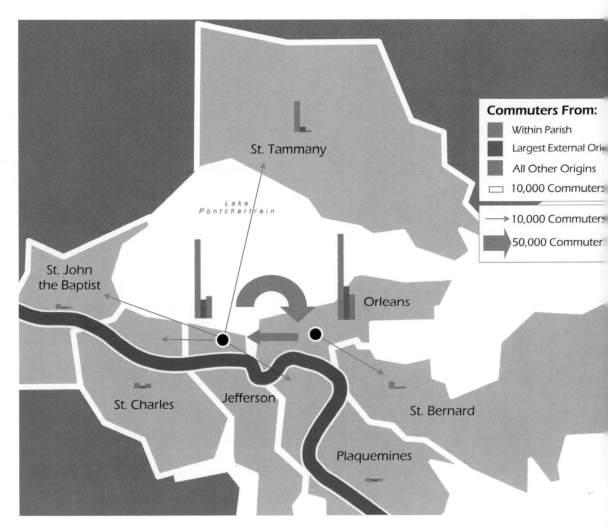

Commuters From:
- Within Parish
- Largest External Ori[gins]
- All Other Origins
- 10,000 Commuters
- 10,000 Commuters
- 50,000 Commuter[s]

St. Tammany

Lake Pontchartrain

St. John the Baptist

Orleans

St. Charles

Jefferson

St. Bernard

Plaquemines

PLATE 13. Parish to parish commuting by job location.

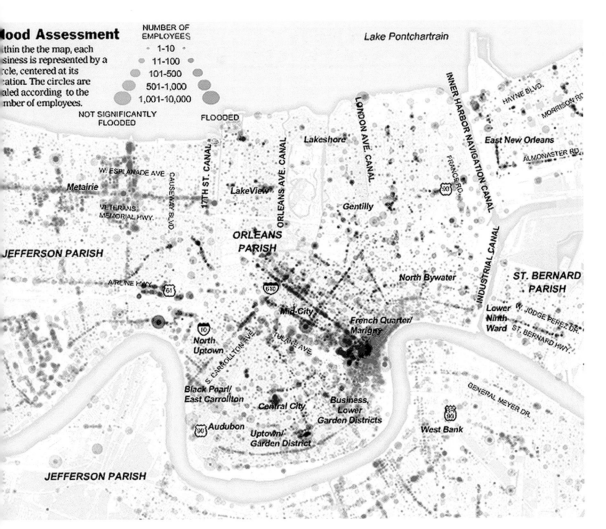

PLATE 14. Distribution of employment in pre-Katrina New Orleans. The map shows both concentrations of employment in the Central Business District, Mid City, and French Quarter, but also an overlay of small- and medium-sized employers spread out across the city. New York Times Graphics, 2005.

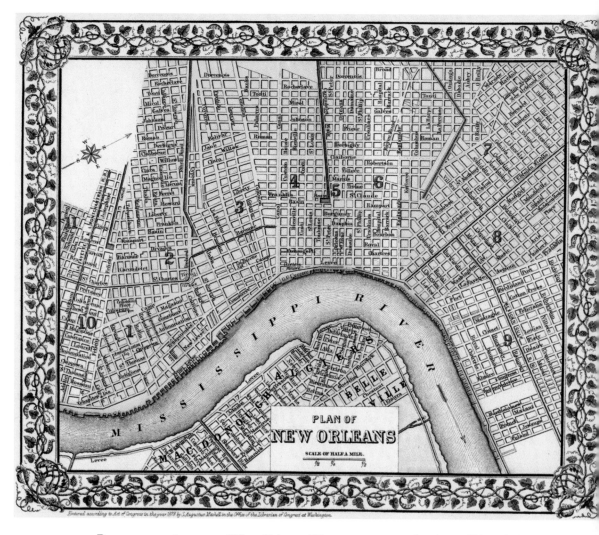

PLATE 15. 1877 map of New Orleans. The map captures the view of New Orleans through the lens of economic values: the complexity of the emergent city and its cultural landscape are radically reduced; the city is represented as a collection of blank lots. The arrangement of streets and blocks represents only the information essential for real-estate transactions. University of Alabama Historical Map Archive, courtesy of Robert M. Baker.

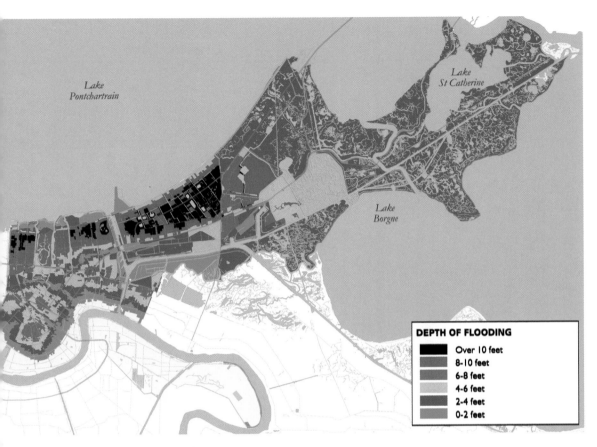

PLATE 16. Depth of floodwater in New Orleans.

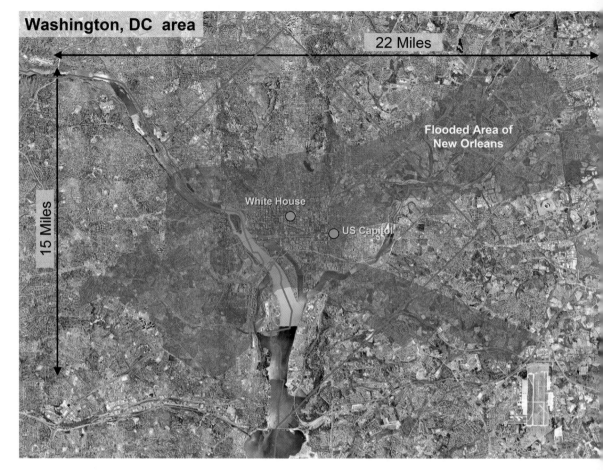

PLATE 17. Scope of the reconstruction problem in New Orleans. The image shows an outline of the flooded area of the City of New Orleans alone over an aerial photograph of the District of Columbia at the same scale.

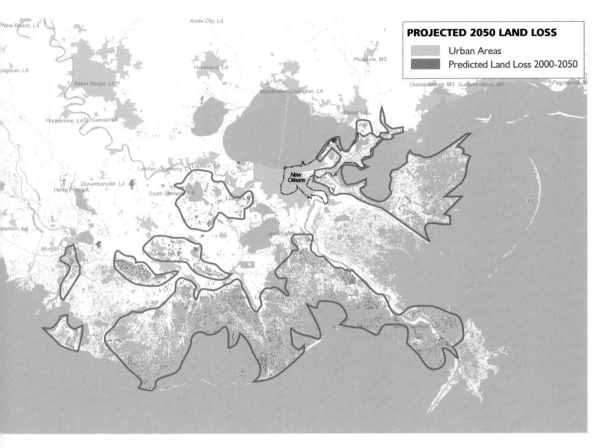

PLATE 18. Predicted loss of wetlands between 2000 and 2050.

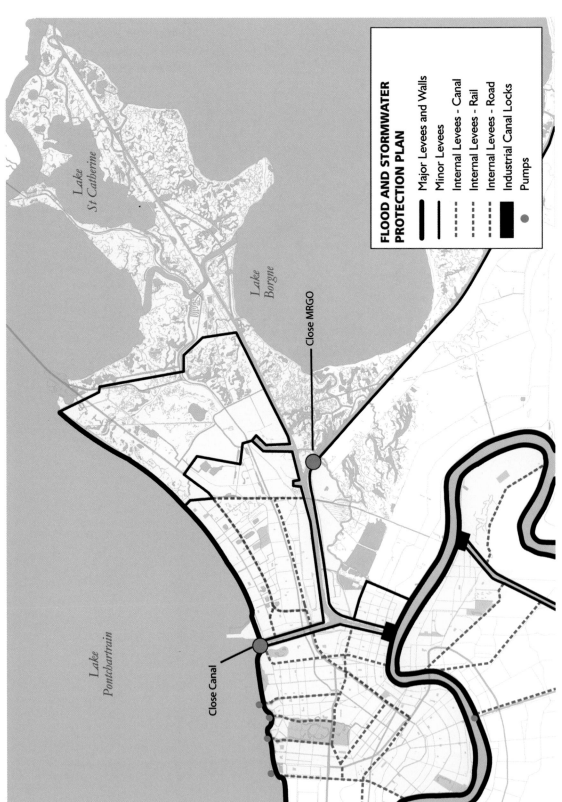

PLATE 19.  Flood and storm water protection plan.

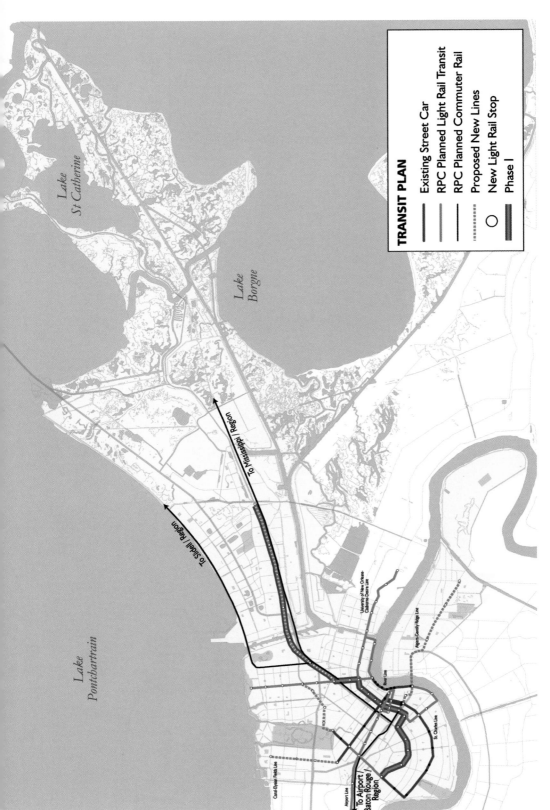

PLATE 20. Transit and transportation plan.

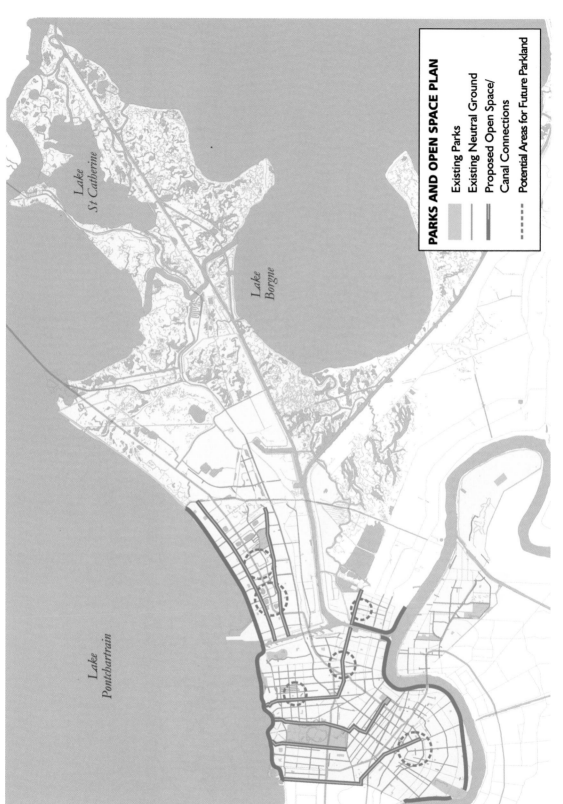

**PARKS AND OPEN SPACE PLAN**

Existing Parks

Existing Neutral Ground

Proposed Open Space/
Canal Connections

Potential Areas for Future Parkland

*Lake
St Catherine*

*Lake
Borgne*

*Lake
Pontchartrain*

PLATE 21. Parks and open space plan.

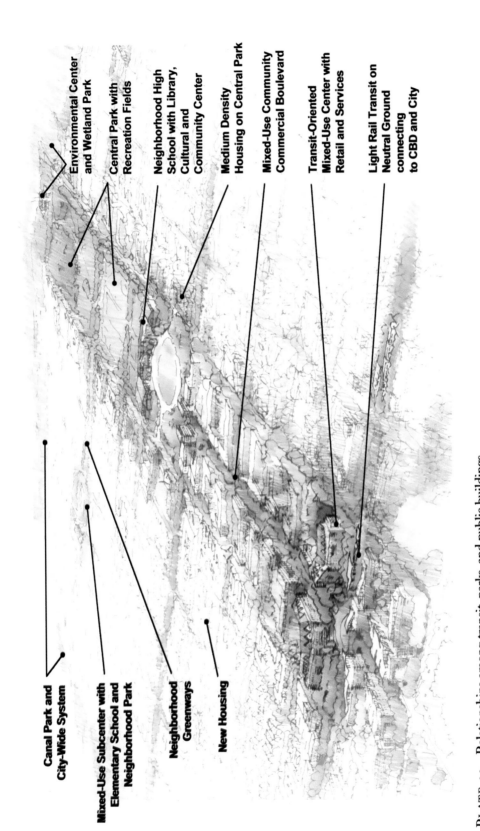

**Canal Park and
City-Wide System**

**Mixed-Use Subcenter with
Elementary School and
Neighborhood Park**

**Neighborhood
Greenways**

**New Housing**

**Environmental Center
and Wetland Park**

**Central Park with
Recreation Fields**

**Neighborhood High
School with Library,
Cultural and
Community Center**

**Medium Density
Housing on Central Park**

**Mixed-Use Community
Commercial Boulevard**

**Transit-Oriented
Mixed-Use Center with
Retail and Services**

**Light Rail Transit on
Neutral Ground
connecting
to CBD and City**

PLATE 22. Relationships among transit, parks, and public buildings.

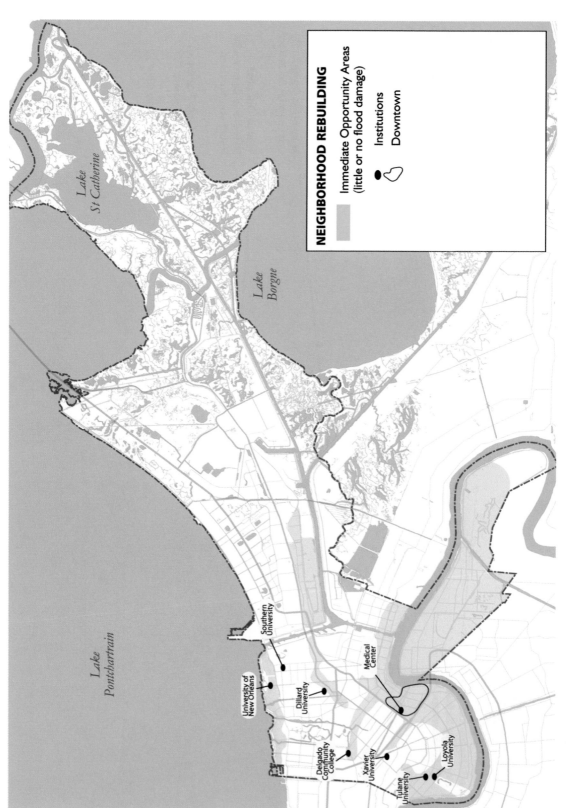

**NEIGHBORHOOD REBUILDING**

Immediate Opportunity Areas
(little or no flood damage)

Institutions
Downtown

*Lake Pontchartrain*

*Lake St Catherine*

*Lake Borgne*

Southern University

University of New Orleans

Dillard University

Delgado Community College

Xavier University

Tulane University

Loyola University

Medical Center

PLATE 23. Immediate Opportunity Areas.

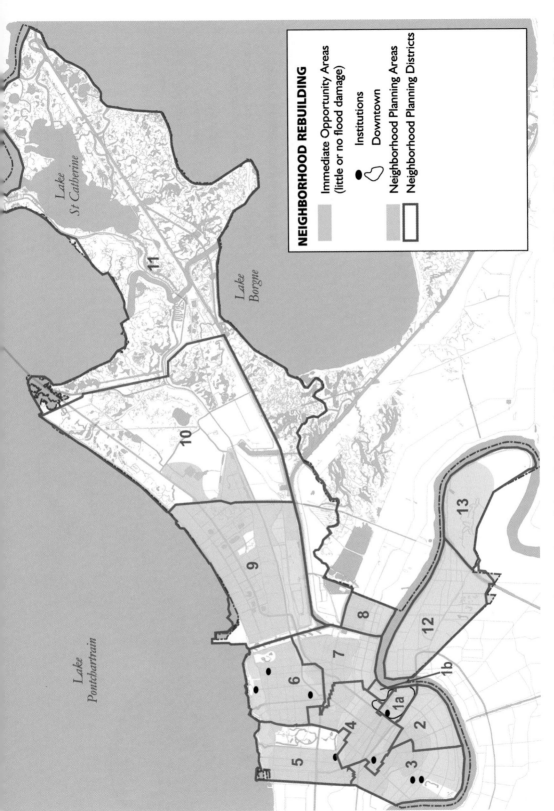

PLATE 24. Neighborhood Planning Areas are located throughout the city with the fourteen designated Planning Districts established by the New Orleans City Planning Commission.

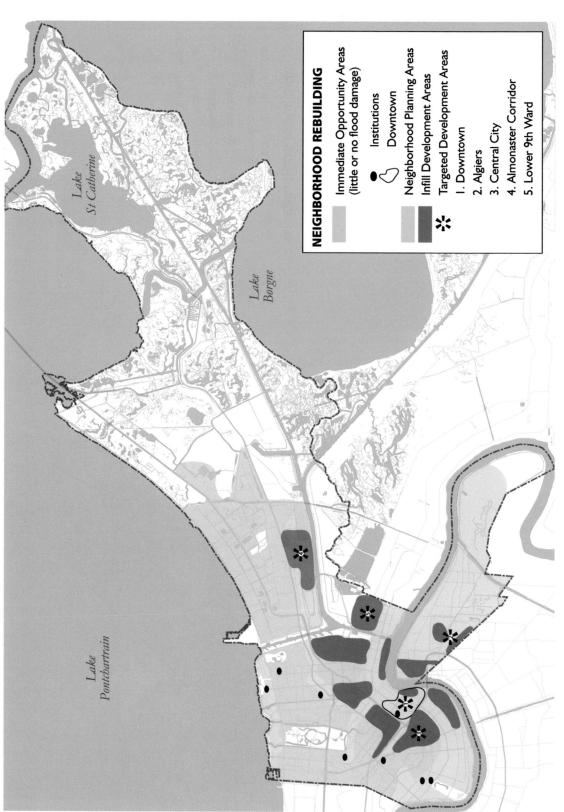

**NEIGHBORHOOD REBUILDING**

Immediate Opportunity Areas
(little or no flood damage)

● Institutions
⬮ Downtown

Neighborhood Planning Areas
Infill Development Areas

Targeted Development Areas
✳
1. Downtown
2. Algiers
3. Central City
4. Almonaster Corridor
5. Lower 9th Ward

*Lake Pontchartrain*

*Lake St Catherine*

*Lake Borgne*

PLATE 25. Infill Development Areas.

# Restoring Urban Viability

Lawrence J. Vale

It is not only difficult to rebuild urban places after disaster; it is also difficult to *evaluate* the rebuilding that has occurred. This is true partly because the act of "rebuilding" can be defined literally in bricks-and-mortar terms or can be a more metaphorical judgment about the broader pattern of recovery or human resilience, issues that are much harder to measure (Vale and Campanella 2005a). Similarly, it is difficult to know at what point in time it becomes possible to measure either the quality or the quantity of rebuilding that has occurred "after" a disaster. There is a vast difference between critiques of initial disaster recovery efforts and reflective analysis of some broader pattern of rebuilding. The latter cannot be measured in weeks or months, but must be assessed in terms of years or even decades. And, for those trained to think in more geological sorts of timeframes, even the perspective of several decades may not be sufficient to judge whether a particular process of rebuilding and rehabitation of a dangerous urban zone was a sensible thing to have undertaken.

Post-disaster economic challenges, at base, are inseparable from social, political, and physical conditions. Similarly, rebuilding is only a small part of anything that truly deserves the name "recovery," especially in places where economic health was not widely shared before disaster struck. Economic viability is therefore inseparable from the challenges of neighborhood planning, community development, and social repair.

For cities on the rise—such as Chicago before its 1871 Great Fire or San Francisco before the earthquake and fires of 1906—the post-recovery period often unleashes a continuation of an underlying trend. For New Orleans today, however, bouncing back must also contend with the disastrous socioeconomic conditions that Katrina's arrival exposed to the world. Post-disaster Chicago and San Francisco enjoyed the immense resource value of a supportive hinterland untouched by the devastation that destroyed the central city. These were disasters with clear boundaries, both spatially and temporally, where rebuilding could commence even before the last embers had been extinguished. Post-disaster Chicago and San Francisco were places where reinvestment of all kinds eagerly awaited the chance to jump in with the heady and hearty mixture of opportunity and opportunism that disasters always present. Residential displacement, though significant, entailed no broad scattering of the population, and industries could be restocked with raw materials supplied from outside the affected areas. Earthquakes and fires, while certainly perils that can recur without warning, are nonetheless regarded as sufficiently infrequent to permit confident rebuilding. Reconstruction in flood-prone and storm-vulnerable areas with inadequate levees, such as New Orleans, adds another layer of uncertainty for those who would commence rebuilding in New Orleans. As the citizens of New Orleans struggle to revive their city, it is worth recalling the earlier experiences of Chicagoans and San Franciscans. In those places, local voices profoundly affected the post-disaster dynamics. Working-class residents demanded that any new city must be rebuilt for them, not simply for the wealthy.

## Learning from Chicago and San Francisco

Although the disasters that struck Chicago and San Francisco so many decades ago are very much artifacts of dramatically different political and economic systems (and also differ in significant ways from each other), many issues from these earlier American experiences with calamity continue to resonate with the unfolding events along the post-Katrina Gulf Coast.

Everyone touts the dramatic recovery of Chicago after the Great Fire of October 1871. It is a story beloved by city boosters then and now, and remains redolent of a particularly American "can-do" attitude (Smith 1995). In the very first week after the Chicago fire, for instance, carpenters built over a hundred long, low warehouses to provide temporary quarters for a wide variety of wholesale and retail establishments (Sawislak 1995, 169). Yet even Chicago's dramatic rebirth was not without controversy, much of it centered on the same sorts of questions about property rights, class relations, ethnic group tensions, and jurisdictional authority that engulf New Orleans today.

In the winter that followed the Great Fire, ordinarily something of a frozen interregnum for the construction industry, Chicagoans debated the feasibility of constructing a "fireproof city." They did so even as most recognized that this was an impossibility—given the prevalence of wooden structures that had survived outside the boundaries of the fire, combined with the broad discretion property owners could exercise over the use of their land. In the Chicago of 1872, not wholly unlike the New Orleans of 2006, citizens faced dilemmas over how to rebuild on a landscape of risk.

Pre-fire Chicago had been a city of shoddy construction and lax regulation; after the fire, debates raged over whether the right to rebuild private property should be tempered by consideration of a broader "public interest" to have a less risky city of masonry that would be more reassuring to future investors. "Such an abstract vision of civic obligation and such optimistic predictions about the economics of fireproof construction," Karen Sawislak observes, "soon ran head-on into the reality of class difference." Because the Great Fire had devastated thousands of worker-owned pine cottages that had served as the basis for much of Chicago's low-cost housing, sorting out how to rebuild the city forced engagement with the highly diversified financial circumstances of the populace (Sawislak 1995, 139). In Chicago, as in New Orleans 135 years later, those who advocated building in accordance with a fireproof agenda willfully ignored the disconnection between increased regulation and decreased affordability.

For working-class Chicagoans of limited means, the vagaries of the insurance industry, especially when coupled with the loss of their workplaces, meant that their only viable alternative entailed construction of a temporary wooden shanty on their property. Efforts by city leaders to push for bans on new wooden structures across the city as a whole, and to forestall construction deemed risky, carried serious consequences for those who had lost everything to the disaster. As Sawislak puts it, "If the city legally barred a property holder from rebuilding with wood, and he or she could not afford brick or stone construction, this site lost all value for its owner. A lifetime of work and savings might evaporate; only the cut-rate prices offered by speculators would seemingly be left to such unfortunates" (1995, 139–40).

In other words, the newly elected leadership of the city talked in rational terms about the civic duty to build back better, but these demands fell hardest on those least able to afford the costs of any new standards. Working-class Chicagoans viewed the proposed restrictions as something imposed by a cadre of downtown property owners who, already once-burned, wished to protect their investments by insisting that lower-income people should not build "fire-traps" anywhere else in the city. Moreover, Sawislak shows, some ethnic groups viewed the restrictions as designed by nativist proponents as a means to undermine their ability to rebuild as an ethnic enclave. Despite the constraints of winter weather, many devastated homeowners rushed to rebuild in wood, seizing a last chance to act before prohibition could be imposed and enforced. In Sawislak's words, to working-class petitioners "a de jure prohibition of wood construction equaled a de facto denial of the ability of all Chicagoans to remain full citizens of their community" (1995, 141–45). Violent protests disrupted the City Council meeting in January 1872, largely fomented by immigrant groups seeking to protect the value of investment in their wooden homes and neighborhoods. A month later, the Council passed a heavily compromised fire protection bill that stopped short of extending the restrictions citywide. And, perhaps of even greater import, the legislation passed without any mechanisms to ensure enforcement. Ward-based local politics had superseded efforts by a reform-minded mayor to impose a stricter order upon the city as a whole.

Within a year after the fire, the "Great Rebuilding" transformed the city with mind-boggling speed. Construction speed also led to shoddy use of building materials, especially bricks, and local unions faced an unprecedented influx of "foreign" workers that kept wages low and jobs scarce for Chicago's own laborers. Moreover, as the new arrivals flooded the city, housing prices rose for the locals as well. As Sawislak comments, "The most economically vulnerable people in the city, those who had not owned property prior to the Fire and those who had not immediately been able to rebuild on their lots, now faced another harsh result of the disaster: a much-inflated rental market" (1995, 180–82).

There are, of course, countless differences between the Chicago of the 1870s and the New Orleans of the present day, but the reverberations are still palpable. Now as then, agendas for rebuilding are contested along class and ethnic lines; elected city governments struggle over how to represent the public interest; ideological commitment to homeownership dominates public policy, but is tempered by tensions over the regulation of risky construction; and the need to restore a local employment base is constrained by the arrival of reconstruction workers from more distant locales who also need housing.

Chicago after 1871 faced many different circumstances, however. Most obviously, the city encountered little of the jockeying for position between and among city, state, and national levels of government that has characterized the situation in the post-Katrina Gulf region. For better or worse, Chicago largely set its own course and the factions that mattered were largely fissures *within* the city itself. Chicago's recovery was a market-driven phenomenon, at a time—at least until the Panic of 1873—when demand for business in the city was strong and accelerating. This market economy, however, pressed hard on the circumstances of the local workers endeavoring to rebuild their city: wage rates remained stagnant while housing costs for their families continued to rise (Sawislak 1995, 184).

San Francisco also rebounded rapidly after the 1906 earthquake and fires, despite similar tensions that emerged when city leaders attempted to extend "fire limits"—parts of the city where wooden structures would be prohibited— into areas where residents feared that new regulations would price them out. As in Chicago thirty-five years before, downtown business interests feared a lack of reinvestment in the city if insurance premiums were too high due to the risks associated with nearby combustible structures. Predictably, smaller businesses objected that they could not afford to pay for brick construction. Lower-income homeowners also feared that they would not be able to afford to rebuild, and they organized protests to complain about class discrimination. As one Catholic priest put it a rally, "Better a city of shacks owned by the people than a city of skyscrapers owned by Eastern capitalists. The extension of the fire limits will be our ruin. . . . Frame buildings are our safeguard" (quoted in Kahn 1979, 206). Others complained that the new regulations would represent a virtual confiscation of their property. Their protests proved convincing to a previously skeptical Mayor Eugene Schmitz, who told the city's supervisors: "I do not think the fire limits should be extended until the small property owners have been given an opportunity to sell their property or rebuild. I would recommend that the fire limits not be extended" (quoted in Kahn 1979, 207).

The supervisors concurred with this assessment, but the net result was a rash of speculative construction by larger landowners who responded opportunistically with shoddily built firetraps in the hope of attracting high rents from desperate low-income households. Meanwhile, swift intervention by the U.S. Army and the Red Cross assisted greatly by implementing a system of temporary camps that provided tented shelter for tens of thousands of people. In Kevin Rozario's analysis, "The camps certainly were an impressive exercise in social organization. They boasted latrines, washing facilities, and hot and cold running water. Army officers, engineers, and charity workers maintained strict sanitary standards, disinfecting latrines, clearing garbage, placing gauze over cooked food to protect it from flies, airing tents daily, testing water samples for typhus, vaccinating refugees free of charge, and moving the sick to hospitals." Moreover, the popularity of this external assistance from the army and the Red Cross encouraged ordinary San Franciscans to be more willing "to sacrifice private rights in exchange for the stability and order offered by local elites and experts" (Rozario 1996).

San Francisco rebuilt rapidly but, as Judd Kahn puts it, "the rebuilding was almost wholly the work of people and firms pursuing their own interests" (Kahn 1979, 210). Daniel Burnham's grand plan for the city, presciently prepared in 1905, did not get implemented (Douty 1970, 233–36). Once again, the dreams of imperial planners fell victim to the realities of democracy in capitalist America. In a similar manner, the early calls by some planners and ecologists to prevent large swaths of the lowest-lying parts of New Orleans from being rebuilt have also been substantially rebuffed. The inertia of prior investment, not surprisingly, still trumps the supposed rationality of big plans.

## BETWEEN MARKETS AND PLANNING

The challenge of rebuilding modern day New Orleans entails the need to steer a course between the vital forces of market behavior and the desirability of having some coherent overlay of planning. Both Chicago and San Francisco, despite their long-term successes, demonstrate the dangers of rebuilding too fast and too randomly. Then as now, the post-disaster economic climate invites opportunism even as it makes it more difficult to seize legitimate opportunities. A fine line runs between capitalizing on an unexpected traumatic disruption as an opportunity to pursue some much-needed improvements and the more dubious practice of using devastation as a cover for more opportunistic agendas yielding less obvious public benefits. The dual reconstruction of Chicago after the 1871 Great Fire illustrates the problem perfectly: the razed city was rebuilt once in a shoddy form and then, in reaction to that, rebuilt again with the grand and innovative skyscrapers that gave the resurrected city a bold new image and lasting fame (Miller 2002). By ignoring the Burnham plan of 1905, San Franciscans initially did little after 1906 to make systematic improvements to the pre-fire city (though eventually the city embraced City Beautiful planning in smaller doses such as the Civic Center). City leaders did better after the 1989 Loma Prieta earthquake, however. San Francisco officials exploited the damage done to the Embarcadero Freeway by treating it as an opportunity to demolish this eyesore and enhance the public amenities of 1.5 miles of downtown waterfront by creating a music pavilion, a new plaza, an extended trolley line, a revitalized historic ferry building and farmers' market, and enhanced ferry service (Vale and Campanella 2005a). The annals of urban recovery are replete with such examples where rebuilding yielded improvements over the pre-disaster built environment, often relating to transportation and other infrastructure, and future redevelopment of New Orleans will surely attempt to make such gains.

The market-driven recoveries of Chicago after 1871 and San Francisco after 1906 raise important questions about how economic revival emerges in risk-prone cities. It is worth underscoring the important role of citizen activism that forestalled the possibility of city-wide constraints on the use of wooden construction, a regulation that could have made city life far less affordable for low-income residents and small businesses. While clearly a victory for market forces, this was a victory of market forces in service of greater equity. Similarly, the relatively modest sorts of new constraints placed on house elevations in the most flood-prone areas of New Orleans in April 2006 suggest an accommodation to the widespread wish to repair or rebuild private homes (Nossiter and Schwartz 2006). Even so, flood-elevation constraints will fall hardest on those who cannot afford to rebuild according to the new standards, and who may not be able to afford insurance.

## RECOVERY FROM DISASTER: STORIES, SYMBOLS, AND POLITICS

Examination of other cities that have recovered from disasters underscores several other themes that remain relevant for the fate of New Orleans. First, the effort to rebuild after disaster is, in part, an effort by urban elites to develop a dominant story line that is plausible to both locals and outsiders. Government leaders—seen to have failed in their duty to protect citizens even if the destruction could be blamed to some extent on "natural forces"—need to regain legitimacy and trust. They tend to do so by making large promises to "build back better than ever." New Orleans has had several versions of this, ranging from presidential pledges of federal largesse to Mayor Ray Nagin's Bring New Orleans Back commission, but restoring urban vitality to the city will need a much greater consensus about the reality of such progress-centered narratives than has been present to date. Rather—as was the case in post-disaster Chicago and San Francisco—the dominant complaints in New Orleans have questioned *whose* New Orleans will be brought back. Since so much of the interpretation of disaster recovery depends on who gets to tell the dominant story, it is vital to listen to local voices. There is always a need to demonstrate "progress," but often the most visible evidence ignores local sentiment. If New Orleans disproportionately loses those of its pre-Katrina residents who were both black and poor, the city will be a vastly different socioeconomic place (Dujardin 2006). Large corporations, often based outside the region, had the largest capacity to marshal necessary resources and landed many of the major contracts for recovery services. For effective long-term solutions, however, indigenous community knowledge must be requested and valued. Otherwise, the polarizations that preceded Katrina will only worsen in its aftermath.

A key aspect of "recovery" entails reconciliation, which is distinct from rebuilding. The latter is physical and social, while reconciliation is community-centered and focuses on creating enhanced trust between the low-income black population and local, state, and federal institutions. This community is not simply physically and economically decimated, it is also culturally and politically alienated. Former residents must be encouraged to feel they have a right to return to their city and its environs. New Orleans will suffer at a fundamental sociopolitical level if displaced residents with low incomes are made to feel that the future city is not being built for them, with them, or by them (Vale 2005).

Although any comparison to the experience of post-quake San Francisco social relations is hardly a direct parallel, here too there is some resonance with that earlier disaster, especially with regard to the fate of the Chinese who lost their homes and businesses. In April and May 1906, local officials repeatedly relocated the displaced Chinatown residents into temporary camps, where they faced considerable uncertainty about whether Chinatown would be reconstructed in its original location or relegated to a peripheral spot. As it turned out, Chinatown did get rebuilt in the same place, but this was largely because most of the land was owned by non-Chinese who wanted to continue to extract substantial rents from the densely inhabited area and who needed a central site to promote tourism (Douty 1970, 308–11). In this sense, the reconstruction of Chinatown (recast in a sanitized form using ersatz Chinese architectural elements) hardly represented a victory for Chinese voices. Still, many Chinese gained new solidarity from the rapid rebuilding, and thousands gained citizenship rights by taking advantage of destroyed city records to assert that they were American-born, thereby permitting their "paper sons" to immigrate from China to join them (Henderson 2005, 134, 228). As one journalist put it in 1906, "The Chinese are everywhere coming to a knowledge of the fact that they have rights, and are preparing to assert themselves to see that they actually get them" (quoted in Henderson 2005, 227). Still, as in other disasters, post-disaster rebuilding intensified pre-disaster segregation and disparities. In San Francisco, just like New Orleans a century later, part of the challenge of disaster recovery is the fight of the disenfranchised to have their stories heard and judged to be important.

A second common theme for post-disaster recovery is an emphasis on symbolic milestones. These range from efforts to restore architectural landmarks (such as the plan to repair the New Orleans Superdome in time for the Saints to begin the fall 2006 football season) to the resumption of signal events (such as Mardi Gras, just six months after the hurricane). Such key symbolic moments have served other cities well. Chicago's grand rebirth was signaled initially by the Inter-State Industrial Exposition, staged in an enormous iron-and-glass "Crystal Palace" structure to commemorate the second anniversary of the Great Fire, and the city's comeback was marked most dramatically two decades later by the World's Columbian Exposition of 1893 (Smith 1995, 95). Similarly, San Francisco countered the stigma of disaster by hosting the Panama Pacific International Exposition in 1915. To underscore the point, exposition planners used the occasion to remove the last of the refugee cottages from the waterfront area, while building the "dream city" on adjacent landfill. As Mayor James Rolph put it, "No sooner had the fire stopped smoking than San Francisco began to build again. Evidences of what she has done are visible on every hand, and we are glad to show the city to our guests from all over the world" (quoted in Henderson 2005, 230).

The downside of such an emphasis is that dominant symbols can be allowed to mask the less visible parts of the city, especially as marketed to outsiders. To those yearning to return to some semblance of normal life in the heavily damaged and largely depopulated neighborhoods of New Orleans, the return of tourists to the French Quarter may offer no more than a compelling façade of normalcy, not unlike the efforts of the White House to import temporary lighting to Jackson Square to illuminate the background of the president's speech a couple of weeks after disaster struck. City rebuilding after disaster thrives on, even depends on, the power of architecture and celebratory festivals to symbolize recovery. Urban reconstruction of prominent landmarks—whether restored or newly conceived—can convey an almost heroic sense of renewal and wellbeing. At the same time, though, these can distract attention away from the necessary insistence that the whole city and its region be monitored for progress.

Finally, all post-disaster situations are inextricable from the politics of redevelopment. In the aftermath of disaster, the very legitimacy of government is at stake. Citizens have the opportunity to observe how their leaders respond to an acute crisis and, if they are not satisfied, such events can be significant catalysts for political change. After the 1985 earthquake in Mexico City, for instance, residents saw that the existing bureaucracy lacked the flexibility and the will to place the needs of homeless citizens first. By criticizing the government's overriding interest in calming international financial markets, grassroots social movements gained new primacy. Cultivation of a sense of recovery and progress therefore remains a priority for governments. Certainly, governments conduct rescue operations, channel emergency funds, and decide upon redevelopment policies first and foremost as humanitarian gestures, but they also do so as a means of saving face and retaining public office. Within two days after the worst of the Great Fire was over, Chicago Mayor Roswell Mason entrusted the "preservation of the good order and peace of the city" (quoted in Smith 1995, 64) to Lieutenant General Philip Sheridan, and assigned the management of relief to a private organization, the Chicago Relief and Aid Society—thereby providing both clear leadership and a structure for government partnership with both the private sector and the military. By contrast, post-Katrina New Orleans may well be remembered as a classic case of infighting among all levels of government—city, parish, state, and federal—which has yielded a destructive inability to cohere around a single plan for recovery (Hsu 2006).

Such infighting may be common, but it is worth recalling that many of the most celebrated instances of disaster recovery—such as the rebuilding of Lisbon in 1755 after its devastating earthquake and flooding—have depended on a level of centralized political and economic control that simply would not be tolerated in a modern-day democracy. Tangshan, China—a city of a million people victimized by a massive earthquake in 1976 that killed at least a quarter of the population, maybe even half—was dramatically rebuilt within a decade by a command economy so that it could resume its important position in the industrial output of northeast China (Chen 2005). Similarly, in postwar Warsaw, both the reconstruction of the Old Town and the creation of modernist housing estates in adjacent areas depended on the power and flexibility assumed by a strong central government (Goldman 2005). Rebuilding is the logical and necessary way to jump-start employment and spending, and thereby casts in bold relief the values and priorities of government. In democratic regimes, however, especially those with a federal system of nested and overlapping jurisdictions, the task of directing disaster recovery in a manner that respects local wishes and priorities is simply much more difficult.

## MEASURING DISASTER RECOVERY

When measuring post-disaster recovery in economic or any other terms, it matters greatly what sociospatial unit of measurement is counted. Sometimes, analysts treat recovery as synonymous with restoration of the pre-disaster population level or, alternatively, of pre-disaster economic activity. Warsaw, which lost the vast majority of its population during World War II to death and displacement, regained its numbers by the late 1950s (Goldman 2005). Even Tangshan was back up to its pre-quake size within a decade (Chen 2005). Galveston, Texas, has three times the population now that it did just before it was destroyed in 1900, but in this case the mere return of population fails to account for its regional eclipse in the face of the massive growth experienced by nearby Houston, the chief beneficiary of Galveston's misfortune. Large disasters affect not just cities but also their surrounding regions, often affording many benefits to nearby places that had once been secondary. Similarly, as much as pundits may despair over the population decline of cities such as Detroit or St. Louis, even such declining urban areas may still have thriving metropolitan regions that actually gain population. The losses suffered in New Orleans are, in part, balanced by economic infusions to suburban parishes and to cities such as Baton Rouge, which now has its own major problems over scarce affordable housing (Moses 2006). A few months after Katrina, for instance, as a whole the multi-parish metropolitan area surrounding and including New Orleans had regained much of its population, even while Orleans parish and other hard-hit areas such as St. Bernard's and Plaquemines parishes remained severely depopulated.

Restoring an urban economy to viability means that job growth must occur in tandem with restoration of housing and the array of social networks and educational institutions that make it possible for people to work while also attending to necessary commitments to family and other social relations. Restoring economic viability therefore entails attention not just to workplaces, but also to the variety of "homeplaces" that must be reestablished to sustain a workforce. In the aftermath of massive displacement, restoring economic viability means developing communication mechanisms to permit shredded networks of neighbors to reconnect, implementing training programs to make sure that the new jobs of the reconstruction economy can be filled by those who wish to return to the city, and providing strategies for coordinated provision of appropriately located transitional housing.

In implementing such programs, it will be important to work at the most meaningful scales. As a map prepared by the *New York Times* makes clear,

FIGURE 1.    Video store, New Orleans. Small businesses, like this one in the Lakeview neighborhood, form a vital part of local community economies. © Will Steacy Photography, 2005.

pre-Katrina New Orleans had three major spatial concentrations of jobs: clusters in the Central Business District (CBD), the French Quarter, and Mid-City, some of which were more flooded than others. But this city—like most cities—also featured a broad array of small-scale employment locales scattered across the neighborhoods of Orleans parish, many of them is the most decimated areas of the city (Plate 14). These places also need careful nurturing if their surrounding communities are to return to viability. From the abandoned malls and shopping centers of New Orleans East to the myriad corner stores and retail strips that punctuate many older neighborhoods, the revival of residential neighborhoods is intricately connected to the web of workplaces. In addition to economies at the citywide and regional scale, there are smaller-scale economies built around neighborhood-centered lives (Figures 1, 2, 3). These include the informal economies of bartered goods and favors, as well as the casual interdependencies of neighbors who provide such necessary services as the childcare that permits a parent to sustain a job outside the home. As the citizens of New Orleans struggle to repopulate decimated neighborhoods, these neighborhoods require a rededication to small-scale institutions that can

FIGURE 2.    Flavor Barber Shop, New Orleans East. In addition to the massive
residential devastation in New Orleans East, most of the retail centers were heavily
damaged. This image, taken seven months after Katrina struck, shows a piece of a
neotraditional strip development, adjacent to a large mall that also remained shut
down. © Lawrence Vale, 2006.

FIGURE 3. B&K Food Store, Tremé. In addition to supermarkets and major job centers, many neighborhoods lost local corner stores. © Lawrence Vale, 2006.

provide both identity and resources to support the viability of hundreds of sub-neighborhood districts that have services as well as residences.

## NEIGHBORHOOD RESILIENCE CENTERS AS A SPATIAL ORGANIZING PRINCIPLE

The New Orleans of early 2006 is a landscape of uncertainty, just like Chicago in 1872 and San Francisco in 1907. Some neighborhoods vital to the tourist economy came through the 2005 hurricane season with relatively little damage and have resumed much of their previous economic activity. The greater challenges affect those places where persistent post-Katrina flooding forced long-term mass evacuation, and where former residents have faced protracted uncertainty about the legality, terms, and costs of rebuilding their homes (Russell, Donze, and Maggi 2006). This is coupled with the even greater uncertainty about the availability of work that could provide the income necessary to finance rebuilding. Many who seek work are caught in a trap whereby jobs are available, but local residents cannot take them because they lack a nearby place to live (Kucinich 2006). Such problems are exacerbated by lingering uncertainty about the future of schools to serve households with children (Figure 4). Moreover, given that most early policy decisions have

FIGURE 4.   Barge and school bus, New Orleans. Residents of the Lower Ninth Ward faced large obstacles in efforts to reopen schools and restore homes. © Will Steacy Photography, 2005.

been directed at assisting homeowners, those who had rented their homes have faced still greater uncertainties, especially if they felt attached to the neighborhood where they had resided even though they did not formally own a stake in it. Barbara Johnson, senior vice president of Greater New Orleans Inc., a nonprofit organization that promotes local businesses, puts it this way: "Our No. 1 economic development issue is housing. Our critical industries— health care, manufacturing, the convention business—need workers, but there is this huge bottleneck because of the lack of housing" (quoted in Konigsmark 2006).

Both the cause and the effect of this uncertainty have been a series of competing plans and initiatives proffered by widely scattered government and nonprofit organizations. Some of these plans make contradictory assumptions based on incomplete information about neighborhood viability and the criteria used to judge it. Many plans proposed by small organizations appear in isolation from similar ideas put forth by others. Equally destructive, many local community groups and nonprofit organizations have also acted as rivals rather than partners in the revival of the city, forestalling progress and raising questions about how and where national foundations and other groups should

FIGURE 5. "Neighbors Let Me Gut Your House," New Orleans East. In the aftermath of Katrina, homeowners in many neighborhoods faced uncertain prospects for rebuilding, and contractors searched for opportunities. © Lawrence Vale, 2006.

invest funds aimed at assisting neighborhood recovery. The result of such a disjointed network of decision makers is a situation that is less decentralized than a market, but still far short of a comprehensive plan. According to one New Orleans building inspector, as of early 2006, the process of building permit approval in some neighborhoods has been "really fly-by-night, chaotic, Wild West, get-what-you-want." The net result is "a plan by default" (quoted in Nossiter 2006a). Without some further effort to structure the processes of rebuilding in a way that looks like more than just the sum of random individuals acting on their own, the future of some whole neighborhoods may be unnecessarily put at additional risk (Filosa 2006a) (Figure 5). As in the Chicago and San Francisco of earlier eras, one core issue is that low-income residents of New Orleans legitimately fear that they could be priced out of their city by the costs associated with rebuilding.

In Chicago and San Francisco, working-class citizens had sufficient political clout to ensure that the city acknowledged their interests when formulating post-disaster building regulations. In New Orleans, by contrast, in the months following Hurricane Katrina lower-income residents have remained disproportionately displaced from the city, making their political participation in municipal elections difficult and, more broadly, limiting their ability to be heard in the debates surrounding the future of their neighborhoods. This displacement has been exacerbated and extended by many months of uncertainties about the nature of post-Katrina building regulations (especially the delays in issuing FEMA flood elevation maps) and a lack of clarity about plans for reoccupancy of most of the city's public housing developments, even those that suffered relatively little damage. The larger economic picture is even more worrisome: unlike the earlier post-disaster situations in Chicago and San Francisco, New Orleans lacks both a thriving economic hinterland and the dynamism of a pre-disaster pattern of urban economic growth. In short, the challenges of reviving the urban economy of New Orleans are significantly greater and would seem to require a more interventionist approach that could direct and coordinate neighborhood-based recovery efforts in a highly visible manner.

One way forward could involve creation of a series of Neighborhood Resilience Centers (NRCs). Each of these could provide home to one or more existing community-based organizations, and could serve as an information clearinghouse for former-residents contemplating a return to within a quarter-mile of that place (Figure 6). Leaders of the NRCs would endeavor to identify the full range of landholders and other stakeholders in each small jurisdiction—perhaps an area of no more than a half-mile square—and would work to communicate with, and determine the needs and wishes of, each of these households and individuals, as well as the businesses and other institutions of the area. These NRCs could also become the point of entry for volunteer labor as well as philanthropic donations. Local universities, perhaps in partnership with more distant academic institutions, could provide student and faculty liaisons to assist the staff of each NRC. Not every NRC would need to provide all services or the same services as every other, but each NRC would need to be able to publicize a list of those services it did offer so that the range of available services would be clear to residents of the city. If a checkerboard blanket of NRCs could serve the city of New Orleans, as well as smaller cities elsewhere in the region, this could provide an organizing structure for reinvestment. Many organizations in New Orleans are discussing the value of "centers"; the NRC concept is intended to emphasize the urgency of having a comprehensive and networked approach to such centers. If implemented citywide, the NRCs could provide a clear way for both locals and outsiders to visualize the structure of support networks across New Orleans, thereby helping to both define and facilitate urban resilience.

The NRC concept facilitates attention to the three aspects of disaster recovery set out earlier: stories, symbols, and politics. First, the NRC system could serve as a reliable source of information, and a way for residents who seek to return to do so in a well-resourced manner. Post-disaster Chicago and San Francisco did not need NRCs because those places were not burdened by

FIGURE 6. Ujamaa Square, Tremé, 2006. The Ujamaa Community Development Corporation, based in the Tremé neighborhood, is developing a community center that could form the basis for a Neighborhood Resilience Center. © Lawrence Vale, 2006

a protracted and widespread diaspora of residents struggling to calculate the costs and benefits of return. In New Orleans, by contrast, the majority of the city's population has remained displaced long after the disaster, and many people are understandably ambivalent about how, where, and whether to rebuild their homes and their lives within the vulnerable bounds of the city. The key goal of the NRC concept is to enable residents and policy makers to gain some kind of collective predictability about who and what will come back where and when. If individual NRCs could gather together a reasonably complete database of intent, it would be possible to demonstrate the feasibility of reconstructing a full neighborhood fabric of inhabited residences and open businesses in coordinated tandem. This, in turn, would enable individuals and institutions from the city's most depopulated areas to speak more authoritatively to city, state, and federal officials about their near- and longer-term viability as urban places. A return of neighborhood voice, spatially anchored to particular localities and bolstered by data, could alter the overall narrative structure of the disaster recovery dialogue in the city.

Second, the NRC network would carry symbolic value by giving a structure of visual images to the New Orleans neighborhoods currently known to outsiders only by their official names and bureaucratic boundaries. These visible nodes, in turn, could be rallying grounds for demonstrating progress and harnessing further resources. Places such as the "Lower Ninth Ward"—now seen as single vast symbolic landscape of devastation—could be reimaged as a set of concentrated points of action. Instead of a single large undifferentiated space, the neighborhood could be seen as a disaggregated collection of smaller sub-neighborhoods centered on institutions taking action on behalf of local residents. Since the NRC concept builds on the existing presence of community-based organizations and schools, this can be another way to gain more media exposure and financial backing for local institutions that have struggled to keep their existing staff, let alone expand to meet the new demands they face.

Finally, an empowered and visible network of NRCs could provide some of the political coherence that the city currently lacks. If these could be recognized as legitimate sources of authoritative information by federal, state, and local officials and, in turn, serve as repositories for up-to-date policy advice, the NRCs could help overcome jurisdictional divisions and help individuals and groups across the city see what is possible, and where.

The New Orleans of early 2006 seems stymied by a lack of reliable communication, an ever-changing cacophony of allegedly authoritative voices that provide contradictory messages emanating from diverse and overlapping jurisdictions. One key element in urban viability for New Orleans entails making sure that its existing residents—and its potential residents—understand their options. More important still, these options must be structured to enhance—

rather than restrict—their participation in the revival of the metropolis. The dramatic rebirths of Chicago and San Francisco demonstrate that urban viability can be restored even after half the residential population loses its homes and the economy is devastated. Post-Katrina New Orleans faces even greater challenges, however, and its revival will need not just the cumulative opportunism of markets but also the carefully considered contributions of neighborhood planners.

# CHAPTER 11

# Housing Displaced Families

## Jeffrey Lubell

Nearly six months after Hurricane Katrina devastated New Orleans, the Mississippi coast, and other parts of the Gulf Coast region, the rebuilding of the homes necessary to house the people that will help restore these areas' economic vitality has barely begun. Part of the problem, certainly, is the magnitude of the disaster, as well as its complexity. Even as temporary housing is being arranged and provided to hundreds of thousands of people, many complicated questions related to building codes, flood insurance, and (in and around New Orleans) the reconstruction of the levees need to be resolved before rebuilding can move forward.

At the same time, it seems clear that one of the principal reasons for delay is the lack of an adequate policy structure for meeting the housing needs of displaced families and devastated communities. Without a clear playbook for providing temporary and permanent housing for families displaced by Hurricane Katrina and the other major storms of 2005, Rita and Wilma, progress has been painstakingly slow. At times, it seems as if the rules are being made up on the fly, and to some extent they are. If there is one single lesson we can learn from the current disaster with respect to housing, it is the imperative to develop a more comprehensive and effective set of housing policies for meeting the temporary and permanent housing needs of displaced families and devastated communities *before* the next large-scale disaster occurs.

Rebuilding delays have both human and economic costs. From a human perspective, families displaced by a disaster have a need and a right to know whether they will be able to return to their homes, and if so, when, and who will cover the costs of rebuilding. So long as their ability to return home, and the terms of any such return, are unclear, it will be difficult for displaced families to move forward with their lives and start planning for the future.

From an economic perspective, the well-being of the devastated communities depends to a significant extent on their ability to reattract residents who have been relocated off-site to help rebuild the communities' job and property tax bases. In a large-scale disaster such as Hurricane Katrina, the extent of damage to local economies and the insufficient availability of nearby housing mean that the only practical option is to relocate families off-site, in the vacant housing of other cities and regions. While there are several factors that are likely to affect the decisions of displaced families about whether or not to return to help rebuild the economy of a devastated community, timing surely ranks high on the list. The longer it takes to restore economic viability in a devastated community, the more relocated families will settle into their new communities—with kids making friends at school, parents finding jobs, and so forth—and fewer families will return. This is one of many reasons why it is essential that both relocation and rebuilding policies be worked out *ahead* of time, so that they can be implemented as quickly as possible following a disaster.

This essay seeks to contribute to the development of a more effective set of policies for meeting the housing needs of families and communities impacted by a large-scale disaster by examining the current policy framework and recommending changes. While the nation's experience with Hurricanes Katrina, Rita, and Wilma provides the principal context for these observations, they are equally applicable to other large-scale disasters.

Since the particular focus of this essay is on the role of housing policy in restoring the economic viability of devastated communities, the subject of temporary relocation is addressed only briefly (Katz et al. 2005; Sard and Rice 2005). Rather, this essay focuses on two main questions: (a) what policies are needed to help devastated communities rebuild their housing stock and provide permanent housing for families that choose not to return? and (b) whose job is it to set these policies—the federal government or state and local government? Since the latter question is a key threshold issue that may bear on the nature of the housing policies adopted, it is addressed first.

## FEDERAL VERSUS LOCAL POLICY DEVELOPMENT

Before examining which policies are most needed to meet the housing needs of disaster-stricken families and communities, we must first determine whose job it is to develop them. Is there a need for uniform federal policies, or should state and local governments be empowered to devise their own housing policies? If the answer is that both levels of government have a role, what is the right allocation of responsibilities? (The private sector will obviously play an important role as well, but there is little question that government needs to intervene to help families and communities recover from a disaster.)

There appears to be consensus among policy makers that federal funds should be the principal source of government financing for rebuilding. But while some parties have argued for a strong federal role in determining the nature of the assistance to be made available to individual families, others have contended that the federal role should principally be to pass the funding along to local governments who should make the decisions themselves. This is not merely an academic question; disagreement about whether the federal government should play a leadership role in guiding redevelopment efforts appears to have been a significant cause of delays in allocation of federal funding for rebuilding efforts following Katrina.

In essence, the question of how to define the federal government's role is one of the main disagreements between supporters of the principal rebuilding plan to emerge from Congress following the 2005 hurricanes—the so-called Baker Bill (H.R. 4100), which would establish a federally chartered redevelopment authority to purchase property from displaced families in Louisiana, settle outstanding mortgage debt, and reassemble land for redevelopment—and the administration's proposed remedy, which appears to rest largely on providing the affected states with flexible Community Development Block Grants that they can spend more or less as they choose. While the Baker Bill describes a robust role for local decision makers in guiding the operations of the redevelopment authority, it provides a definitive framework for the delivery of federal aid—for example, guidelines for how much compensation homeowners and mortgage lenders will receive if a property is sold to the redevelopment authority. By contrast, the administration has called on the affected states to develop their own plans for spending the more than $11 billion in Community Development Block Grants allocated to date. In rejecting the Baker Bill, the President's appointed coordinator for Gulf Coast rebuilding, Donald Powell (2006) wrote: "State and local leaders—not those in Washington—must develop the recovery plan. . . . If federal bureaucrats determine the path of rebuilding, local insight and initiative will be overrun and local needs overlooked."

The administration's deference to state and locally developed plans for spending federal disaster rebuilding funds is consistent with the general allocation of responsibility in today's affordable housing programs. Over the past twenty to thirty years, housing policy decision making has steadily devolved from the federal to the state and local levels. The three principal sources of government subsidies for new affordable housing development today—the Low Income Housing Tax Credit and the HOME and Community Development Block Grant programs—all involve federal funds allocated to state and local governments which then determine how these funds are spent.

The general rationale offered for the devolution of housing policy decisions is that states and localities are better able to tailor housing programs to meet the unique needs of different communities. Some communities may want to focus more on homeownership, others may prefer to focus on rental housing; some communities have a particular need to increase the housing supply, while others may be better off providing tenant-based assistance that helps low-income families better afford the cost of existing housing.

For the same reasons, an argument could be made that states and localities should have principal responsibility for setting the housing policies to meet the needs of families displaced by a large-scale disaster. Every housing market is different, so why not let the governments that are closest to the people determine how best to meet the needs of their residents?

Clearly, the local governments of disaster-stricken areas and the states in which they are located have a central role to play in determining how those communities are to be rebuilt. No one is suggesting that the federal government unilaterally impose its vision on how communities should be rebuilt. But it is equally critical for the federal government to assume a major leadership role in managing disasters, especially when it comes to determining the *basic benefits to be accorded to all affected families*. It is that federal leadership—both following the disaster, in speedily determining how to most effectively house displaced families, and prior to the disaster, in developing the policies to guide disaster preparation and response—that was so clearly necessary and so disappointingly lacking in connection with the 2005 hurricanes.

To succeed in meeting the housing needs of displaced families and devastated communities, it is essential that the basic housing policies governing both relocation and rebuilding be developed ahead of time so that they can be implemented quickly and effectively. For a number of reasons, this can be done efficiently and effectively only at the federal level.

First and foremost, there is little question that the federal government is best positioned to bear principal financial responsibility for helping families and communities struck by a disaster. State and local governments simply do not have the funding reserves or fund-generating capacity to meet these needs on their own. Part of the advantage of living in a federal union is the ability to share risk across a broad and diversified set of regions that comprise our nation. If we are one country, we all have an obligation to help meet the dire needs of U.S. citizens wherever they arise. The federal government is the fiscal agent best suited for meeting this challenge.

So at a minimum, states and localities need guidance on how much the federal government is willing to spend to help meet the housing needs of disaster victims. Without that guidance—which has been very slow to emerge following Hurricanes Katrina, Rita and Wilma—states and localities cannot determine how best to spend those funds to meet families' housing needs. But even if the basic federal funding parameters were agreed upon ahead of time, it is unrealistic to think that states and localities would be able to develop effective disaster response plans *before* a disaster occurs. It is hard enough getting policies developed to meet existing needs, let alone prospective ones.

This point is most obvious with respect to the policies governing the immediate relocation of families displaced by a disaster. If a disaster were to occur tomorrow in Cincinnati, Ohio, what policies would be used to relocate the affected families? It simply is not realistic or practical to expect Cincinnati or any other city to have its own fully developed and *executable* relocation plan in the off chance that a large-scale disaster were to occur. On the other hand, it is both realistic and imperative for the federal government to develop a single set of relocation policies that can be implemented *immediately* whenever and wherever a disaster occurs.

Relocation policies also involve an interjurisdictional element that would be difficult, if not impossible, to negotiate without federal intervention. For example, in a large-scale disaster such as Hurricane Katrina, where there is insufficient habitable housing in the surrounding area, far too much damage to the underlying economy, and far too many displaced families to be housed effectively with mobile trailers, the most practical solution is to house families temporarily in vacant housing in other cities. Since many of the displaced families will have low incomes, some mechanism is needed to help them afford the rents. Clearly, local governments are ill-positioned to manage the relocation of families from one jurisdiction to another and the subsidization of rents in other cities. (The obvious solution to the affordability problem, used successfully after the Northridge Earthquake, but not, for inexplicable reasons, after Hurricane Katrina, is to use the federal Section 8 housing voucher program, which provides a subsidy to owners to cover the difference between the market rent and the rent families can afford to pay.)

The same basic points apply to the broad parameters—though not necessarily all the fine details—of a plan to permanently house residents. First, while the timeframe is obviously different, the development of permanent housing solutions is every bit as time-sensitive as that of a relocation plan. The longer it takes for a rebuilding plan to be developed and for families to understand whether they will be able to return to their community and, if so, under what circumstances, the harder it will be to reattract the families needed to rebuild the economy. Ideally, the basic ground rules will have been decided ahead of time, so that all residents understand their basic rights and can plan their lives accordingly. Since the odds that a large-scale disaster will hit any particular community are low, but the odds that a large-scale disaster will strike again within the United States are extremely high, only the federal government has the strong incentives necessary to develop the basic ground rules for a permanent housing solution on a prospective basis—before the next disaster occurs.

As with immediate relocation, the question of how displaced families will be permanently housed also has an interjurisdictional component. Given the tremendous dislocation these families have suffered, displaced families deserve choices about whether to return to their original communities, to stay in the community to which they relocated, or to move to still another community. It is impractical to ask each community around the country to develop a separate policy for how to deal with the families that have relocated there after a disaster that took place in some other community altogether. The federal government has to step up to the plate and define the nature and amounts of assistance available to displaced families—including for any assistance provided to help meet families' long-term housing needs—wherever they choose to live.

The final concerns necessitating a prominent federal role all involve consistency—consistency of benefits across communities and across disasters and the consistency of rehousing policies with other key national policies, especially insurance and mortgage lending policies. If the basic parameters of how much assistance is provided to displaced families, and in what form, is set by local government, rather than the federal government, then the treatment of individual families (and their ability to recover economically) could vary widely from one disaster to another, or (as appears will likely be the case following the 2005 hurricanes) from one community to another following the same disaster. This seems inconsistent with basic principles of fairness and the expectations of federal taxpayers that they are all equal in the eyes of the law and government. A decision by one community to be particularly generous could also lead to expectations on the part of residents of other disaster-stricken communities that simply cannot be met, creating friction and ill-will that impedes the essential process of reattracting residents to rebuild the economy.

It is important to remember that there are multiple national systems that are affected by the housing policy choices following a disaster and that these systems can operate most efficiently under a consistent set of federal policies. Insurance is one category of policies, for example, that will be heavily influenced by the government's housing policy decisions following a disaster. The question of whether uninsured homeowners (or uninsured owners of business or rental property) are compensated for their losses, and under what circumstances, is widely believed to have an impact on the long-term health of an insurance market. (Specifically, the concern is that if we compensate uninsured homeowners for their losses, we will create the "moral hazard" that, in the future, some families will choose not to purchase insurance because they expect to be bailed out by the government.) The finances of mortgage lenders are also heavily affected. Without a coherent and consistent set of federal policies for responding to a large-scale disaster, it is extremely difficult for either the insurance or mortgage markets to operate efficiently.

For all these reasons—that the federal government controls the purse strings, that the federal government is far more likely than any particular city or state to face a natural disaster within its borders (and thus is the most efficient body to develop housing policies for responding to a disaster), that many of the elements are interjurisdictional, and that there is a need for consistency across disasters and with other national policies—it is imperative that the federal government take the lead in defining the housing benefits to be made available to families and communities impacted by a disaster.

This does not mean that state and local governments have no role to play. To the contrary, state and local governments clearly have a central role to play in the decision-making process regarding rebuilding, but that role should be against the backdrop of clear federal standards. In my view, it is the federal government's job to determine the nature of the basic financial assistance to be provided to displaced families—for example, how to meet families' immediate shelter needs, how to help uninsured homeowners rebuild their homes, and so forth. On the other hand, it is the state and local government's job to determine how a particular affected community will be rebuilt—where rebuilding will be allowed, how basic infrastructure will be restored, what architectural guidelines will apply to the rebuilding, if any, and so forth.

This recommended allocation of responsibility between federal and local government more or less mirrors current law, at least as it was applied prior to the 2005 hurricanes. The federal Robert T. Stafford Disaster Relief and Emergency Assistance Act (the Stafford Act) defines specific financial assistance to be provided to families affected by a disaster. As discussed in the next section, however, the assistance provided to homeowners whose homes have been destroyed has proven inadequate to meet families' needs. Rather than strengthen the baseline assistance package, so that all families impacted by a disaster receive the same level of assistance, the emerging response to the 2005 hurricanes has been to augment these individual benefits with assistance provided to state and local government—notably Community Development Block Grants to states.

It is possible that this impromptu policy "band-aid" will eventually lead to the development of new norms for federal assistance that are clearly defined and thought out ahead of the next disaster. If not, then when the next large-scale disaster comes along, we will be stuck with the impromptu approach, under which displaced families will still not know how much assistance they will ultimately receive—particularly, whether it will be enough to enable them to return to their homes—and precious months will go by while the federal government decides how much funding to provide and in what form. Additional time will elapse once the federal government makes up its mind while state and local governments determine how to respond to the federal assistance offer. These delays will lead to reductions in the number of families that return to their original communities, depriving the local economies of the people needed to get things going again. At the same time, families affected by the identical disaster, but living in different communities, may well receive different levels of benefits. And families that choose, after months of waiting and settling into their new homes, to move on with their lives and not move back to their original community, will likely receive far less in federal benefits than those that choose to return.

If there are problems with the basic benefits structure provided in the

Stafford Act—and, as discussed below, I believe there are—we should amend that Act or other components of federal law to provide for more effective solutions. This will ensure that all citizens impacted by a disaster will receive equal treatment. It will also expedite the process significantly, so that families and communities can start rebuilding.

## Strengthening Federal Rebuilding Policies

There is a substantial need for the federal government to play a leadership role both in funding rebuilding efforts and in establishing the baseline set of benefits to be provided to impacted families and businesses. A solid foundation of federal rights and benefits will ensure that states and localities have a clear sense of the assistance to which families and businesses will be entitled and can apply toward rebuilding efforts. While local circumstances may well necessitate additional aid to address particular issues—the rebuilding of the levees in New Orleans, for example, or the need to purchase land for greenfields redevelopment on the Mississippi coast—a comprehensive and effective set of federal policies establishing baseline assistance levels will go a long way toward expediting the rebuilding process after the next large-scale disaster.

Among the key disaster-related housing issues that need to be addressed at the federal level are the following:

1. *Temporary relocation.* How will the temporary housing needs of families displaced by a disaster be met?
2. *Displaced homeowners.* What assistance will be provided to help displaced homeowners rebuild their homes, or purchase a home in a new location?
3. *Displaced renters.* What long-term housing assistance, if any, will be provided to help displaced renters afford the cost of rebuilt housing in their original communities, or the cost of existing rental housing in a new location?
4. *Affected rental property owners.* What assistance will be provided to help rental property owners rebuild their properties?
5. *Flood insurance.* How can the federal flood insurance system be improved to maximize the chances that most losses are covered by insurance, minimize future charges on the federal treasury, and create the right incentives for minimizing risky building?
6. *Building codes.* What building codes should be adopted to minimize future risks from flooding, wind, earthquakes, and other potential disasters? (While building codes are normally a local issue, the fact that many of these properties will seek federal flood insurance necessitates an examination of this question at the federal level.)

While addressing aspects of several of these questions, the balance of this article focuses principally on the question of how best to provide assistance to displaced homeowners. In general, the shortcomings in the current policy framework for dealing with assistance to displaced homeowners are illustrative of the need for reexamination of all federal disaster-related housing policies. To inform a more thorough examination of these other issues in the near future, I conclude with a few observations on selected additional issues.

## ASSISTANCE TO DISPLACED HOMEOWNERS

### *Assessment of Current Federal Rebuilding Programs*

At present, there are two main forms of federal assistance available to help homeowners whose homes have been damaged or destroyed by a natural disaster:

- SBA Rebuilding Loans. The Small Business Administration (SBA) is authorized to provide home repair/rebuilding loans of up to $200,000 at both market and subsidized rates of interest.
- FEMA grants. Under the Stafford Act, the Federal Emergency Management Agency (FEMA) is authorized to provide grants to families that cannot qualify for a SBA rebuilding loan. Currently, the grants are capped at $5,200 for home repairs and $10,500 for home replacement. Additional FEMA grants are available to cover the incremental costs (beyond simply rebuilding) of steps to mitigate future hazards, such as raising homes off the ground to reduce the likelihood of future funding.

While there has not been an official acknowledgment by Congress or the administration that these existing tools are inadequate to meet the needs of displaced homeowners, that assumption clearly underlies much of the policy debate. In his public statements, Donald Powell has suggested that states use their Community Development Block grants to help displaced homeowners rebuild their homes (Powell 2006). Representative Baker's bill also embodies a judgment that far more federal assistance is needed to help displaced homeowners than what is currently available.

This implicit assessment of the inadequacy of the primary federal rebuilding tools for impacted homeowners is right on the money. Clearly, the FEMA grants of $5,200 for home repair or $10,500 for home replacement provide far too little assistance to enable families whose homes have been destroyed or substantially damaged to rebuild a habitable home. During an Urban Land Institute forum in New Orleans in which I recently participated, for example, local developers indicated that it would normally cost at least $120,000 to build a modest home of decent quality. (Shortages of labor and supplies may well drive up prices, though hopefully, economies of scale, such as modular construction, could be used to bring prices back down at least to historic norms, if not lower.)

The SBA rebuilding loans provide a much higher level of funding (up to $200,000), but the form of assistance makes it unworkable for many families. According to a *New York Times* editorial (2005), some 82% of the families whose home rebuilding loan applications have been processed by the SBA have been rejected on the grounds that their incomes are too low or their credit scores are inadequate. While it is impossible to say whether the SBA's decisions have been fair or not, it seems likely that much of the problem lies with shortcomings of the loan product itself, rather than with the SBA's administration of it. As with any other standard amortizing loan, the SBA expects to receive regular payments on the loan from families' monthly incomes, and therefore is reluctant to issue a loan to families whose incomes are too low to afford their monthly payments, or whose credit scores suggest they may not be a particularly good risk.

Much has been made of the severe poverty of New Orleans residents (Berube and Katz 2005; Logan et al. 2006) and a similar point can be made about the Mississippi coast, which was also devastated by Katrina. Perhaps less well known is the fact that many of these low-income families were homeowners. According to Logan et al. (2006), despite the fact that the storm disproportionately struck poor and minority families, some 47% of families with flood-damaged homes within the City of New Orleans and some 55% of families with flood-damaged homes in the metropolitan areas of New Orleans and Biloxi-Gulfport were homeowners, rather than renters. Clearly, many of these homeowners cannot afford to service a regular, amortizing mortgage, even at a subsidized interest rate. Consider an elderly homeowner on a fixed income. Many such homeowners were already struggling to meet their housing expenses for property taxes and home repairs. It simply is not feasible for them to service a loan for $120,000 to rebuild their homes.

Nor is it clear that it is fair to ask them to do so. Again, consider the elderly homeowner. She has paid off her mortgage and is likely just scraping by. Along comes a hurricane that wipes out her home. Is it fair to ask her to take on a huge loan burden just to rebuild her home? Or consider a poor, working family, also struggling to get by on low wages. Where is the family to get the funds to cover the reconstruction of a new home, and how is the family going to meet its shelter costs if it cannot rebuild?

In addition to being inadequate to meet the needs of displaced families, the current system of federal assistance for displaced homeowners falls short of meeting the core economic needs of devastated communities. Economies need people, and people need housing. To the extent that displaced homeowners do not have the means to rebuild their homes, they may very well choose not to return. (Indeed, even those families that have the means to rebuild may choose to stay in their new communities rather than take the risk of returning to an area with an uncertain future.) This analysis suggests a somewhat different lens with which to view government rebuilding assistance following a major disaster. Rather than simply a matter of kindness to assist distressed families, or an example of when the government needs to step up to meet a need that cannot be met solely by the private sector—although surely it is those too—government rebuilding assistance may well be a prerequisite for long-term community survival and sustainability. Government rebuilding assistance can be the carrot that encourages displaced families to return to help rebuild the devastated communities' economies.

### Addressing the Gaps in the Current Federal System for Financing Rebuilding

Clearly, there is an important interplay here with the nation's flood insurance policies—if everyone were required to contribute to the flood insurance program, or to some more general disaster insurance program, in proportion to perceived risks, then everyone would have insurance and much more of the rebuilding costs would be paid for through insurance. This would be a vast improvement over the current system. But under the system we currently have, there are two main gaps in insurance coverage that need to be addressed.

First, there are families with mortgages living outside the floodplain that were not required by their mortgage lenders to purchase insurance. According to estimates provided for an Urban Land Institute forum by GCR & Associates, Inc., some 7,000 of the New Orleans homeowners who suffered damage from Hurricane Katrina lived outside the floodplain and lacked flood insurance. That's roughly 11% of the 63,000 New Orleans homeowners whose homes were damaged, and roughly 29% of the 24,000 families in this group that lacked flood insurance (Urban Land Institute 2006).

Second, many homeowners did not have mortgages and thus had no requirements to purchase flood or property insurance. According to the 2004 American Housing Survey for the New Orleans Metropolitan area, some 140,000 (43.4%) of the area's 323,000 homeowners owned their home free and clear of any mortgage or other home debt. This percentage is even higher among families with incomes below the poverty line; in 2004, some 63.8% of poor homeowners in the New Orleans Metropolitan area owned their homes free and clear. This is probably because poor homeowners are more likely to be elderly than non-poor homeowners, and thus to have paid off their mortgages (HUD and Census 2005).

While there may well be modest numbers of additional families that fall between the cracks, in general, these two groups of families that lack flood insurance—either because they live outside the floodplain or because they lack significant mortgage debt—represent the bulk of the population for whom current rebuilding policies are inadequate. This is because the vast majority of other families with damaged homes have mortgages that required them to have property insurance and (if they live within the floodplain) flood insurance.

The policy options available to meet each group's rebuilding needs are dictated to a large extent by each group's debt situation. Families in the first group have outstanding home debt. Unless their debt load is relatively minor or their rebuilding costs particularly low, these families are unlikely to be able to qualify for or afford additional debt. For example, if a family has a $150,000 mortgage on a $180,000 home that is completely destroyed by a flood but lacks flood insurance because it is outside the floodplain, the family is unlikely to be able to assume an additional loan of $180,000 to replace the home. That would give the family a total $330,000 in debt on a home valued at no more than $180,000.

These families will clearly need a significant amount of grant assistance to rebuild their homes. One option, currently under consideration at the state level in both Mississippi and Louisiana, would be to provide outright grants to enable these families to rebuild their homes. In Louisiana, the proposed grants would be capped at $150,000. The justification is that these families were not required to purchase flood insurance, and thus should not be penalized for not having it. Without this or comparable assistance, many families in this group would be forced to default on their mortgages, damaging both their individual financial situations and those of the financial institutions that funded the mortgages. To the extent that the lack of assistance prevents these families from returning to their original communities, the local governments would also suffer from reduced property tax revenues.

Families in the second group—families inside the floodplain without flood insurance—mostly lack flood insurance because they have no mortgage debt. Because these families do not currently have mortgage debt, they may be in a position to assume some level of debt to refinance their properties. The problem with the current system is that many low- and moderate-income families cannot afford a standard amortizing mortgage. One option to consider for these families would be a "silent mortgage," or a combination of grants and a silent mortgage.

Silent mortgages are mortgages in which no payments of principal or interest are due until the home is sold (or the homeowners pass away). Silent mortgages could provide the funds needed to repair or rebuild the homes of tens of thousands of families whose homes were damaged or destroyed by the hurricanes, but who lack adequate property and/or flood insurance to pay for the damage. Silent mortgages are being used successfully (on a smaller scale) in affordable housing programs around the country; they are also similar, in certain respects, to reverse mortgages.

Consider, for example, an elderly homeowner within the floodplain whose home was valued at $60,000. She had no flood or property insurance because she had no mortgage and thus no requirement to purchase insurance. Assume that it costs $120,000 to build a basic modest-quality home to replace the one that was destroyed. (The rebuilt home will certainly be of higher quality than the one that was destroyed, but it makes no sense to rebuild a substandard home.) If she is provided with a grant to cover 20% of the rebuilding costs ($24,000) and a silent mortgage to cover the rest ($96,000), she will have a modest cushion of equity to get started and a loan to cover the balance on which she owes no payment until the home is sold. When the home is sold (or the homeowner passes away), the $96,000 loan is paid back, together with a portion of the home price appreciation (above the market value at the time of reconstruction, defined as the pre-hurricane land value plus the estimated replacement costs of the improvements after rebuilding/repair) as interest.

There is nothing magical in the percentage of assistance provided in the form of a grant, rather than a silent mortgage—it can be higher or lower (indeed, even 0%)—depending on how much of an equity cushion we want to give families and how much the nation feels it can afford. The most likely source of financing for silent mortgages is the federal government—either directly through new legislation or indirectly through Community Development Block Grants. Additional design and funding options are reviewed in Lubell (2006a, b).

This approach has several advantages over the potential alternatives. First, unlike the current SBA loan program, silent mortgages are affordable to families with very low incomes, as they require no payments of principal or interest until the home is sold. Because the source of repayment is the sale of the home, rather than the family's income, poor credit history is also a much less significant problem. On the other hand, silent mortgages are clearly less expensive than grants as the government eventually gets its funds back (plus a share of home price appreciation as interest). The recovered funds could either be returned to the treasury or used to capitalize an affordable housing trust fund to meet future housing needs. For those concerned with the moral hazards of making uninsured homeowners whole, silent mortgages have the additional advantage of not completely returning families to the position they occupied prior to the disaster. (The bulk of assistance is, after all, a loan, not a grant.)

*Decisions to Prohibit Rebuilding*

A separate problem arises when some level of government determines that rebuilding is not going to be permitted. In this case, insurance payments may well prove inadequate, as they do not provide for the purchase of new land, and may only provide funds for repairing a home, when (due to the decision to prohibit rebuilding) a full reconstruction is needed. Families without insurance will have similar problems affording the purchase of new land on which to build.

In these cases, the only effective *retrospective* solution is to provide grant funding to fully compensate families for the extra costs. While it would ultimately be more effective to make a realistic determination of where it is safe to build *before* families purchase a lot and build on it, that solution is not available on a retrospective basis.

### Helping Homeowners Who Choose Not to Return

While this essay is focused principally on the housing policies needed to reattract residents to rebuild the economies of devastated communities, it is important that society respect and support the decisions of families that have been displaced. If families displaced once by a disaster settle into their new communities and choose not to uproot their families again to return home to an uncertain future, their decisions ought to be supported. For the most part, these families can be served effectively by providing them with the same financial benefits provided to families that choose to rebuild—either rebuilding grants if they did not have flood insurance because they lived outside the floodplain or a combination of grants and silent mortgages if they lived inside the floodplain but did not have flood insurance because they had no mortgage debt.

There is one additional type of assistance that will be needed by families that choose not to return—a mechanism for these families to sell their homes in the displaced communities and receive meaningful compensation. To the extent that families are prohibited from rebuilding, they clearly should receive full compensation for the value of their home—ideally, at pre-hurricane land values. To the extent that families have the option to rebuild, but choose not to, a mechanism needs to be established to help them safely sell their properties. In the immediate aftermath of a disaster, property values in the devastated areas are likely to plummet (even as property values in surrounding areas increase, due to a restriction in available supply of buildable land). To help recover from the economic shock of the disaster, many families may feel compelled to sell their homes at bargain basement prices, losing the equity needed for future financial well-being.

To counter this problem, and help assemble parcels for efficient rebuilding, some type of land bank or redevelopment authority is needed—whether at the federal level, as in the Baker bill, or at the state or local levels—to purchase properties at fair value. This could be at a multiple of pre-hurricane land value or at post-hurricane values, with a mechanism that allows homeowners to share in any increase in property values that occurs between the time of purchase and assemblage and sale for redevelopment.

In addition to helping displaced families that choose not to return to move forward with their lives, such an approach would also provide a unique opportunity to assemble a land bank of properties that could be used to meet future community needs, such as for affordable housing, schools, and parks. For example, a portion of the assembled properties could be devoted to a community land trust that would provide affordable homeownership opportunities on a long-term basis.

## OTHER DISASTER-RELATED HOUSING POLICIES

While space constraints prevent a complete examination of all the many components of housing policy needed to help displaced families and devastated communities recover from a disaster, I believe the shortcomings identified in the current set of policies for helping displaced homeowners are generally illustrative of the need for a thorough reexamination of all aspects of disaster-related housing policy. To this end, the following are limited observations on two additional housing issues: relocation and the reconstruction of affordable rental housing.

### Relocation Policies

While the final bill is apparently being tallied, initial reports are that, within days of Hurricane Katrina, FEMA purchased 200,000 trailers to meet the temporary relocation needs of displaced families, at a total cost of $3.3 billion, and then another 100,000 trailers for a total cost of $4.9 billion (Dinan 2005). As of February 20, 2006, more than 10,000 of these trailers were sitting empty in a pasture in Hope, Arkansas, waiting for someone to use them (Vlahos 2006). Among other problems, many of the locations in southern Louisiana that could benefit from the trailers are in a floodplain, and thus unable to serve as acceptable temporary housing locations under federal law. Another problem is that many communities simply do not want them.

While it is easy to poke fun at this predicament, it seems clear that FEMA was simply playing by the playbook in place at the time: when a disaster hits, relocate families nearby in trailers or other temporary housing until their homes can be rebuilt. The problem, of course, is that this playbook did not make much sense for a disaster of the magnitude of Hurricane Katrina. Nearby relocation works well when the extent of damage is fairly modest and the local economy is basically intact. Keeping families near their jobs and support networks helps sustain displaced families and minimizes difficulties associated with reattracting them to help rebuild the local economy.

But when an entire economy is devastated, as occurred with Hurricane

Katrina, it simply is not fair to ask displaced families to wait around in an area for years without a job or schools for their children as the community gradually rebuilds. Rather, families need to move on with their lives, at least for the short and medium terms, which means relocating to a community that can provide the housing, jobs, schools, and other community amenities families need to resume a normal life. Of course, after Katrina, there was not nearly enough close-by housing for displaced families to occupy, so nearby relocation was never a realistic option for the bulk of families. Given the understandable opposition of local communities to massive trailer-cities—and the fear that such a temporary solution will prove indefinite—trailers are not a realistic option either.

Notwithstanding the government's anomalous decision not to use it following Katrina, the Section 8 housing voucher program, which provides rental property owners with monthly payments to cover the difference between actual rents and the rents families can afford to pay, is well structured to help displaced families relocate to new communities in nearby states, and indeed throughout the country, and the government would be well advised to plan to employ it quickly after the next major disaster. Yes, this will necessitate incentives to encourage families to return home to rebuild their economies, but there simply is no other realistic option.

## Reconstruction of Affordable Rental Housing

As part of its package of assistance to help communities impacted by Hurricanes Katrina, Rita, and Wilma, the federal government has allocated billions in Low Income Housing Tax Credits to affected states. These credits will go a long way to helping to rebuild the affordable rental housing stock.

It is important to remember, however, that without additional assistance, Low-Income Housing Tax Credits generally provide housing that is affordable to families with incomes between 50% and 60% of the area median. In New Orleans, by contrast, roughly half the renters living in flooded buildings had incomes *below* 50% of the area median income (Urban Land Institute 2006). To provide rental housing that is affordable to these very low-income families, additional assistance will be needed.

While there are many options for structuring this additional assistance, one option worth considering would be to provide funding for a pool of "thrifty vouchers," a new policy option introduced in legislation (but not enacted) in 2002 by members of both parties[1] to help cover the gap between normal tax credit rents and the rents of families with incomes below 30% of the median income. Thrifty vouchers differ from regular Section 8 vouchers in that they are designed solely to be used with a production subsidy, such as the Low-Income Housing Tax Credit, which means their total cost can be capped at an amount that does not exceed 75% of the normal payment standard (which determines the voucher's subsidy level).

## CONCLUSION

A thorough review of federal disaster and rebuilding policies is needed to better prepare the country to meet the housing needs of displaced families and devastated communities following the next large-scale disaster. In addition to updating and clarifying the federal benefit structure, that review should address the relative allocation of responsibility among federal, state, and local governments. While there is a need for more effective tools for meeting families' rebuilding needs, such as greater use of silent mortgages to help uninsured homeowners rebuild, the basic package of benefits for displaced families should continue to be determined by federal law, with additional federal aid flowing to state and local governments for use in rebuilding local infrastructure.

## Note

1. S. 2721 (2002), Housing Voucher Improvement Act of 2002, sponsored by Senator Paul Sarbanes (D-Md.); S. 2967 (2002), Affordable Housing Expansion Act of 2002, sponsored by Senator Christopher S. Bond (R-Mo.).

CHAPTER 12

# Assessing the University's Role

Lester A. Lefton and Yvette M. Jones

Universities are anchors to communities. In some ways they are similar to a major department store like Nordstrom that is an anchor at a mall, providing employment and services. But in other ways, they have a deeper role. Rooted in their communities through their histories, their investments in campuses, and their identities and culture, they are not as footloose as commercial enterprises might be. They are closely associated with their host cities. Everyone knows that Harvard is in Cambridge, Yale is in New Haven, the University of Pennsylvania is in Philadelphia, and Tulane is in New Orleans.

More than half the nation's colleges and universities are located in cities (Rodin 2005). These urban universities have a central role in the life of their cities as employers, purchasers, real estate developers, incubators of business, educators of the workforce, and civic leaders (Perry and Wiewel 2005; Hahn 2002; Initiative for a Competitive Inner City 2002). As universities are large, stable community resources on multiple levels in their cities—both large and small—local government, policy-makers, and the community look to them to be good citizens, partners, and agents of change. All this is true for Tulane University.

Tulane is the largest employer in Orleans Parish. As the only Association of American Universities private, research university in the state of Louisiana, it maintains a major healthcare system, a medical school, a law school, and well-known, highly regarded graduate and undergraduate programs. Through these enterprises, Tulane University pursues its mission to create, conserve, and convey knowledge, and it fosters community-building initiatives, as well as scientific, cultural, and social understanding that integrate with and strengthen learning and research.

Hurricane Katrina—arguably America's worst natural disaster—challenged Tulane at all levels. Two-thirds of the main campus was under three feet or more of water and the health sciences campus was submerged completely. We sustained damage of more than $200 million to our buildings, and suffered the devastating loss of at least $100 million in research assets, including tissue samples collected for over 25 years, as well as other important medical and historical data. Additionally, our operating losses for the year were staggering. Following the storm we were trying to survive as an institution and reinvent ourselves. Throughout fall 2005, we cleaned up the campuses, maintained contact with our students, most of whom were dispersed throughout the United States in the many institutions that took them in, moved our medical school to Houston where the students continued their training relatively uninterrupted, and prepared to reopen in the spring semester. And in January 2006, 91% of our undergraduates did return to New Orleans.

Beyond that we were challenged to be a leader in rebuilding New Orleans. As an institution, we responded and embraced our responsibility to reach out to our community as we were rebuilding ourselves. We did this in three ways: as a partner, as a convener, and as an agent of change.

## PARTNER

As a partner we reached out to help rebuild all aspects of New Orleans, including helping other universities in the city. Members of the Tulane faculty and administration continue to work with the city and local community agencies and organizations individually and collectively to lend their expertise so that the city might rebuild itself. As the largest employer and part of the city's strongest industry, we had an arsenal of resources and expertise to draw upon in a variety of different areas. To optimize these resources we partnered both with the city and with other universities, such as Loyola University, our next-door neighbor. Together we reached out to Xavier and Dillard Universities (two historically black universities) who were especially hard hit by Hurricane Katrina. We offered these institutions assistance in a variety of ways. First, we allowed their students take classes in spring 2006 at Tulane and Loyola at no charge. Second, we offered administrative and classroom space, and we told their students they could use our library, physical education facilities, and dormitories, based on availability. As with many challenges, opportunity often lies within. In this case, as we reached out to our sister institutions in the same way that other higher education institutions across the country reached out to us as our students were displaced from New Orleans during the fall semester, our students were able to meet students from different schools, different races, and different cultural backgrounds in ways they otherwise might not have done.

## CONVENER

As a convener the university is working with different organizations, funding agencies and foundations, and has organized a series of conferences, discussions, and debates. For example, as the students returned in January, Dean Richard Marksbury of the School of Continuing Studies organized a seven-week series entitled "Perspectives on Katrina: An Interdisciplinary Approach to the Study of Katrina at Tulane University." It included twenty-one different programs, all free and open to the public. One of these sessions dealt with the U.S. Constitution and how our fundamental political system contributed to the crisis. Another focused on Habitat for Humanity's Operation Home Delivery. Our goal was to bring a panel of individuals together to examine carefully what the antecedents were for Katrina and how this natural and manmade disaster affected our lives. Because of our standing in the academic community the university is able to bring in experts from around the country, as well as draw from its own faculty, to examine everything from disaster preparedness to issues of race and poverty. Furthermore the university can serve as a conduit for resources into the community through foundation support.

## Agent of Change

The university's faculty, staff, and students have served as volunteers, ambassadors, and conduits to vital resources such as foundations, government agencies, and an array of nonprofit organizations. To address the needs of a community now in crisis and to facilitate the changes necessitated by Katrina, Tulane constructed a Renewal Plan that established a Center for Public Service. The Center centralizes and expands the scope of public service activities at Tulane, as well as strengthens and expands the connections between academic study and public service by creating new initiatives and providing clear and deliberate integration and collaboration among existing programs. For example, through the Center for Public Service, Tulane is establishing a "Semester in New Orleans" program. Traditionally, many students travel to Paris, Washington, or Sydney for semester abroad study. Now, many students from around the country are looking to spend a semester of service in New Orleans, and we are providing such an opportunity. The Center for Public Service is also the coordinating body for a new public service requirement that will be a part of the core curriculum at Tulane. The Center is providing research opportunities and coordinating with other university centers and departments that will engender organic service learning opportunities for students.

To further our role as change agent, Tulane University has also established an interdisciplinary federation called the Partnership for the Transformation of Urban Communities. Its mission is to build and rebuild healthy, sustainable communities locally, regionally, and throughout the world. This partnership will sponsor educational programs, generate research initiatives, and produce activities of national and international relevance, many of which will emanate from the Hurricane Katrina experience. Because of its breadth of resources, Tulane can draw on the expertise of the university's entire faculty, especially those in social work, architecture, the school of public health and tropical medicine, and social science and science departments to bolster this unique endeavor.

The partnership will also collaborate with other universities to develop and expand programs that address issues of social justice, emergency preparedness, and disaster response and recovery. For example, the Tulane University School of Architecture has a long and distinguished record of contributing to the built environment. In the post-Katrina era, our School of Architecture with its new dean, Reed Kroloff, is seeking to redefine itself, and in doing so it is adding programs to address the specific challenges of creating healthy, sustainable cities, both here and elsewhere. This new emphasis on urban studies will complement our strengths in building design and historic preservation. Additionally, the forthcoming Tulane City Center will be a locus for community-based design and urban development. Located in the heart of the downtown New Orleans business district, it will house faculty and students working on urban projects. Through initiatives with other schools, the Tulane University School of Architecture is planning a new interdisciplinary undergraduate degree in urban studies with the hope of leveraging its human and intellectual capital to offer rich, holistic solutions to global problems of rapid urbanization.

As we made arrangements for reopening Tulane we undertook many new tasks. We provided housing for our faculty, staff, and students, a task we went about with considerable vigor, including renting a cruise ship. We knew that shelter addressed only half of what was now missing from a once viable city: a public school system. The New Orleans public school system had closed in the wake of Katrina. Unlike the housing issue, the New Orleans Public Schools presented a tremendous opportunity for Tulane to affect change in an otherwise ailing system. To seize this opportunity Tulane quickly mobilized its resources to charter a public school. This was no easy task as the process normally—in good times—takes a year or more. However, again the university's resources were tapped, and law professor and interim Chief Information Officer Paul Barron, with the support of Tulane's president, Scott Cowen, told the state that we would pay for the start-up costs of the new charter school as long as the children of our faculty, students, and staff had an opportunity to attend. Within two days the school board and other entities passed the necessary paperwork to allow the Lusher School to open. In winter 2006, with nearly one thousand students, the school was one of only eight functioning public schools in New Orleans. At its inception, the children of Tulane University faculty and staff filled over four hundred seats in this very vital and special school. To further assist the New Orleans public school system, President Cowen serves as the chairman of the Bring Back New Orleans Commission Education Subcommittee. President Cowen and other Tulane faculty members continue to infuse the resources of our institution into a critical facet of the community.

Many critics of universities throughout the United States think of faculty and administrators as individuals who live in ivory towers, disconnected from the reality of community life. In the case of New Orleans, the faculty, staff, and administrators of Tulane University have strived to be a beacon of organization. Under the leadership of our president we have marshaled our intellectual capital, our financial resources and our loyal alumni and students, to lead the way in building a better New Orleans. This has, in part, taken place through the individual dedication and hard work of committed citizens through dogged determination. It has also taken place by putting policies, theories, and ideas into action. If any university is ever to be taken seriously as an incubator of ideas that can transform communities, Tulane University is that institution. Our goal, before and after the disaster of Katrina, is to serve as a strong anchor in the community and to put policy into practice.

Part III

# Responding to the Needs of the Displaced: Issues of Class, Race, and Recovery

# CHAPTER 13

# Inadequate Reponses, Limited Expectations

## Elijah Anderson

Hurricane Katrina was a natural disaster that caused great loss of life and property and profound distress among people of all stripes. But it was also a disturbingly unequal human disaster. The devastation revealed two underlying problems that had been hidden from view: the government's inability to cope with a catastrophe of such magnitude, and the socioeconomic stresses and strains that beset the Gulf Coast region. Racial inequality rooted in the legacy of slavery and segregation has been exacerbated by the structurally impoverishing impacts of deindustrialization and globalization. In the ongoing shift from a manufacturing base to a service and high-technology economy in an increasingly global context, so many people are left behind. Many lack the "human capital"—the formal education, access to career pathways, and geographical mobility—now necessary to survive, and when the social safety net is cut, their situation is even worse. Public policies and private development have generated a growing gap between poor black people and the ground floor of opportunity in America. This reality was made visible by the human disaster that accompanied Katrina.

While the hurricane impacted everyone, the poor were affected disproportionately, and a disproportionate number of these poor people were black. The poor were unable or unwilling to get out of New Orleans because they lacked ready money and transportation or had no place to go—no cars, no credit cards, no family or friends in other places who could take them in. Accustomed to a daily struggle for survival in a hostile environment, many succumbed to fatalism; those who were aware of the constant peril that living below sea level entailed gave in to complacency. Some calculated correctly that they could survive the hurricane, but were swept away in the flood; many others died during the human disaster that followed (Dewan and Roberts 2005). When the wall of water surged over the city after the wind had subsided, chaos reigned. People trying desperately to save themselves and others sought refuge in public spaces that were not equipped to shelter them or awaited rescuers who never arrived. Bedraggled groups of black survivors were blocked from crossing the bridge into predominantly white Jefferson Parish by local police who were moved by defensive fear rather than compassion or reason. The images shown in the national and international media of poor black people stranded on rooftops and milling about in distress outside the Superdome and Civic Center opened up old wounds. It became painfully clear that as a country we have not moved forcefully enough to resolve the racial strain directly attributable to slavery, Jim Crow, and second-class citizenship and the persistent poverty and geographic isolation that are its peculiarly malignant—and usually invisible—form in the twenty-first century.

Now in the aftermath, the racial divide is being revealed in terms of who is able to return and who is not, who decides how New Orleans and its public institutions are to be rebuilt, and what funds and services are made available to aid the poorest victims. Proposals have been advanced not to rebuild the major black neighborhoods in the city, since they were the lowest-lying districts in the city. Those with money might be allowed to rebuild at their own risk, but with no guarantees of physical safety and financial security. Replacing the public housing that sheltered so many is simply not on the agenda. Homeless families living "temporarily" in other cities are being evicted from motels and told to rent apartments when market rates far exceed their government vouchers and they are prohibited from making up the difference with their own earnings. Most displaced black residents lack the financial resources—savings, insurance settlements, and borrowing capacity—required to go back home.

The racial divide in this country became visible not only in the experience of Katrina but also in the differing perspectives on the issues involved in reconstruction held by black citizens and white citizens, both locally and nationally. All too often, these views are divergent, even polarized, reflecting differing presuppositions and reinforcing the racial divide. One of the major problems that appeared in the news media after the hurricane was that workers were brought in from Mexico and Central America to remove debris and rebuild when local people desperately needed jobs. Should the "free market" search for corporate profits override the common good, or should public policy ensure that hurricane-affected people are able to rebuild their own lives while they rebuild houses, schools, and infrastructure and that money spent on reconstruction circulates within affected communities? The substitution of lower-paid foreign labor for readily available and employable local black citizens by the national corporations awarded government reconstruction contracts is symptomatic of how globalization positions African Americans. Displaced residents of New Orleans rally for the right to vote in city elections from their temporary lodgings in other cities and states, worried that once again the masses of black people will be disfranchised. As national black leaders rally for polling places near displaced citizens, where are the non-black defenders of voting rights?

Katrina was one of the increasingly common natural calamities, such as the tsunami in the Indian Ocean and the earthquake in divided Kashmir, that reveal chronic poverty and persistent ethnopolitical conflict on a global scale. Other recent catastrophes are entirely socioeconomic, such as the riots among the marginalized children of African immigrants in the suburban ghettoes of Paris and other French cities. In Katrina, social rupture compounded natural disaster and engineering failure. Although whites' fears of armed gangs looting New Orleans after the defection of the forces of law and order were more paranoid than justified, blacks' fears that public servants would save themselves and abandon poor people to the flood were all too fatally confirmed. The question is how we can go about making victims whole and bridging the racial divide. Katrina shows the world how the United States, which more often responds to emergencies abroad, handles a disaster within our own borders and responds—or fails to respond—to the suffering of its most vulnerable citizens. Internationally, it exposes us to criticism if we can't get our own house in order, especially while the U.S. tries to impose its authority overseas. In Europe and around the world, there is a lot of cynicism about America's power and our racial divisions. A woman from Paris told me that her mother phoned her when these images were on TV to say how sad she was for black people in America. We call again on the Bush administration and Congress to investigate what went on, and why, in order to do right by the communities and the people who have been so damaged. Only if we make New Orleans, the Gulf Coast, and its people whole will we make the nation whole again. That would bring about healing in this country and demonstrate to the rest of the world that such an achievement is possible.

We are beginning to hear more incisive analyses of what happened during the hurricane and what is likely to happen in its aftermath that address the sensitivities and concerns of all people involved and of poor black people in particular. Preliminary death statistics by the State of Louisiana and a simplistic analysis by Knight Ridder suggested that Katrina was an equal opportunity disaster that killed those who were old and infirm without regard to poverty and race (Simerman, Ott, and Mellinik 2005). More sophisticated statistical analyses, especially the recently released study by John R. Logan and his colleagues at Brown University funded by the National Science Foundation, demonstrate that Katrina disproportionately affected poor and black residents of New Orleans, who were concentrated in the city's lowest-lying areas (Logan et al. 2006). If we fail or refuse to attend to the issue of racial inequality we will simply exacerbate the racial divide as people view the media images through their presuppositional frames. We *attend to people with regard to race* in this country, and people are ready to see race everywhere, even when it does not exist. Black people certainly see racial oppression everywhere. And in New Orleans, racial competition for resources did show its ugly face. Whites cleared out, while the people sleeping in the Superdome, the corpses rotting on the street and floating in the water, and the people camped out along evacuation routes were black. The racial divide is such that black people assumed from the outset that they would bear the brunt of the devastation, and that does seem to be what happened. Black neighborhoods were disproportionately destroyed, and it now appears that the destruction of black communities will be permanent. Logan and his collaborators estimate that up to 80 percent of black residents, as opposed to 50 percent of white residents, may not return. In consequence, the population of New Orleans will shrink to about 150,000 from its pre-Katrina total of about 484,000, and it will shift from a majority black city to a majority white city. These are telling projections.

The racial divide is starkly revealed when we look at the media images and examine the data that answer this question: who was able to leave New Orleans before the hurricane and flood, and who will be able to return? The elephant in the room in this conversation is race. Although those who suffered from the natural disaster were not only black people, those who suffered—and still suffer—in the human-made disaster were disproportionately black. Literally as well as figuratively, poor black people were left behind, and many felt that the government had abandoned them. A lot of black people assume that they will get the short end of the stick as New Orleans is rebuilt. Whether this assumption is right or wrong remains to be seen, but people do hold that belief, and it shapes their responses to the situation. In this great urban renewal project, the task of "Negro removal" was accomplished by Katrina, but the dominant American pattern for reconstruction excludes the poor black people whose communities have been destroyed. The displaced are convinced that black people will not be brought back to New Orleans. The privatized, consumerist paradise planners' project looks like a white city. Mayor Nagin reassured everyone that it's going to be a "chocolate city," but he took a lot of flack for that comment from all sides. Displaced black people ask who is going to raise hands for them. It seems like the country has a dog in this race—that is, that even outsiders have a stake in the outcome of the mayoral election and in the contest over "whose city will be rebuilt" (Logan et al. 2006).

Katrina precipitated a diaspora of the people of New Orleans. The poor black people who were evacuated in the aftermath of the hurricane and flood are now scattered all over the country. They are not distributed entirely randomly, however. Some went to places they had kin; others were sent wherever they would be received on an emergency basis. Some people who were scattered among strangers have moved again, reuniting families and kinship networks in places outside New Orleans, such as Shreveport and Atlanta, Chicago and Philadelphia. Many more remain in Houston, the first major city in a nearby state to offer material aid. Houston has retained many displaced denizens of New Orleans because it already had a vibrant black community, and those who were arbitrarily delivered to that destination have not felt entirely like aliens, as many black families did in the predominantly white urban and small-town communities where they were sent. Yet even in Houston, New Orleans people have been stigmatized, blamed for an alleged increase in crime and for stresses on the school system and housing market. Now Texas cries that the federal government has reneged on its promise to pay for the costs of caring for displaced persons and protests that the state cannot bear this burden alone. The nation has yet to reckon with the assertion of those displaced by Katrina that they are not "refugees": they are not foreigners arriving on our shores fleeing a natural or political catastrophe, but United States citizens who belong to the body politic.

One of the most important consequences of the disaster was a rediscovery in America of the problems of race and poverty, if only for a short time. The graphic images shown on TV revealed what black people had always known and liberal whites had suspected prior to the hurricane. This discovery is both salutary and dangerous. Making white people aware of racial inequality is an essential precondition for policies that address its causes. Yet reminding black people once again of the wounds of race and class and of the malign neglect and outright bad faith of the white-controlled power structure deepens the racial divide. Here the ethnographic perspective widens, deepens, and focuses our inquiry. As I have traveled across the country talking with people about the human disaster on the Gulf Coast, I have heard the more encompassing, more deeply rooted meanings they attach to these events and have become acutely aware of the vast disparity between whites' and blacks' viewpoints as they set this calamity in the context of their understanding of life in these United States.

Black people have a restricted social place in this country. Indeed, for poor black people in inner city neighborhoods, that place is often so confining as to render them invisible under normal circumstances. Interracial interaction is highly regulated, even ritualized. Black folks know the boundaries that circumscribe their lives and the etiquette required when crossing them—even in New Orleans, despite its reputation for multicultural gumbo. I remember one black man from New Orleans who talked about the fact that he had a white neighbor who would go fishing and come back with fish. He would call him and pass fish over the fence, and he was very friendly in that respect. But never in the twenty years that they had been neighbors had this black man been invited into the home of the white man. This story is very provocative: a white man and a black man could trade things over the fence, but the white man simply assumed that the black man was not going to come in his house. And the black man knew full well what that meant, though he never said so—except to me. Racial etiquette enacts the caste-like relations that still shape the social landscape in the South, where some black folks and white folks live next to one another.

In other situations, even proximity is denied, and racial boundaries are erected and defended at the cost of people's lives. The incident of the black people who were trying to cross the bridge into Mississippi being stopped by the white people on the other side was broadcast on national TV and still resonates powerfully in discourse and memory. This provocative image has historical echoes and is quite biblical to a lot of people. African Americans recall the confrontation at the bridge on the Selma-to-Montgomery march, when civil rights protesters were halted by the police and beaten up by white supremacists with official connivance, and then, after gathering supporters, both black and white, finally marched triumphantly across the river. It seemed a moment to celebrate in a long exodus toward freedom. The uniformed defenders of order who stopped the exodus from New Orleans at the bridge over the Mississippi to protect their white enclave in Jefferson Parish were acting as whites have always done since slavery and Jim Crow, black people are convinced. Every now and then an event occurs that reminds people of the status quo and how it is related to the racial past. Every time this happens, it makes the wound ever more difficult to heal.

The 1927 Mississippi River flood is almost beyond living memory, but its history resonates deeply—and disturbingly—with recent events in the region. *Fatal Flood*, a 2001 documentary by Chana Gazit and David Steward for the WGBH/PBS series, *American Experience*, recounts the "human storm" that followed devastating spring floods (Gazit and Steward 2001; Barry 1997). The white planters who ruled the Delta were determined to save their lucrative cotton crop and to keep the black sharecroppers whose low-paid labor was essential to their enterprises from fleeing the region; they feared that if black working people fled the rising waters temporarily, they would never return. So local police, sheriffs' deputies, and National Guardsmen rounded up black men and boys and forced them at gunpoint to keep adding sandbags to failing levees until they were swept away as the dikes crumbled. After this catastrophe at Mounds Landing, black residents of Greenville were held in a makeshift camp on the levee while white residents of the town were evacuated. Black people were forced to live under impossible conditions and distribute relief supplies to other refugees. This concerted attempt to halt black laborers' "escape from peonage" was ultimately unsuccessful, for those who survived departed for the North soon after the flood subsided. This fatal sequence of confinement, death, exodus, and diaspora produced by the confluence of racism and poverty echoes in our minds today.

Many Southern blacks are resigned to this situation. Their feeling is that that's just how white people are. The idea is simply to get along with them without taking them seriously as friends and associates, because in a pinch they'll always let you down. They are not to be counted on. I had an intriguing and disturbing encounter while visiting the Mississippi Delta for a funeral recently. I was on the shuttle bus at the airport, and the driver, a black man about sixty years old, was listening to a Christian radio station. I said to him, "Tell me this. What do you think about Katrina? What do you people think about Katrina down here?" And he said, "Well, that's how white people are." And I said, "What do you mean?" And he said, "Well, you know, I don't trust them. I don't know about you. Did you see all those people trying to go across the bridge, and they kept them from going across the bridge? And the response from the government was so slow. I don't trust them." I said, "But yet you drive this Hertz bus around, and you have to deal with white people all the time." "Yeah, but I don't trust them." This man is cordial and pleasant, not mad and hostile, but he doesn't trust white people. This is powerful. I talked to many other people down there about this, and I kept hearing the notion that white people are not trustworthy. You have to live with them, you deal with white people every day, but they are not to be trusted. The bus driver and others I spoke with were not angry about this, just resigned. They do what they need to do: get along with white folks as well as they can, but watch out for themselves and their own when they must. Blacks I spoke with in the South keep saying that the country could have done more in response to Katrina. The authorities could have sent buses to evacuate people; they could even have dropped inflatable boats from helicopters. Instead, black people saw their relatives floating face down in the water. The local knowledge held by black folks in rural and urban communities across the South and shared by African Americans across the nation says that if it had been white people stranded and seeking refuge, the government would have done something. Black people in America, they are convinced, are treated as if they do not belong to the body politic and are dispensable in a disaster.

All of this is premised on this presuppositional frame of race relations that people know. They just know that black people are mistreated by whites. This is what a lot of people assume, so they look at this situation and assign a racial meaning to it. One guy from Memphis whom I met on a plane from Florida said, "If you've always mistreated me as a white person and then you come to me, even in this situation, am I to expect something other than further mistreatment from you?" The past has set people up to believe certain things about white people. Whites will always let you down in a pinch. You may work with white people as a black person, but you don't rely on these relationships. No matter how friendly people act or how civil they are to one another, you know that you can't trust them. To me that seems like a horrible way to live, and yet so many people in the South that I've been able to talk with have expressed just that—I mean black people. White people seem not to notice.

Living with each other without full trust on either side—especially when facing life-and-death situations—is an indication that the racial divide lingers, ready to be opened up with the next social test. Unhealed wounds are re-opened with such events as the Rodney King beating and the O. J. Simpson trials, which become defining racial stories. Blacks and whites do not see the problem as the same order of magnitude. For whites each crisis tends to be a separate issue, but blacks remember previous instances of the same problem each time it recurs. Blacks and whites blame each other. Blacks see it as the caste system at work, with whites privileged and blacks oppressed and disrespected. Liberal whites understand that the country is more divided than we like to pretend, but most whites ignore this reality when it is not in the news and resent blacks for bringing up the subject. We all just accept the racial divide and keep on keeping on, remembering how we and our people have been wronged or denying that we belong to a group that has wronged others.

We still have a lot of work to do racially in this country. Generally we can pretend everything is all right, or at least manageable, until there is a crisis. Then racial fault lines open up. One side want to protect and defend what they regard as normal society. Such people tend not to scrutinize what is normal but to blame the victim for what has happened, not looking to see that the victim lacks the rights, duties, and obligations they have. The other side say that is simply how it is; whites are just not trustworthy. If a white man saw a black and a white in need of help, he would choose to help the white. People make decisions based on tribal connections. This particularism goes against the ideal of human universalism that is central to our national ideology, but it is what many blacks believe to be our social reality. What does this say about us getting along as people? In these United States, black people have only a provisional status, while in their eyes white people are on probation. Each group waits for the next disaster, when the marginality of black Americans and the mistrust of white Americans will be revealed.

# CHAPTER 14

# Educational Equity in Post-Disaster New Orleans

## Vivian L. Gadsden

The devastation of Hurricane Katrina brought to the surface a range of educational problems—poor schooling, inequity, and low academic achievement—that have long plagued New Orleans and the Gulf Coast region and that have been at the center of debates among policy analysts, researchers, and practitioners for decades. In the process of rebuilding, educators, politicians, policymakers, and residents have unprecedented opportunities to rethink issues of educational equity and to reform the educational system for the better. Unfortunately, the actions taken by the state and federal government since the hurricane have failed to allay fears that longstanding issues of educational equity and quality schooling for the most vulnerable will not be addressed. A future-oriented effort toward educational change and equity for New Orleans and other areas in the region must redress past failures to ensure equity while committing to the elimination of potential inequities of quality and access to resources and opportunity.

New Orleans, the largest urban center of the affected areas, has been a particular focal site, because of both its location in relationship to the remainder of the state and the quality of its public school system, considered by many experts to be among the worst in the country (Hill and Hannaway 2006). Prior to the hurricane, the Louisiana Department of Education, challenged by problems of uneven resources for urban and rural parishes in the state, had determined that New Orleans was in academic crisis (Center for American Progress 2005). Since the hurricane, the state has reportedly taken over more than 100 of 117 schools that performed below state accountability standards. The state government perks for the formation of charter schools have yielded relatively little thus far, with barely a handful of schools having been given charters. In most cases, schools are so storm-damaged that they are likely to remain vacant well into the future. As of January 18, 2006, 17 schools with 9,000 students had reopened in Orleans Parish (*New York Times*, January 18, 2006). The same week, an Education Commission report with recommendations for next steps was disseminated, and a mayoral committee set out a plan to decentralize the city's troubled schools.

Without educational leadership to address the problems facing post-disaster cities, the incremental efforts now taking place in New Orleans are likely to result only in a shortfall of durable approaches to systemic problems. There is enormous potential for malaise if the problems facing schools and the educational system more broadly are not addressed directly, particularly in relationship to the city's poorest children and families. An alternative to such malaise is the formulation and implementation of well-conceptualized policy that promotes monitoring of change over time. Thus, policy planning that leads to transformation in equity and a long-term agenda that reduces racial and class divides must begin immediately.

Neither new nor even sound policies alone will stem the tide of problems faced by the city and region. Policies and plans for program implementation must be constructed with an eye toward the realities of housing, health, employment, and social welfare that will confront poor and minority children and families returning to New Orleans as well as those who have remained. They must be complemented by systematic efforts that center on the needs of children and families, disproportionate numbers of whom were victims of poverty, poor schooling, and inequity of schooling prior to the hurricane. As several public and academic commentaries have suggested, the hurricane, despite its broad-scale devastation, provides New Orleans, the Gulf Coast region, and the country an opportunity to examine policies, structures, and practices across multiple services—such as education, social services, and health care—and to reframe them in ways that promote equity. While almost all American politicians would agree that education is necessary to create social equity, establishing equity at the educational level has deviled most of the United States, with several states focusing more directly on adequacy rather than equity. As Edwards suggests, however, "Without some conception of adequacy, the promise of education is a right without a remedy" (Edwards forthcoming, 2). The concept and practices associated with educational equity draw heavily upon evidence from education and the social sciences, economic perspectives, and legal analyses, especially in relationship to the intractable national problem of segregation in urban school districts and the isolation of poor and minority children and families in these communities (Orfield and Lee 2005). Koski and Levin (2000) remind us of the disjuncture between our stated commitment to equity and the reality of our practices. They write, "in preparing our young for citizenship and economic participation, there is a yawning chasm between reality and our democratic ideals" (480).

Educational equity is the context in which we can examine the tensions of "past and future" in rebuilding New Orleans and other urban settings. Focusing principally on the problems and potential to change the circumstances of poor African American families and the poor in general, this chapter underscores the intricacies of race and poverty prior and subsequent to the hurricane. Educational equity also provides an important context to examine racial and economic disparities and their relationships to educational access, school achievement, and educational opportunities. Moreover, the effects of the hurricane and the displacement and relocation on children, especially their experiences in the schools receiving them, show that children may continue to be placed at risk. Finally, it is imperative to redress the past problems in New Orleans through viable alternatives that reduce these problems and shape the future.

## EDUCATIONAL EQUITY AS HISTORICAL CONTEXT IN AN UNCERTAIN FUTURE

From a race and class perspective, the inequities of the past in the New Orleans education system are sure to be the inequities of the future without targeted efforts and a vision for change. Hurricane Katrina made public the perennial problems in the Gulf Coast region and the schools in it. The hurricane destroyed most of the New Orleans public education system—such as its physical school structures, with fewer than 20 of the 120 school buildings being usable (Hill and Hannaway 2006). Katrina also destroyed local and state tax bases, the district's primary source of revenues. Among the children and families who left the city after the hurricane were teachers and administrators, many of whom have relocated to other communities in and out of state. The superintendent and other top administrators have reportedly returned to the city, but few teachers have returned; recent accounts lead the public to believe that many children and their parents will not return either. Although Catholic schools, which account for almost half of the children educated in New Orleans, have been comparatively more successful in finding spaces for their students in other parishes in the state, their future is equally uncertain.

Prior to the hurricane, students in the public schools were disproportionately poor and African American. High school dropout rates were high, and achievement scores were low. Educational inequity was further evident in low teacher salaries and high unemployment and underemployment among the parents of children in the school system. Single-mother births accounted for more than half the births in poor families (Golden 2006). A culture also existed among whites and blacks in which few questions were asked and traditions that reinforced race and class barriers were rarely challenged.

Although the problems of educational equity are not unique to the Gulf Coast region, the states and cities in the region have received considerable attention in educational policy analyses, particularly funding for poor and wealthy districts. Disparities in school funding are both derived from and affect the economic disparities in communities. Poor neighborhoods, made up of overwhelmingly African American residents and other minorities, shoulder the burdens of these inequities. In 2004, African Americans constituted 68 percent of the population of New Orleans, and the median earning of those 16 years and older was $18,939 (Center for American Progress 2005). In the affected areas, 90,000 people had incomes of less than $10,000; New Orleans, which is located in the second poorest state in the nation, had a poverty rate 76 percent higher than the national average in 2004 (Center for American Progress 2005).

The issues of quality, equity, structure, and operational competence have challenged almost all school districts. They are visible in statistics that show the inequity of funding and states' failure to remedy the inequity. For example, although unequal funding has been ruled unconstitutional in ten states and litigation is pending in many more, only 33 states have targeted poor districts for more funding. Louisiana was one of two states that had the unintended consequence of providing more state funding for wealthy districts than for poor districts as a result of targeting. Such targeting has become fairly common and has affected funding equity in the states where it has been implemented. Programs are far from universal and have often been instituted only after litigation (Education Trust 2003). In 1991, Louisiana targeted more aid to poor districts than to wealthy districts. As the state targeted poor districts, affluent districts raised taxes so that by 1995–1996 funding for students in wealthy districts rose by more than $700 per child while spending per child in poor districts increased by only $504 per child.

This disparity does not result from a failure of poor communities to participate in self-taxing; in fact, poor communities often over-tax themselves (Hoff 1997a). When these poor communities over-tax themselves, the funding disparities decrease, but only slightly and only over the short term. Communities with low property values have low per student funding levels, and communities with high property values have high per student spending levels, despite low property tax rates. With existing formulas, poor districts can never achieve comparable funding to wealthier districts. In addition, wealthier districts may have other financial and human resources that cannot be factored into state funding formulas.

The impact of different funding approaches varies by state and is not confined to the Gulf Coast states. Comparisons of state funding in 2002–2003 show Gulf Coast states such as Alabama, Florida, and Mississippi with the lowest median expenditures per student for instruction (teacher salaries and classroom supplies) in the U.S. and considerable disparity between wealthy and poor districts (Hill and Johnson 2005). When considering all states, it is possible for the average school in a wealthy district to receive as much as 24 percent more state funding than the average school in a poor district, with wealthy districts in some states such as Missouri receiving as much as 70 percent more funding than schools in poor districts. Yet, in other states such as Oklahoma, wealthy districts receive 6 percent less funding than poor districts. Higher state funding to poor districts, in the absence of other resources such as employment, may not address sufficiently the severity of the problems facing children and their families, particularly in Gulf Coast states such as Mississippi where there is widespread and deep poverty for large numbers of residents.

Policy researchers agree that the history of New Orleans's school district provides "few guideposts" to help in the transformation that is necessary for the future (Hill and Hannaway 2006). Moreover, in a financially depressed state such as Louisiana, the state educational agency is caught in a tangled web of responding to poor rural and urban settings while being pressured by wealthier districts to maintain or increase support. The inequities of public spending are harshly affected by the region's cultural practices around education, including historically large numbers of private and parochial schools and religious academies. These schools existed prior to desegregation, and many have maintained their enrollments into the present. Some may serve as refuge for the children of segregationists while others may be an alternative for parents (white, black, and other minority) who are concerned about failing schools and have the money to pay for an alternative (Orfield and Lee 2005).

Funding disparities reveal racial and class disparities, if not bias. Funding disparities relate directly to students' ability to succeed academically. Students in under-funded school districts typically score lower on standardized measures than do students in well-funded districts, regardless of family income. In a longitudinal study of 40,000 students in the late 1990s by the U.S. Department of Education, students in poor schools scored, on average, two grade levels lower in mathematics and four grade levels lower in reading than students in wealthy schools (Hoff 1997b; Taylor and Lang 2005). The achievement gap increases with age and unimproved quality of education such that by the time students reach seventh grade, those in wealthy schools score 50–75% higher in both reading and math. As one might expect and as any observer of schools and poverty knows, poor quality school experiences and low achievement levels coupled with high dropout rates in poor districts guarantee high levels of unemployment/underemployment. These byproducts of poor quality schools affect a range of other factors that dictate the pathways, experiences, and futures of adolescents and young adults attempting to become wage earners, parents, and citizens and that result in sustained poverty and limited access by historically disfranchised groups.

The achievement patterns for children in New Orleans and Louisiana mirror the problems in the national picture. On some indicators of children's well-being (such as outcomes for young children), the local and state picture in New Orleans and Louisiana is worse than the national picture (Golden and Turner 2005; Annie E. Casey Foundation 2005). Drawing on data from the Louisiana Department of Education, Hill and Hannaway (2006) indicate that in the 2004–2005 academic year only 44 percent of fourth graders in Orleans

Parish were proficient in reading and only 26 percent in math. Eighth graders performed even worse: 26 percent were proficient in reading and 15 percent in math. Almost 75 percent of the schools in the district had received an academic warning or were rated "academically unacceptable" in the 2003–2004 academic year. Moreover, the school district faced a $25 to 30 million deficit for 2005–2006 and was notorious for mismanagement and corruption (Hill and Hannaway 2006).

Like other urban school districts, the New Orleans school district was neither designed for nor prepared to handle the kinds of traumas created by the hurricane. Similar to other school districts, New Orleans and the state educational agency in Louisiana based the system on certain assumptions, especially that there would be a student population of predictable size and neighborhood distribution (Hill and Hannaway 2006). As several policy analysts have asserted, it is difficult to imagine the former Orleans Parish emerging again any time soon or at all. The district will not know for some time how many students it will serve. The size, location, and composition of the student population are likely to shift from year to year, as neighborhoods are rebuilt and the economy revived. Hill and Hannaway (2006) also state that no more than 10,000 students are expected to enroll in the district in 2005–2006, compared to 65,000 in 2004–2005. So many questions remain. Will these children return to a system that is prepared to provide quality schooling? Will the district be able to dismantle the dilemmas created over time by segregation and the accompanying issues of race and class disparities that influence how, when, how well, and with what level of commitment to educational equity? Whether parents decide to return depends on a range of factors, not limited to the quality of schools. It is likely that many parents will make their decision to return, based on how well the district progresses in providing quality schools and a system that attends to the diverse needs of children and families. However, parents may not know how well planning and implementation of programs are being achieved for some time, making the likelihood and timing of their return even more unpredictable. Other parents may not have the wherewithal or resources to return, irrespective of whether the schools have improved.

Issues around equity cannot be solved by the New Orleans school district without external support from state sources and expertise available from other states and localities. The federal government must contribute more financial and strategic assistance to equalize school funding through programs that it supports as well. The district's past failure rests largely on its inability to secure better and more equally distributed resources for its children, families, and teachers in the face of restricted local, state, and federal allocations for those in the most low-resourced communities and schools. As the U.S. General Accounting Office (1997, 1998) suggests, states such as Louisiana have a role to play in increasing equity, but solutions must address the different complexities that local districts experience. It noted that in order for states to address funding gaps, they would have to increase state equalization efforts and impose constraints on local tax efforts.

The region and nation must commit itself to change. Interventions that might have alleviated the problems prior to the hurricane were not implemented. Although their implementation would not have forestalled the hurricane, they would have provided the fundamental infrastructure and safety net to address much-needed policy and on-the-ground efforts of the present. New Orleans is in one of the most difficult situations of modern history—rebuilding a city that has lost almost everything for most of its residents. Turner (2006) reports that only half of New Orleans's 500,000 pre-Katrina residents expect to return by 2008. However, it is likely that this number may be dramatically higher, depending on the experiences of the displaced in their new homes, the degree to which kin and other social networks are created, and the availability of employment, housing, and schools for their children.

## DISPLACED AND RESETTLED CHILDREN: PUTTING A FACE ON THE HURRICANE AND THE NEED FOR EQUITY

Equity issues often take on a different look when they are associated with individual faces. As the post-Katrina images pierced the nation's sensibilities about the apparent absence of government relief and prompted efforts to help disaster victims find respite, *NBC News* presented the striking commentary of Charles Evans, a nine-year-old boy from New Orleans who poignantly captured the frustration, despair, desperation, and fledgling hope of the displaced. He became their voice, and in a series of targeted statements caught the incredibility of both the disaster and the government's response. He became a representative persona of the complex issues related to child well-being, safety, and education facing the Gulf Coast region's displaced and as a lens to the past, present, and future for children whose health and well-being are in jeopardy. Evans stood as the image of the area's loss and past and of its promise and future. In describing Charles, MSNBC wrote:

> And about young Charles Evans, the little boy who is just so extraordinary: So many people have come forward and there are such big plans for him, please rest assured that if just HALF of it comes through, his future will be much brighter. It's important to all of us who have been touched by his life that he have a good future, but more immediately that he have a childhood and gets a good education.

Since Charles's interview and the outpouring of concerns about his future, he and many other school age and preschool children are now attending schools in other parts of Louisiana, Mississippi, and cities throughout the United States. While news reports highlight the conditions of these displaced children and families and, more recently, of the increased crime rates in cities such as Atlanta and Houston (described as a byproduct of the relocation), fewer reports have addressed issues of education and schooling—either the efforts of the schools and school districts that now house the Gulf Coast region's displaced or the plans of local agencies in the region to address the needs of displaced/returning students and their families. One can imagine that an assumption guiding current efforts is that once housing and other basic needs are addressed adequately, the reorganization of the schools and educational systems will follow. This assumption is problematic.

Charles, should he return to New Orleans, and other children who will return will be different children from when they left. They will have been relocated to school districts and settings that are unfamiliar to them; they will have had positive and negative experiences, with some children experiencing more negative than positive. They will return with memories of their past. Some of these may be fond; depending on their experiences in their new homes, they may recast these memories to make them more appealing in anticipation of their return. However, they will not change ethnically, and they probably will not be significantly better off economically. Broad and equitable policy reforms are needed to address the pre- and post-Katrina damage to these children.

Charles is an especially strong and compassionate face to put on the disaster. He is not just another little boy, however, and his face represents only one of many deeply affected by past educational policies and the storm. As *MSNBC* suggests, Charles is in many ways extraordinary—articulate, bright, and confident. As he spoke for and about people such as his grandmother, his primary caregiver, it was easy to be attracted to his careful analysis and forthright presentation of the problems he and others traumatized by the disaster faced. After hearing him, one could well say that the New Orleans's schools did not fail with Charles.

Or did they? The answer is not at all clear. His ability to provide such a cogent analysis is indicative of a certain kind of lived experience which is as likely to be the result of a nurturing, engaging grandmother as of quality teaching and schooling. It may also be, as Linda Burton (2001) might suggest, a form of child adultification in which children faced with hardship take on the personas and responsibilities typically associated with adult roles. This behavior is often seen in children with an ailing parent or aged caregiver, children responsible for other siblings, children who serve as language brokers for their parents, or children whose parents are low-literate. According to Burton, the child's birth order, ethnicity, and class only partially explain the ability of such children to act in adult roles since children with different places in the birth order, from different ethnic groups, and across income levels have been known to assume these primary roles of spokesperson, caregiver, and protector.

At the same time, Charles is both strikingly different from and similar to other children whose lives have been changed by Katrina as well as children in other parts of the country experiencing hardship. He is a member of the largest subset of Katrina-affected residents: the socially disfranchised. His black male status also renders him more vulnerable to a number of problems in school and society, especially as he becomes an adult. In other words, he represents the historical face of racial and economic disparity that had come to be taken for granted in New Orleans and the country.

Charles is also the face of promise. For example, Charles's appeal is enhanced by his apparent resilience. There is much discussion about children's resilience in stress-ridden, poor homes. Such children show a remarkable ability to construct life approaches that allow them to persist in the face of adversity. However, the impact of experiencing poverty and observing trauma and undue stress of the magnitude and duration experienced by the children and families of the Gulf Coast region may be massively underestimated. Moreover, even in the absence of natural disaster, there is a curious pattern of unstated adult expectation of these children: the children have at their disposal a package of strategies that they can access readily to rise above any adverse circumstance. This view does not lead to the creation or implementation of needed support for children. Instead, children are revered for their persistence and resilience—to get along with so little and to be able to withstand hardship—but not necessarily relieved of the weighty responsibilities for self-care and survival (Gadsden 1995). As Kotlowitz (1991) suggests in his popular text, *There Are No Children Here*, media reports capture only a part of the lives of these children, often highlighting the one child who "made it," yet forgetting those who did not.

While Charles may well be resilient, he is also vulnerable not only to typical developmental transitions and the effects of their Hurricane Katrina experiences but also to the ambivalence of a society that continues to wrestle with issues of access and opportunity for the poor and minorities. Like Charles, the thousands of displaced New Orleans children and families who have relocated in other cities are predisposed to a range of residual effects of their displacement, the trauma of the disaster, and the apparently indeterminable response to their plight. Children such as Georgnell Addison and Nicholas Wright, who have been featured in the press, were forcefully wrenched from known, cherished possessions, familiar locales, and family and friends and relocated to places that are different along multiple dimensions (*New York Times*, December 18, 2005). Many have been accepted in districts as a function of legal mandates, not just human generosity. (Prior to the passage of the

Hurricane Education Recovery Act, public schools were required to take in school-age evacuees under the McKinney-Vento Homeless Assistance Act, which guarantees homeless children equal access to public education.)

A common thread runs through the reports of and commentaries from school districts that have received the students—almost always referring to the children's loss of place and of a sense of safety and well-being. News stories chronicle the differences in academic expectations of students, such as in the courses and sequence of courses for high school students as well as the complexity of social relationships. In school districts such as Houston and Atlanta, where the highest percentage of African American students are relocated, tensions run high as children from the disaster-affected areas attempt to recover their sense of place by asserting how tough they are or simply bringing problematic behaviors with them. Differences in colloquial expressions, slang, dialect, dress, or hairstyles often become defining features and dividing factors for children making transitions to new schools.

Not surprisingly, the relocated children experience difficulties. The trauma of the disaster coupled with the uncertainty and temporal nature of their resettlement disrupt the developmental transitions of childhood and adolescence. Research on the well-being and welfare of children in developmental psychology, psychiatry, medicine, and other disciplines highlights the real and potential impact of trauma for children in different parts of the world (Jones et al. 2001). In the U.S., some of this work has addressed the experiences of children and families affected by natural disasters such as the response to Hurricane Andrew and Hurricane Hugo (Kreuger and Stretch 2003). It shows "varying and divergent estimates" of a causal link between disaster and psychopathological consequences, among them, affective disorders, post-traumatic stress disorder (PTSD), behavioral difficulties, or general emotional distress yet identifies four factors as predictive of psychological distress: (1) the characteristics of the stressor (loss, threat to life, fatalities, and physical disruption); (2) cognitive processing of the traumatic event, including general coping strategies used in dealing with the event (magical thinking, appraisal, conceptual understanding of the cause of the event, and intrusive and avoidance symtomatology); (3) individual characteristics (demographics); and (4) characteristics of the environment, pre- and post-disaster (reactions of the family members, interruption of the routine, peer and school support systems, and general life events) (Green 1991; Earls et al. 1988; Kreuger and Stretch 2000).

The degree to which race exacerbates these factors has been studied with some consistency of findings. For example, some research (Marchet al. 1998) demonstrates that race as well as gender leads to differential outcomes following a disaster. After both Hurricane Andrew and Hurricane Hugo, African Americans (both male and female) were more likely to exhibit PTSD than whites, white women exhibited it more than white men, and African American youth reported greater numbers of PTSD symptoms than either Caucasian or other minority youth (Loniganet al. 1991; March et al. 1998). Three studies are of particular relevance. Lonigan and his colleagues' (1991) study of children three months after a hurricane found a correlation between increased disaster exposure and increased anxiety among females. Riad and Norris (1996) found high levels of stress in children six months following a disaster, while Prinstein and his colleagues' (1996) study of coping assistance with 606 elementary age children found that a considerable amount of PTSD persisted ten months after Hurricane Andrew. Researchers are typically cautious in generalizing findings from studies focused on brief disasters, such as hurricanes, to longer-term extended disasters. However, in the case of Hurricane Katrina, the failure of the government's response shifted the disaster from a short-term incident with serious implications to a protracted experience of uncertainty and anxiety that is unlikely to disappear soon.

Although reports indicate that the local school districts where children, families, and teachers have relocated have been accepting, if not gracious, the other reality is that problems of multiple proportions and complexity have emerged. The results have been mixed and perhaps counter-intuitive. For example, most of the relocated African American children attend schools where the demographics of the student body are similar to those of the schools that they left. Of the eleven cities with the highest numbers of displaced families, half are predominantly black, and the poverty rates among blacks are two to four times higher than the percentage rates of poor whites (see Table 1).

Poor African American children in these cities have been as likely to be shunned as welcomed in urban districts as in suburban, predominantly white districts. In Houston, many displaced African American students attend Scarborough High School, where most of the 950 students are from poor African American and Latino families (*Wall Street Journal*, December 2, 2005). In 2004–2005, the school failed to meet federal guidelines for progress in math and language arts, encountered low graduation rates, and had few of its graduates attending college.

In comparison to the schools the displaced students left, the new schools exhibit little difference in terms of these performance data. For the poor African American students in schools such as Scarborough, their current experiences and future hopes appear inextricable from past neglect. Moreover, the relocated students experience marked differences, especially the fundamental reality that the new school represents the unknown. One social worker from Scarborough reported that black students entering the system "were threatening to the black kids" already in the district while another suggested that the students from New Orleans moved quickly into a "survival mode," attempting

TABLE 1.   Cities Receiving Highest Numbers of Relocated Children and Families: Comparisons by Poverty and Race (percentages)

|  | White | Black | Poverty rate | Whites in poverty | Blacks in poverty |
|---|---|---|---|---|---|
| United States | 75.1 | 12.3 | 12.4 | 9.1 | 24.9 |
| New Orleans | 28.1 | 67.3 | 27.9 | 11.5 | 35.0 |
| Atlanta | 33.2 | 61.4 | 24.4 | 8.5 | 33.0 |
| Baton Rouge | 45.8 | 50.0 | 24.0 | 12.8 | 33.8 |
| Dallas | 50.8 | 25.9 | 17.8 | 12.1 | 24.1 |
| Houston | 49.3 | 25.3 | 19.2 | 13.7 | 44.0 |
| Jackson (Miss.) | 27.8 | 70.6 | 23.5 | 9.0 | 29.1 |
| Little Rock | 55.1 | 40.4 | 14.3 | 6.3 | 24.7 |
| San Antonio | 67.7 | 6.8 | 17.3 | 14.7 | 21.7 |
| Shreveport | 46.7 | 50.8 | 22.8 | 8.5 | 36.0 |
| Cleveland | 41.5 | 51.0 | 26.3 | 16.6 | 33.8 |
| Las Vegas | 69.9 | 10.3 | 11.9 | 9.3 | 23.7 |
| Oklahoma City | 68.4 | 15.4 | 16.0 | 11.0 | 29.9 |

Source: Figures compiled by the Urban Institute using 2000 U.S. Census data.

to maintain a little semblance of self and dignity (*Wall Street Journal*, December 2, 2005). Bereft of other resources, the children relied on elements over which they had control, their personal and physical strength. This often created confrontational situations that exacerbated rather than reduced their problems. The results in some cases have been quite troubling, as reported by the *Wall Street Journal*: "several troublesome New Orleans students dropped out, and administrators reassigned some belligerent Houston students to another school" (*Wall Street Journal*, December 2, 2005).

News reports of students' experiences tend to fall in two categories—(1) those depicting poor African American children attending schools where the majority of students are also poor and minority, and (2) those reporting on African American and white children relocated in more affluent districts. The first typically highlight the race of the students and focus on disciplinary not academic issues, while the second rarely mention race but discuss academic transitions and socio-emotional adjustments.

All evacuees, regardless of age, social position, or responsibility, face uncertainty about the future, their perceived status in new communities, and perceptions of those in the receiving communities. Displaced children were often separated from their families for extended periods of time which compounded their trauma. Parents who were able to find their children early faced questions of where to turn and how they and their children would fare in new settings. Teachers with varying levels of teaching experience who had to relocate suffered in ways that have yet to be examined while having to learn about new systems, curricula, and expectations.

Children relocated to new dwellings and new schools have had to adapt to new situations, new students, new ways of working in school, and new expectations. Their lived experiences point to the hardships they have endured and to the promise they hold. If and when they return to New Orleans, they will need to return to a system of promise as well.

## Supporting Children to Achieve Their Promise: Equity, Access, and Opportunity

That the work toward rebuilding the educational system in New Orleans is on its way is evidenced by the report of the New Orleans post-disaster Education Commission released on January 17, 2006. Providing an administrative framework including leaner district offices, charter schools, and partnerships with parents and communities, its thirty-three recommendations also include new goals, approaches, and services.[1] At the time of this writing, the future of New Orleans's schools is uncertain. The future of New Orleans's children is also uncertain, particularly with regard to the reforms needed to make sure that their education will prepare them to assume critical roles in society. Rebuilding will require both vision and considerable investment of time, energy, and work. Because of the magnitude of the devastation and the complexity of the relationships between the state and the local school district, no single or foolproof plan has emerged. However, several promising ideas have been suggested. The efficacy of these ideas may vary, depending on how many children and families return and over what timeframe. Whatever the plan, it must situate the most vulnerable children and families to achieve, making the circumstances of their birth secondary to the potential that is evident in children such as young Charles Evans.

In recent monographs by the Urban Institute as well as short commentaries in other printed venues, a range of models have been presented to rebuild and remake New Orleans. For example Hill and Hannaway (2006) suggest that "demography will be destiny," referring to the reality that the New Orleans of the future may have a dramatically different population than the New Orleans of the past. However, it is unlikely that the city will be constituted with upper-middle-income families only. Indeed, the poor—African American, other minority, white, or immigrant—will also constitute the city. Demographic shifts may dictate increases in different kinds of services, from bilingual educational programs to intensive literacy efforts for children and parents, after-school programs, and early childhood initiatives.

There are multiple concerns that different levels of government must work together to address. These should be the concerns of educational institutions (in other school districts and in colleges and universities) that have the capacity and expertise to contribute. Hill and Hannaway (2006) propose four factors that New Orleans and Louisiana should consider in creating and enacting next steps: (1) provision of quality schooling for children who return to New Orleans, as soon as they arrive and whenever they arrive; (2) matching the needs of the student population and the diversity of schools and instructional programs; (3) provision of the most qualified, competent, and committed teachers, prepared to take on the uncertainties and the certain difficulties of rebuilding; and (4) investment in building, instructional programs, and people who meet the needs of the district in the present, with an eye toward the future but without promises in an uncertain future.

In addition, if New Orleans is going to move forward, it must develop along with the state a plan to de-complicate the mission of systems that undermine the development of effective and positive change and that increases the likelihood that children will succeed. Because the state cannot assume oversight for all of the city's schools, the number of charter schools and externally contracted schools has received considerable attention, although the potential for either to address the problems of equity and access cannot be assured. Moreover, the significant support for charter schools is both a plus and minus if there is concern about equity and quality teaching. Charter schools vary vastly in quality and cannot serve as the single response to a multi-tiered complex problem.

In much the same way that wealth influenced the funding levels of districts in old formulas, charter schools located in affluent areas will likely have access to more resources, higher expectations of children, and quality experiences. Grappling with demographic shifts, linguistic differences, and cultural, racial, familial, and poverty challenges in most urban school systems such as New Orleans requires a certain level and type of knowledge, preparation, and commitment not necessitated in past periods or in other settings. In both charter schools and externally contracted schools, local, state, and national governments will need to be determined, demanding, and vigilant; build upon the compassion, commitment, and support of the public; and construct appropriate systems change.

Systems change has at least two faces that should be considered in the effort to align local and state goals in the rebuilding. The first highlights the historically adversarial relationships that exist between large urban centers (and their school systems) and state education departments. Urban centers are seen by both state government officials and by residents in small towns and rural areas as liabilities. That is, there is a shared perception that cities are a drain on the resources of the state, fed by a variety of negative images of cities and portrayals of the people in them; large urban school districts often differ dramatically in demography from other areas throughout a state. Second, politics—and resources—tend to favor the communities that occupy the majority of the state rather than their urban centers.

Hill and Celio (1998) suggest that in asserting systems change urban school leaders should not attempt to transform every part of a district's program at the same time. Rather, they should conduct a careful survey of the field of issues, past and present programs, and the people within the systems to determine where the potential points of convergence, possibility, and opportunity lie—that is, between identifiable and emerging problems and possible or proven remedies. Determining what constitutes a problem may depend upon whether, or the degree to which, the problem debilitates students, families, and teachers or the likelihood that solutions will provide results, be replicable, and increase learning for students and for administrators and teachers trying to effect change and implement strong programs, not only in response to emergencies and immediate needs but also over the long term.

In addition, any effort intended to identify the needs of children and families returning to New Orleans should bring together the multiple agencies focused on children and families within and outside of schools—such as social services and health systems—as well as systems such as the court and corrections systems that have traditionally not focused on the children of their constituency. If the New Orleans school system is decentralized, as is planned, organized teams of school and municipal leaders, teachers, and parents will enhance the development, implementation, and review of the processes of implementation.

Last, teachers' commitment, administrators' support of students, teachers, and parents, and teachers' and administrators' commitment to engaging students through interesting and relevant curricula serve as a primary ingredient to children's achievement and educational success. Teachers are essential to the rebuilding of the system—that is, teachers who place appropriate and necessary importance on building reciprocal relationships of trust and respect within classroom settings, the expectation of excellence, motivating students, and investing in tasks that will help students achieve their learning potential. The planners and implementers must be sure to raise the ceiling for achievement and educational success. Schools must not become stuck at getting children to grade level, reveling in the short-term gains. Instead, they must use these gains as a mechanism to spur the development of sound pedagogy and high-quality schools with quality teaching.

## CLOSING CONSIDERATIONS

Promise for children of the Gulf Coast region lies in two aspects of the post-disaster city. The first is that the individual and systemic educational problems facing displaced children and families are not situated in schools and school systems alone. The second is that a focus on educational systems and schooling will not happen naturally—that, in fact, such a focus at the outset of any effort is perhaps an unnatural act, given the range and severity of needs of families and the comparably limited resources. Any consideration of the past must include redress of the past. Any consideration for the future must accept the challenges of the present facing schools and of the transitions that children and families are now forced to make. Any effort for the future must construct an image of promise in which the multiplicity of needs and prospects, and of problems and possibilities, for children and families are imagined, wrestled with, and addressed.

The problems of New Orleans are the problems of the nation, and efforts to improve the schools and the well-being of children in the city requires the investment of the nation. There is little doubt that urban school districts such as New Orleans and the poor children and families in them are increasingly isolated and vulnerable, not simply by the day-to-day complexities of urban life but also by the intergenerational legacies of unemployment, hardship, inadequate resources, crime, strained family and community life, and a range of other circumstances. Despite the problems created by the hurricane and the ensuing distress and anger, children and families who return to New Orleans will, as they have in the past, depend on the system for help and will expect their confidence in the system to be merited, unlike their experiences in the past. On the one hand, the schools and school system can be seen often (or remembered by parents) in less complimentary ways: that is, as unfriendly buildings, spaces of discontent, sources of cultural discontinuity, or places for failure. On the other hand, schools and other educational resources can be seen as sites for and of learning, places of safety, community resources, gathering spaces, or sources of caring.

The author thanks the following graduate students for their assistance at different points in the writing of this essay: Susan Bickerstaff, Malik Edwards, Cleo Jacobs, and Jie Park.

*Note*

1. The Education Commission Final Report, http://www.bringneworleansback .org.

# CHAPTER 15

# The Lost and Forgotten
## Richard J. Gelles

The aftermath of Hurricane Katrina revealed an inadequate local and national response system to major disasters. More important, the inadequate preparation and response to the hurricane disproportionately impacted on the poor and disadvantaged who, having no means to flee, were left behind in a flooding city to fend for themselves. The plight of two groups in particular remains largely unknown, unnoticed, and still uncovered by the media: children in foster care and battered women who had fled their abusers and were in shelters. These women and children were already dispossessed when Katrina hit. That they remain dispossessed and largely unaccounted for is an even deeper tragic consequence of the storm.

On August 29, 2005, when Hurricane Katrina struck the U.S. Gulf Coast, there were nearly 13,000 children placed in foster care in Louisiana, Alabama, and Mississippi (U.S. Department of Health and Human Services 2005b).[1] More than 50% of these children were from minority populations. In addition, an estimated 129 women resided in shelters for victims of domestic violence in the greater New Orleans area.[2] By September 1, 2005, it was estimated that hundreds, perhaps thousands, of foster children, and all 129 women in shelters had joined the approximately 350,000 to 600,000 individuals displaced by Hurricane Katrina (Katz et al. 2006; Tierney 2006).

The situations and predicaments of foster children and women in domestic violence shelters in the hurricane-affected areas share a number of unique characteristics. First, and most obvious, the two populations were already displaced by the time the hurricane struck. Second, and this is especially true for the children in foster care, the two populations were primarily comprised of minorities who were largely economically disadvantaged and who already had suffered dislocations and disruptions of their normal family support systems. Thus, any safety net that might have protected these two populations was already fragile. Moreover, the information systems in place that kept track of foster children and victims of domestic violence in shelter care were (and continue to be) inefficient and inadequate. Six months after Katrina, an intensive search for the whereabouts and well-being of foster children and abused women displaced by the storm yielded negligible reliable and factual information. Finally, from August 30, 2005 until March 31, 2006, the situation of these foster children and victims of domestic violence remains completely off the media and public policy "radar screens." While there have been numerous newspaper and television accounts regarding pets and other animals abandoned and displaced by Katrina, there is but one media article on either foster children or battered women affected by the storm, and that was a CNN report from September 16, 2005 that stated:

> BATON ROUGE, Louisiana (CNN)—Louisiana officials working to rebuild families torn apart by Hurricane Katrina are being especially challenged in trying to locate some 500 foster children still unaccounted for by guardians.

This essay examines the impact of Hurricane Katrina on these two vulnerable populations. Largely ignored during the preparation for the hurricane, they remain forgotten, still, six months after the hurricane. Yet the needs of these two "re-displaced" populations may far exceed the needs of others displaced by the hurricane. It is unknown when and if children in foster care will be reunited with their parents. It is unknown and uncertain whether the children, foster caregivers, and parents are receiving financial support, medical services, and social services. It is unknown whether battered women will remain safe, secure, and protected from their abusers. Even though the remaining child protective service system and informal networks that aid battered women continue to try to reach out and locate children and women and provide assistance, the potential for harm and tragedy—an already significant risk for foster children and battered women—may well have increased exponentially as a result of the general lack of attention to these two populations.

## ALREADY OFF THE RADAR SCREEN

The "back-story" of foster care and battered women who seek shelter first must be understood in order to understand the needs and ongoing struggles of these two groups. The situation of victims of domestic violence is more straightforward in its explanation, while the plight of foster children is complicated by the web of federal, state, and local responsibilities and funding streams.

### Victims of Domestic Violence

Prior to the mid-1970s, violence against women, or what was often referred to as "woman-battering," was largely a "private trouble" that afflicted women in the privacy of their homes, and for which there was no social service or publicly organized system of services or protections. The Women's Movement of the late 1960s and 1970s placed domestic violence on its advocacy agenda, and over the next twenty years a patchwork of grassroots, private, and public responses was assembled and financed. The initial, and still core, services provided to victims of domestic violence were refuges or shelters. These were small, grassroots-organized "safe houses" to which women could go and be protected from continued abuse at the hands of their husbands, boyfriends, or partners. No more than six such shelters existed in the United States in the mid-1970s, and the number grew to about 500 by the end of the decade (Straus et al. 1980).

During the 1980s, the number of shelters neared 1,000 (Gelles and Straus 1988), and the number finally approached 2,000 in the mid-1990s (National Research Council 1998). Although advocates and academics were quick to point out that the number of shelters for pets exceeded those for female victims of domestic violence (Gelles and Straus 1988), the patchwork of shelters, and the advocacy and services provided by the shelters, had become the backbone of a private-sector service system for battered women. Financing for shelters—largely accomplished through donations—became more firmly established with the enactment of the Violence Against Women Act of 1994 and the $250,000,000 in grant and service funds authorized by federal law.[3]

The structure, rules, and culture of shelters vary, but common to all shelters is that they have undisclosed locations and are designed to protect women from being located, and possibly harmed, by abusive partners. Shelter advocacy focuses on providing female victims with "safety planning," to better protect themselves and their children, and to lay the groundwork for possibly leaving their abusive situations.

For the 129 women in domestic violence shelters in the greater New Orleans area in August 2005, and the perhaps equal number in the greater Mobile area as well as southern Mississippi, shelters provided a life raft and support system. In addition, it offered female victims protection from being further abused by their abusive partners.

Because privacy, protection, and support are the core shelter functions and missions, "management information system" or centralized registry of women needing and seeking shelter do not exist. When Hurricane Katrina struck, it scattered victims of domestic violence and service providers in all directions. The providers understood, however, that no matter where they were displaced, they had to protect the privacy and confidentiality of their clients.

## Foster Care

A full presentation of the structure and function of the American child welfare system is well beyond the scope of this essay. In brief, by the end of the 1960s, the United States committed itself to a policy of mandatory reporting of suspected cases of child abuse and neglect. While the federal government provided a model reporting statute, guidelines, and a modest funding stream, states and counties were left to draft their own definitions of child maltreatment, determine who would be required to submit a report, and create and fund a system that would investigate reports of suspected child maltreatment.

State and local child protective service offices receive about three million reports of suspected child maltreatment each year (U.S. Department of Health and Human Services 2005a). The nearly 3 million reports involve about 5.5 million children. Some reports are screened-out due to a lack of complete information, while others are screened-out because the suspected abuse does not meet the state's legal definition of child maltreatment. In 2003, the last year for which there are available data, states and localities conducted 1.5 million investigations, involving 3.5 million children. Of the children examined for possible victimization, some 906,000 were deemed victims of some form of child maltreatment. The rate of child victimization in the four Gulf Coast states impacted by Hurricane Katrina and its aftermath (Texas, Louisiana, Alabama, and Mississippi) was between 5.1 and 10.0 victimized children per 1,000 children in the state (U.S. Department of Health and Human Services 2005a). This is lower than the national average of 12.4 maltreated children per 1,000.

Nationally, nearly 60% of maltreatment is neglect. However, in the Gulf Coast states affected by Katrina, the proportion of victims of child maltreatment who were neglected ranged from 39.6% in Alabama to 76.9% in Louisiana. Throughout the U.S., physical abuse comprises 19% of all victimizations, while the range in the Gulf Coast states was as high as of 38.6% in Alabama to 22% in Louisiana. Sexual abuse is the least common reported form of child victimization, constituting 10% of reports nationally. Sexual abuse made up 24.7% of victimizations in Alabama, but only 7.4% in Louisiana (U.S. Department of Health and Human Services 2005a).[4]

Once victims are identified, state and local agencies respond with a range of services. Many of the services are designed to keep children in their homes while reducing the risk of further maltreatment. However, where the danger to a child is so great that services alone cannot ensure protection, child protective service agencies, with the approval of a juvenile or family court, may remove the child from the home and place the child in out-of-home care. In 2003, more than 100,000 children were removed from their homes (U.S. Department of Health and Human Services 2005a).[5]

Once a child is removed from his or her home, a combination of federal and local funding becomes available to support children in foster care and the administrative and training costs associated with such placements. The guiding federal laws are the Adoption Assistance and Child Welfare Act of 1980 (PL 96–272) and the Adoption and Safe Families Act of 1997.[6] (PL 105–89; Amendments to Title IV-B Subparts 1 and 2 and Title IV-E of the Social Security Act). In brief, the federal government provides an open-ended entitlement to states that matches the state's costs for children in foster care. The state sets what is called the "board rate," based on the level of care a child requires and what type of placement a child is in (foster care, residential care, and special needs). The federal government matches the board rate and cost of administrating foster care, as well as training workers and foster care providers. In order to continue to receive the federal matching funds, states must maintain detailed records on each child in foster care. Foster care is a "record intensive" endeavor. Caseworkers are required to maintain detailed notes on contacts, services provided, and progress toward case goals such as reunification or adoption. These records are necessary, as each case of a child in foster care is reviewed by juvenile or family court.

The federal government has established requirements for states with regards to data on children in foster care and has supported states in developing appropriate management information systems. There are two standardized management information systems in place in child welfare agencies. These are mandated and partially funded by the federal government. The first is the Adoption and Foster Care Analysis and Reporting System (AFCARS). The AFCARS is a federal data collection effort that provides child-specific information on all children covered by the protections of Titles IV-B and IV-E of the Social Security Act. On an annual basis, all states submit data to the U.S. Children's Bureau concerning each child in foster care and each child who has been adopted under the authority of the state's child welfare agency. The AFCARS databases have been designed to address policy development and program management issues at both the state and federal levels. The data are also useful for researchers interested in analyzing aspects of U.S. foster care and adoption programs. Thus, AFCARS is a "legacy" management information system that gathers information on what child welfare systems *have done*, but does not provide information on a daily basis as to what the system *is doing*.

The second system is the State Automated Child Welfare Information System (SACWIS). The federal government provides funds to support efforts at the state level to develop automated child welfare information systems, including the costs associated with planning, design, and installation. The funding is an "open-ended entitlement" in which the federal government provides a 75% match for state expenditures. Once implemented, it matches the operational costs at a rate of 50%. Federal funding for the initial two years (1998–1999) was $191 million. Funding for fiscal year 2002 was $243,113,029 (U.S. House of Representatives 2004). In total, the federal government has provided $2 billion in funding to develop SACWIS. The most recent data from the U.S. Department of Health and Human Services, Administration for Children and Families is that SACWIS is operational in 28 states, in development in 16 states, and not in planning or implementation in 7 states (U.S. House of Representatives 2004).

The adequacy of state management information systems was questionable even before Hurricane Katrina tested the local child welfare systems along the Gulf Coast. According to a report issued by the United States Inspector General, most child welfare systems nationwide fail to see maltreated children placed in foster care at least once a month, as prescribed by state law. Children are seen once a month in only five of the seventeen states that require monthly visits (U.S. Department of Health and Human Services 2005b). More important, according to the Inspector General, most states have *no information* or data management systems to determine how often children in foster care are actually seen by caseworkers. Only nineteen states and the District of Columbia can even report how often visits occur.

## The Data on Children in Foster Care in Affected States

State and federal government reports on child maltreatment reporting and the status of children in foster care are lagged by two years. Thus, the most recent reports from the U.S. Department of Health and Human Services on children in foster care pertain to 2003. Therefore, estimates of how many children were in foster care on the day of the Hurricane Katrina can only be developed from data as of September 30, 2003. This is a severe limitation. As noted at the beginning of this chapter, those data yield the following estimates of children in foster care in August 2005:

| | |
|---|---|
| Louisiana | 4,353 (56.4% African American) |
| Alabama | 5,200 (55% African American) |
| Mississippi | 3,196 (59% African American) |

Neither Alabama nor Mississippi has county level data on children in foster care, so it is not possible to estimate how many children in foster care were in the path of Katrina. Louisiana data are available from the state's "Kids Count" (http://www.agendaforchildren.org/kidscountdata.htm). Figure 1 presents county-level data for the children in foster care in the direct path of the hurricane. Orleans County, where New Orleans is located, had an estimated 477 children in foster care. The CNN report cited above seems to confirm that number, in that the state was trying to locate nearly 500 foster children two weeks after the hurricane hit.

How difficult a task it would be to locate foster children after the hurricane is, in part, dependent on how closely the children were being monitored prior to the hurricane. According to the U.S. Inspector General (U.S. Department of Health and Human Services 2005b), both Louisiana and Alabama had standards for monitoring children. Thus, at least in principle, the parish

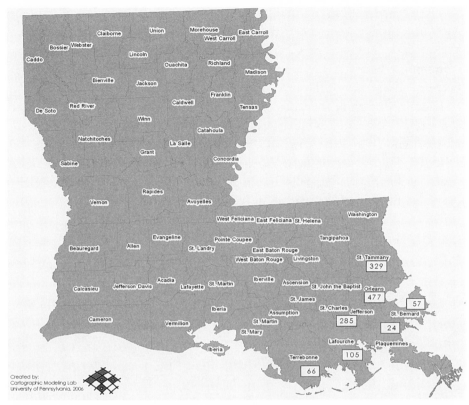

FIGURE I.   County-level data for children in foster care in the direct path of the hurricane. Map produced by the Cartographic Modeling Laboratory, University of Pennsylvania.

or county child welfare agencies were seeing foster children at least once per month. Mississippi has no standard for face-to-face contacts, and thus it is impossible to know, without data from the state, how often caseworkers had face-to-face contact with children in foster care.

Unfortunately, it is impossible to know whether children in foster care were being seen by their caseworkers, as neither Louisiana nor Alabama had management information systems that could actually track whether children were being seen.[7]

## THE IMPACT OF KATRINA

My research assistant, Christina Arena, and I attempted to piece together the impact of Hurricane Katrina on children in foster care and female victims in shelters for domestic violence. Since New Orleans was near "ground zero" for the hurricane's impact and flooding, and since the state had the best county (parish) level data available, we focused on the impact of Katrina on that city and Orleans Parish.

We searched for data in all types of directions. We made calls to John McInturf, Acting Director of the Louisiana Department of Social Services; Walter Fahr, Division of Child Welfare Program Development, Office of Community Services, Louisiana Department of Social Services; Joe Bruno, Section Administrator, Foster Care, Office of Community Services;[8] faculty and administrators at the Tulane University School of Social Work; officials at the Child Welfare League of America; the American Bar Association Center for Children and the Law; and, the American Public Human Service Association. The result of these extensive contacts, six months after Katrina struck, yielded an incomplete and hazy picture of the current structure and function of child welfare services in New Orleans.

## Background

The aforementioned contacts in New Orleans described the city's population as one of the least mobile of any urban area throughout the U.S. The city consists of 73 distinct neighborhoods each with a unique identity and geographic isolation. In the hard hit Lower Ninth Ward, even though this was one of the city's poorest neighborhoods, most residents owned their own homes.

From the point of view of this description, New Orleans appears as a city that, while poor, has a strong network of family, extended kin, and neighborhood support for families under stress. One possible test of this hypothesis is to compare rates of child maltreatment among African American children in Louisiana to the rates in other states. The national rate of victimization experienced by African American children is 20.4, with a high of 65.9 per 1,000 in Alaska, and a low of 5.8 in Virginia. In Louisiana, the rate was 11.7 per 1,000 African American children. A further test is how many children are removed from their homes. In Louisiana, in 2003, there were 4,829 children in foster care in a state with 1,185,674 children, for a rate of 4 children per 1,000. Philadelphia had a population of 421,334 children in 2003, of which 7,896 were in foster care, for a rate of 18.74 children per 1,000. According to the National Center for Children in Poverty, 38% of children in New Orleans live in poverty (National Center for Children in Poverty 2006). The percentage of children in Philadelphia who live in poverty is 28% (U.S. Census 2006). While this is at best a crude and gross analysis, it indicates that, despite having a greater proportion of children living in poverty, and thus more vulnerable to child neglect, the removal rate of children in New Orleans is less than one quarter the rate in Philadelphia. Perhaps the pre-hurricane poor neighborhoods of New Orleans had more social capital and support for at-risk children than a northern city with a lower poverty rate. If this is true, the dislocation of children from New Orleans may have significantly increased the likelihood of post-hurricane maltreatment given the disruption and dislocation of support and social capital.

## The Impact of the Storm

The Louisiana Office of Community Services (OCS) estimates that 1,800 to 2,000 foster children resided in Katrina-affected areas. This number seems to be consistent with the data obtained from Louisiana "Kids Count."[9] Louisiana OCS estimated that 1,601 providers, and therefore the foster children under their supervision, were also affected by Katrina. Lastly, caseworkers also felt the blow, and the affected parishes had an estimated 738 caseworkers and staff.

As Louisiana had no comprehensive management information system (per the U.S. Inspector General report), follow-up after the hurricane was arduous and labor intensive. The state "cut checks" for foster care providers and contractors, but had no means of actually finding the providers. Thus, OCS and staff from the National Center for Missing and Exploited Children (a private nonprofit that receives substantial federal government funding), visited shelters and asked foster care providers to identify themselves. OCS set up an 800 number so that parents and foster care providers could call to receive their monthly Title IV-E "board rate" payments. The National Foster Care Association attempted to link foster care providers in other states with displaced foster parents from the impacted areas.

Children in foster care are eligible for Medicaid health care coverage, and the coverage continued after the children and their providers were displaced. However, anecdotal information provided by officials from Louisiana seems to indicate that some states would not accept the Louisiana Medicaid care.

Not only are the children and their foster care providers' lives disrupted, but so are those of the 1,408 parents and relatives of the children in foster care. Many, if not most, of these relatives were receiving services designed to lead to a return of their children.

Since Louisiana has a county- (parish-) based system for receiving reports of suspected child abuse and neglect, the hurricane shut down, for all intents and purposes, Orleans Parish's system for receiving and investigating suspected reports of child maltreatment. Orleans Parish received no reports of suspected child abuse and neglect for the first several months after Katrina. On the one hand, officials said there were no children in New Orleans anyway. If there were children remaining in the city and if they were maltreated, there was no one to whom to report any harm and nothing that could be done about it.

At the time of the hurricane, an unknown number of reports of suspected child maltreatment were open and under investigation. OCS printed out a list of open cases, triaged the cases as best they could, and then classified the cases according to risk. This was only possible for the cases that were in the system (that is, the caseworkers had actually entered their notes into the management information system) and for which safety assessments had been completed. Given that there is often a delay in caseworkers entering their notes and completing safety assessments, it is likely that on August 29, 2005, the information on open cases was not current.

Cases where the families could not be located (and this may well have been the majority) were closed. Cases classified as "low risk" were also closed. Cases that were open for services but the families could not be located were also closed. This latter group would be families in which the agency had "substantiated" or found sufficient evidence that a child was maltreated, but whose children were allowed to stay in the home. In all likelihood, these families were not highly motivated to keep in touch with Orleans Parish child welfare services, since being released from child welfare scrutiny outweighed the benefit of the services. Finally, cases that were deemed "moderate" or "high" risk received a "protective services" alert that was distributed to other states. Under normal circumstances, states are often reluctant to investigate abuse cases that cross state boundaries. Thus, "protective service alerts" would be useful only if the open case from Orleans Parish were reported for suspected maltreatment in their new location.

Subsequent to the hurricane and the scattering of child protective service cases, foster families, families from whom children had been removed, and many of the child welfare system workforce, additional problems affected child welfare services. The Louisiana child welfare system saw its funding cut by $6,000,000. Since Louisiana continues to face economic problems, additional funding cuts are likely. Foster care and service contractors were dislocated; thus, the agency lost existing contracts for case management and services. As mentioned, state and contract agency workers were displaced. Many agency workers are still without homes, some continue to live in other states, and many of those who returned to work were relocated to other offices.

The Office of Community Services was unable to move back into its offices until February 2, 2006. The office staff face the same challenges as all other returnees to the city—disruption of basic communication systems. The St. Bernard Parish child welfare office was completely destroyed, and all its records were ruined.

Thus despite the apparent best efforts of the remaining administrators and staff, the child protective service system in Orleans Parish and the surrounding parishes was essentially destroyed by Hurricane Katrina. There is no evidence that the child protective service system is yet able to respond to reports of suspected child maltreatment, protect children who are risk of maltreatment, and meet the needs of children in foster care. For the children in foster care the immediate prognosis is frightening, given that rates of maltreatment of children in foster care in Louisiana, without the stressors of the hurricane and subsequent dislocation, are already nearly one in a hundred (U.S. Department of Health and Human Services, Administration on Children and Youth 2005a).

## Victims of Domestic Violence

Information on displaced victims of domestic violence is scant but slightly more hopeful. According to Julie Fitch, Community Outreach Coordinator for the Louisiana Coalition Against Domestic Violence, many women and children went to other domestic shelters in northern Louisiana (personal communication, February 2006). Other women and children went to stay with family and friends. For those that evacuated to other domestic violence programs, services continued.

## THE AFTERMATH

Children who are victims of physical abuse, neglect, sexual abuse, and other forms of maltreatment are dependent on the child protective service safety net. Their lives, safety, and very futures depend on a system that can receive reports of suspected maltreatment, carry out a careful investigation, make critical decisions as to whether maltreated children can stay in their homes or should be removed and placed in some form of out-of-home care, and provide social, psychological, and economic support to the children, their parents, and foster care providers. Nationally, child protective service safety nets are generally fragile and often inadequate. Hurricane Katrina destroyed the entire fabric of the safety net in Orleans Parish and seriously damaged the net in the other hurricane-impacted regions. The children with the greatest need, who were the most vulnerable, and required the most vigilant monitoring, are children in foster care. For these children, the hurricane was even more devastating than for the other individuals and families in the path of Katrina.

Children in foster care make up a mere four-tenths of one percent of the population of children in Louisiana, and the same tiny proportion of children in the other states affected by Hurricane Katrina. They are monitored and provided services and protection by systems that are notoriously under-staffed, under-funded, and over-worked. Given how minimal the safety net was for the hundreds of thousands of poor and disadvantaged individuals and families in New Orleans and the Gulf Coast, it is no surprise that there was virtually no disaster planning for a possible large-scale disruption of the child welfare system.

A key problem faced by the New Orleans's and other jurisdictions' child welfare systems, and child welfare systems nationally, was the nearly complete inability to track clients (and workers) after Hurricane Katrina. On any given

day, there are more than 500,000 children in foster care in the U.S., and at
least as many children who have suffered maltreatment while still in their own
homes with their cases open to Child Protective Services. High caseloads
often prevent caseworkers from seeing children at least as often as prescribed
by law. The most significant "crack" in the child welfare system in the Hurricane Katrina impacted regions (and nationally), turns out to be the lack of a
management information system that can effectively keep track of children,
and the work of those in the child welfare system.

In areas impacted by hurricanes, as well as other natural disasters, the
child welfare systems continue to be problematic and their ability actually to
protect children appears minimal. The ongoing hope is that there are few
children currently residing in New Orleans, and thus few at risk of abuse. But
the situation for children remaining in foster care is precarious. Foster care
was not designed to be permanent. Parents who have lost their children to
foster care are constitutionally entitled to the opportunity to have their children returned to them. The rights of children and parents are in a precarious
situation, and even more tragically, aside from the dedicated professionals in
the state and local child welfare agencies, few seem to know or care about the
population that was disrupted before Katrina struck. The most critical need
in the wake of the hurricane is to reestablish contact with children in foster
care, foster parents, and biological parents. The next step is to get services and
case planning back on track. It is critical that foster families receive financial
support. Next, caseworkers must revise plans and determine whether and
when children can be reunited. This requires that biological families be con-
tacted and assessed as to whether they will be able to adequately care for their
children. Court reviews must be scheduled so that family or juvenile court
approves the revised case plans. State and federal funding for child protective
services will need to be increased (not decreased) to meet the short-term crisis
needs of maltreated children, their parents, and their foster care providers.
Even a jury-rigged safety net will be better than having no safety net whatsoever.

## Notes

1. This and the other statistics on the number of children in foster care are, at
best, estimates. As will be discussed throughout this essay, the management information systems that keep track of children in foster care have many limitations so that
any discussion of numbers of children in foster care should be taken with the traditional "grain of salt."

2. Information was provided by Julie Fitch, Community Outreach Coordinator,
Louisiana Coalition Against Domestic Violence, February 3, 2006.

3. The Violence Against Women Act of 1994 (VAWA) was passed as Title IV,
sec. 40001-40703 of the Violent Crime Control and Law Enforcement Act of 1994
HR 3355 and signed as PL 103-322.

4. The different proportions of type of victimization across the Gulf Coast states affected by Hurricane Katrina probably has more to do with variations in state and agency policy and practice than the actual occurrence of the forms of maltreatment.

5. Alabama and Louisiana did not report information about children removed from their homes in 2003. In Texas, more than 9,000 children were removed from their homes; in Mississippi nearly 2,000 children were removed.

6. Adoption Assistance and Child Welfare Act of 1980 (PL 96-272); Adoption and Safe Families Act of 1997 (PL 105-89), Amendments to Title IV-B Subparts 1 and 2 and Title IV-E of the Social Security Act).

7. Mississippi reports having a management information system that could track children, but the state had no actual standards that require such tracking.

8. Bruno was on medical leave and had not yet returned to work as of March 13, 2006.

9. http://www.agendaforchildren.org/kidscountdata.htm

# CHAPTER 16

# Temporary Housing Blues

Gary Hack

Katrina exposed a great deal about American society, not the least the fact that we have no accepted models for providing housing for those displaced by natural or manmade disasters. We do better assisting relief efforts in other countries than at home. We appear to have no stockpiles of essential materials and are not organized to quickly mobilize to handle those displaced from U.S. cities. This became painfully evident in the last week of August 2005, as Hurricane Katrina struck the Gulf Coast, and Hurricane Rita followed less than a month later. These storms displaced at least 770,000 families, destroyed at least half that number of housing units (depending upon the definition of "destroyed"), and made hundreds of neighborhoods and communities uninhabitable. They were equal opportunity disasters, affecting large cities like New Orleans, where around 100,000 houses were destroyed, and tiny settlements like Pass Christian, Mississippi, that were largely obliterated. Some of the wealthiest neighborhoods were flooded along with marginal living areas of the poorest citizens in the poorest states in the country. While some communities reacted better than others, none was prepared for the recovery effort needed in the weeks and months following the storms.

Dealing with the needs of those displaced is a complex subject, mired in debates about the appropriate distribution of responsibility among levels of government. Providing housing for those displaced is one of the most tangible needs that must be addressed in the wake of a natural disaster. The immediate decisions about housing will have profound long-term consequences for the speed of recovery and ultimate physical form of communities. At the same time, each response from a natural disaster can allow long-term improvements to communities that may have not been possible without displacement.

In responding to the needs of those displaced, we have tended to triage our response into three time scales:

- *Refugee housing* that satisfies the immediate housing needs of those who must evacuate their homes and neighborhoods.
- *Temporary housing* that provides interim accommodation for families who wish to return to their home cities or neighborhoods to resume their jobs and work on making their houses inhabitable.
- *Permanent housing* that often requires reconstructing housing and neighborhoods that are damaged beyond repair.

The problem is divided in this way for institutional convenience, since agencies that deal with the immediate needs of those displaced are not the same organizations that deal with the longer-term needs for shelter. It is worth noting that the situation need not be parsed in this way. A system to mobilize for rapid repair of permanent housing may make temporary housing unnecessary. Or a supply of temporary housing that can be mobilized quickly will reduce the need for refuge housing. However, inadequate planning in any of the three areas can have serious consequences for the others. The difficulty in siting temporary housing in New Orleans has both over-stressed the refugee housing arrangements and made it practically impossible for individuals to get on with repairing their permanent homes. The implications are far reaching: these delays have led to thousands of decisions by families not to return to their former towns and cities.

## Housing for the Displaced

In New Orleans and along the Gulf Coast, each family's network of relatives and friends was the first line of support for immediate accommodation, and perhaps the only reliable system. This was not the first time that coastal residents had faced evacuation, and on past occasions they were able to return to their homes after a few days. Many knew where to go, and were able to pack their cars quickly and head to the homes of those who they knew would welcome them. Others had no fixed destination in mind, but luckily found accommodations in hotels, motels, and campgrounds on high ground within a few hundred miles of their homes.

Most residents of New Orleans safely evacuated either before Katrina or in the days immediately following. However, a large and highly visible minority either could not leave the city or chose not to do so. These were the thousands seen on television, on rooftops, balconies, or other high ground. Many thousands more found their way to temporary shelters in the Superdome, Convention Center, and other locations, where they were urged to go. They assumed they would be back in their homes in a day or two, which proved not possible as flooding persisted for several weeks. What was assumed to be a problem of housing soon became the need to evacuate large numbers of individuals and accommodate them in temporary facilities.

The psychology of why people did not evacuate New Orleans and other Gulf Coast towns is complicated (Tierney 2006). Some simply did not believe the warnings; they had heard them before and rode out the previous storms. People may have been numbed by the constant drumbeat of impending storms on television, many of which never live up to their advance billing. Some residents had pets they did not want to leave behind, since pets are typically not allowed in temporary shelters. Others were disabled or incapable of assessing the risk or what to do about it. Still others were worried about the looting of their possessions, and they remained to protect them. About one quarter of New Orleans households did not have cars, making evacuation even more difficult. But interviews also indicated significant gaps in preparedness. Many residents had no idea where to go if they left the city, or how they could find accommodations, or how they would pay for them. The lack of understanding options surely contributed to the slow evacuation.

Federal, state, and local officials scrambled to provide decent temporary shelter for the evacuees, including those who had spent days in the New Orleans Superdome, the Convention Center, and other local refuges. Emergency tent cities were created in several locations, with the intention of moving people back to their communities as soon as possible. Thousands were accommodated in the Astrodome in Houston (see Figure 1), the Reunion Arena in Dallas, Kelly/USA in San Antonio, a former military base, and various state parks in Arkansas and other states. Public and private groups organized thousands of smaller shelters in gymnasiums, churches, and other facilities within several hundred miles of the Gulf Coast, an extraordinary outpouring of good will. Private hotels, motels, and apartments inland and in nearby cities were flooded with evacuees. Several cruise ships were leased to provide additional housing, particularly for police and other public officials who needed to be near their home communities.

After a delay, FEMA offered funds to assist families in covering the costs of immediate accommodations. In all, 700,000 Gulf Coast residents received rental assistance. FEMA set a three-month limit on temporary payments, but as more permanent housing was not available, it was necessary to extend the deadline several times. By March 2, 2006, six months after the disaster, thousands of families were forced to leave their temporary hotel rooms and cruise ships as the FEMA allowance expired. Exceptions were made for police and other essential employees. The bill for the 1,276 households accommodated on cruise ships totaled $236 million, the 10,266 living in hotels cost $529 million. and rental assistance paid to displaced homeowners totaled $3.1 billion (Tierney 2006).[1]

Communities receiving the displaced faced huge burdens. More than 150,000 new residents were added to Baton Rouge overnight, and along with other localities, it struggled with accommodating children in schools and providing medical services and other needs. As the stays in emergency housing stretched from days to weeks to months, the lack of more permanent housing became a political issue in host communities and a critical deterrent to the reconstruction of areas devastated by Katrina. With hotel space filled with evacuees, and the winter tourist season on the horizon, towns and cities hoped that refuges would return to their home communities soon. But providing

Figure 1. Houston Astrodome shelter. Ed Edahl/FEMA/www.illinoisphoto.com

temporary housing in home communities proved more difficult than imagined.

## Temporary Housing

The use of manufactured homes and trailers as interim accommodation was the solution favored by FEMA. The objective was to get residents back to their original communities or at a minimum closer to their homes. However, several difficulties confounded this hope. Without an inventory of trailers, they had to be manufactured, and were slow to materialize. Even as trailers rolled out of factories, lack of agreement about their distribution and siting meant a delay of several weeks in transporting them to the Gulf Coast. Sites would need sewer and water service, and receiving communities would need to deal with school and health care needs, and provide other facilities for residents located in the temporary housing. There was no way to provide guarantees about when the temporary communities would be removed. Horror stories circulated about lawless temporary communities in Florida that remained in place many years after they were created to house evacuees. Ironically, sizeable numbers of manufactured homes sat empty in Florida, where they had served the needs of families dislocated by previous hurricanes. Lacking sites and transportation to the Gulf Coast, they were of little use.

The difficult task of securing locations for the temporary communities fell to FEMA. While the site options available varied among communities, generally there were three choices: create large neighborhood scale temporary settlements, complete with infrastructure and facilities such as schools, usually on greenfields on the outskirts of metropolitan areas; or find smaller sites within cities, such as parks, abandoned industrial areas or school playgrounds where clusters of housing could be located near the residents' original neighborhoods; or disperse trailers in the front yards, driveways, or other areas attached to the homes of evacuees (Figure 2). Each option had risks, and local politicians became the voices of fear and resistance to absorbing sizeable numbers of trailers in their communities.

First among the fears was that temporary communities would become permanent and that jobless families would need to be absorbed in their communities. Residents of some recovering neighborhoods resisted allowing trailers in front yards or driveways of damaged homes, worrying that they would be there for an indefinite period, detracting from the appearance of their street. Other residents worried about whether it would be possible to reclaim parks and school sites given over to temporary communities. In New Orleans, city council members—including those who had lost virtually their entire constituency and were calling for a speedy return of residents—voted against most of the temporary housing sites the mayor proposed.

FIGURE 2. FEMA trailers in front yards of houses, New Orleans. Robert Kaufman/FEMA.

The slow pace of restoring essential electricity, gas, sewer, and water services, and the absence of a consensus on whether badly flooded neighborhoods should be rebuilt, confounded plans to locate temporary housing in New Orleans. The slow return of residents also delayed the reopening of schools, local commercial services, and other essential facilities. By mid-February 2006, only 5,191 households had been accommodated in temporary housing in New Orleans (Orleans Parish), and many of these were in federally owned housing that had been vacant before the storm, and on cruise ships. This represented about 5% of the households whose units were seriously flooded. Finding relocation sites has been difficult in other parishes as well, but vacant fringe sites have proved slightly more feasible. By mid-February, 12,707 units of temporary relocation housing were occupied in Jefferson Parish, and 2,825 units were occupied in St. Bernard Parish, New Orleans's nearest neighbors.

Temporary housing sites have been designed in the most rudimentary ways, usually rows of trailers angled along roadways to allow quick delivery and removal (Figures 3 and 4). While the site plans allow for easy and economical installation of sewer and water lines, there is little attempt to plan them as living communities. There are minimal or no community facilities and most lack even small play areas for children or other amenities. The site is sometimes fenced to provide security to and from the residents. The message of the planning is clear: the sites should not encourage residents to stay

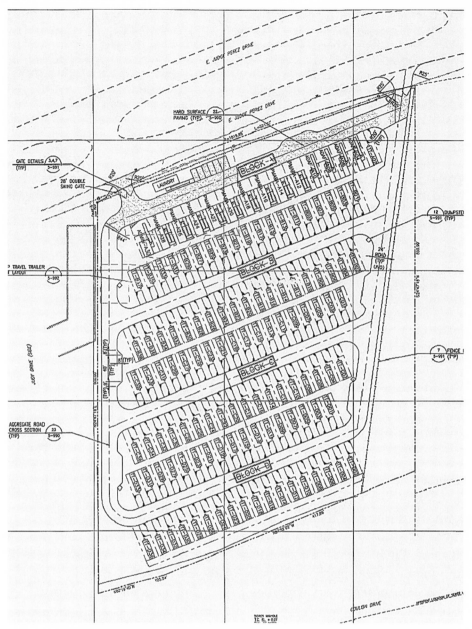

Figure 3. Lattimore temporary housing site plan, St. Bernard Parish, Louisiana. Fluor Corporation/FEMA.

FIGURE 4.   Installing infrastructure, FEMA site, Belle Chase, Louisiana. Robert Kaufman/FEMA.

longer than necessary. Many of the developments are being built on private lands leased for the purpose, and one enticement for owners to lease the sites to FEMA has been the prospect that the infrastructure would remain for long-term use. Another strategy might be to design that infrastructure so that it has long-term value.

The design shortcomings have their roots in the rigid separation of thinking between temporary housing and permanent settlements. Instead of constructing compounds of travel trailers (designed to be removed as soon as possible), these settlements might be the groundwork for new permanent neighborhoods. With unit costs of travel trailers approximating those of modest sized manufactured homes, componentized housing would have been an attractive alternative. It could be designed as starter homes, capable of being added to as residents can afford additional rooms. The new neighborhoods would then need walkable streets, open spaces for recreation, and community and religious facilities incorporated into their pattern. While some of the first occupants might leave when their original houses were again inhabitable, others might stay and make the neighborhood their permanent home. Many of the residents of New Orleans would find such a community a distinct step up from their previous situation.

As the months have passed and the amount of temporary housing has fallen far short of the needs, many evacuees have dealt with the uncertainties in their own ways. They have sought permanent jobs in the communities where they had relocated after the storm, and have moved into long-term rental apartments or more permanent housing. With only a few schools re-opening in New Orleans, teachers are searching for permanent appointments elsewhere. Medical personnel, unsure whether their hospitals will reopen, have found that there are abundant opportunities in other cities. Residents with the greatest choice—including skilled workers and those with modest savings beyond their home—have shown reluctance to move back into tempo-rary settlements, particularly with economic uncertainty about how quickly their city will rebound. Economic revival will depend upon attracting back these residents. In New Orleans, the middle-class neighborhoods were the most greatly affected by floodwaters and the last to have services restored.

## Restoring Permanent Housing

The rebuilding process has become a prisoner's dilemma for former residents of New Orleans and other communities. Residents are deterred from return-ing or rebuilding homes by the lack of assurance that their neighbors will follow suit, and the logical thing to do is wait and see. However, the unwill-ingness to commit to return also deters their neighbors from returning. And those who live at the margins of the society, whose only equity was their homes or who rented low cost housing that has been destroyed, are largely closed out of the options to return.

The debate over rebuilding neighborhoods has been joined in ways that make decisions exceptionally difficult. Politicians in New Orleans, seeking to resurrect their constituencies, argue that every citizen has a "right of return," borrowing an incendiary phrase from conflicts in the Middle East and other volatile parts of the world. Community activists from ACORN and other organizations have also promoted the right of every New Orleans resident to return, not just to the city, but to the home he or she occupied before Katrina. Activists from outside New Orleans have outnumbered neighborhood resi-dents at demonstrations seeking to stop the removal of demolished houses in low-income neighborhoods such as the Lower Ninth Ward. Many of the houses in the poorest neighborhoods carried no flood insurance—the owners had been persuaded that they were not in a flood zone and therefore did not need insurance, and New Orleans was among the minority of governments that did not make conformance to FEMA flood elevation regulations manda-tory. More than 100,000 houses in New Orleans were flooded with more than 3 to 4 feet of badly polluted water (Figures 5 and 6). As a practical matter this requires the entire first floor of the unit to be gutted, dried out, and rebuilt, a

FIGURE 5. Damaged house in the Lakeview neighborhood, New Orleans. Gary Hack.

FIGURE 6. Damaged houses in the Ninth Ward, New Orleans. Gary Hack.

costly proposition. Many houses were swept off their foundations, and a large number ruined beyond repair.

The most flooded New Orleans neighborhoods—with over 8 feet of water for up to 6 weeks—are a band of middle-class white and black neighborhoods built after World War II. Many of the houses are brick veneer bungalows, built on foundations that are concrete slabs on grade. A significant number have mortgages now in default, after six months of forbearance by lenders. Owners face several uncertainties in addition to the question of whether enough of their neighbors will decide to reinvest in their homes to create a neighborhood without huge gaps in its fabric. Will there be enough residents to support neighborhood schools, commercial outlets, and religious facilities? Will FEMA flood regulations, to be issued in March, require them to raise the ground floor level of their houses—a practical impossibility for most of the homes? If they repair their houses, will there be buyers when they wish to sell? Alternatively, will the much discussed buyout program, using federal funds, actually materialize? Many of the former residents are paralyzed by the uncertainty. Coupling these issues with the declining job prospects in the city, many New Orleans residents have decided not to return. Recent RAND projections suggest that the city will have only half its former population in five years.

As difficult as conditions in New Orleans are today, many communities along the Gulf Coast of Mississippi that faced the dangerous side of Katrina were literally wiped off the map. In these areas, the fundamental question is whether to rebuild at all, knowing now the vulnerabilities of their coastal location. Rebuilding may require stringent FEMA flood elevation standards to be met, which at a minimum requires that new patterns of construction be adopted and expensive flood protection be installed for low-lying areas.

New Orleans and other Gulf Coast communities are in the midst of a debate whether they should restore their towns and cities to their previous pattern, which consisted largely of post-World War II automobile-oriented suburban development, or worse, scattered and unplanned sprawl. One alternative image is to seek more compact development, with modestly higher densities and a greater mix of residential and commercial uses. Planners and designers organized by the Congress for New Urbanism, argued in the Mississippi Renewal Forum for the return to development patterns that are more characteristic of the best early twentieth-century towns of the region. Such a change will require greater capacity to plan, regulate, and carry out redevelopment efforts than currently exist in any Gulf Coast communities. The new state chartered reconstruction commissions in Louisiana and Mississippi could become the lead entities, but such a move would represent a significant increase in governmental intervention in urban development activities in these states.

ORGANIZING FOR HOUSING THOSE DISPLACED IN THE FUTURE

The Gulf Coast has become a landscape of uncertainty, which is itself the most significant factor that must be overcome as it seeks to reconstruct its cities and towns. Hurricanes and natural disasters are, by definition, unpredictable—although the scenario that unfolded in New Orleans was not unfamiliar to long-term residents who had seen floods before, and to hazard recovery specialists who had gamed events that were hauntingly similar. What was lacking was an organized response.

We might look to other ways that our society deals with uncertainty for cues about possible responses. Our military efforts are one such model. Dealing with uncertain threats from abroad has motivated the creation of a large and extraordinarily expensive response system, organized around contingencies, and employing intelligence and planning. Most imaginable threats have been considered in advance, and people positioned and materiel stockpiled to address such a threat. Suppose we fought a war in the way we have dealt with Katrina: Our military units would wait until the onset of conflict to order the equipment they need to go into battle, the transportation required to put troops and materiel into the field would not be organized in advance, and we would have to design the communications facilities required for maintaining command and control after the battle began. The units would be scurrying around in the midst of conflict to secure forward deployment areas and to identify sites for those displaced by battles.

While the strength of the military depends upon a network of centrally organized units and locally maintained guard detachments, they are unified in their command structure once battle begins. There is no debate as to who should be determining the deployment of troops. There is much to learn from this articulated system of planning and response.

We know that the Gulf Coast will be struck by future hurricanes, and can in hindsight estimate with some precision the needs that will follow—immediate shelter, temporary power and other utilities, high capacity pumps, facilities and staff for schools and medical services, accommodations for residents when they return to their home neighborhoods, financial arrangements for damages, and so on. It should be possible to stockpile the essential items in convenient and protected locations, while making standby arrangements for the specialized skills that will be necessary for their deployment. Learning the lessons from Katrina, refuge areas, and areas for temporary housing, should be secured in advance, not after the event.

While many potential emergencies had been gamed by emergency planners, including a scenario hauntingly similar to that which occurred in New Orleans, the problem was the absence of resources or organizations with the capacity to follow through. And residents had no knowledge of the key aspects of evacuation plans. Evacuation routes were marked by road signs, but not the destinations.

Taking emergency planning seriously might also lead to changes in the way we construct our environments and educate the public about preparedness. Areas in cities might be set aside for temporary settlements and provided with the infrastructure needed to be occupied. In Tokyo, local development regulations and plans mandate the creation of outdoor refuges for occupants of each area of the city in the event of earthquakes and fires. Disaster drills are held regularly to test preparedness and to educate citizens about how to react, much in the way fire drills are conducted in many of our buildings. For those most vulnerable in our society—the sick, elderly, infirm, and those with limited capacities—testing the emergency preparedness system may be critical to their survival. Some of the great failures of the New Orleans evacuation were in nursing homes and health care facilities.

When small probability but catastrophic events rise to the level of public consciousness, they will affect community and building design in other ways. During the 1960s, the threat of nuclear fallout (however real or manufactured) led to a national program of fallout shelters and the creation of public refuge areas. Design competitions were held for imagining schools that could serve as radiation shelters while providing good environments for education. Federal funds were allocated to construct prototypes. Taking seriously the need for refuge areas within communities might affect the design of all manner of public facilities. It should not be necessary to house thousands of those displaced in sports stadiums that lack essential facilities, or in schools with inadequate facilities to feed those who are sheltered. And perhaps there ought to be areas of cities with standby infrastructure so that temporary housing can quickly be attached to it and serve the needs of those displaced.

Finally, the best policy for recovery is minimizing the impacts of hazards that make a response necessary. An abiding lesson of Katrina must be that if the public is expected to provide relief after natural hazards, there have to be tough standards to minimize the risks. Adopting flood protection standards, having building codes which can withstand known winds and stresses, and paying for public improvements such as flood control protection would seem to be minimum qualifications for any assistance from higher level governments. The loss of wetlands east of New Orleans, and of barrier islands along much of the Gulf Coast, will necessitate massive regional efforts to lower the hazards communities face. This is an effort that is at least 50 years overdue, and there is little excuse for delaying it further.

Planning settlements so that they avoid areas with the greatest natural hazards would seem to be common sense. New Orleans and most of the Gulf States did not meet such a criterion. One failure may be forgiven, but this is not the first instance, and we should insist that the price of assisting the recovery is ensuring that there will not be a recurrence.

*Note*

1. Brookings Institution, Katrina Index Tracking Variables of Post-Katrina Reconstruction, March 2006.

# CHAPTER 17

# Lessons from Sri Lanka

## Thomas L. Daniels and Harris Steinberg

On December 26, 2004, an undersea earthquake registering 9.3 on the Richter scale erupted off the western coast of Sumatra, Indonesia. It was the fourth most powerful recorded quake in the previous hundred years. The quake triggered a massive tsunami, with walls of water up to 50 feet high traveling at speeds up to 500 miles an hour toward twelve countries rimming the Indian Ocean. The tsunami killed an estimated 165,000 people, mainly in Indonesia, India, Thailand, the Maldives, and Sri Lanka. The tsunami wave fanned around Sri Lanka from the southeast up the east coast and around the south coast and partly up the west coast, impacting an area 600 miles wide and up to one mile inland. More than 35,000 Sri Lankans were killed (Glancy 2006). Between 500,000 and 800,000 people were left homeless (Jagtiani 2006; World Bank 2005).

World sympathies resulted in massive relief efforts to Sri Lanka and less than a year later, in November 2005, the United Nations High Commission for Refugees (UNHCR) declared its post-tsunami relief work complete in Sri Lanka. The Sri Lanka government recorded the quick restoration of basic health and the effective rebuilding of infrastructural and educational systems that resulted from the "quick combined response by the government, local communities, local NGOs, private sector and the international community" (Government of Sri Lanka 2005).

In comparison to the tsunami, Hurricanes Katrina and Rita left far fewer fatalities (1,405 dead), an equal number of displaced (760,000), and affected an 108,000-square-mile area spanning four states (Louisiana Recovery Authority 2005). Unlike Sri Lanka, where the losses mainly occurred in 54 small and poor villages, the destruction in New Orleans and the Gulf Coast occurred in urban places (Glancy 2006). Furthermore, as observed in February 2006 by the U.S. House of Representatives, the response to Katrina was a "national failure, an abdication of the most solemn obligation to provide for the common welfare. . . . At every level—individual, corporate, philanthropic, and government—we failed to meet the challenge that was Katrina" (U.S. House of Representatives 2006, x). It is ironic that one of the world's poorest nations could mount a more successful response to a widespread natural disaster than the wealthiest. The United States can learn from Sri Lanka's example, especially in the realm of housing.

One set of lessons revolves around the design and delivery of affordable housing. Both Sri Lanka and Gulf Coast of the United States are places that have populations characterized by relatively large numbers of low-wage workers and people living below the poverty line. These conditions create special recovery issues related to the provision of inexpensive permanent dwellings in hazard-resistant locations and linking rebuilding to economic development. An associated concern is building healthy communities that include housing precincts that will not become slums (as has been the experience of many so-called "FEMA-villes" that were created post-hurricane in Florida and elsewhere and have become permanent mobile home or trailer settlements without amenities, variety, or safety). Moreover, the rebuilding efforts must assist in restoring the sense of place to areas that have lost much of their identity through the natural disaster.

Within fourteen months, Sri Lanka, which under normal conditions built 5,000 new units annually, dramatically multiplied its housing production: in six months, it constructed 55,000 temporary shelters, and by 2006 it had organized the construction or repair of 60,000 units (Jagtiani 2006; World Bank 2005). While Sri Lanka still struggles to provide the entire supply of needed housing, it took an important step in the linking of temporary and permanent shelter programs, developing simple prototype permanent housing, while putting fewer resources into temporary units and fostering economic development projects in conjunction with housing. In addition, Sri Lanka implemented regulations and incentives for rebuilding in disaster-resistant locations, relocated especially vulnerable villages at suburban densities, and developed an organizational structure for shelter delivery blending central and decentralized functions. Furthermore, Sri Lanka produced these results at a fraction of the cost that the U.S. is predicting for shelter efforts. The Sri Lanka response has flaws that also provide instruction, including difficulties in setting boundaries for rebuilding on completely disaster-resistant sites, creating uniform standards for dwelling units, and delivering relief efforts in areas with racial tensions. The following general overview and case studies illustrate the various lessons.

## GOVERNMENT STRUCTURE AND GENERAL POLICY

With any disaster response, the two main issues are the speed and the scope of the relief and rebuilding efforts. Unlike the United States, Sri Lanka established a national oversight and implementation structure, delegating responsibility to three agencies: the Task Force to Rebuild the Nation (TAFREN), the Urban Development Authority (UDA), and the National Physical Planning Agency. Through this structure, Sri Lanka coordinated with nongovernmental organizations (NGOs) that have provided the bulk of temporary and permanent shelter. By December 28, just two days after the tsunami struck, the Sri Lanka government had appointed TAFREN, a ten-member body outside direct government control, to set the general strategy for reconstruction. Within the national government and influenced by TAFREN's policies are the UDA and the National Physical Planning Agency. The UDA has drafted master plans for reconstruction and new town developments and authorized NGOs to construct both temporary and permanent housing. The National Physical Planning Agency has worked to restore basic infrastructure. In November 2005, the Sri Lankan government created the Reconstruction and Development Agency (RADA), both to replace TAFREN and to function as the single government agency responsible for all reconstruction and development activities relating to post-tsunami relief throughout the nation.

Political and economic factors played a role in the effectiveness of Sri Lanka and the ineffectiveness of the United States. As a highly centralized, socialist democracy, Sri Lanka has no local planning. This eliminates consultation with or approval-seeking from local planning or zoning boards. This compares to the three levels of government—federal, state, and local—in the United States that responded to Katrina with a remarkable lack of coordination or direction. Such an ineffective response is even more amazing, given the vast wealth of the United States. Moreover, the United States has received or accepted very little help for Katrina relief from the international community, highlighted by President Bush's rejection of Cuba's offer to send doctors to the Gulf Coast. By comparison, the Sri Lankan central government had very limited funds to respond to the tsunami, and it recognized that NGOs could provide essential relief in health care, food distribution, and shelter. The Sri Lanka central government agencies, working with the UNHCR and NGOs, chose to emphasize the construction of new houses for tsunami refugees while simultaneously providing tents or primitive supplies for temporary shelter. This approach not only proved acceptable given the mild local climate, but also kept the population in place rather than widely dispersing it as has occurred with the Katrina victims. This effort was viewed as an interim measure and stepping stone to the construction of a durable solution—the construction of simple, traditional, and functional homes (D'Urzo 2005). The permanent units, described below, are not unlike the Katrina cottage that has recently emerged as a U.S. alternative to the trailer or mobile home (Figure 1).

Eight months after the tsunami struck, all the emergency camps had been dismantled and very few of the tsunami victims were living in tents (D'Urzo 2005). For the Sri Lanka government, the very real concern had been that temporary housing sites might deteriorate into permanent slum settlements.

FIGURE 1.    Katrina cottage. Jeffrey K. Bounds, 2006.

## RECREATING A SENSE OF PLACE

In conjunction with the housing program, the Sri Lanka government, through the UDA, directed attention to recreating a sense of place in rebuilding. While this goal may sound like a luxury in the midst of widespread destruction, creating places rather than a group of houses contributed to instilling a sense of ownership in the residents. A key feature of a sense of place is security. For Sri Lanka, this has involved relocating people away from the coast, an action not without controversy. (D'Urzo 2005). Immediately after the tsunami, the Sri Lanka government through its Coast Conservation Advisory Council declared a conservation buffer zone along 1,000 kilometers of coastline prohibiting rebuilding and new construction. The buffer varied in width: in the south it was 100 meters and along the east coast it was 200 meters. Many viewed the ban, an attempt to safeguard the country from future flooding disasters, as a government land grab to promote the lucrative tourism trade. The resulting public outcry ultimately caused officials to relax the blanket post-tsunami ban; it is now 15 to 40 meters in some places based on the less stringent 1990 National Coastal Zone Management Plan (Sandra D'Urzo, personal communication, February 8, 2006). An estimated 56,000 houses remain within this no-build area and the government plans to resettle their inhabitants outside the buffer zone (World Bank 2005).

FIGURE 2.   One of 647 permanent houses at Hambantota built by the Tzu Chi Foundation of Taiwan. Tom Daniels, 2006.

While establishing the no-build zones, the UDA made land available for new housing. Although the land was mostly government-owned, the UDA also employed eminent domain to acquire some private property. The UDA also assisted in developing master plans for the new areas. Thus, through administrative and regulatory devices, Sri Lanka established a structure and policy for rebuilding, applying it in varying ways as the following case studies underscore lessons that can be applied to rebuilding and reshaping New Orleans and the Gulf Coast.

## HAMBANTOTA: A SWIFT AND DEDICATED RESPONSE

The tsunami swept through the heart of the south coast city of Hambantota, destroying hundreds of homes and killing as many as 1,000 of the city's 11,200 inhabitants. Four days later, on December 30, 2004, staff and volunteers from the Taiwan Buddhist Tzu Chi Foundation arrived in Hambantota. The Foundation immediately established emergency facilities, including a free clinic for medical care and food distribution services, and erected 296 tents for temporary shelter. The staff and volunteers then quickly embarked on a plan to build 647 permanent homes, known as the Tzu Chi Great Love Village Homes (Figure 2). The village is part of a 4,000 unit mixed-use addition to the city,

FIGURE 3.   New houses in Hambantota, NGO Association for Lighting a Candle (AFLAC). Harris Steinberg, 2006.

located a safe one mile from the coast across an ancient salt pond still used for salt production.

The following principle informed the redevelopment process: "Be aware the families who will be settled in identified sites will come from 'divers [sic] social and family backgrounds.' Therefore people need an 'outlet to recapture their self esteem and resourcefulness for their socio-economic upliftment'" (Urban Development Authority 2005) Notably, this principle centers first on the social, cultural, economic, and psychological—not the architectural— needs of the families.

The UDA prepared the master plan for the development. The plan maintained a visual connection with the sea through the use of view corridors from the high ground of the new settlement to the coast. As many of the relocated families drew their livelihood from the sea, this visual connection provided a psychological link to the ocean. The plan also established road networks, surface drainage systems, solid waste disposal, and open space. To establish a sustainable framework for the new development, it gave special attention to rainwater harvesting, tree planting, and renewable energy sources (such as solar and wind). A participatory planning process based on a UN-Habitat/ United Nations Development Programme model guided the community development process (UN Development Programme 2003). The Hambantota victims of the tsunami who originally lived within the no-build zone qualified for free 500-square-foot houses (Figure 3). Constructed of site-fabricated mud brick covered in plaster with a red tile roof and a front porch, these houses emulate traditional Sri Lankan dwellings. Each house is one story with two bedrooms (one larger than the other per government standards), a kitchen (for wood-fired cooking), a sitting area, and a bathroom (accessible from the outside per local tradition). Not fancy, but these structures are nonetheless sturdy, functional houses set within a community. The Tzu Chi Great Love Village will be complete by the end of March 2006 and the Tzu Chi Foundation will begin planting 300,000 trees throughout the entire 4,000-unit new development to intercept storm water and provide shade.

Fourteen months after the tragedy of the tsunami, the Hambantota new town is preparing for its first permanent residents. Subsequent development phases will include schools, an assembly hall, and commercial areas. The Hambantota project is not emblematic of all rebuilding projects in Sri Lanka, and its success lies in the strong team structure implemented by the Hambantota District office of the UDA, which coordinated the work of all agencies and donors for the first six months after the tragedy, enabling the rapid design and construction of the 4,000-house new town. Ultimately the central Reconstruction and Development Agency (RADA) took over this function.

## OLUVIL: UNIVERSITY AS A DRIVER OF ECONOMIC DEVELOPMENT AND SOCIAL INTEGRATION

At the remote fishing village of Oluvil on the central east coast, an area dominated by Muslims, the international engineering and design firm, ARUP, is designing a major expansion of the South Eastern University of Sri Lanka (SEUSL). While SEUSL and Oluvil were spared the brunt of the tsunami that devastated the surrounding areas, the aim of the project is to use the opportunity presented by the tragedy to strengthen a civic institution that will draw together Muslims, Tamils, and Sinhalese to help overcome the nation's political strife. Under this plan, the university, which currently occupies the buildings of a former rice mill, would increase its student enrollment from 1,200 to 5,300. It will become a regional center of Islamic studies and biotechnology (Figure 4).

The plan calls for a novel creation in Sri Lanka: a residential college house system so that the "subtle arts of comity can be developed and communicated from one generation of students to the next" (ARUP 2006). To accomplish this, the physical site plan proposes a rich intermingling of formed spaces responding to the natural contours of the landscape. The plan deftly weaves together residential quarters, academic buildings, gardens, courts, water features, and other academic and social facilities to create a new academic campus evocative of a local village main street.

FIGURE 4. Existing campus of South Eastern University of Sri Lanka in Oluvil, Ampara District. Harris Steinberg, 2006.

The environmentally sensitive physical plan will more than triple the existing campus (from approximately 15 to nearly 55 acres). The plan respects the 200-meter setback from the ocean to the east in addition to a 100-meter setback from a tidal river to the north, placing sports fields and other low impact uses in the flood plains. Furthermore, all new buildings will be placed on high ground with ground floors designed to withstand floods both programmatically (no living spaces) and structurally. The ARUP team is working with natural ventilation and shading devices, siting buildings to respond to prevailing seasonal winds and paying careful attention to microclimates that are created between buildings. They are investigating the use of building materials that are durable, easy to obtain, cost effective, and sustainable. The plan even proposes the use of bio-diesel fuels made from local crops; this move would not only help the local economy but also point to a sustainable way to reduce dependence on foreign oil.

The ARUP plan creates a new physical connection between the remote campus and the adjacent fishing community with a new road that literally and figuratively extends higher education to the local fishing villagers. The campus also connects with the rest of the country and the world through innovative advanced communication technology, e-learning and bio-engineered bamboo transmission towers that will be distinctive visual marks in the landscape. Phase One of the expansion is awaiting the required cabinet level approval by the current government (Ratnayke 2006).

## Batticaloa District: Joining Relocation, Job Training, and Housing

In the Batticaloa District on the east coast, GTZ, the German government's sustainable development corporation, is facilitating the permanent relocation of three fishing villages to higher and safer ground. The tsunami leveled the 500-home fishing village of Passekudah, located on a small peninsula thirty kilometers north of Batticaloa, and the nearby village of Kalkudah with 700 homes located just outside the buffer zone. In cooperation with other local NGOs, GTZ simultaneously built temporary and permanent housing for families displaced and affected by the tsunami. GTZ is also working to make up the gap between government funds and actual needs for those families forced to rebuild on their own outside the buffer zone.

Working quickly, GTZ helped coordinate relief efforts in the east with the Tamil revolutionary government, the Liberation Tigers of Tamil Eelam (LTTE), and other NGOs by helping to distribute 12,000 tents to the victims within the first three months after the tsunami. By June 2005, tents were replaced with 16,000 temporary shelters made of simple pipe frames, which the local families covered in coconut thatch and other indigenous materials. Simultaneously, GTZ and the other NGOs in the area worked with the UDA on acquiring nearby government land and began the participatory planning process of creating permanent new villages for 16,000 new homes.

At the village of Paddiyadichenai, 30 kilometers north of Batticaloa, GTZ is building a new village for 130 families displaced by the ravages of the sea. GTZ's goal is not only to rehouse people, but also to provide training and new skills for a changing workforce. Because the demand for new housing in Batticaloa is staggering and the skilled workforce required to build new houses is virtually nonexistent, GTZ established three construction-training centers that are part of their housing developments. As a result, families participate in building their homes and family members learn new trades that are transferable across the island when the housing boom abates on the east. Additionally, GTZ is facilitating the creation of community groups and homeowner organizations to help the relocated villages find a political voice and restore a sense of community.

GTZ's holistic skill and community-based building process is exemplary, not only restoring housing, but also fostering economic development and a sense of community pride. As a bonus, GTZ's temporary housing is often built on the same lot as the resident's eventual permanent housing and people are adapting the temporary shelters to chicken coops and other ancillary uses, sensibly extending the useful life of post-tsunami aid (Figure 5).

## Weaknesses in the Sri Lanka Rebuilding Process

The Sri Lanka system is far from perfect. While New Orleans has been criticized as being politically disorganized, the situation in parts of Sri Lanka can

FIGURE 5.   New houses in Batticaloa District by GTZ, the German government's international enterprise for sustainable development. Harris Steinberg, 2006.

only be described as worse. Since 1982, the ethic minority Tamils have waged a civil war against the majority Sinhalese government to establish an autonomous state in northern Sri Lanka. In 2002, the Norwegian government helped broker a truce. But after the tsunami hit the Sinhalese government withheld relief funds from damaged areas under Tamil control along the northeast coast. In late 2005, Mahinda Rajapakse, a Sinhalese hardliner, was narrowly elected president. Soon sporadic fighting broke out between the two ethnic factions. At the time of this writing, no resolution had been reached on post-tsunami reconstruction in the Tamil-held areas although the two parties agreed to meet in Geneva in February 2006 to resume talks.

A further political obstacle is the centralized political control in the capital city of Colombo. Although the national government has worked effectively with several NGOs, it is widely criticized for corruption, while local governments have little funding available for reconstruction. Ferial Ashraff, the Sri Lankan Minister of Housing, explained that in her home province of Ampara on the east coast, 30,000 homes were destroyed and only 300 permanent houses have been built (Ashraff 2006); meanwhile, NGOs stepped in to provide 18,000 temporary shelters within six months (Glancy 2006).

Despite government mandates for minimum house size and room types, there are great inconsistencies between the works of the various NGOs. Projects range from providing the bare housing minimum to offering larger, more substantial structures (Figures 2 and 3). Coupled with the government's seemingly random line of demarcation between those who get a free house (formerly living within the no-build zone) and those who get partial assistance to rebuild (regardless of the extent of damage to their house), there are questions being raised about fairness and equity. Dr. Dietrich Stotz, senior advisor to GTZ, estimates that the value of the new housing built by NGOs on the east coast in the Batticaloa District ranges from approximately U.S.$4,000 to $20,000, underscoring the equity challenges raised by the ad hoc rebuilding program (Stotz 2006).

## CONCLUSIONS

Sri Lanka's response to the tsunami offers several lessons for the United States in reconstructing New Orleans and the Gulf Coast. In both Sri Lanka and New Orleans, the speed of the response has been a key factor. Sri Lanka has largely delivered timely relief and rebuilding, thanks to a combination of international NGOs, the central government's TAFREN and Urban Development Agency, local governments and nonprofits, and reliance on a traditional extended family structure. In Sri Lanka, the national government served as a facilitator in helping NGOs get on the ground quickly and in making land available for the NGOs to build temporary and permanent housing. In greater New Orleans, the federal, state, and local responses to Katrina have been largely uncoordinated and poorly directed; reconstruction to date has been minimal.

The Sri Lanka experience also suggests that nonprofit organizations often working in tandem with the central government and local residents may be more effective than only governments or only NGO relief efforts. The Sri Lanka central government welcomed the NGO and international relief aid. The United States has rejected international aid. Based on the Katrina experience, the United States appears to have no faith in its national government and the large NGOs, which, except for Habitat for Humanity, are not oriented toward building houses.

The Sri Lanka strategy to build permanent homes while simultaneously providing temporary shelter appears to have been the correct decision; this strategy has helped to restore local economies while enabling local residents to help themselves (Stotz 2006). Traditionally, emergency response focuses on the first steps of providing health facilities, food temporary shelter, and basic infrastructure (especially water, sanitation, roads, and schools) and later tends to deal with permanent housing. But the permanent housing must follow closely behind the temporary housing to begin the creation of permanent communities where residents feel a sense of security and ownership. The Sri Lanka example also demonstrates the design and use of indigenous architecture for the permanent housing. Finally, the master plans for the new housing communities include amenities and environmentally sensitive layout, and walk-able connections.

Political obstacles, such as friction among different levels of government and between governments and nonprofit organizations, and a certain amount of corruption can be expected. Sri Lanka's ethnic tensions have impeded reconstruction efforts in the northeastern part of the island. The inability of politicians to decide which areas of New Orleans to rebuild first, and the "Right of Return" policy have confused those displaced by Katrina as well as those planning for reconstruction.

The true lesson for the United States from Sri Lanka is a call for humility and cooperation and an end to the blame game. Disaster is no time for political bickering. While the rebuilding in Sri Lanka is far from perfect and inequities are inevitable, the combination of NGO-driven design and construction with government oversight and assistance, has allowed for over 54,000 temporary shelters to be swiftly built with permanent housing quickly following—often on the same plot, so that families need not move twice. In opting to strengthen a center of higher education as a means to help repair their civil society in the wake of the tsunami, Sri Lanka tells the world that there is more to rebuilding a country than houses alone. Indeed, it is the civic institutions that are the matrix for a democratic way of life. This small Third World island holds some big lessons for America.

Part IV

# RECREATING A SENSE OF PLACE

# CHAPTER 18

# Promoting Cultural Preservation
## Randall Mason

Housing, the regional economy, racial discrimination, education, health care, environmental restoration, and public safety are the frequently listed key considerations in rebuilding the post-Katrina landscape. Cultural values are missing from the list. Often overlooked, they are difficult to measure and, by definition, "priceless." New Orleans and the Gulf region, however, are places of immense cultural value—as distinct from their economic values—making the fate of culture an urgent issue in their redevelopment.

While the scope of the disaster is vast, it creates unique opportunities to rethink all aspects of a city and region. The lengthy rebuilding process will likely be dominated by debates about economic development, physical geography, and political will, resulting in the weakening or disappearance of cultural values. This does not have to be the case.

This essay argues that cultural preservation, the conscious conservation of a place's cultural values, should be a core part of post-disaster rebuilding. In calling for a values perspective, it distinguishes cultural and economic values, discusses the cultural values of New Orleans, traces the evolution of cultural preservation through the work of cultural geographers in articulating the meanings of urban places and presents a case study of Valmeyer, Illinois, a community relocated after the Mississippi River floods of 1993, as an example of cultural preservation.

## DISTINGUISHING BETWEEN CULTURAL VALUE AND ECONOMIC VALUE

The values perspective asserts simply that every place exhibits a number of different types of value simultaneously.[1] For example, an urban park has economic value (as a piece of real estate, as something that increases surrounding property values, or as a place to sell a lot of ice cream), artistic value (as a place designed by a famous landscape architect or a locale for a sculpture by a distinguished artist), historic value (as an engine for development of the surrounding neighborhood or the site of notable events), ecological value (as a remnant of old forest or a place with a stream running through it) (Avrami, Mason, and de la Torre 2000; Mason and Avrami 2002). While every place has a number of values, its specific values are different. Not all parks or historic houses or Southern cities carry precisely the same values. Different people will describe the values of a place differently. And in shaping the meaning of a place, wide public and expert consultation is critical to its full understanding. Furthermore, various values of a place often conflict, making trade-offs necessary. (For example, realizing economic values may degrade historic or ecological values.)

In the scholarly discourse about values, a cleavage emerges between economic and cultural values (Ackerman and Heinzerling 2004; Porter 1996). But economic and cultural perspectives on value are two ways of slicing the same pie. All places have both economic and cultural value; they are distinct characteristics. In a society increasingly driven by quantifying the value of things, and using markets to make decisions about what is important, cultural meaning—the richness and idiosyncrasy of human experience, creativity, all the things one would describe as "priceless"—is often lost.

Economic values are quantifiable, defined by market. They have two forms: "use values," those with actual prices gained through market transactions; and "non-use values," those with estimated prices because markets for them do not exist.[2] An archaeological site, for example, might have values that include revenues from admission prices and concessions or agricultural products produced on surrounding lands; its non-use values might include the way the site informs the identity of an indigenous culture, the value for researchers who derive information from excavating the site, or the beauty of the place.

Cultural values are the qualities or characteristics of a place. In articulating cultural values, the sort of things economists label "non-use" values govern—qualities like beauty, feeling, meaning, and symbolism. Not generally quantifiable, cultural values lack a unanimous shared theoretical basis for their evaluation. Assessing cultural values relies on qualitative (narrative, visual) measures and depends on connoisseurs, artists, and other creators, not markets, as arbiters.

The two approaches are not neutral toward each other. The epistemology of neoclassical economics is not only scientific but colonial and pretends to account for *all* kinds of value. The epistemology of cultural value is fractured, fickle, contingent, and (at least tacitly) criticizes the scientific, mathematical discourse of economics. Cultural experts insist that beauty, historical meaning, and symbolism have no dollar expression, while economists assume that individual actors account for all values when they make a decision about the price they are willing to pay for some thing or some experience (Mason 1999; Throsby 2001).

The cost-benefit analysis advocated by many is well tooled to handle the economic values but fails in assessing cultural values (see Daniels, Kettl, and Kunreuther 2006; Ackerman and Heinzerling 2004). Making decisions based only on economic values underestimates (if not ignores) cultural values. Preservationists tend to view economists as the bogeymen, while they are often guilty of the same value bias when they favor cultural values over economic considerations in conservation decision making. Nonetheless, being easier to measure, economic benefits often take precedence over the more difficult to measure cultural benefits when it comes to decisions about resources or redevelopment in a market-centered society.

Recently, social science and humanistic discourses have been challenging the hegemony of economics as the main arbiter of value (Brooks 2006). Additionally, in the field of historic preservation a new "values-based" trend is emerging calling for a broad understanding of the varied qualities defining the uniqueness of every place (Mason 2006). These trends are converging in the area of cultural preservation, where practitioners define the problem thus: conservation and development have to be brought in to some kind of balance in order to achieve "quality of life" in the fullest sense. They acknowledge that, while conservation and development both happen in cities, the devil is in the details when it comes to determining which places are to be conserved and which (re)developed. They assert that the best decisions about achieving this balance result from considering the *full* range of values of a place, arguing that basing decisions on a single value is a recipe for unbalanced urbanism and unsustainable development.

Today, more and more preservationists are aware of, and fluent in, economic values; more economists and business interests are willing, and even eager, to embrace cultural values on cultural terms. Guiding the way is the theoretical work of economist David Throsby (2001), which narrows the gap between cultural and economic modes of analysis regarding values. Throsby argues that economic and cultural goods are distinct and separable. Labeling them economic capital and cultural capital, he suggests that each generates flows of benefits that are measurable.

This insight has two applications. The first enables the articulation of distinct economic and cultural flows for use in decision-making frameworks that employ factors like sustainability to balance them. The second adds the notion of cultural capital flows into market-centered analyses of mainstream economics. Crafting sensitive assumptions about the unique nature of cultural values, and using sufficiently elegant mathematics, this could yield useful estimates for weighing economic and cultural values.

Other fields, such as international development, have already incorporated culture into their approaches. Responding to a critique against development decisions being made with insufficient regard for culture, Nobel economist Amartya Sen (1999) asserts that there are no universal development approaches, no blind applications of economics. He argues that cultural well-being must be considered a component of overall social well-being, and part of any sort of successful "development." He calls for development policy that is responsive and respectful of the cultural conditions of the places where the policies are applied.

## WHAT ARE THE CULTURAL VALUES OF NEW ORLEANS?

The larger subject of this chapter is how cultural aspects of a place enter into decisions about redevelopment. But the specific challenge is thinking about rebuilding urban places, and specifically New Orleans. Perhaps more than any other American city, New Orleans's identity rests on its cultural uniqueness, as its "most important attributes spring from a history and a geography that are eccentric to the mainstream of American urban experience" (Lewis 2003, 4).

The cultural values of New Orleans include celebrated cuisine, music, architecture, literature, and events (Mardi Gras and Jazz Fest) that fuse Old and New Worlds, North and South Americas, Latin and Protestant worlds and gregariously mix races and identities. In American culture and memory, it is the nation's most interracial and international city; it is a place of tolerance and creativity. New Orleans's cultural values bridge historic and contemporary periods; they relate to the built environment as well as the more immaterial, ephemeral expressions of culture. Others have articulated some of these cultural values very vividly (this volume; Abrahams et al. 2006).

While New Orleans's culture is clearly unique, it is also typical of American cities in some respects—its racism, devastating tolerance for inner-city poverty, and ignorance of environmental health. Past decisions to build on marginal land, many would agree, should not be valued, let alone replicated or looked upon with reverence. But these ideas—certainly part of the contemporary culture of the city—should be put on the table, available for memorialization.

This phenomenon reveals a problematic aspect of cultural preservation: cultural values are not only the celebrated or tourist-friendly ones but also the undesirable ones. Geographer Peirce Lewis, in a landmark essay, called the cultural landscape "our unwitting autobiography," representing likeable and unlikable qualities (Lewis 1970). All of it—under the rubric of cultural values—warrants consideration in the conservation-redevelopment balancing act.

Why do cultural values matter for New Orleans? First, they have an enormous influence on people's decisions to live in New Orleans and are the basis for the hospitality industry. Second, they frame very different ways of understanding the place. Asserting their importance in rebuilding discussions is a means of resisting the hegemony of markets in dictating how value is

FIGURE I.   Walker Evans's photographs of southern towns and landscapes capture
the richness of cultural values attached to these places. As with this 1936 image of
Vicksburg, Mississippi, the life of the place is represented in the people, their
buildings and streets, and, with a little imagination, their lives. OSA/FWI Collection,
Prints and Photographs Division, Library of Congress, LC-USF342-008076-A.

debated, decided upon, and traded off, making the distinction between economic and cultural values strategically important.

Plate 15 and Figure 1 illustrate the distinction between economic and
cultural values and its implications for thinking about urban redevelopment
around the Gulf. In Plate 15, a map of 1877 represents the emergent city as a
collection of empty lots and emphasizes the economic values of New Orleans.
It says little about its cultural landscape, for in only showing the arrangement
of the streets and blocks it provides information essential for real estate transactions and nothing else. In contrast, in Figure 1, photographer Walker Evans
captures the life of Vicksburg, Mississippi, in 1936 through his portrayal of
people along with buildings and streets. With a little imagination the viewer
can grasp some of the complexity of their lives, and the culture of inhabiting
the place pictured. Comparing these two images shows how discourse limited
to economic values reduces the complexity of the place, while assertions of
cultural values valorize the complexity of the place.

In terms of the concerns raised above, current efforts at cultural preservation in New Orleans rebuilding are fraught with problems. While traditional historic preservation tools deployed throughout the region have yielded some limited successes and the press has reported widely on recovery efforts by artists, arts institutions, and other cultural forces, the work of the Cultural Committee of the Bring New Orleans Back Commission, appointed post-Katrina, is worrisome. To judge from its recent report, the Commission is unduly emphasizing the aspects of culture that serve economic development goals (Bring New Orleans Back Commission 2006). Using the language of marketing and inferring that culture is foremost an industry—an economic activity like making cars or frozen peas—the sixteen committee members, described as "leaders from creative industries," define culture narrowly. For example, while they realize that "in the wake of Katrina, the city's very existence has been threatened and its cultural economy has been decimated," they also assert "Culture is business in New Orleans"; "Culture can and should serve as the catalyst to rebuild New Orleans"; and " culture . . . will stimulate our economic revival." They offer only a few noneconomic assertions about culture such as "Culture defines the Soul and Spirit of the City" and "The culture of the City is essential to its well-being—it will die if it is unattended."

The committee calls for a three-year investment strategy to rebuild the cultural economy of New Orleans. Its recommendations, based on institutional aspects of culture, are marketable and measurable. (They include the following: rebuild our talent pool of artists, cultural groups, and cultural entrepreneurs; support community-based cultural traditions and repair and develop cultural facilities; market New Orleans as a world-class cultural capital; teach our arts and cultural traditions to our young people; attract new investment from national and international sources (Bring Back New Orleans Commission 2006). The Committee's economic argument for the preservation of culture is not illegitimate, but it is limited, since it is the *only* argument offered about the fate of culture in the post-Katrina situation. Important aspects of culture are likely to be devalued, if not ignored, if this vision of culture and development prevails.

The most damaging aspect of this approach lies not in the predominance of economic discourse about New Orleans's culture, but in the segregation of culture as something altogether separate from other rebuilding issues. Undoubtedly, the mayor had important political and pragmatic reasons to create a "Culture Committee," but this separation may do more damage than good. A more effective strategy would be one of cultural preservation.

## EVOLUTION OF CULTURAL PRESERVATION

The cultural preservation approach suggested here embraces a new way of thinking about a place. First, it balances the many values, including economic and cultural, that are associated with a place and makes connections among natural, cultural, social, and economic systems, strengthening the health of *all* of the systems, not just *some* of them. Second, it defines culture as neither static nor monolithic, valorizing it as a process. Third, it broadens the historic preservation field's approach to culture and rebuilding. Fourth, it demonstrates the relevance of the cultural landscape interpretations in addressing the problems of large-scale cultural preservation such as posed by the post-Katrina situation. Fifth, it showcases the concept of "cultural confidence."

## Defining Culture

Cultural preservation has at its base a thoughtful definition of culture and some theoretical insight about how culture works vis-à-vis other social phenomena. Culture is not easily identifiable, knowable, and definable. It is an encompassing and complex concept, described by cultural critic Raymond Williams as "one of the two or three most complicated words in the English language" (Williams 1985, 87). Despite its complexity, culture is not beyond the reach of having an operable definition for praxis, one that rejects the predominant ideas implying that culture is static, primarily material, and separate from economics, politics, and other spheres of life. A useful definition should have several qualities.

First, culture is always evolving and being remade. Anuradha Mathur's chapter in this volume makes a similar point about mistaken perceptions of land in the Mississippi Delta. Culture is a physical reality, but it is governed strongly by processes that are in some sense predictable and in other senses unpredictable.

Second, culture has both material and immaterial aspects. Knowledge, habits, traditions, memes, and other immaterial phenomena are as constitutive of culture as its material expressions. A New Orleans-specific example is represented by Creole plasterer Earle Barthe: the moldings and rosettes he creates as well as his knowledge about how to do the plastering work are culture. In another example, the culture of jazz consists of both material aspects (the instruments, the places where jazz is played, the recordings) and immaterial aspects (performances, styles of playing, the sounds themselves). Overemphasizing material aspects of culture tends to devalorize its intangible aspects.

Third, a definition of culture is captured by the simple phrase "ways of living together" (UNESCO 2000), a notion that encompasses the everyday and habitual as well as the visible, famous and celebrated. It also includes material and immaterial phenomena, artifacts as well as processes; it is something shared, not limited to individuals; it covers the historic and the contemporary, things marketable and unmarketable. Culture is not an apolitical notion. Quite the opposite: as noted above, culture is not just what society chooses to embrace or what is marketable; it also includes all "ways of living together," even ones that many would disavow or be ashamed of. And in its very nature "culture" invokes the idea of exclusion by presuming that some people are part of it and some are not—you are an insider or an outsider.

Such a catholic understanding of culture would of course also encompass economic behavior as an aspect of "living together." And at the urban scale culture has a geographic meaning, the spatial experience of being in the world; foregrounding relations between environments (natural and human-made) and human activity; understanding spatial distribution of activities, meanings, systems, processes, and other social phenomena.

Finally, culture is not a separate part of society but a separate way of looking at the totality of society. Economy-centric ways of looking at the world are rooted in both neoclassical and Marxist economics, which argued for the primacy of economic relations in shaping society. The perceived separateness of cultural concerns from other, more important economic or political concerns is a symptom of the over-specialization and over-professionalization that dominate contemporary academic and professional discourse. To look at corporations, for instance, as only economic entities denies their influence on culture. Or, to think of the political establishment of New Orleans in terms only of politics, without considering economic and cultural forces at play in governance, gives only a partial picture of what is happening.

## Broadening the Approach of the Field of Historic Preservation

Historic preservation is centrally concerned with saving, repairing, and interpreting buildings. It has a privileged position in that it enjoys a broad public mandate to act as a steward of culture—at least of culture as represented in the built environment—and, by dealing with buildings it often negotiates the worlds of cultural *and* economic values. Traditionally, historic preservation has had a strongly artifact-centered view of culture, as seen in its two-pronged approach: to preserve buildings as unchanging artifacts to contrast with the changefulness of modern society (by arresting decay and otherwise repairing buildings); and to fix their meaning in time (by recollecting some historical period through detailed investigations of the buildings, historical scholarship, and didactic exhibits) (Mason 2003).

This static notion of culture stems from the field's roots in art conservation (in which focus rests on retaining or regaining an original, clearly defined artwork) and from historic preservation's function in the broader culture, creating islands of stability in a sea of change. The words of an early twentieth-century preservationist capture this latter role: "in the midst of the many changes in our fluid city we need some permanent landmarks to suggest stability, and to connect one generation with another in the higher things of life" (American Scenic and Historic Preservation Society 1912).

At its worst, historic preservation has become so focused on building preservation for its own sake that it verges on taxidermy of cultural artifacts, propping up the dead facsimiles of the past. Typically, preservationists think in terms of "levels of intervention," in order of increasing seriousness of intervention into the conditions of historic architectural fabric. The National Park Service defines them as "preservation, rehabilitation, restoration and reconstruction" (National Park Service 2001). This very static, artifact-centered way of organizing preservation underestimates the changeability of buildings' uses and meanings—a changeability demanded by social and cultural processes. It also ignores a dictum of insightful urban designer Kevin Lynch, "preservation is not simply the saving of old things, but the maintaining of a response to those things" (Lynch 1972).

In the past few decades, the historic preservation field has broadened its mandate considerably. At its best, preservation has pursued its core mandate while responding to broader, more process-centered ideas about culture. Faced with multifaceted threats to historic buildings and built environments, it has developed more flexible, adaptable notions about preservation—purposefully connected to cities' economic, social, and political dynamics. The last generation has witnessed a real expansion in the work of preservationists beyond narrow concerns with architectural fabric, evident in the broad successes of the National Trust for Historic Preservation-sponsored Main Street Program, urban conservation tools such as conservation districts, and a new orientation around issues of suburban sprawl (Moe and Wilkie 1997; Stipe 2003). The historic preservation field is learning how to be more adaptive and less reactive.

### Cultural Landscape

The cultural landscape concept comes from the field of human geography, which has been concerned with understanding culture in the fullest sense: how it takes form and is expressed in space. The landscape tradition in geography is a powerful lens because it looks at human environments ("places") holistically: through time, across natural and political boundaries, as a complex of things and processes, zones and lives. The cultural landscape idea merges physical geography with human geography. It is important to this argument because it connects the encompassing definition of culture outlined earlier to its expression at an urban/regional scale and to the management of actual environments.

The cultural landscape concept was first coined by American geographer Carl Sauer in the 1920s, who held that "The cultural landscape is fashioned from a natural landscape by a culture group. Culture is the agent, the natural area is the medium, the cultural landscape is the result" (Sauer 1963, 343). Postwar geographers, led by writer J. B. Jackson, revolutionized and humanized this mechanistic model. Jackson's impressionistic accounts of vernacular landscapes opened a whole new front to human geographers, whose detailed investigations of ordinary places revealed deep layers of cultural meanings.

Emblematic of this movement is geographer Peirce Lewis's urban biography of New Orleans (2003). His essential insight was seeing the city and its region as a cultural landscape—not as an artifact of French colonization, nor a point in the shifting physical geography of the Mississippi Delta, nor a collection of hybrid architectural forms, nor an important exchange point in the national economy, nor a crucible of race relations—a set of connected logics and dynamics incorporating all these things.

The starting point for Lewis's rendering of New Orleans is the region's physical geography. As seen in Figure 2, he uses Erwin Raisz's landform map showing the historic outlet of the Mississippi, the Atchafalaya Basin, the Delta, and the lowlands around New Orleans, to argue that the old courses of the Mississippi framed the possibilities for human geography: "New Orleans has preserved its exotic individuality because it is a cultural island. And . . . the city is a cultural island in part because it was first a physical island" (Lewis 2003, 12). This geomorphological reality remains an issue of great importance in post-Katrina rebuilding (see Robert Giegengack and Kenneth Foster's chapter in this volume). The cultural landscape concept links the realities and complexities of human geography and physical geography by offering historical and geographical explanations of racial patterns, development history, and the ongoing natural hazards playing out at local and regional scales.

Lewis's notion of a landscape asserts natural processes as a basic structuring element as well as source of changefulness—geomorphological, ecological, hydrological, and other natural processes never stop. More recent innovations in cultural geography and cultural landscape studies have raised more forcefully issues of economic, social, and political dynamics (Groth and Bressi 1997; Mitchell 2003; Olwig 2002) and demonstrated the power of the cultural landscape concept as a way of seeing, through art and design, as well as a mode of preservation (Mathur and da Cunha 2001; Alanen and Melnick 2000).

The connectedness of cultural and natural dynamics is the central interest of those studying cultural landscapes, and understanding this connectedness—as an historical resource as well as a contemporary condition—is crucial to achieving cultural preservation in the context of rebuilding.

## Cultural Confidence

The organizing idea of cultural preservation is "cultural confidence," which refers to the idea that a place's insiders remain confident (or alternatively comfortable) that cultural forms represent their ways of life, even as these forms change. Inspired by the anthropologist David Maybury-Lewis (Getty Conservation Institute 1998), the term is based on theories of culture as an

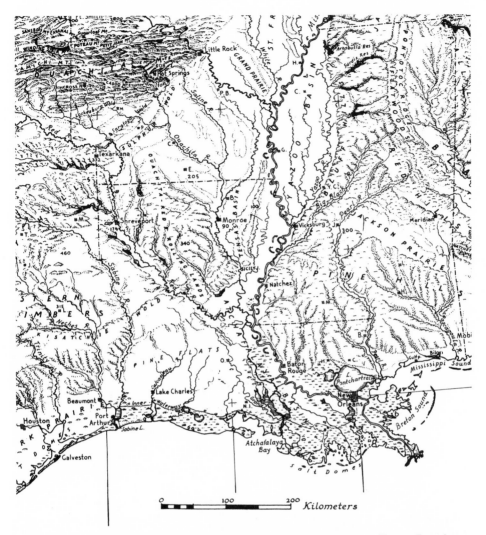

FIGURE 2. Excerpt of Erwin Raisz's map *Landforms of America*. Erwin Raisz's
cartographic masterpiece, reproduced here from Peirce Lewis, *New Orleans: The
Making of an Urban Landscape*, 2nd ed. (Charlottesville: University of Virginia Press,
2003), vividly portrays the bones of the region's geomorphology—including the
historic outlet of the Mississippi down the Atchafalaya Basin, the delta accreting out
into the Gulf of Mexico, and the lowlands surrounding the site of New Orleans.
Courtesy of Raisz Landform Maps.

evolutionary process and emphasizes the processes of cultural change, instead
of focusing on static cultural conditions.

When change that is too fast or too drastic occurs, it threatens cultural
confidence and social instability could result. An excellent example of this
phenomenon occurs in the widespread debates about globalization and its
effects. At the center of the debates are the opposing contentions that (a)

globalization is destroying cultures around the globe by inflicting unwanted, alien changes (through the vectors of market neoliberalism and multinational corporations), and (b) globalization is a positive cultural force because it enables greater prosperity and increases the freedom to compete in markets (Appiah 2006).

Preservation based on the idea of cultural confidence allows for change, but protects against change that is too disruptive or alienating. In other words, cultural confidence assumes that change will happen and can move in a number of directions which cannot be a priori judged as good or bad. The presence of change is not the issue—it is assumed. More important are the pace of change, the character of change, and who has power over it. To retain "confidence," culture should change within limits, and those limits should be determined by the holders of the culture themselves.

Sustainability, or sustainable development, is often invoked as a standard that rebuilding has to meet. Most often, sustainability is debated in terms of economic indicators and/or ecological indicators. Cultural confidence can be thought of as a way of conceptualizing the sustenance of culture and cultural process—a way to imagine what sustainability might mean for the region's culture.

In the planning field, there already exists a technique to carry out this sort of process. Called "limits of acceptable change," it is used in environmental, natural-resource planning, as a more consultation-based and culturally sensitive alternative to carrying capacity studies. It has occasionally been used in relation to cultural-resource planning. Who sets the limits? This model pushes forcefully in the direction of public participation, as opposed to relying on expert knowledge.

Centered on the idea of cultural confidence, the rebuilding debate needs a new model of large-scale yet decentralized preservation of culture. It is just an idea for now; obstacles to implementing such a model are many. For one, there are no established measures, indicators, or methods for engaging members of a culture in a discussion about cultural confidence. Do we just "know it when we see it"? Scholars can speculate about it, and experts can draw conclusions about it, but a widely validated way to sample cultural confidence is somewhere in the future. Another obstacle is the absence of institutions that could take responsibility for even establishing a conversation about cultural confidence. American governments lack coordinated cultural agencies, and what government and nonprofit agencies do exist tend to think about culture most in terms of what is measurable about it (the economic use values).[3]

The assertion of cultural values should at least stimulate conversations among New Orleanians about what they treasure and what they would happily lose as their shared culture, and how they would project their collective memory in the form of preservation activities and rebuilding investment. But this

FIGURE 3. Aerial photograph of Valmeyer, Illinois, 1996. The photograph (north is at the top of the image) shows the old townsite of Valmeyer, Illinois, at the center of image and the new townsite, to the east and slightly north. The Mississippi River runs north-south, on the left of the image. USGS/TerraServer.

does not address directly the tough, urgent, material questions—for example, what will be the fate of the buildings, lots, lives, and stories of the Lower Ninth Ward, Lakeview, and other areas of great physical destruction?

What would a cultural confidence/limits of acceptable change approach to cultural preservation look like? What would happen if cultural knowledge—of the kind lived by generations of New Orleanians and embedded in historic landscape and buildings of the region—was indeed factored in to redevelopment decisions in the ways suggested here?

## THE EXAMPLE OF VALMEYER

Instead of attempting the gargantuan task of answering these questions empirically, or proposing a design to solve all the problems, I will let the experience of a place in Illinois called Valmeyer serve as an example, albeit extreme, of cultural preservation.

Valmeyer is a small town near the Mississippi River, about a half hour's drive south of St. Louis. The 1993 Mississippi floods covered the town with 20 feet of water, destroying 90% of the buildings. In the aftermath of the floods, two-thirds of the citizenry (900 residents total) took the remarkable decision to move the town to a new, nearby site.

Figure 3, an aerial view of the area, shows the locations of the old and new town sites. The new site, 1.5 miles east of the old one, is farther away from the Mississippi. More important, it sits atop a bluff, 400 feet higher. While most of the town moved to the new site—houses, school, church, fire station, businesses—it is not a replication of the old forms. Some elements of the old buildings were removed and reused, but urbanistically and architecturally the place has quite a different sense and feel, as reported by residents. The new Valmeyer feels more like "a suburban subdivision"—with vinyl siding, curving streets, a "squircle" instead of a town square, and a lack of big trees—than an early twentieth-century farming town. One of the losses incurred in the move, according to Mayor Knoblock, was the mix of new and old houses. On the plus side, Valmeyer's residents can see the site of their old town (indeed, a few of the houses on higher ground are still occupied), smell the familiar smells of river and earth, visit the old town site to see if their perennials bloom in spring, and inhabit mostly the same riverside landscape they knew before (Brown 1996).

Does this mean that the changes Valmeyer has experienced fall within limits of cultural confidence? This is a question that needs deliberate study, but it would seem, given the available evidence, yes: that the majority of the town's residents feel comfortable with the move. In a radio interview, one resident said, "People are happy . . . happy with the decision . . . you hear good things" (Sepic 2005).

Financing the move was a challenge. A mix of government grants and assistance ($35 million), along with insurance proceeds, personal savings, and new mortgages, were needed to fund the new site acquisition ($3 million) and bridge the time of several years it took to realize the move. The per-resident cost was high (Aguirre 2002).

Think of Valmeyer as a radical example of cultural preservation: its citizens retained and reused some aspects of the old town and its buildings but wholly and purposely changed other aspects. To preserve the town in the wake of the wholesale destruction of its built fabric, relocating its people and social networks was the only choice. Is it still the same Valmeyer, or is it some new place, also called Valmeyer? There are big questions, unanswered as far as the literature reports, about the effects of these decisions on the cultural values of Valmeyer. But it was remarkable, on the face of it, as a collective action to create a long-term solution instead of a quick fix.

Valmeyer is a special case, to be sure—the small scale of the town, the large majority who agreed to the move, the strong leadership of the mayor, the high per capita cost. It is certainly not a model replicable for all of New Orleans. But can the ideas and strategies be any kind of guide to dealing with the Lower Ninth Ward or other highly devastated areas of New Orleans? Is there some land in or around New Orleans where relocation within the viewshed of destroyed communities—within the bounds of their cultural confidence and landscape—could be realized?

Relocation, as a preservation strategy, is one possible solution to the thorniest problems of post-Katrina rebuilding—thinking specifically of the mostly destroyed areas like the Lower Ninth Ward and the east end middle-class neighborhoods. Could places be traded or relocated like Valmeyer? There are many uncertainties. Is there other land available nearby? Can any meaningful consensus be reached? Can it be financed? Would the folks who once lived in these places want to return to a new place, as nearby and as similar as possible? Possibly within eyeshot, or a walk, of the places they had to leave behind? Creating such aesthetic connections between a new place and their old place could perhaps preserve a sense of cultural confidence.

## FINAL THOUGHTS AND PROPOSITIONS

In the wake of such physical destruction and social dislocation, culture is affected but not destroyed. The question is how to protect and rebuild sufficient cultural infrastructure for the place's culture to continue evolving and repairing itself. Clearly, the answer is not to think in terms of a zero-sum game: the culture is destroyed or intact; it is restored or ruined. The cultural confidence of New Orleans is intact but threatened. Having recognized the cultural value of region, it follows logically that some kind of cultural preservation approach to the whole place is warranted. Is it left to chance? No. The experience of Valmeyer suggests that more adaptive, flexible preservation strategies than we're used to may work—that maintaining culture and landscape, ways of living together, traditions of inhabiting the land—may be more helpful objects of preservation than buildings.

In light of the distinction between cultural and economic value, the proposals of paying people who are not permitted to rebuild their place are problematic—you cannot just exchange "place" or "home" for money. People reject this as an unfair trade; congruent with the other debates about economic and cultural ways of valuing, this is pricing the priceless. It treats their homes as property, not as place, which is a fundamental misunderstanding of what place and culture means, and what it contributes to our lives.

Sufficient cultural infrastructure, knowledge, and material exist for the New Orleans landscape to be able to sustain itself—traditions of literature, decoration, music, food, spiritual life, architecture, inhabiting the land, and on and on, are intact. Indeed, as this is being written, Mardi Gras celebrations are reported on the front page of the *New York Times*; and seemingly countless colleagues around the country are engaged in the myriad efforts to reframe, guide, or do the rebuilding.

The reality is that some large-sale interventions will be needed to address this large-scale disaster. Large-scale intervention is at cross purposes to culture. Made up of a thousand different things mixing together—"ways of living together"—culture is much more likely to respond to incentive policies than to command policies. This is the opposite of the approach required for the ecological management, transportation, and housing interventions needed in the region.

A final note about time and duration: One of the key contributions of preservation is thinking about the long term. Duration—the sense of time having passed—has become a more valuable aspect of culture, in light of broader society's increasing orientation to short-term business thinking and breakneck cultural change. Asserting cultural preservation as part of the discourse on post-Katrina rebuilding will help enforce long-term thinking, and this makes sense whether one is worried most about culture, about the economy, about the environment—and it's up to those of us without a personal stake in the region to hold up this end of the conversation. Time is also a precious resource, and spending some of it to explore the virtues of slower processes of rebuilding would enable more decentralized processes of rebuilding and allow the influence of local knowledge and local culture to grow.

## Notes

1. "Values," as used here, do not refer to ethics, morals, or principles by which decisions are made.

2. One final, important point about the concept of economic value is that it is not synonymous with business value. Businesses have profit-making as their goal, and all values are shaped by that purpose. Economic values stems from a social-scientific purpose of analyzing how societies assign value, and as an intellectual enterprise they seek understanding not profit. Although business interests obviously use economic value discourse as their fundamental means of analysis, economic and business values are not one in the same.

3. An exception to this has been the discourse on cultural policy that was maintained robustly for several years by the Pew Charitable Trusts, the Center for Arts & Culture, research centers at Princeton and some other universities, and other foundations. Some excellent publications resulted from this over the last decade (Bradford, Gary, and Wallach 2000; McCarthy et al. 2004).

# CHAPTER 19

# Understanding New Orleans's Architectural Ecology

## Dell Upton

New Orleans's future must include its historic architecture and cultural landscape, both because so much survives and because the city's economy depends on the tourism and lifestyle migration that its distinctive built environment attracts (Banay 2005; "Mayor Moves" 2005). But the landscape is more than a magnet to outsiders. It is a stage for the Crescent City's everyday life and, no less important, a complex record of the human history of the city, region, and nation. The fate of the city's historic architecture is a quality-of-life issue as much as an economic one, and as an ensemble, the landscape provides the kind of visually and psychologically rich environment that gives our lives meaning.

This architecture is in great danger. The damage from the hurricanes, the flood, and the short-term actions in the wake of the disaster, such as the suspension of historic preservation regulations and of restrictions on demolition and construction, may eventually pale in the face of the long-term threat posed by planning and policy decisions during reconstruction (Eggler and Russell 2005; Nossiter 2005). While very few people openly deny the importance of New Orleans's historic landscape, many treat it as a secondary or even irrelevant aspect of the city's recovery. Few reconstruction and replanning proposals show more than a superficial grasp of the city's historic environment and the processes that produced and maintained it. Obviously the technocratic and bureaucratic proposals to move New Orleans to a new site are unacceptable for many reasons in addition to historic ones (Jacob 2005). Less drastic proposals promise equally disastrous results—a homogenized city along the lines of contemporary planning ideals or a tourist-oriented caricature of the past. New Orleans's historic architecture deserves as careful and sophisticated a consideration as that which has been devoted to the city's economic and political future. A proper consideration should take into account the diversity of New Orleans's architecture, its intricate interrelations, and the ways the city's architectural fabric has fared in past disasters and reconstructions.

## A Varied Architecture

Tourist images of New Orleans emphasize the cast-iron balconies of the French Quarter and the mansions of the Garden District. To those who know

FIGURE 1.   Early twentieth-century shotgun houses and Creole cottage, 800 block Hampson Street, Carrollton, New Orleans. Dell Upton.

a little more about the city, shotgun houses and Creole cottages seem even more characteristic of its built environment. These are only the beginning, the distinctive or idiosyncratic elements of an urban landscape made of a diverse repertoire of local, regional, and national architectural forms. Certainly shotgun houses and Creole cottages *were* important working-class housing forms into the interwar period of the twentieth century (Figure 1). However, they have always coexisted with other kinds of houses, many of a kind found in any other American city, including urban row houses, cottages, single-family houses for the middle class, mansions, bungalows, public housing and apartment buildings, postwar tract houses, and even plantation and farm houses that have been engulfed by the growing city (Figure 2). As a multi-ethnic society, New Orleans also boasts hundreds of houses of worship of all dates, sizes, and denominations, ranging from tiny African American spiritualist churches to enormous, architecturally ambitious nineteenth- and twentieth-century churches and synagogues.

The Crescent City owes its existence to its location at the intersection of the Mississippi and Caribbean basins, which placed its merchants and manu-facturers in an advantageous position to buy, sell, and process commodities traveling in both directions. It is an advantage that they retain. The city's warehouses, factories, and commercial buildings have housed everything from cotton presses and sugar mills to modern-day food processing plants (Figure 3). As an example, New Orleans boasts a rich array of early to mid-nineteenth-

FIGURE 2.    Early twentieth-century bungalow, 1439 Broadway, New Orleans. Dell Upton.

century waterfront and wholesale stores of a kind once thick on the ground in all United States ports, but which cities such as New York, Philadelphia, and Boston have demolished. Despite its best efforts, New Orleans has not been able to keep up with the pace of destruction they set.

The way we understand the variation of New Orleans's architectural diversity will affect their fate during post-Katrina reconstruction. How can we categorize these structures and landscape elements? How did they come to be built in New Orleans and to be distributed through urban space and time as they are?

## HISTORIC ARCHITECTURE AS A RESOURCE

The first step in making sense of any historic landscape, disaster or not, is to know what is there. Typically, a state or a locality conducts a survey of historic architecture and makes a master building-by-building inventory. New Orleans has been fortunate to have had many local historians and architectural preservationists who arduously and carefully surveyed its built environment over the past half century. The Vieux Carré Survey, conducted from 1961 to 1966, examined all the surviving buildings in the French Quarter and correlated its findings with the documentary and photographic record (Jumonville 1990). Shortly after the completion of the Vieux Carré Survey, the Friends of the Cabildo sponsored a project to survey the remainder of the city. Eight vol-

FIGURE 3. Blue Plate Foods factory, New Orleans. Dell Upton.

umes have been published to date, all focusing on districts that were built before 1900 (Friends of the Cabildo 1971–). They followed the lead of the Vieux Carré Survey in supplementing brief descriptions of individual structures with information derived from land records and other written sources detailing each district's urban development. In addition, the city's Notarial Archives, a rich depository of visual and legal documentation of the city's early architecture, has been undergoing conservation and cataloguing in recent years. The Southeastern Architectural Archives, the Historic New Orleans Collection, and the city's archives at the New Orleans Public Library also hold extensive collections relating to the city's historic architecture.

Nevertheless, there are limitations to basing our understanding of the city's historic landscape entirely on these sources. As is usually the case in historic preservation surveys, these sources emphasize the earliest and the most visually appealing buildings. The Friends of the Cabildo volumes, for example, focus on New Orleans's most conventionally "historic" districts, those built up during the antebellum period and late nineteenth- and early twentieth-century districts built by the urban elite. Most of the city, including the areas most devastated by the 2005 disasters, is much less thoroughly documented. Even in the areas treated in the published surveys, coverage emphasized the antique and the extraordinary.

Most surveys grade the buildings they inventory by age, "integrity" (the degree to which a building or site retains its original form and details), or visual interest. In New Orleans, the Vieux Carré Survey (stealing a jump on the Department of Homeland Security) devised a system of color-coded categories for the French Quarter's buildings. They ranged from purple, for buildings "of national architectural or historic importance," to brown, for buildings that were "objectionable or are of no architectural significance" (Jumonville 1990, 4). Usually after such an exercise the most "important" buildings are restored or rehabilitated, often at public expense or with the assistance of special tax relief and other public financial incentives. These restored structures are used to define the "character" of a city or a district. Middling buildings typically become available to private owners, who are urged through preservation agencies, publications (Heard 1997), and the example of neighbors to recognize and emphasize those architectural details of their properties that are oldest or most distinctive and that enhance their value as cultural and economic commodities. When the survey and subsequent educational campaign are successful, tourism and rising real-estate prices "revitalize" the lucky city or neighborhood.

As the color-code system of the Vieux Carré Survey implies, this is a figure-ground view of the built environment. The historic stands out against the dull background of the insignificant and the positively objectionable, which may freely be pruned away. Historic buildings are treated as resources whose value can only be increased by removing buildings that are (in the terminology of the federal National Register of Historic Places) "intrusions," or "noncontributing" elements in historic areas. This way of categorizing the historic landscape informed the New Orleans Historic District Landmarks Commission's announcement that only 172 (1%), of 16,000 "historic" buildings in New Orleans were seriously damaged by the 2005 hurricanes and flood (Roberts 2006a). By "historic" the commission meant "significant" buildings standing in formally designated historic districts. At the same time, many similar buildings outside the thirteen official districts remain unprotected, despite their architectural similarity to their historic counterparts (Roberts 2006b). Many of these will be demolished without official notice or constraint.

We might call the buildings-as-resources stance the "Confederacy of Dunces" approach, after one of the best-known novels about New Orleans (Toole 1980). John Kennedy Toole's comic novel sets its hapless protagonist Ignatius J. Reilly on a collision course with the kinds of outrageous New Orleans personalities, landmarks, and institutions that a tourist might know or associate with the city. Collectively, these encounters strike the reader as a collection of idiosyncrasies rather than as an integrated portrait, comic or otherwise, of the city.

Similarly, the resource approach to history creates a postcard view of a city defined by its exceptional or idiosyncratic structures. This caricature is, at the same time, a generic historicized landscape whose styles of renovation, landscaping, and street signs, types and mix of businesses, and often race and class of residents and visitors identify it to outsiders as a "heritage" site worth visiting (Judd and Fainstein 1999, 12–13).

## Architectural Ecology

There is another way, however, one we might call the "Moviegoer" approach. Again, I borrow the name, this time from Walker Percy's renowned New Orleans novel, which is still one of the best portraits of the city's white elite (Percy 1961). Percy's narrator Binx Bolling is as hapless as Toole's. Destined to a certain kind of career and to a mate designated by his elders, Binx undergoes a crisis of confidence and briefly tries to break away. At the conclusion of the novel his domineering aunt, disappointed at Binx's fecklessness, delivers a soliloquy about the gulf between "us" and "them," the responsible white elite and the undisciplined black majority. As the speech unfolds, the reader comes to understand how intricately entwined, how inseparable, and how similar "us" and "them" are, and indeed that "them" make "us" possible. In the same manner, as Bolling moves among his family's Garden District headquarters, his own residence in a Gentilly suburb, and the raw new development along

Lake Pontchartrain, Percy never allows us to forget the ways that these disparate districts (and the unnamed African American districts of the city) depend on one another.

Percy understood that a city is defined by relationships. The same is true of architecture. Each building's significance is defined by the presence of all the others. That is, the urban landscape is better seen as an ecology or economy of architecture, a system of relationships, than as a collection of resources. Let me illustrate the point using New Orleans's architecture of the first half of the nineteenth century, the era I know best. The twentieth- and twenty-first-century cities hang on the armature created in those antebellum decades and my story might easily continue unfolding unbroken to the present.

The relationships that define New Orleans's architectural ecology include "cultural" origins of the sort studied by anthropologists and folklorists and celebrated in museum exhibitions and tourist literature. For example, the shotgun houses and Creole cottages of New Orleans are varieties of house types that are widely distributed throughout the Caribbean basin. They were brought to the Gulf Coast in the late eighteenth and nineteenth centuries in the course of continual migrations among the French- and Spanish-speaking Caribbean islands and the North American mainland. The folklorist John Michael Vlach has called shotgun houses an "African architectural legacy," a New World synthesis of African, French, and indigenous ideas, while anthropologist Jay Edwards has added Spanish architecture to this mix (Vlach 1986; Edwards 1976–80, 1994).

In New Orleans, however, these house types quickly became surer indicators of social class than of race or ethnicity. They housed middling and lower-class urbanites of all racial categories. By the end of the nineteenth century, shotgun houses were popular choices for developers when they sought working-class custom. So while shotguns and Creole cottages can be found in many of the oldest neighborhoods of New Orleans, they are thickest on the ground in the poorer ones. Their occupants' richer neighbors were building other kinds of Euro-American urban houses less often identified with particular ethnicities (Edwards 1994).

Social and racial hierarchies determined the distribution of building types within the New Orleans system. Nineteenth-century New Orleans's ethnic and racial divisions had a clear spatial order. The so-called French Quarter *was* heavily Francophone. It was the location of most of the major French institutions, including the Roman Catholic cathedral, the St. Louis Hotel, which served as the French merchants' exchange and first-class hotel, and the French Opera. Land records collected by the Vieux Carré Survey show that property owners in the district were more likely to bequeath or sell their properties to other people with French surnames, even to people living in France, than they were to Anglo Americans in New Orleans. The upriver Faubourg

Sainte-Marie, on the other hand, became "the American Sector," the location of the St. Charles Hotel, which was the American first-class hotel and exchange, and Protestant churches. The downriver and "back" faubourgs such as Tremé and Marigny were dominated by free people of color and European and Latin American immigrants (Friends of the Cabildo 1971, vol. 4; Shenkel, Sauder, and Chatelain 1980, 27, 57). Between 1837 and 1852, New Orleans was divided along these lines into three separate municipalities to defuse ethnic rivalries.

Yet within these basic geographical divisions there were economic subdivisions. The downriver lake corner of the French Quarter and the adjacent faubourgs were already poor areas at the beginning of the nineteenth century. The residents of what is now Governor Nicholls Street were acknowledged by the city council in 1805 to be too poor collectively to pay the taxes levied for sidewalk building, while the Faubourg Marigny was dismissed as the "faubourg de la Pauvreté" in 1829 (New Orleans City Council 1805; Boze 1829). Yet the Francophone elite built their large houses along the Esplanade, the street that separated the Faubourg Marigny from the Vieux Carré, splitting the poorer neighborhoods.

In the second quarter of the nineteenth century the Anglophone elite began to build suburban villas uptown (upriver) of the growing American business district in the Faubourg Sainte-Marie. These upriver faubourgs, now known as the Garden District, were first incorporated as the City of Lafayette, then absorbed into the city of New Orleans when the three municipalities were collapsed once more into a single urban government. Between the villas and the Mississippi, near the stretch of riverfront where flatboats were broken up at the end of their journey and close to employment on the levee and in slaughterhouses, cotton presses, and iron works that lined the river, another faubourg of poverty formed, one occupied by Irish, Germans, and other immigrants. It became known as the Irish Channel.

Woven through this already complex landscape were the homes and workplaces of free and enslaved blacks. Many of them lived in and around the houses of white employers. Through seemingly minor techniques such as changes of elevation between sections of a house, the construction of blank walls facing the windows of adjacent houses, the careful placement of entries, and the enclosure of yards and working spaces, the architectural fabric was intricately adjusted to maintain customary social separations in very densely packed neighborhoods (Upton 1995). In the nineteenth-century uptown suburbs, the houses of well-off whites line the boulevards that follow the radiating lines of the old faubourg boundaries and the circumferential avenues that link them. A stroll through the center of one of the "superblocks" defined by these avenues still reveals a population that becomes poorer and blacker and houses that become smaller as one approaches the center (Lewis 2003, 50–51).

By the middle of the nineteenth century, New Orleans had attained the spatial structure on which the twentieth- and twenty-first-century city was built. The historic architectural landscape maps these racial, economic, and class divisions in the mixture of house types and the distribution of factories, churches and synagogues, and warehouses and commercial buildings.

In addition, of course, the architectural ecology was shaped by other urban patterns, including the ebb and flow of the New Orleans and national economies, real-estate development practices (speculative building of multiple houses and stores appeared in New Orleans early in the nineteenth century), craft organizations, municipal reform efforts, and, most of all, the refinement of technologies to restrain and drain the ever-present water. As early, passive systems such as earthen levees and open drainage canals were supplemented in the early twentieth century by sophisticated systems of open and below-ground drains attached to massive pumps, New Orleans's white residents dispersed through the backswamp and low grounds to build less densely and to sort themselves in less subtle but more definitive ways than they had in the nineteenth century.

One could multiply factors shaping the architectural ecology, but the point is clear: rather than separating buildings into individual examples, good, bad, or objectionable according to their formal or physical qualities, the entire corpus of buildings must be seen as a system of relationships. Even where social practices have undergone considerable changes, these have been accommodated by tweaking the landscape rather than by radically reconstructing it. Newly built areas of the city extended the system rather than redefining it, so the Garden District and Faubourg Marigny and the French Quarter must be understood in relationship to Gentilly and the Lower Ninth Ward and all the other regions of the city: somehow one has to hold them all in mind at once.

## INVISIBLE RELATIONSHIPS AND MEANINGS

A corollary of the "Moviegoer" or ecological view of architecture as a system of relationships is that the most significant architectural relationships are usually invisible. For example, the plans of houses—the relationships among their interior spaces—are as interdependent as the corpus of urban buildings as a whole. House types—the arrangements of spaces that appear in house after house in a particular time and place—are typically compromises between widespread patterns of domestic life and the idiosyncrasies of individual households. They fit neither perfectly, but they fit each well enough, with minor refinements, to make the effort of developing a new plan for each house unappealing. Minor adjustments and major remodels adapt individual houses to changing patterns over short and long periods of time.

The house also connects to its immediate surroundings. Nineteenth-

FIGURE 4.   Backbuildings and service courts, Julia Row, New Orleans. Each of
these 13 identical houses has a rear service ell that defines a courtyard cut off from the
street by a wall and from its neighbors by a blank rear wall. Dell Upton.

century New Orleans was a courtyard city. Relatively small Creole cottages as
well as large mansions fronted rear courtyards defined by perpendicular or
parallel service buildings and enclosing walls (Figure 4). They were small,
barely visible microcosms of the city. Owners often rented space in the courtyard to mixed groups of whites and blacks, slave and free, and to craftsmen.
It was possible for a fugitive or an escaped slave to evade detection for weeks
or months in the warren of courtyards that laced the old city. Even in the
smallest houses, however, porches or simply deep overhanging eaves drew the
sidewalk into domestic space, as on shotgun houses and some Creole cottages
(hence their nineteenth-century name "banquette," or sidewalk houses), while
encircling galleries or rear porches extended household space into the yard
(Figure 5). At the moment we know too little about New Orleans domestic
patterns in the past or the present to be able confidently to interpret the
meanings and uses of these spaces or to dictate spatial patterns in a rebuilt
New Orleans.

Invisible patterns extend beyond the individual household to the city as
a whole. The meaning of a shotgun house or a Lakeside ranch house to its
residents and neighbors rests on local knowledge of the alternative kinds of
houses and neighborhoods one might occupy and of who lives in them. Everyone in New Orleans understands the city's historic socioeconomic and political patterns (Thevenot 2005; Bowean 2005). They understand what "shrinking

FIGURE 5.    Late nineteenth-century shotgun houses, 1300–4 Chartres Street, New Orleans. Dell Upton.

the footprint" implies because they know whose neighborhoods are the toes (Dao 2006). They understand what the phrase "chocolate city" implies because they know how and by whom decisions about the city's form and social organization have always been made in the past, when Storyville was destroyed, when New Deal and postwar public housing was planned and sited, when the Riverfront Expressway was planned and abandoned, when desegregation was undertaken, when gentrification began to move into the Faubourg Marigny and Bywater (Baumbach and Borah 1981; Rogers 1993; Baker 1996; Lewis 2003; Pope 2006). They see familiar patterns coalescing in the debates over the allocation of resources and the location of temporary housing during recovery (Levy 2005; Moran, Bazile, and Boyd 2006).

## THE SPECIFICITY OF NEW ORLEANS

From the point of view not only of the artifactual qualities of historic buildings, but also of those aspects of New Orleans's life that insiders and outsiders both value, an understanding of the city's historic architectural ecology must be embedded in any reconstruction plans. Any scheme that fails to take into account the variety of the built environment, the specific processes by which it was built and used, and the invisible patterns of significance residents understand is doomed to failure.

So the many technocratic and professional solutions proposed so far by

FIGURE 6.   737 Touro Street, New Orleans, a narrow Creole cottage remodeled in recent years, is an example of the ways disparate architectural tastes create New Orleans urbanism without excessive uniformity. Dell Upton.

planners and civic leaders are destined to fail. Their generic quality, derived from contemporary fashions in urban-design theory, pales before the specificity of the city's historical geography. In particular, the racial and class structures that have shaped the city since its inception cannot be wished away simply by appealing to good will and an apocryphal common good.

Demands to "keep it historical" feed into the resource approach (Conty 2005; Elie 2006). This is most evident in the New Urbanist schemes that seduce many political, civic, and business leaders (MacCash 2005; Thomas 2005). They promise to promote an idealized communal life using formal codes based on visual and spatial relationships. These kinds of codes show no understanding of the invisible relationships and local meanings of New Orleans architecture. The Katrina cottage, a model house produced by New Urbanists at the Mississippi Renewal Forum in January 2006, is a good example of the strengths and weaknesses of the approach. The project is an admirable attempt to imagine high-quality, low-cost temporary housing, but it is wrapped in a faux-shotgun envelope, the result a "308 square-foot tribute to coastal Mississippi style." As in the resources model for assessing historic structures, the shotgun house stands for local "style" stripped of its particular history (AlSayyad 2001). The significance of shotgun houses in New Orleans and on the Gulf Coast lies in the specifics of where, when, and for whom they were built. Their simple presence means little—it is their place in the larger *mix* (as shopping-center managers call it) of local, regional, national, and international practices that is significant. To reproduce shotgun houses in great numbers seventy years after they lost their place in the local repertoire would create a picture-postcard New Orleans, not a living landscape.

## WHAT IS TO BE DONE?

New Orleans has been through disasters many times before, even if none approached Hurricane Katrina in scale. In the nineteenth century a series of levee breaks (locally known as crevasses) inundated the city. Macarty's Crevasse (1816), Sauvé's Crevasse (1849), and the Bonnet Carré Crevasse (1871) were the most dramatic, with water often remaining for months. The great Mississippi Valley flood of 1927 would have drowned New Orleans had someone not chosen to cut the levee and inundate farmers instead. In 1969 Hurricane Camille brought devastating floods.

Each time, New Orleanians have rebuilt their city, often with little or no outside aid. They did so piecemeal, as best they could, and the slow, individualized nature of reconstruction is responsible for the continuity in the built environment that is visible today. I say this not to argue against outside aid, for I believe that it is our national responsibility to provide massive aid adequate to the rebuilding task. It is to argue that to approach rebuilding on an economies-of-scale basis, with decisions based, like postwar urban renewal, on the greater convenience of large-scale building on a clean site, would be fatal for New Orleans's architectural ecology. It is important not only that residents have a strong say in the comprehensive plans, but that final, building-by-building decisions be as individual and as dispersed as possible. Within basic parameters of public health, allow individual homeowners to decide whether and how to rebuild, how much of it they want to do personally, and how long they are willing to take to do so (see Klein 2005; Donze 2006; Filosa 2006a, b). While the process will take longer and while the results may not be the picturesque New Orleans tourists love, it will still be New Orleans, and it is more likely to be a New Orleans that citizens of the city can and want to live in.

CHAPTER 20

# Reconstructing New Orleans: A Progress Report

Jonathan Barnett and John Beckman

In early November 2005, the Urban Planning Committee of Mayor Nagin's Bring New Orleans Back Commission asked our firm, Wallace Roberts & Todd, LLC, to help develop a preliminary plan for the reconstruction of New Orleans. The resulting "Action Plan for New Orleans" was presented to the Mayor and the City Council of New Orleans on January 11, 2006 and to the Governor of Louisiana and the Louisiana Recovery Authority two days later. The next phase will be the production of a Recovery Plan that meets the requirements of the Federal Emergency Management Authority.

This next phase of planning needs to include city-wide strategies for repairing and operating heavily damaged infrastructure, replacing schools and other public buildings, and creating new citywide parks and transit systems, as outlined in the Bring New Orleans Back Commission Report. Citizens should participate in plans for every neighborhood in the city, probably organized by planning district, and coordinated with the city-wide plans. The public planning process has to be brought to New Orleans residents temporarily living elsewhere.

Hurricane Katrina struck New Orleans on August 29, 2005. Flood walls and levees failed in multiple locations the next day, which left much of the city uninhabitable, and then the rain from Hurricane Rita on September 23 and 24, 2006 overwhelmed temporary patches in the flood protection structures, reflooded areas that had been pumped dry, and made things worse in the large areas where the city was still inundated. This disaster has been much bigger than most people can imagine. An extensive coastal region of the United States has been devastated; two thirds of New Orleans's population is still unable to return home. President Bush made a strong statement of commitment in New Orleans on September 15, 2005:

> I also offer this pledge of the American people: throughout the area hit by the hurricane, we will do what it takes, we will stay as long as it takes, to help citizens rebuild their communities and their lives. And all who question the future of the Crescent City need to know there is no way to imagine America without New Orleans, and this great city will rise again.

It is essential that the U.S. government continue to honor this pledge, as the reconstruction of New Orleans and the recovery of the whole Gulf Coast region is dependent on aid from the federal government.

Our firm has a long history in New Orleans; we know the city well and have many friends there. We understand the terrible losses that people have suffered, and have been impressed by the ability of so many people to put aside their own pressing personal concerns to meet with us about the future of the city. The work of all the sub-committees and committees of the Bring New Orleans Back Commission has given us a strong basis for developing the Commission's planning proposals.

We have also been able to review the summaries and findings of the many conferences and meetings that were convened in New Orleans after the disaster by organizations such as the American Planning Association, the Brookings Institution, the United States Green Building Council, the National Trust for Historic Preservation, and the American Institute of Architects. Perhaps the most influential of these panels was organized by the Urban Land Institute (ULI), just before we started work. This panel addressed some of the major institutional issues that the city must resolve, such as the need to create a powerful development corporation to manage the work of reconstruction. The ULI panel also took on the most politically charged issue of all: where and when people could return to their homes. The ULI panel distinguished three location categories within the city: (1) the places that suffered wind and rain damage but were not flooded, where reconstruction could begin immediately; (2) the locations where the flooding was relatively shallow and did not go on for too long (in these places, the ULI claimed that recovery could proceed in accordance with area reconstruction plans); and (3) the vast, low-lying areas of the city, where the flooding was both deep and prolonged, and caused the worst damage. In these areas, the ULI panel recommended not going forward with reconstruction until the effects of the storm had been thoroughly studied and the future land needs of the city assessed.

When this triage map appeared on the front page of the New Orleans *Times-Picayune*, it seemed to confirm the worst fears of many. The parts of the city where damage was lightest included the downtown, the French Quarter, the Garden District, and Uptown. The most severe flooding had taken place in areas where the residents were predominantly African American, with the exception of the middle-class Lakeview neighborhood in the northwest corner of the city. East New Orleans, where middle-class African Americans were most concentrated, suffered some of the worst flooding. Many of the severely flooded neighborhoods were places that had large proportions of poor people. The map in the newspaper, plus the statements by some business leaders that New Orleans would have to accept being a smaller city in the future, looked to some like a conspiracy to exclude African Americans from the city, and—by eliminating several hundred thousand predominantly Democratic voters—swing Louisiana to the Republicans in state and national elections.

It was important for the ULI to address the location and priorities for reconstruction and bring it to the forefront of these discussions. Yet it was difficult for the ULI to deal with the full complexity of these issues during the week we were in New Orleans. We have come to some different conclusions, but have had a hard time disassociating ourselves from the Urban Land Institute's triage map, as people cannot always distinguish the official Bring New Orleans Back Commission plan from the ULI recommendations. We have also had to contend with statements from other experts that all or parts of New Orleans should never have been built because of its vulnerable location. But New Orleans is no more vulnerable than Rotterdam, Amsterdam, and other cities in the Rhine-Meuse Delta in the Netherlands. Part of the pump technology that protects those cities was originally developed to protect New Orleans. Although there are arguments to relocate New Orleans, most fail to provide a specific locale for the new city. It turns out to be very difficult to secure approval for a few thousand temporary Federal Emergency Management Agency trailers in the jurisdictions around New Orleans, much less for relocating the entire city.

It is understood, but easy to forget, that all the cities on the West Coast of the United States are at risk for a major earthquake. It is less well known that St. Louis, Boston, and Charleston, South Carolina, are also in zones where there are serious earthquake risks. East Coast U.S. cities are at risk for hurricanes as well. A hurricane striking New York City may not be likely, but it is a possibility. The official hurricane evacuation maps for New York City show that even a Category 1 hurricane could flood lower Manhattan, parts of East Harlem, and both Kennedy and LaGuardia Airports. The Holland and Brooklyn Battery Tunnels, all the major subway lines, and possibly the Amtrak and Long Island Railway tunnels could flood, as well as the Lincoln and Queens Midtown Tunnels. A direct hit by a Category 3 storm would produce a true disaster movie scenario, with 30-foot flood surges rolling up lower Manhattan and over Jamaica Bay and Kennedy Airport. All the tunnels would flood. One hopes that the mayor of New York City, faced with a possible direct hit from a hurricane, will have the political courage to evacuate the vulnerable areas of the city and close down the subways and rail and auto tunnels before the storm arrives. All New York City's utility services are underground and would be likely to flood. How long would it take to pump salt water from the tunnels and restore the electrical systems, heavily damaged by submersion in salt water? Windows in high-rise buildings on the sides facing the storm are likely to blow out. How long would it take to restore buildings and utilities? How would the city manage in the meantime? These questions give us a little perspective about what has happened to New Orleans.

In any case, we now know that what happened in August 2005 was not just an act of nature, but also the result of multiple failures in the New Orleans flood protection system. Investigations have shown that the flood walls along the canals failed, not because they were overwhelmed by a storm stronger than their capacity, but by forces that were well within the intended capacity of the walls, which are now reported to have been improperly designed and constructed. If not for these failures, flooding would have been minimal and it would have been short. The real disaster has been the deep water that remained over a long period of time in large areas of the city. Plate 16 documents the depth of floodwater in New Orleans. The red shadings indicate areas with more than six feet of floodwater. The brown shadings are areas with more than ten feet of floodwater. These conditions persisted for weeks until the breaches were closed and the pumps removed the water. Deep standing water, particularly if it is brackish, is far more destructive than a short immersion. Approximately one-half of all New Orleans households had over four feet of floodwater. Only the areas that are shaded in green had less than two feet of water. Even as little as two feet of water can destroy machinery and electrical systems.

Plate 17 shows the scope of the reconstruction problem in New Orleans by placing an outline of the flooded area of the City of New Orleans alone over an aerial photograph of the District of Columbia at the same scale. All of central Washington, including the White House and the U.S. Capitol, would have been under water for weeks. Much of the remainder of the District as well as large portions of the suburban metropolitan area in Maryland and northern Virginia would also have remained under deep water.

Figure 1 shows the diaspora of displaced New Orleans citizens across the United States. The size of the dots indicates the number of people. Those who have been displaced are not just in the south and the southeast, but in the four corners of the country creating deep personal and financial impacts for these citizens and for their hosts.

Estimates prepared by the RAND Corporation and local consultants GRC Associates indicate that out of the pre-Katrina New Orleans population of 485,000, close to 150,000 people had managed to return by January 2006. Estimates are that by September 2006, the start of the next school year, there may be approximately 181,000 people in the city. A September 2008 population of approximately 247,000 people is the best guess at present. These figures are based on national and international experience and estimates of the speed with which damaged homes can be repaired and made habitable. It is important to understand that the lack of housing is now the biggest constraint to people moving back. People who have jobs have trouble finding places to

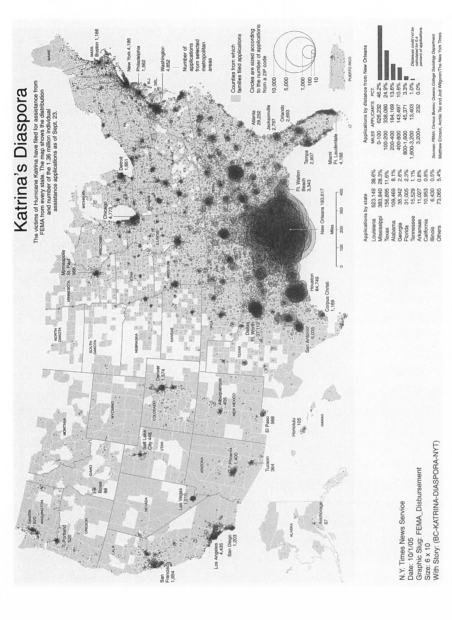

FIGURE 1. Katrina's diaspora, showing the distribution of the 1.36 million individual assistance applications to FEMA as of September 23, 2005. New York Times Graphics.

live. Employers with openings have trouble finding employees with a place to live close enough to permit them to accept the job.

## THE VISION

The Urban Planning Committee of the Bring New Orleans Back Commission gave much thought to developing a vision for a future New Orleans based on the best of its legacy and on not perpetuating the many inequities and functional problems that beset the city before the hurricane. This is the objective the Committee adopted:

> New Orleans will be a sustainable, environmentally safe, socially equitable community with a vibrant economy. Its neighborhoods will be planned with its citizens and connect to jobs and the region. Each will preserve and celebrate its heritage of culture, landscape, and architecture.

We did not consider rebuilding only as a way to replace what was damaged, but as an opportunity to create an even more livable and beautiful city—not just for people to return, but also to attract others from around the world to visit and live. It may be a long time before the city gets back to its former population, but planning for this is the only practical way to proceed. The people who talk about creating a consolidated city—that would be half the size, but much more efficient than it was before the storm—are being both defeatist and profoundly unfair. It is defeatist because the less damaged central area of the city needs the people who lived in the rest of the city in order to operate, and it is unfair to exclude the people whose homes were ruined because of the failures of the flood protection system.

## OUR APPROACH TO PLANNING

Our charge was literally to create order out of chaos. We needed to address the immediate problems of environmental safety and the provision of habitable houses. At the same time, we needed to create a comprehensive, citywide framework for a long-term sustainable city that could only be New Orleans. The solutions to each issue had to be direct, efficient, and equitable. They had to enhance citizens' quality of life and create opportunities for future evolution of the community toward achievement of its vision. All these tasks needed to be accomplished without ready access to most of the data we needed, as the local and regional planning agencies were operating with sharply reduced staff and resources, and some of the pre-Katrina data and maps appear to have been lost. To be effective we also had to produce a finished plan in the time frame that in a conventional planning process would be devoted to gathering preliminary information. We were fortunate to have had the support of the members of the Commission and its committees and subcommittees, who were able to fill in many of the gaps for us.

## A CITYWIDE FRAMEWORK FOR RECONSTRUCTION

There are three essential elements that are needed to support rebuilding all the neighborhoods in New Orleans. Obviously the first step is to secure the city against a repeat of the kind of flooding that followed Hurricane Katrina. The second has to do with making all parts of the city accessible so that every location is part of a desirable neighborhood. The third is planning for the parks and open space, which can do so much to attract returning and new citizens and make the city more sustainable. These three components support the most critical action, which is rebuilding each neighborhood with its necessary public facilities and services.

## FLOOD AND STORM WATER PROTECTION PLAN

New Orleans's location requires a specific approach in response to the characteristics of the enormous, but shrinking, Mississippi Delta, the subsiding soil, the raised elevation of the Mississippi River, and the high probability of future hurricanes. From the preliminary findings of various experts, we have put together what we hope will become a comprehensive system with multiple lines of defense to protect the city.

The first step, already in progress, is for the Corps of Engineers to rebuild the floodwalls that failed along the canals within the city so that they attain the level of safety they were already supposed to have had, the ability to withstand a Category 3 hurricane. This work needs to be complete before the next hurricane season begins.

As shown in Plate 19, the next step is to redesign the drainage canals so that they no longer bring storm surges into the heart of the city's neighborhoods. This means putting flood gates at the mouths of the canals so that they can be closed off during a storm event. The city's pump system also needs to be reinforced with pumps at the perimeter levees and floodwalls. During and after Katrina, pumps located in central areas where the edge of the city had been 100 years ago were trying to take water from Lake Pontchartrain that had broken through from the canals and pump it back into Lake Pontchartrain. All pumps must also have their own back-up generation capacity so that they can continue to work even if the power grid fails.

We also recommend closing and ultimately filling in the Mississippi Regional Gulf Outlet, a short-cut for shipping now seldom used, which turned out to be a short-cut for the storm surge to come into the center of New

Orleans. The Industrial Canal should be closed at the lakefront because commercial boat traffic does not need that access. We recommend also that the Industrial Canal locks be completed to provide another line of defense.

The dashed lines on the Plate 19 map show still another line of defense, a series of internal levees similar to the Dutch polder system. This provision has more to do with managing storm water than floods. New Orleans's frequent torrential rains create temporary floods, and the current pump system is not designed to handle them in all parts of the city. The internal levee system takes advantage of existing high ground, such as embankments and railroads that are elevated even as little as a foot or two above surrounding areas. These stretches of slightly higher ground can be used to form self-contained "cells" that can isolate storm water and permit it to be removed with pumping systems designed for each separate area.

These measures will protect New Orleans from all but the worst imaginable storms, and certainly would have been more than sufficient to protect New Orleans from the kinds of flood damage suffered as the result of Hurricanes Katrina and Rita.

Protection from flooding during Category 4 and 5 storms also requires a regional approach. A most important part of any such regional system is the restoration of coastal wetlands to reduce the effect of the storm surge in a big hurricane. Every 2.7 miles of coastal wetlands between the storm and inhabited areas is said to reduce the height of a storm surge by one foot. Before Katrina there was a plan for restoration of the wetlands along the Gulf Coast by 2050. Plate 18 illustrates the loss of wetlands predicted between 2000 and 2050 if such a plan were not implemented. We have outlined the greatest concentrations of predicted loss, shown by small red dots, and highlighted the city in the center of the map. The best estimate now is that 100% of the New Orleans area's projected 2050 wetland loss occurred in 2005. This is a sobering, perhaps terrifying, number.

Challenges so large require a superbly organized response. However, there have been multiple levee districts in the region, many of which have been criticized for being agents of political patronage rather than professional organizations. The Bring New Orleans Back Commission recommended creation of a single levee district and further recommended that the Corps of Engineers be responsible for implementing the restoration of the coastal wetlands and for funding, building, operating, and maintaining all regional levees and pumping systems. The Corps of Engineers has claimed that it would have been able to provide better flood protection for New Orleans, if it had not been for the intervention of the Levee Boards. The Louisiana legislature has now voted to create two levee boards, one for each bank of the Mississippi, which goes some way toward fulfilling the Commission recommendation. Consolidation of the levee boards is not the only issue, however. Actual flood protection responsibilities should belong to an independent entity, with oversight of the Corps of Engineers, responsible for the whole regional system along the Gulf Coast, and it should be led and staffed by qualified and experienced professionals.

The flood and storm water protection plan diagram (Plate 19) presents the city's lines of defense from flood and storm water, which can be implemented immediately while the larger regional protections are still in preparation. The thick lines show the major levees and flood walls. These are located along Lake Pontchartrain and the Mississippi River. Minor levees are shown in a thinner line, east of the Industrial Canal on both sides of the Intracoastal Waterway. The map shows the canal pumps relocated away from the center of the city to the lake. Moving the pumps to the lake and protecting them and the canals will provide a higher level of security not only from hurricanes, but also from the seasonal downpours that have caused flooding in New Orleans. The lines indicating the proposed "polder" system can also be seen on the map, as well as the protections for the Industrial Canal, and the measures to close the Mississippi River Gulf Outlet.

On December 15, 2005, President Bush promised New Orleans a levee protection upgrade to provide a levee system "better and stronger than ever before" that must be completed in 2007. But he made no commitment to a specific plan for how to accomplish this objective. Our plan brings together what the components of this upgrade should be.

A critical element of the reconstruction of New Orleans will be the release by the Federal Emergency Management Agency of maps that show the elevations individual buildings must attain to qualify for flood insurance. In the past, these elevations have been adjusted to take account of the city's levee and floodwall system. We are hoping that improvements to the existing flood protection system will be part of the considerations that FEMA gives to delineating the new floodplain maps. This process is closely held, however, and at the time this chapter is being written we do not know the outcome.

## TRANSIT AND TRANSPORTATION PLAN

Our transit and transportation plan creates a citywide, high speed light rail transit network that connects neighborhoods to other neighborhoods, to downtown, and to other employment centers. The vehicles can look as historic or modern as desired, but they will make fewer stops and move faster than the familiar New Orleans street cars, so the service can become more competitive with the automobile. We know from national experience that light rail creates value in downtown real estate and the neighborhoods where the light rail lines run and provides a catalyst for reconstruction and redevelopment. We also recommend a regional rail transportation system to link the city to the airport, and then on to Baton Rouge, and also eastward to the entire Gulf Coast, of which New Orleans can be considered to be the capital. In addition, when new arterial roads are planned or existing arterials reconstructed, we recommend that they be designed with the wide park space running down the center that is traditional in New Orleans and is called locally "neutral ground." This wide median system provides space for pedestrians, bicycles, and transit as well as landscaped park space.

The recommended system (Plate 20) incorporates many previous transportation plans and adds some new ones. The connection to the airport and Baton Rouge largely uses existing rail rights-of-way. The new rail lines running out through East New Orleans connect to Slidell along the lakefront, and out Chef Menteur Highway to the Mississippi Gulf Coast, where the train can connect with that state's proposed system. New Orleans needs to work with the states of Louisiana and Mississippi to plan for the commuter rail connections to the airport and Baton Rouge, Slidell, and then to the Gulf Coast.

Within the city, we recommend fifty-three new miles of light rail transit service. Many of these have been studied and proposed before. We combine and add to these to create a network where the station areas will support concentrations of activity and investment.

Immediate transportation priorities include repairing the existing streetcar lines and rolling stock and restoring bus service. The first phase design for the light rail lines needs to be done immediately, as well as more detailed plans for the rapid transit to the airport and Baton Rouge, because developed plan concepts can help implementation happen more quickly. Because of the disaster, the city now may have higher priority for federal matching grants. In addition to providing transit, there has to be a priority to repairing and improving the streets that transit will run on, and their associated drainage systems.

Not every light rail line can be built right away, so our plan provides for bus rapid transit service in the short term. This bus service, typically on exclusive rights-of-way that later will be used for rail transit, would operate more efficiently than traditional buses, reaching the lower end of the range of speed and efficiency possible with light rail. As the population returns, New Orleans can convert the highest-use bus rapid transit routes to fixed rail; we are proposing a phased transit system that brings high service everywhere upfront so that it can become the means for planning concentrations of population during the rebuilding process.

The New Orleans transit proposal is comparable to successful new light rail transit systems in other U.S. cities. Portland, Oregon, has created a famous prototype for a citywide light rail system that serves the existing population and also helps determine the location of new development and strengthen existing population centers. Denver, Colorado, which already has two light rail lines in operation, now has five new light rail and commuter lines approved for implementation. The system in Dallas, Texas, while only partly constructed, already has much higher than expected use with new lines in planning and construction to respond to their popularity and to help the city manage growth and development.

## PARKS AND OPEN SPACE PLAN

Our plan recommends providing parks and open space in every neighborhood. This may seem a simple goal, but it was not achieved in New Orleans before Katrina. The parks will be part of a citywide public and green infrastructure system that will serve multiple functions:

- Recreation and outdoor social space;
- Variety in the visual environment;
- Urban forest "services" including carbon sequestering and carbon dioxide conversion to oxygen, particulate capture, reduction of urban heat island effects, phyto-remediation of contaminated soils, wind amelioration, and habitat creation;
- Storm water management;
- Connections through a citywide network that serve movement, social, and habitat creation values.

As Plate 21 shows, the city already has a number of large parks, including Audubon Park, City Park, Pontchartrain, and Joe Brown. We recommend building on an additional asset unique to New Orleans: the Neutral Ground system. As noted earlier, these wide landscaped spaces run down the center of major streets, making connections between neighborhoods, and providing spaces that can be used as the right-of-way for transit as well as for neighborhood parks and storm water management. Wherever a major new street needs to be constructed or a damaged one reconstructed, comparable Neutral Grounds should be included in the design.

Canal rights-of-way should be incorporated into the park system as well. We have shown these as the large green lines on our map. A comprehensive flood protection plan will mean that these canals are now primarily for drainage into Lake Pontchartrain. Some canals can be put in box culverts, turning the space above the culvert into landscaped open space corridors. Other canals can become water features.

We have identified a number of areas, shown by dashed circles, within which future neighborhood planning is likely to be able to find locations for additional parks. The circles are large to indicate that we have not identified properties; those will be determined with citizen involvement in a process described later in this chapter. The new parks should perform many functions: creating new recreation and open spaces, reducing heat radiating from paved surfaces and rooftops, helping purify the air, and acting as part of the citywide storm water protection and management system.

A small portion of the Mississippi riverfront is accessible to the public now. The plan recommends that the riverfront walkway be extended along the Mississippi from the Industrial Canal to Jefferson Parish. In some places this can occur directly on the riverfront; in others, for example, where active port uses take place, it will need to be located on the closest available street or other place. The Trust for Public Land already has a proposal in planning for an approximately one-mile long extension upriver from the Riverwalk. By extending the Riverwalk for more of the City's frontage along the Mississippi, New Orleans can provide more connection among neighborhoods, enhance the value of adjacent land, and help give people a sense of their relation to the riverfront, which is hidden behind the levees.

## Rebuilding Neighborhoods Plan

Flood protection, transit, and parks provide the framework for the central task of the reconstruction plan: creating opportunities for every citizen to return and making New Orleans so attractive that newcomers will desire to move there. New Orleans has always been a city of neighborhoods, and most of the neighborhoods are made up of individual homes.

These houses vary from the grand mansions of the Garden District to tiny shotgun houses on narrow lots. Some houses are in historic districts, others look like more ordinary urban and suburban style houses. Many low-income families own their own homes; sometimes these houses have been in one family for generations and any mortgage was paid off long ago. The people who had hurricane insurance are finding that some of the insurance companies are claiming that the flooding was not covered. Few houses were covered by flood insurance, because owners relied on the levee system.

U.S. Representative Richard Baker (R) of Louisiana has introduced a bill that calls for a Louisiana Recovery Corporation (LRC), as distinct from the state Louisiana Recovery Authority (LRA). The proposed LRC could purchase property from people who wanted to sell, who would be paid compensation for the equity they have in their house, and, if they have a mortgage, have their entire loan obligation settled so that they can move to a different location in their neighborhood, move to a different neighborhood, or make a new life outside New Orleans. The LRC could then pay for cleaning up the land and provide the infrastructure improvements necessary for it to be redeveloped, facilitating the rebuilding of whole blocks and larger areas by contracts granted through a competitive bidding process. The LRC could also help finance rebuilding efforts by owners who want to stay in place.

Baker had originally hoped that his bill could pass the House and Senate and be sent to the President before Congress adjourned in December 2005, so that the LRC could be set up before the grace periods in mortgages started expiring six months after Katrina. The bill did not get to the floor of the House, however. Baker reintroduced the legislation in January 2006 and continues to make hopeful statements about passage, although the White House has let it be known that it opposes the bill.

The Governor of Louisiana is now proposing an alternative approach that would channel federal funds through a state agency and would focus more on reconstructing houses on site and less on buyouts. Without something like the Louisiana Recovery Commission, or a locally funded equivalent, New Orleans homeowners face excruciatingly difficult questions. If they rebuild their house using insurance money or their own resources, will their neighbors rebuild also? When will services be restored to their neighborhood? Should they write off their property and let the mortgage holder foreclose? If their property is their sole major asset, how and when can they realize its value?

As planners, we assume that something like the proposed Louisiana Recovery Corporation will be created somehow, if not by the federal government then by the state or the city. We believe that the federal government has a responsibility to the people of New Orleans because of the failures of the design and construction of the flood walls, which were a federal responsibility. Without federal funds to back up a recovery corporation, rebuilding New Orleans will take longer, and will impose terrible hardships on many families.

In any case, decisions about the recovery plans for New Orleans neighborhoods should include the people who live there, or used to live there. We have designed a planning process that tries to reach as many citizens as possible through public meetings in New Orleans and also in cities which have major concentrations of displaced New Orleans families. In this process planning teams would work on plans for fourteen districts of the city, following district boundaries drawn by the New Orleans Planning Commission.

All the planning teams are intended to follow a Neighborhood Center model. We are starting the process by postulating neighborhood populations between approximately 5,000 and 10,000 people. There should be enough people living at a sufficient density to permit the delivery of public infrastructure, services, and utilities in an efficient manner. The planners will follow the Bring New Orleans Back Commission Education Committee's proposal for rebuilding the public school system with relatively small, neighborhood-based schools: two K-8 public schools and a shared high school to serve a population of approximately 11,000 people. Other aspects of a full and satisfying daily life that need to be included in neighborhood plans are places of worship, access to convenience retail, health, community, and cultural facilities, parks and open space, accessibility to the rest of the city and region by transit, and contiguous relationship to other neighborhoods.

The illustration (Plate 22) showing the relationships among transit, parks, and public buildings such as schools might apply to many places in the city of New Orleans, places that need to be rebuilt dramatically, or that just need new houses to fill in the empty lots. It might be Lakeview, the Lower Ninth Ward, Central City, New Orleans East, or elsewhere.

The drawing shows a major street with a light rail transit line and a station. We know that access to transit generates investment; therefore we see a mixed use center with retail and other services for residents and transit riders around the stop. The neutral ground model is used, with the open space leading from the transit stop into the community, with mixed use commercial and higher density houses along it. There is a central park around which are located the community high school, public library, cultural and community center, and perhaps health facilities. Beyond are recreation fields which are jointly used by the high school and the community. Going farther, there is the opportunity for an environmental center and a wetland park, one of the neighborhood parks described earlier that also function to detain and manage storm water. Around these areas are existing houses, new houses, neighborhood greenways connecting the elementary school, and city parks, connecting to the citywide system. This is not a neighborhood in isolation; it is connected to the rest of the city in every way by transit, by open space, and by roads. The neighborhood plans need to be completed in a few months, not only to help people make decisions about their houses, but also to draw up definitive reconstruction costs that FEMA can submit to Congress in the next budget cycle.

Opportunities for neighborhood rebuilding throughout the city can be divided into Immediate Opportunity Areas, Neighborhood Planning Areas, and Infill Development Areas. Each has different characteristics.

### Immediate Opportunity Areas

Immediate opportunity areas are locations that suffered little or no flood damage. People have already moved back and started repair activities in these areas which include the downtown concentration of commercial, medical, residential, entertainment, cultural, and hospitality activities as well as educational and medical institutions. The planners for these areas need to work with the institutions to address their immediate needs so they can rehire their employees and return to a fully functioning role in the city's economy. Repair and construction in these areas can begin using current rules and regulations.

Plate 23 shows the Immediate Opportunity Areas with a yellow tone. They include the West Bank, large areas on the East Bank, and parts of New

Orleans East. In addition, we have indicated major educational institutions with dots. These include Dillard, Delgado, Loyola, Southern University, Tulane, the University of New Orleans, Xavier, and the medical center in downtown. We have outlined the downtown here because it had relatively little flood damage and is the economic powerhouse of the city and the region, poised for return.

## Neighborhood Planning Areas

Other neighborhoods contain properties that were deeply flooded and heavily damaged. Individual decision making in these areas will be more difficult. FEMA's revised Base Flood Elevation maps will likely have a significant effect on many residents' decisions. Because these maps are not now available, it would be irresponsible to guess their effect. Plate 24 shows that these Neighborhood Planning Areas are located throughout the city with the fourteen designated Planning Districts established by the New Orleans City Planning Commission. Because of differences in severity of damage, some planning districts will require more in-depth attention than others. Many neighborhoods had pre-Katrina plans that can serve as the basis for this effort. Some have already initiated post-Katrina efforts that also can facilitate completion of the neighborhood planning work.

## Infill Development Areas

The third type of neighborhood rebuilding area contains places that offer the opportunity for immediate infill development. They include land that is privately and publicly owned, blighted and adjudicated properties, brownfields, underutilized sites on high ground, or those requiring demolition and clearance. To take advantage of these opportunities to bring the city back quickly, the city will need to consolidate public and private ownership to create parcels of land that can accommodate urban development. We have identified Infill Development Areas in Plate 25. They vary in their characteristics from place to place. For example, there are areas of Algiers where there is relatively little development or underutilized land that could easily provide more housing for returning residents. They are on De Gaulle Drive, south and west of De Gaulle, and in Algiers Point.

On the east bank, there are areas appropriate for infill along the riverfront including Irish Channel and the Lower Garden District (upriver from the bridge), the downtown, and the Marigny and Bywater areas. There is a series of opportunities for construction of infill development to support returning residents located in a band going across the center of the city. In varying degrees, they contain blighted and adjudicated properties, public land, public housing authority property, and other areas of publicly owned land, all of which can become seeds around which new or revitalized communities can grow. The character of each will be determined through the neighborhood planning process described earlier. There is an unusual infill opportunity in the Almonaster corridor, an area not subject to deep or long flooding. This area is next to a proposed light rail corridor that helps create the opportunity for both residential and employment investment and growth. The Bring New Orleans Back Commission has already received unsolicited expressions of interest for this type of housing and jobs development in the area.

### Neighborhood Planning Process

The Plan recommended a neighborhood-based planning process to address the different rebuilding opportunities across the city over time, to level the playing field in terms of expertise and resources available to each neighborhood, and to mesh with the citywide coordination plan described below. Neighborhood planning teams will be assigned to each of the 70-plus self-identified neighborhoods, but grouped in clusters using the City Planning Commission's fourteen Neighborhood Planning Districts. Each neighborhood planning team will consist of neighborhood residents supported and led by experts in planning and urban design, historic preservation, mitigation, environmental health, public health, finance, and community outreach. The outreach plan describes a series of work sessions in the city as well as in other cities with large concentrations of residents who have not yet been able to return. These sessions will bring information to citizens, elicit their views and preferences, and work through a process that balances individual and neighborhood desires with public fiscal and physical realities. The teams will have administrative and technology support and include representatives of the City Planning Commission. The teams will be guided by the sustainable neighborhood center model described in the plan, an understanding of residents committed to return and the population numbers and density necessary to support equitable and efficient delivery of public facilities and services, structural and environmental safety, and neighborhood culture and history.

## CITYWIDE COORDINATION PLAN

Citywide coordination will hold the neighborhood planning efforts together and will lead to a draft Master Plan recommendation to the City Planning Commission. The citywide effort will include:

- Standard base maps with common data layers;
- Data file for common use including socioeconomic, physical, and policy elements;
- Information coordination and management;
- Flood protection and storm water management plan;

- Transit plans;
- Parks and open space plans;
- Interim citywide development guidelines leading to a focused update of the zoning ordinance
- Assistance structuring the Design Review Committee, its guidelines and procedures

The success of the neighborhood and citywide planning efforts will require people in New Orleans to put aside political differences and deeply felt grievances to present a unified list of funding requirements to the federal government. It will require the federal government to recognize responsibilities that derive both from its role as a national government and its failures in the specific task of protecting New Orleans from flood damage.

These are some of the implementation measures that need to be in place soon, if recovery plans are to succeed.

- There needs to be a Louisiana Recovery Authority as proposed by Congressman Baker, or a locally funded equivalent, to provide financial assistance to people who want to rebuild their homes, or to buy heavily flooded and damaged homes at 100% of their pre-Katrina market value, less insurance recovery proceeds.
- The neighborhood planning process needs to be completed and the reconstruction measures for infrastructure, transit, schools, and houses agreed upon in these plans need to be funded by Congress through the Federal Emergency Management Authority.
- The city must create a Recovery Corporation to manage and direct the reconstruction process.
- Individual priority projects in target development areas need to be started immediately to provide housing and jobs so people can come back.
- The light rail transit system needs to be given a funding priority in Washington and initial design on the most important routes, such as the connections to the airport, to the Ninth Ward, and to East New Orleans, should go forward as soon as possible.

Throughout this process New Orleans should remember the vision that informs the reconstruction process: creating a city that is environmentally, socially, and economically sustainable; building a city on the best of its legacy. Our vision and goal is and will remain to re-create a New Orleans that resumes its place as one of America's leading cities.

# CHAPTER 21

# Rebuilding the "Land of Dreams" with Music

## Nick Spitzer

In "Basin Street Blues," blues composer Spencer Williams wrote:

> Won't you come along with me, to the Mississippi?
> We'll take a boat to the land of dreams.
> Steamin' down the river, down to New Orleans.
> The band is there to me us,
> Old friends there to greet us.
> Now Basin St. that's the street
> Where all the dark and light folks meet
> Way down in New Orleans
> That's the land of dreams . . .

As music helped build New Orleans, helped give it a face and a feel, now it is necessary to rebuild the city. Only music—and related cultural expressions that conjoin New Orleans's deep history with its once vibrant neighborhood traditions of cuisine and carnival, jazz funerals and saints' shrines, costumery and vernacular architecture—can lead the city famous for its urban culture to a future that is not terribly different than what existed prior to the deluge. I mean "terribly different" in two ways: "very different," in the sense of a huge disconnect from the past; and a future that is literally "terrible" to all those who have valued New Orleans for the soulful creativity, diversity, and complexity of its cultural life as an American urban center of global distinction.

In antediluvian days, the city's cultural landscape was expressed in neighborhoods filled with identifiable forms like Creole cottages and shotgun houses in an array of variations; music from jazz and R & B to soul and funk—often within an African Caribbean framework of rhythm . . . and the sound Jelly Roll Morton called the "Spanish tinge"; and rituals and public celebrations from Mardi Gras to the "second line" parades of social aid and pleasure clubs. In all these ways and others, New Orleans is identified as a part of the Caribbean as much as a part of the American South. The historic and ongoing creolization of French-, Spanish-, African-, African Caribbean-, Native- and English-derived American cultures, has long set the city, south Louisiana, and the Gulf Coast apart from much of North America. The comingling of older cultural forms to create new expressions and identities that, while connecting with historical sources, are rarified and living examples of newly made Gulf South/American sensibilities, offers a model for better understanding similar, less explicit cultural processes in the nation as a whole. New Orleans offers a creolized counterpoint to "Americanization" as assimilation (Hirsch and Logsdon 1992) to a world where "black" and "white" are bounded entities. The city's in-between Creole legacy is an excellent starting point for reinterpreting the creation of diverse cultural communities in the United States not as atomized islands, but as part of a process of interrelationships.

Now post-hurricane, ensuing flood, and months of indeterminate reconstruction, a perilous passage continues for this tattered but worldly city-state of art and culture. New Orleans, with its African-Mediterranean cultural inheritance—never nearly so enamored with WASP variations on Puritanism and Calvinism as the South or the rest of America—is a place rare in our country, where the vernacular cultural and artistic expressions of communities have been central rather than marginal to civic identity and the economy.

In addition to the values of traditional cultures and the creation of a shared city/region cultural sensibility that transcends race and class in a manner more consistent with Latin-African-Caribbean societies than with the Anglo/African American South, New Orleans and the surround suffers from many problems associated with so-called Third World societies. It has an old colonial legacy of overseas capitalism and slavery, manifest today in a highly inequitable social order topped by a small, mostly white elite—one not given to dynamic leadership promoting social and economic growth or a fully realized sense of "public good." The city's large, poor, mostly black and Afro-Creole underclass faces huge problems of unemployment, nonliteracy, substance abuse, and, most of all, exclusion from social advancement. Some whites and Afro-Creoles (also known as Creoles of color), together with new, in-migrant professionals, make up a modest middle-class and slow-growing upper-class meritocracy, but historic patterns of "white flight" have, as in many American cities, drained New Orleans of this historically small center in this semi-feudalistic urban social order.

As much as one applauds the legacy of cultural creativity in New Orleans, one is saddened by a history of weak and corrupt governance, poor institutions (especially schools), a lackluster economic base (never terribly strong in the industrial sector to begin with), and a historic disregard for environmental concerns. In the latter realm, the coastal erosion, now made famous by allowing storm surge into populated areas, resulted in part from the very levee system meant to protect the city. The levees—many poorly engineered—have until now largely prevented urban flooding, while depriving the lowland marshes of silt needed to maintain the coastal elevation that afforded the city natural protection. In the past plantation mono-crop agriculture depleted local soils of the richness needed for more diverse cropping, and more recently the extractive processes of oil field production have often contaminated the landscape or sullied it with navigation canals and salt-water intrusion that furthered the coastal erosion process.

As one of America's old Southern port cities and cultural crossroads, New Orleans has long been a destination for visitors. Often as not, the city has been romanticized as a carefree refuge for those who come to indulge in carnival, cuisine, alcohol consumption, music clubs, festivals, and the visual delights of the city, all in a locally promoted "bon temps roulet" atmosphere. The 1926 Spencer Williams Tin Pan Alley song "Basin Street Blues" proclaimed New Orleans to be a "land of dreams" in which the visitor is enticed to come to a carefree place, enjoy the interplay of "dark and light folks," and spend a happy time among musicians and old friends. "Basin Street Blues" and the 1947's "Do You Know What It Means to Miss New Orleans?"—composed for the film *New Orleans* starring Louis Armstrong and Billie Holiday—are among the best known of the genre: sentimental confection about New Orleans by outside professional song writers. They appeal to a sensual image of personal renewal and play in an uninhibited social setting. Many such popular creations, even very romantic ones concerning New Orleans life, have largely been taken to heart by natives, who used or absconded with them—as local musicians have historically fed the same schmaltz right back to all those tourist and local audiences willing to listen.

In the near term after Katrina, however, the context changed. Even tired songs and halcyon imagery suddenly acquired a new and different emotional urgency and personal significance. There were fewer meetings of the "dark and light folks" or the related creative tensions and interminglings of the place. The "folks"—mostly the "dark" folks—were gone. The city was empty. Magnolia scents and sentiments of "Do You Know What It Means . . . ?" were overcome by other offal experiences. Even the birds were blown away. New Orleans—a town of music makers, big talkers, nightlife, and bon vivants—at least on the surface—was hauntingly silent, especially at night. Suddenly over 1.2 million evacuees had more complicated, nuanced and highly personal answers to "Do You Know What It Means to Miss New Orleans?"

The city's economic leaders and outside commentators like the *Washington Post*'s Joel Garreau immediately raised another question: How many of New Orleans's famed landmark cultural tourism "assets" were left? (2005) They sighed with collective optimism of a superficial sort that, after all, the high ground "sliver by the river"—including the French Quarter, Garden District, and Uptown—was largely intact, though battered and looted in places. What wasn't initially articulated or admitted was that the areas that flooded most—the lower areas of Mid-City and the Seventh, Eighth, and Ninth

Wards—were the very places that fostered many of the musicians, cooks, building artisans, and carnival celebrants revered by the city and the nation—not to mention the taxi drivers, plumbers, street sweepers, and repairmen who maintained and operated the place every day. The city's soul had drowned, while many public figures with limited cultural literacy in the vernaculars that make it great initially, at least, took a laissez-faire attitude toward the importance and fragility of local culture in holding the city together.

In the last decade, tourism, based on cultural and entertainment attractions, has increasingly eclipsed the oil industry in the New Orleans economy. In many studies, tourism is second only to shipping as the primary source of New Orleans business income. Though a "clean industry," tourism and other uses of the culture have not been an unlimited good. Many locals resent Hollywood film crews blocking the streets, tourists clogging favorite restaurants, or drunken revelers from less tolerant places misinterpreting the larger meanings of Mardi Gras. The service jobs that support tourism, it is often claimed, are not the kind on which to build economic equity. Still, if ever a city could argue for a cultural economy—from musicians and musical events to the building arts and a remarkably intact, historically connected landscape—it is New Orleans. The emotional attachment to and reverence for the city's culture and sense-of-place encouraged the outpouring of diverse personal support from around the world post-deluge. Such culture-based appeal also appears directly linked to an initial doubling of federal dollars for levee protection (November 2005), after initial recalcitrance by the White House and Congress. This early assurance was essential in bringing back those neighborhood-dwelling natives and locals that have come home. This process of initial federal reluctance followed by public outcry and then adjusted assistance levels or services has been repeated multiple times as the months passed into a new year.

In New Orleans many artists, musicians, and community leaders began slowly to search for ways to ensure that a cultural perspective was embedded in all planning decisions regarding housing, schools, governance, environmental protection, security, and the economy. Given the extreme romanticization of the city's history and culture by tourists and literary commentators, and by many Uptown and downtown neighborhood dwellers alike, there have been a variety of competing "authentic" pasts invoked in portrayals of what the future might be. Yet the argument one makes for such post-colonial societies in general, and for New Orleans in the opportune moment of post-catastrophe renewal, must be to find a shared vision of what could be called an "authentic future"—one that maintains aesthetic creativity and social continuity in both the material and intangible cultural landscapes, while rejecting the previous regime of regressive limitations associated with provincialism, racism, economic inequity, environmental lassitude, and so on.

If New Orleans is again to be a globally significant monument of living culture, local music, musicians, and related cultural expressions must be paramount in its restoration, re-inhabitation, and rebirth. The most prominent aspects of public culture that express New Orleanians' deepest sense of themselves and their communities writ large are found in music and celebratory occasions. Without these expressions and the individuals and intact neighborhoods central to their realization, it will be difficult for the city to find the continuity essential to family and community life, as well as the economic and social advancement of New Orleans as we have known it and might improve upon it.

At first consideration by an urban planner or social science professional, the thought that music and culture are key in bringing back a New Orleans that is recognizable and can progress in a variety of ways may seem like a nice idea—though perhaps window dressing for the real tasks at hand. After all, New Orleans has been stalled for months on slowly or inconclusively answered major questions of financing reconstruction of homes and levees, safe elevations for building and availability of insurance, reconnection of electricity and gas, reopening of schools and hospitals, and the return of restaurants and grocery stores. "Infrastructure" has been the mantra. But beneath that all-embracing term of repair and the possibility of a new level of facilities and logistical relationships—some suggest we'll have light rail, better schools, and effective governance—is this question: What is infrastructure and its concomitant, an improved economy, a means to, if not a better quality of life for all the citizenry? Indeed it would be hard to argue that native New Orleanians have stayed for so many generations, or that so many outsiders have come to reside here long term, because New Orleans had a great infrastructure in the past. Many places in America "do infrastructure" quite well. New Orleans—which in many neighborhoods offers a genteel rusty-bucket of pleasantly decaying facades at best, and in others a shockingly raw level of poverty often associated with places outside the United States—has never been one of them.

What New Orleans has done well—creating music and culture that have transformed the world, and remain globally beloved—was not orchestrated by local governance or the city's post-colonial social and economic power structure. To the contrary, the creation of distinct vernacular music, food, festival, and building arts—in arguably one of the world's greatest urban cultural landscapes—has remained resolutely based in family, neighborhood, and local communities. That demimonde has been dominated by Creoles and African Americans in complex cultural and social relations to ruling French, Spanish, and later Anglo-American elites as well as working-class immigrant Germans, Irish, Italians, and others. As is well known by now, it is largely that neighborhood culture—from Mid-City to Gentilly and adjacent parts of the Seventh Ward, the newer African American subdivisions of New Orleans East and the economically less powerful and (inappropriately) culturally dismissed Lower

Ninth Ward—that was largely under flood waters. In addition, other neighborhoods, if not as fully flooded—like the Tremé (near the French Quarter) and African American Central City—suffered from wind damage, loss of inhabitants and jobs, and restrictions on return to public housing in their vicinity.

These are the neighborhoods where many of New Orleans's best-known jazz musicians lived and from which they emerged: seminal figures including Jelly Roll Morton, Louis Armstrong, Sidney Bechet, and Kid Ory. They are the neighborhoods of today's brass band street parade "second line" tradition and the sequined-and-feathered Mardi Gras Indian tribes; of corner bars, barbershops, and beauty salons. They are intimate and inspiring places of family-run funeral homes and churches ranging from storefront to elegant, if faded, French Catholic nineteenth-century edifices to grand Baptist congregations. The house forms are many and varied: from the modest shotgun to raised Creole cottages covered with Victorian treatment to wooden camelbacks and stucco bungalows. Elaborate brick semi-suburban homes with yards guarded by pink cement Egyptianate dogs and Virgin Marys lie not far from ramshackle board-and-batten shacks. In the last two decades, these varied vernacular landscapes have been increasingly valued by locals and visitors, preservationists and architects alike, alongside the better-known places and edifices along the high ground.

The local and lateral social structure of life in these neighborhoods is based in history and culture. Their older, core areas were, after the Civil War, home to newly freed African American communities as well as the noted *gens de couleur libres* (free people of color), now known as "Afro-Creoles" or just "Creoles." These communities engendered social aid and pleasure clubs and benevolent societies, which became culturally and musically key, as will be discussed below.

The various people called "Creole" and the notion of cultural creolization—making a new social group and cultural expressions from the comingling of earlier discrete traditions, in this case African, European, and native American—is critical to arguing New Orleans's distinctiveness in the United States and its connection to Afro-Latin aspects of the Caribbean. The "Holy Trinity" of New Orleans music, architecture, and cuisine get mantra-like repetition because they are the best evidence of how cultural creolization embodies a type of creativity where traditions converge into newly transformed cultural wholes. In some ways, this is the story of New World and American culture in general. Underneath the excesses and commodification of our entertainment industry and those mass media productions not grounded in local culture, remains an underlying process of synthesizing eclectic community-based cultural vernaculars that has come to stand for both the *pluribus* and *unum* in our national psyche. New Orleans and its regional environs are the one place in

America where the notion of creolization as a kind of cultural simmering of many tastes—as opposed to a unidirectional assimilation—has the proper noun and adjective, "Creole," to back it up: Creole lady, Creole tomato, Creole language, Creole music—jazz. When arguments are made that New Orleans is the "Creole soul" in American life, the reference is in part to how the African and European minglings in this place have achieved unity in normative creative tension across lines of culture, color, and class in the city (Abrahams et al. 2006).

Many descriptions of New Orleans's specifically Creole cultural qualities focus on the Tremé neighborhood just north of the French Quarter and extending north and east across the Seventh Ward toward the Gentilly neighborhood. In these areas there are the highest concentrations of descendants of the antebellum *gens de couleur*. Many of their ancestors were freed under the eighteenth-century French Code noir and parallel Spanish Siete Partidas. This part of New Orleans is known for its craft workers and building tradesmen—plasterers, bricklayers, ironworkers, and fine carpenters. Its now evacuated middle and upper classes also formed a core of bankers, doctors, lawyers, and family businesses whose transformation into long-term exiles is so worrisome because of the stability and essential cultural influence they exert over community and civitas (Cass 2006). Creoles from these and related neighborhoods are also high in the political class, as surnames of the last four mayors of New Orleans—Morial, Barthelemy, Morial (son), and Nagin—attest. The Seventh Ward and related areas remain dominantly Catholic, with French and Spanish surnames—a few elders speak French or French Creole, something more common in prior generations.

As the promise of Reconstruction in nineteenth-century New Orleans was replaced by the encroaching Jim Crow South, downtown Afro-Creoles—having had traditional privileges and antebellum freedoms such as education in private and Catholic schools (some of the Creole elite went to France for schooling), access to the professions and skilled craft trades, and freedom of association—increasingly, to their great displeasure, found themselves considered, for official socially restrictive purposes, racially and culturally the same as the newly freed "African Americans." The famous *Plessey v. Ferguson* case revolved around a Creole-of-color man, Homeré Plessey, defending his right as a Creole descended from free people of color to ride in a "white-only" section of a train car—that is, not on the basis of discrimination against a person of African American descent.

African American and Creole communities formed social aid and pleasure clubs in the late nineteenth century to protect themselves socially and culturally. These associations helped guarantee medical and death benefits, collaborative home construction, and leisure time entertainments from picnics to carnival. Benevolent societies especially focused on providing insurance and appropriate funerals for members in an increasingly segregated society. Jazz emerged in New Orleans at the turn of the century combining parade music, spirituals, popular classics, ragtime, and blues. Many of the players were part of the same African American and Creole cultural groups participating in the social aid and pleasure clubs and their events. Jazz bands were employed for saints' day parades, sporting occasions, and Mardi Gras as well as jazz funerals—most relevant to the events of life and death that faced the culture then and now.

From this brief description, I hope it is apparent how much of the vernacular culture of New Orleans springs upward in a society that is hierarchical in a classic colonial sense—with a small, powerful elite at the top and large, mostly black and Creole poor and working class on the bottom. Until white flight of the late 1950s, '60s, and afterward, a substantial white working class—of Irish, Italian, and German immigrant backgrounds, mingled with descendents of French and Spanish populations—was also present in Orleans Parish. What New Orleans has long lacked is a large, stable middle class. Many whites who rose into the middle class have fled the city, while racism, a weak economy, and lack of leadership at the top of the social order prevented many blacks from moving up. The downtown Afro-Creoles—some with their own elite connections and legacies—often became a population in between poorer downtown blacks and wealthier uptown whites. From the Depression onward, the long-term departure of talented African Americans and Creoles to more progressive and prosperous places like urban Texas and California left behind a city famous for a high proportion of multi-generation families. This out-migration and brain drain among people of color, as well as white flight, hurt New Orleans in many of the usual indicators of economic and social success.

The continuing political implications of New Orleans's post-colonial structure are that governance and the economy have never served the lower end of the society and its culture(s). This has long been a double-edged sword. On one hand, economic isolation and the earlier depredations of slavery combined with religious (Catholic), linguistic (French), and geographic (coastal flood plain) isolation from the rest of the South and the United States helped to *maintain* the very cultural continuities in music and lifestyle later to be revered by many natives and visitors alike. The value and appeal of a place where music and street performance, visually compelling local landscapes, and a vibrant ritual-festival tradition were not part of a progressive plan for New Orleans—to the contrary. However, the creative traditions that now serve as primary symbols of the city to its dispersed residents, former visitors, and appreciators, as well as current residents, emerged over almost three hundred years of pain and pleasure in the polyglot port that was first Caribbean colonial outpost, then New World *metropole*, and for a time a leading American Southern city. New Orleans faded in stature after the Civil War (in antebellum times of surging sugar and cotton economies, it was the country's second largest port after New York). The Depression and postwar loss of population and energy added to a sense of decay as the city slipped behind Houston, Dallas, Austin, Nashville, Atlanta, and Miami, and even more so as the "Sunbelt" boomed in the 1970s and after.

Despite its strictures, the New Orleans colonial legacy also played a complex role in the city's cultural creativity wherein the vernacular "creative class" (Florida 2002) of New Orleans—its "piano professors," master chefs, decorative plasterers, original thinkers, and others—were effected by and reacted to the high culture aesthetics in their midst. Jazz—with its historic mix of high-minded and down-home sensibilities, its crossover of both opera house and stevedore songs, its continued place in both streets and clubs, its more recent ascension of ghetto-born talent to Julliard recognition, and, finally, its originality as an art form that changed how the world thought about Americans and themselves in terms of personal and group freedom—is the greatest expression of New Orleans's cultural creolization.

Jazz reveals a city that remains socially and economically segregated, but integrated through cultural sharing—some of it based in both geography and biology. In geographic terms, New Orleans is the most integrated American city by virtue of historic neighborhood proximity of servant classes and elites. The appearance of New Orleans's Creoles of color does not argue for biology (or race) as the equivalent in any way of a Creole culture, but suggests that such fluidity of society was possible in an Afro-Latin setting where the identifying lines of color and culture were often transcended or transgressed. The image of social courtship events like the quadroon ball, white males with white families having relationships with separate black female-led families in a *plaçage* relationship, and the emergence of an in-between caste of light-skinned Afro-Europeans was normative in New Orleans history.

One can go on at length about the cultural complexities here, and about how New Orleans offers a condensed model for less acknowledged cultural and social sharing in other American places and times. But the historical situation points to a city where the underclass majority in relationship to others made its own culture for its own consumption—and beyond—as jazz continued to evolve and define American popular music. If the music has long symbolized America's diversity and unity in creative freedom to the world, back home in New Orleans, jazz remained not unlike what some call a "folk" music, or in today's terms: a music socially grounded in community life. While professional musicians have become legendary—from Jelly Roll Morton to the Marsalis family in jazz, and from Fats Domino, Allen Toussaint, and Dr. John in parallel realms of rhythm & blues and early rock and roll—the cityscape has been dominated on nights and weekends by hundreds, if not thousands, of local players who were also, by weekday, plasterers and plumbers, bricklayers and tinsmiths, auto body shop repairmen and school teachers. As in professional sports, behind every star player there are teeming networks of local musicians who back social parades of the Lady Buckjumpers, Tremé Sport, or the Black Men of Labor.

The connection of traditional jazz to the city's building trades is particularly strong among Seventh Ward Creoles. Johnny St. Cyr, Louis Armstrong's banjo player in early bands, was a plasterer who returned to the trade when he tired of touring. St. Cyr supported the notion of jazz in New Orleans as a community-based music, far from the image of the singular, often inwardly focused player that emerged as the be-bop and cool eras of modern jazz took hold in New York and other nationally dominant cities. He asserted that it was New Orleans's skilled tradesmen, not its famous musical professionals, who made the best players:

> A jazz musician have to be a working class of man, out in the open all the time, healthy and strong. That's what's wrong today; these new guys haven't got the force . . . a working man have the power to play hot. Whiskey or no whiskey. (quoted in Lomax 1950)

While St. Cyr's comments were made in a mid-century look back to the 1920s and '30s, New Orleans's deepest musical traditions have remained inextricably tied to the material landscape and its builders. Creole pianist/singer Eddie Bo (Edwin Bocage), from a long line of family craftsmen in bricklaying and carpentry in the Algiers Point neighborhood, notes:

> I love (the craft work) as much as the music. . . . I love to stand back and look at what I've put together. . . . a couple of weeks ago I was in Mississippi and I had to rearrange part of the roof [after hurricane damage].

Likewise, many traditional building artisans see their work as musical. Sixth-generation Creole plasterer Earl Barthé, whose on-the-job musical tastes run from the opera *Carmen* to Muddy Waters's blues, describes his ornate work on cove mouldings, dentils, cornices, and medallions as "in tune" with one another. He speaks of "improvisation" in and "rhythm" of the work (Spitzer 2002, 123). The late Mardi Gras Indian chief Allison "Tootie" Montana, a lather, often told me of blending "speed and quality" in his trade, while one of his fellow workers described the musicality of Montana's work:

> You would watch these guys with total amazement to see how fast they could nail a nail. They formed a rhythm. It's like music being played. . . . He [Montana] knew how to turn the nail so the point is coming out. When he spit the

nail out and put it in his finger, the head [of the nail] is facing downward where he had to hit . . . He put one nail in each stud. . . . When he nailed it, he nailed it with a rhythm. The rhythm would go one nail. The next nail would create a song. In other words it went "bink-bank," "bink-bank," "bink-bank." You hear this sound and he is actually driving nails with this sound. They are making music. So amazing. (Vlach 2002, 45)

For his part, Tootsie Montana has suggested that he'd just as soon be known by his daily work as a lather as by the annual Mardi Gras costume and parading. In a city historically famous for its play and joie de vivre, one is continually struck by the work ethic in the building arts—an aesthetic of labor quality in an occupation that, like music, requires both collaboration and competition of its practitioners. For more on the relationships between music and the building trades, the New Orleans Museum of Art catalog *Raised to the Trade': Creole Building Arts of New Orleans* is an excellent starting point (Hankins and Maklansky 2002).

Clearly the building arts will be essential to New Orleans's recovery. Given the public symbolism attached to these trades and the huge need before the storm to repair much of the city's urban decay, what's now required is a WPA level of training for and building by a new generation of practitioners. The tangible aesthetics and results of the work are especially appealing, when so much that is familiar has been destroyed. The building crafts also offer the chance to train and employ a class of young workers who can continue to create and repair the city with some sense of cultural and occupational continuity, and the potential for ownership.

One painful irony of New Orleans before the catastrophe was that the patina of decay was often viewed as part of its charm: a lopsided set of quarters behind a raised nineteenth-century cottage in Faubourg Marigny; vines overtaking an unpainted shotgun house's roofline in the Ninth Ward; an Anglo-Southern central-hall neoclassical plantation home in the lower Garden District converted into a maze of apartments, each with its own external wooden stairway, all trapped in a spiderweb of electric lines. Now with as much as 80% of the city in ruins, it is hard to romanticize the frailty of the built environment. Indeed the high-ground structures that were in decay pre-Katrina are suddenly prime candidates for renovation. The need is clear for new and renovated dwellings in New Orleans related in style to the cultural landscape as we have known it, using local craftsmen to create that connection. Housing is the link between neighborhood life, the aesthetics of the cityscape, and the building trades for which the city has been revered.

Although much remains unknown about what housing will be repaired, how buyouts will be financed, and various ways government and private sector developers and planners will create new housing, it seems fair here to advocate that New Orleans musicians and their families especially be given housing incentives to return to the city. Rather than detail the ways and means of incentives—better handled by specialists in that realm—let me provide personal narratives from among New Orleans's highly regarded performing artists, as to why music and musicians are so critical to the city's future.

In the confused days immediately after August 29, 2005, many New Orleanians only whispered their grim concern when Antoine "Fats" Domino remained unaccounted for. Domino, who'd lived his entire life—except when touring or in Las Vegas—in the Ninth Ward, grew up speaking Creole and English not far from the modernist yellow- and pink-trimmed house he had built in the early 1960s for his family of eight and six cars. The property was surrounded by a cast-iron fence in the form of a grape arbor. Domino, beloved by several generations of New Orleanians—black, white, rich, poor, old, young—is an icon of the city's grassroots culture and music. His elaborate compound in a poor neighborhood was a sort of African American equivalent of Graceland built from sales of over 110 million records. Until Katrina, Fats lived in an older, elaborately renovated yellow and black double shotgun house (adjacent to the family dwelling), complete with his initials over the doorways and adorned with "Fats Domino Publishing" in neon. When Domino, his family, and entourage were rescued from a second-floor balcony four days after the collapse of the nearby Industrial Canal, many had an early glimmer of hope that New Orleans itself could survive. Months later, television cameras would document the removal of a moldy, warped piano from the house to be part of a museum exhibit. Domino, a notoriously shy man who avoids interviews, could only smile benignly at the sight of his wrecked home and, with a modest grin, say, "I think things gonna get better." Many New Orleanians hung on to and repeated these sentiments from Fats.

Domino's friend and fellow musician Allen Toussaint, the urbane producer, songwriter, and pianist, took an active and articulate role as a symbol of concern about the city's future from the beginning. As the city flooded, Toussaint managed to get out on a commandeered school bus to Baton Rouge and then, after sleeping overnight in the airport, flew to be with colleagues in New York City. Barely two weeks after the deluge, he offered me his critical perspective on the multiple roles of a noted musician and music in bringing the city back.

> I have a bi-level house, a top floor and a bottom floor, nothing was on the top floor but a bed, I just sleep there, but the bottom floor of my house had seven to eight feet of water, so everything in my room where I do my editing and writing and arranging and all of the musical things that I do. It's all gone.
>
> It's my piano room because my Steinway is the most important thing there and everything that surrounds it, like synthesizers, recording equipment and all

of my records and arrangements and things that I am working on now and things that I put in archives in that room, it's all gone, sorry to say. *But, the spirit didn't drown.* (Spitzer emphasis)

I think that I care more about the city than my own personal material losses and I really, really ideally feel that way when I saw such devastation and places that used to be in a certain position and they are no longer there, total rubbish. . . . My most personal possession is life and health, and maybe a running close second, my family and friends and those things seem to be fine and I mean because we are alive and well. But, as for my personal losses, I have thought about those things for a moment, but I immediately begin thinking how exciting it is going to be to rebuild, replace, it's going to be great looking forward in fact. And I am so glad that I was in New Orleans to witness this great event.

Toussaint was among the first to articulate a fundamental reality for musicians. If they survived, they could continue to play, create, and teach music—they could serve as guides to imagining a future for the city even in its darkest days. One of Toussaint's songs from 1970, "Yes We Can Can," an optimistic paean to collective action and the essential soul required to carry it out, was re-recorded as the lead track for *Our New Orleans: A Benefit Album* on Nonesuch Records with proceeds going to Habitat for Humanity. After its release in December 2005, the muscular, funky song pounded insistently out of radios in New Orleans tuned to a wide range of station formats as a kind of "can do" soundtrack for recovery. Some of the lyrics are

Now is the time for all good men to get together with one another,
Iron out their problems and iron out their quarrels, and try to live as brothers.
And try to find peace within without steppin' on one another,
And do respect the women of the world. Just remember we all had mothers.

Chorus: Make this land be a better land, than the world in which we live.

And help each man be a better man by the kindness that you give
And I know we can make it.

Chorus: I know that we can.

I know darn well we can work it out.

Chorus: Oh yes we can, I know we can can. Yes we can can. Why can't we, if we want it? Yes we can can. . . .

Great gosh almighty yes we can, I know we can can. (Allen Toussaint, Screen Gems/EMI Music Ltd)

Toussaint's all-embracing message, plus his new visibility and renewed voice, is one of many "silver linings" of the catastrophe: New Orleanians and the public in general have turned to such enduring performers (and music styles) for a sense of continuity from the past to the otherwise disconnected present. This has encouraged many residents to return or imagine a time when they could do so. Toussaint for his part also recorded a darkly luminous minor-key version of his mentor Professor Longhair's well-known song "Tipitina"—beloved because of how it enfolds or creolizes classical, jazz, rhythm & blues, and soul within one tune. Called "Tipitina and Me," Toussaint's new minor version evokes the atmospheric nineteenth-century classicism of New Orleans's and America's first great composer-performer, the (white) French Creole Louis Moreau Gottschalk. "Tipitina and Me," also on the *Our New Orleans* CD, serves at once as a mourning but hopeful soundtrack for the city—just the sort of symbolic resolution needed from the hands of a master pianist who delivers such ornate delicacies with ease alongside the baseline funkiness of "Yes We Can Can."

The revival of noted musicians' careers is one of the many unexpected good effects of the new focus on New Orleans culture. As Creole jazz banjo-man Don Vappie told me eight months after the flood, "Music that seems familiar from the New Orleans we knew, allows us to imagine we are connected to it, even now as things have changed. The musicians coming back here make us feel like things will be alright. They keep us going."

Given the environment of a major river, lakes, a swamp basin, bayous, flotant marshes, and the Gulf Coast, water has long been a theme in New Orleans and south Louisiana music. Most obvious are the sacred evocations of going "Down by the Riverside" in jazz hymns, and the encouragement to "Wade in the Water" from the broader gospel tradition where water is part of baptism, rebirth, and salvation. On the secular side of music in the city, rain or flooding is often depicted as an extension of tears or overwhelming human emotions. A song like the "swamp pop" hit by Slim Harpo has the remarkable title "Rainin' in My Heart" (1960), while years earlier the Algiers Point New Orleans native known as Memphis Minnie played on her husband Joe McCoy's blues narrative "When the Levee Breaks" (1928).

Water is essential to south Louisiana cultural life as lived by levees, canals, and bayous, in raised cottages and (now rarely) on houseboats. The area was settled originally by the water, built into a trading center because of water (the Mississippi River and port), and became America's largest, most diverse producer of seafood because of its varied water environs (inland fresh, brackish marshes, and salt water of the Gulf) that produce catfish, *sac-a-lait*, crawfish, shrimp, oysters, redfish, red snapper, and more. The final irony in all this is that the very flooding that occurred in pre-levee days not only built up the natural coastline against storms, it created fertile soil ideal for crops ranging from sugar cane to rice grown in flooded paddies, as well as the fecund marshes that support much of the seafood. Flooding, siltation, life, and deathly destruction are inextricably wrapped up in the ecosystem. As such, existence on the floodplain of lower Louisiana and the Mississippi Delta to the north has produced its share of fatalistic songs in blues, jazz, and soul. One could argue that this is a matter of coping with the anxiety of living in such an unstable and low lying area of swamps, marshes, bayous and coasts.

Among the recent events, the experiences and music of the "Soul Queen of New Orleans," Irma Thomas, are exemplary of both the fatalism and the resiliency of New Orleans natives. Her New Orleans East home was flooded and needs rebuilding. Thomas's Mid-City nightclub, The Lion's Den, had over six feet of water and will not reopen. Thomas, who evacuated upriver near Baton Rouge to a relative's home in Gonzalez, Louisiana, spoke with me two weeks after the flood:

> Irma Thomas: It looks like storms have been a part of my life because [1969 Hurricane] Camille made me move to California and Katrina has me moving to Gonzales; but Gonzales is a little closer than California and I don't think that I'll be staying away as long as I stayed in California. This time I'll be able to go back and forth between New Orleans and Gonzales.

> NS: One of your most famous songs is a song about the weather, "It's Raining"—a song you've sung so many times over the years. How does it sound to you when you hear it now?

> IT: Oh, it has a lot more meaning now . . . but you know, "It's Raining" was a love song and it's still going to be a love song as far as I am concerned. It is a love song for New Orleans.

"It's Raining," written by Allen Toussaint, presents a woman alone in her house in a rainstorm, wishing to be with her lover. It has the mordent sadness of so many south Louisiana blues and soul songs. Now, like many familiar pieces of music, it has been symbolically elevated to stand for more than just the couple's relationship. It expresses a longing appropriate to enforced separation from New Orleans, its community and cultural traditions.

Thomas for her part is also "riding a wave" of newfound success. Always popular with old soul fans and a heroine to mothers in the city (for years she did a Mother's Day show in Audubon Park for a strongly female audience as large and enthusiastic as it was diverse as to race and class), she rarely sang blues. Like many urbane artists of her generation, Thomas considered blues old-fashioned and perhaps with associations of a depressed Old South in the life of African Americans. Yet when asked to do a classic blues—Bessie Smith's 1927 composition "Backwater Blues," written in response to massive flooding that year in the Mississippi Valley (flooding that led in part to building the current levee system)—Thomas took a leap to bring new life to the old genre:

> "Backwater Blues" is so poignant, there is a line in there that said that "It thundered and lightening and the winds began to blow," and you repeat that line. The next line, it says "and there's thousands of people that has no place to go." I am one of them. But, I do have a place to go. I can go back to New Orleans when it's rebuilt. And I will.

The aural evidence of a performer leaping genres, shifting style, reaching for something historic and relevant, and having success doing it (Thomas was featured singing the song on *Our New Orleans*, at the Madison Square Garden hurricane relief concert "Big Apple to the Big Easy," and backing up Allen Toussaint singing "Yes We Can Can" on the 2006 Grammy Awards), offered a sense to her many fans that this current hurt could be contained and transcended.

As much as the heroes of New Orleans rhythm & blues, soul, and funk mean to the city, the most powerful musical symbols on the ground are those associated with "second lines," the neighborhood parades devoted to dance, entertainment, and display occasions, as well as with the more solemn jazz funerals. The second lines gather and articulate the people from within and beyond a neighborhood in the streets. They mirror the grassroots governance, social action, and economy that are essential to organization in the black and Creole neighborhoods. Writer Ralph Ellison once suggested that, in lieu of official structures for African Americans to fully achieve freedom in the polity, the creation of jazz and the collective and individual freedoms it suggests make the intangible art form as powerful as the Constitution and Bill of Rights (2002).

The second line is the political freedom document writ small—to the level of the neighborhood. It's the place to see and be seen, to meet friends and rivals, to claim a right to the street as public space, and to articulate the neighborhood space and relationships by moving with the locally produced music and the musicians who make it—who are in turn sponsored by community organizations. The primary argument of this essay, that music is necessary to bring New Orleans back with cultural continuity, hinges on the second line as a social and artistic performance and demonstration of the polity from inside out, from the emotions of home, family, and friends conjoined to the expression and life of the neighborhood. The second line is the public artistic statement of the neighborhood—the largest organic social unit of community and of political life in the city.

Unlike "Basin Street Blues" or "Do You Know What It Means to Miss New Orleans?" the music of the second line arises from within neighborhoods, commenting on them directly, rather than as pop music originating in the mass media or among professional songwriters and used mainly in settings. Paraphrasing the anthropologist Clifford Geertz's now classic formulation about the power of ritual and festival performances, the second line is a "story" the members of New Orleans neighborhoods tell about themselves to themselves (1973).

By bringing people back into the city for events, and into the streets, the second lines driven by music are also the building blocks for the annual Mardi Gras with its proliferation of parades. This is also true of the New Orleans Jazz and Heritage Festival—the official commercial celebration of New Orleans vernacular culture—where a purposeful appeal is made nationally and beyond to have visitors "join the parade," particularly in this moment of potential reemergence for the city as a center for art and performance. The success of the 2006 Jazzfest has been heralded widely as a key to culture and community restoration efforts.

At the second line, the individualism of musical and parade leaders and the collective of the dancing throng that follows, struts, steps, competes, dances, drinks, and sings, embodies the creative tension, and the mix of order and chaos, in New Orleans society. This is music, in the words of one recent writer, that is not just "about" New Orleans; it is "constitutive of" New Orleans (Sakakeeny 2006). Gregory Davis, trumpeter and leader of the Dirty Dozen Brass Band, elder statesmen of the brass jazz sound that was revived in the city in the 1970s, spoke fervently in September 2005 of his desire to return to New Orleans and join a second line as player and marcher:

> I hope that it's a regular, a real down-home second line with one of the . . . whichever social and pleasure club has the ability to form, to re-form and get it together. I hope that's the real one that I see. I don't want to see the one where it's the politicians and we are cutting the ribbon and it's for the cameras and "Hey, look! New Orleans is back!" To me, I can see that as being some kind of television commercial kind of thing. I want to see a second line with the guys sweating it out and just jumping in the street like they always do. I want to see the women in their big hats and their dress (I don't want to say "costume," but you know, "dress" whatever it is). That is what I want to see, with the sashes and the umbrellas. I want to see a real second line. I want to see the umbrellas that the guys make for themselves. I don't want to see one that comes out at some shop from the French Quarter. I want to see the guys. . . . One of the

Mardi Gras Indian Parades. I want to see that where they had time to sew their feathers and get the whole suit together.

When I go back I want to see the real thing . . . a second line with just that tension that exists from being in a crowd that is too crowded. You don't have enough room to move, everybody is jumping, but it's real peaceful. That is what I want to see.

Sadly there have been shootings and deaths at recent post-catastrophe second lines—an extension of the young male turf rivalries and gunplay that have so long hurt these neighborhoods. These occurrences, perhaps more than any other recent single act, have provoked fear and outrage as community members become wary that a new New Orleans cannot emerge in a city that remains hostage to street violence. In part the violence grows in reaction to a local hierarchy that ignores or, worse, denies better opportunities for African Americans. Regardless of cause, it raises the question whether New Orleans may not be worth the effort of return. For all these reasons, a joyous, safe second line is critical to the restoration of the city's population.

For its part, the Dirty Dozen Brass Band offered an ironic and humorous take off on the old minstrel routine in their performance of "Feet Don't Fail Me Now" on the *Our New Orleans* recording. This is quintessential second line party music for the deepest of street play and an ironic comment on the flesh in flight from and now in return to the 'hood, according to Davis and his bandmate, saxophonist Roger Lewis.

The most ritualized and emotionally powerful kind of second line parade is the jazz funeral, partly because a prominent community member's death and life are being both solemnized and celebrated. The jazz funeral has nineteenth-century roots in its New Orleans formulation, where uniformed bands lead by stoic grand marshals mixed hymns and dirges at a slow, respectful pace from the funeral home or church to the cemetery. Carried in a horse-pulled hearse, the body was (and is) attended to by immediate family, the band, and the somber celebrants. Once the cemetery is reached and the interment takes place, the band—which by now has gathered a crowd of curiosity seekers, neighborhood followers, and in the last fifty years, local culture mavens, media documentarians, and tourists—turns back toward town and follows the drummers' rhythmic transition to pick up the tempo from dirge to fast blues or breakdown. It is the balance in this moment, moving from dignity and mourning to joyous play and celebration, that so enthralls the participants and people of the larger world who have come feel the jazz funeral's emotional complexity. In formal terms, the funeral as a performance moves from structure to anti-structure, formality to celebration, and enfolds in a culturally Creole way the European funerary and parade traditions with a West African use of ecstatic music and dance to invoke the spirit world and celebrate the dead. It can also be pointed out that Christianity in the American South, especially, has long been an avenue for poor blacks and whites to express hope for salvation on "the other shore," or "Over in the Gloryland" (the name of a hymn)—the chance to sing "I'll Fly Away" to a better place than the current one where governance, the economy, and social order are stacked against you.

Lest one think that the jazz funeral as a sort of metaphor for New Orleans life moving from grieving to celebration and hope is a well-kept secret, President Bush's speechwriters made it a primary trope in his address to the national television cameras on an otherwise empty Jackson Square on September 15, 2005, invoking the emotional transition in a jazz funeral and promising to do "whatever it takes" to bring New Orleans back. Many Louisianians were dubious of the President and the federal government's level of commitment. Still, the community intelligentsia and musicians have been mindful of the metaphoric progression of the jazz funeral from death and grieving to celebration and rebirth for several generations. A local public discourse has arisen as to how the meaning of a jazz funeral applies to the rebirth of a city that was socially ailing long before the events of August 29, 2005.

For All Saints Day, November 1, 2005, a communal jazz funeral/second line was organized by community leaders to honor all the deceased as well as the death of the city as we knew it. The event was attended by those representatives of brass bands who could make it back to New Orleans. Shortly after, the young jazz composer and trumpeter Irvin Mayfield—a proponent of a new modernism in New Orleans jazz and, in terms of composition, an acolyte of Duke Ellington and Wynton Marsalis as much as the community-based parades in which he marched and played as a youth—premiered "All the Saints" with his New Orleans Jazz Orchestra. Commissioned by the Episcopal diocese, and held at the cathedral on Uptown's grand St. Charles Avenue, "All the Saints" attracted a new, intimate cross-section of neighborhood leaders from flooded, working-class, mostly black areas as well as white Uptown leaders in the arts, business, education, and politics. Mayfield's father was still missing two and a half months after the flood (the body was discovered drowned only days after the premiere), and Mayfield used the jazz funeral fully as a conceit in the work that included traditional New Orleans jazz with modern, cool orchestral jazz and the overtones of classical program music. "All the Saints" begins with a jazz funeral's mournful moments and ends an hour and a half later with an artfully constructed version of a second line.

> Irvin Mayfield: In the classical music realm, every great composer has a requiem. And, for New Orleans our requiem is a dirge from a jazz funeral. . . . I just needed that call that we all know in the city of New Orleans that means somebody has passed.

NS: Who's passed in this case?

IM: I think a lot of people passed. My father has passed. Our city, of what it used to be, The 9th Ward has passed. I think the leadership that we've had has definitely passed. I think us thinkin' that we're a great city but mediocre in our approach and our delivery has passed. I think, not appreciating our culture has passed.

In between are passages about the Mardi Gras Indians, street life, and the need for locals to metaphorically get to "higher ground" (the name of a musical section)—a personal, cultural, and political effort.

I was thinking to myself, we're in a 911 [emergency] situation right now. And it's time for the Mayor and for the Governor and especially for the citizens, we've all got to get to higher ground. If we don't do that, we're not going to be able to seize this opportunity. Because this is an opportunity. Is it a tragedy? Yes. But this is an opportunity for us to redefine ourselves and to really create a Mecca for culture and make a masterpiece, you know . . . like what Kenneth Clark says in his book, *What Makes a Masterpiece*—a masterpiece is many men thick. And I think that that's what I'm saying in that song, you know, "Got to get to higher ground," you know, "people of the city."

Myself, I hear a lot of people always saying, "What are we going to do? What's the Mayor gonna do? What's the Governor gonna do?" Now is the time for people to stop looking toward politicians. That it's time for the trumpet players to play the trumpets. It's time for the mayors to be the mayors. And we need to stop looking around for somebody else to do something.

Traditional jazz clarinetist Dr. Michael White, a chaired professor in the humanities at Xavier University of New Orleans—the only black Catholic university in the Western hemisphere, one positive result of the Latinate side of the city's post-colonial legacy—has focused his thinking about jazz funerals. He has played in them for years with his Original Liberty Street Jazz Band, studied them, and recently post-storm held a conference about their social and poetic impact. He did all this in the wake of his own precarious situation: losing thirty years of manuscripts, nearly forty rare musical instruments, his collection of recordings, original Jelly Roll Morton sheet music, rare photos of musicians and more at his home near the London Avenue Canal levee breech. After a long interlude in Houston where he helped evacuate his ailing mother and aunt—both primary musical influences in his life—White has centered himself by trying to teach and play on:

A large part of me was in that house. But I realized when I left that I still have the music and what all of these older musicians gave to me through the love and the spirit and beauty of the music is still there. And for that I feel very fortunate, because I'll take that with me wherever I go.

White had just completed a project the year before devoted to newly composed music in the style of traditional jazz, and had spent much time on the concept that New Orleans's departed musicians are, in the title of his CD, *Dancing in the Sky*. He echoed others' comments that this unprecedented event could spur great creativity—something that would help the broader local populace in the way that music as symbolic artistic work and play has always done.

> Well, you know one of the things that happened was of course I am definitely writing songs now. I wrote a song that has two parts to it. But the last part is . . . the first part is like an old dirge. And the second part, though, is a joyous uptempo song with the words "I'm gonna be there when New Orleans comes back home." That's what I'm looking for. That's what I'm thinking. We have to get back to New Orleans. We have to get our culture back and, start over. . . . That was just a little water. Jazz is much more powerful than that.

At White's packed early 2006 conference at Xavier University on jazz funerals, his band struck up an old hymn commonly heard in the street to the tune of "Red River Valley," but with these emblematic words sung by trumpet player Greg Stafford:

> We shall walk through the streets of the city
> Where our loved ones marched on before.
> We will meet on the banks of the river.
> There we'll meet to part ne'er more.

The lyrics more explicitly address the social power in crossing the familiar urban landscape of home than any other sacred song in the jazz funeral repertoire. They recall the past departed souls and saints while depicting the banks of the (Mississippi) river as the place of salvation—that symbolic, shared, natural space with its metaphoric healing and cleansing power. The hymn concludes with the promise of uniting with the lost soul of the departed beyond the earthly landscape.

It's the comforting vision of a believer in the sacredness of the music, where life passage, and the larger cultural envelope within which this ritual performance resides, by analogy suggests hope for the city as a whole . . . and hopefully not only in the hereafter, but soon on this flooded earth! As a counterpoint, the secular songs like "Back Water Blues," "It's Raining," and "Yes We Can Can" seek resolution to the pain of life in the here and now.

Taking their cue from the narrative structure of a jazz funeral in first honoring death then celebrating life, the Rebirth Brass Band also embodied a sense of tradition reborn as they emerged in the second generation to follow in the footsteps of the Dirty Dozen—while adding more soul, funk, and rap to the mix. Phillip Frazier is the tuba player and leader of Rebirth, now considered the model for yet another generation of even younger bands. He offers a concerned narrative about the place of music and culture in the city's return, and about New Orleans's role as the soul in American life:

> The brass bands is a part of New Orleans culture and if we stay out of New Orleans, how can we refurbish the culture, teach it to the next generation? All these other places are nice and stuff, but ain't nothing like New Orleans, it's unique, the music is unique, the people are unique. So I cannot abandon the people, I cannot abandon where I started at, so I am hoping that one day everything will settle down, that they get this levee straight. I mean, the city will come back to how it used to be . . . it may never be the same, but I will go back and try to be an ambassador and make sure that "Hey, we are going to keep this going" get the second lines back rolling, get it back rolling, it's just something that can't die. New Orleans is part of American culture. Without New Orleans, there is no America.

In the weeks just after this catastrophe—now widely regarded as the largest "natural"—I always add "cultural"—disaster in American history, several commentators suggested that New Orleans was a kind of new Pompeii: facing a trial by water rather than fire. Some network television news reporters with whom I was encamped in the media compound on the Canal St. neutral ground days after the floodwaters rose, had just returned from Iraq—noting the occasional gunfire and black-shirted security guards—and called the place a "wet Baghdad." The latter was a characterization I resented. Though there was some thuggish malfeasance on the part of a few of those left in the city, we learned soon after of the much larger bureaucratic malfeasance on the part of the Corps of Engineers whose levee design and maintenance was found so lacking—that, plus the slowness of FEMA's response to the disaster. Perhaps worse was the active refusal by the police force from the West Bank town of Gretna to allow the evacuation of nearly a thousand persons, mostly African Americans, over the main downtown bridge to escape life-threatening conditions in the Morial Convention Center. Warning shots were fired. All these actions or inactions left local citizens perceiving a kind of civic "original sin." They mourned their city's near-term demise and remain frustrated by the pace of its long-term recovery.

To these moral injuries of insensitivity, engineering neglect, and antisocial behavior, remains the backdrop of the Iraq war. No matter how one feels about its beginnings or current status, the view of a wide range of commentators in New Orleans is that the war weakened the ability of the United States government to provide men, materiel, and focus to the city in a timely way. The Iraq war looms still as a huge financial and moral drain on the ability to ensure security for this part of the "homeland." So it is that the bumper stickers have emerged here: "Rebuild New Orleans, Not Baghdad"; and the widely seen T-shirt: "Make Levees, Not War."

From the urban historians and futurists alike, we hope for a better metaphor for New Orleans's prospects than Pompeii. Another ancient city, Venice, on the Adriatic Sea, comes to mind. Both New Orleans and Venice are great cities of arts and culture that capture the world's imagination and surely deserve defense against the water of a flood plain or the daily tides. The fear is that, like Venice, now less lived in than visited, New Orleans will become mainly a tourist attraction for its most visible high culture monuments and high-ground neighborhoods, so losing the soulful aspect of its vernacular culture, much of it nurtured in "back-a-town" neighborhoods.

In this difficult passage, our citizenry are being asked to think expansively about the future at a time when some are still grieving loss of a family member or friend—many bodies will never be recovered. Many hundreds of thousands have lost homes, jobs, and a lifestyle embedded in a sense of place. Those who remain or have returned are being asked to rebuild new and better infrastructure, restart schools from the ground up, hold jobs, take care of our families and others, while planning to shrink and fortify the cityscape. It's a lot to ask of anyone. It's harder to ask when a break in cultural continuity has occurred.

New Orleans music—embodied in the sounds and sentiments of a jazz funeral and other second lines, found in soul, funk, rhythm & blues, and other styles—remains a "balm of Gilead" for residents at home or dispersed. The deep sound of New Orleans traditional jazz offers hope as the mourning ends and a new day begins.

There is no water line on this music . . . at once intangible and so powerful as a symbol. There is no water line on the spirit and soul of the city it represents.

If art forms and culture that are close to people's hearts are ever to be accepted as having the power to heal and remake a society by providing a new, shared understanding and intimacy between formerly contentious groups as to what the future can be, it is in New Orleans that this can happen. Music and shared culture provide the framework for a collectively self-authored social order. To be successful, it must account for continuity of tradition, improvisation, and creativity to a future grounded in, but not beholden to, the past.

Whether New Orleans offers the promise of a new, improved "Land of Dreams," a place where "Yes We Can Can" do better, a resurgently spiritual "Gloryland," or some combination of these secular and sacred visions, the city and America have everything to lose by not embracing the cultural links between past and future. The dirge is over . . . it's time to pick up the tempo, collaborate . . . and celebrate . . . as the jazz funeral hymn would have it, "Down by the Riverside."

> I'm gonna lay down my burdens down by the riverside
> I ain't gonna study war no more.
> I'm gonna lay down my sword and shield down by the riverside
> I ain't gonna study war no more.

All interviews with musicians, except where noted otherwise, were conducted between September 15 and December 15, 2005 as part of the *American Routes* (Public Radio International) *After the Storm* series of seven programs. Thanks to the artists quoted, but especially to Earl Barthé, Eddie Bo, and Michael White for their help in thinking this through. At the Penn Urban Institute and Penn Press, thanks to Peter Agree, Genie Birch, Amy Montgomery, and Susan Wachter for tolerating my difficulties writing in the midst of an unrecovered, distracting city that vacillates between frenetic frontier village and silent ghost town—depending upon time of day and neighborhood. Thanks also for support in presenting these ideas at a time when colleagues have been more valued than ever: Dan Ben-Amos and Mary Hufford at Penn; Bill Ferris at the University of North Carolina; Allen Tullos at Emory University's Institute of Liberal Arts; Judy McCulloh at the Society for Ethnomusicology; Robert O'Meally at Columbia University's Jazz Institute; Daniel Usner at Vanderbuilt University; Steve Siporin and Jeanie Thomas at Utah State University, where portions of this essay comprised the 2006 Fife Honor lecture; and two mentors and men of words about music and culture, Roger Abrahams at Penn and John Szwed at Yale.

# CHAPTER 22

# Walking to Wal-Mart: Planning for Mississippi and Beyond

Sandy Sorlien and Leland R. Speed

A scant six weeks after Katrina, at the behest of the Governor of Mississippi, two hundred urbanists led by architect-planner Andrés Duany convened for six days on the Gulf Coast for a massive planning charrette known as the Mississippi Renewal Forum.[1] One-hundred-twenty participants arrived from all over the country (and a few from Europe); about eighty more were locals. They produced an astounding amount of physical design work. They did more than just brainstorm about plans; they produced them. Their drafting tables and computer stations filled the ballroom of the hurricane-damaged Isle of Capri Hotel in Biloxi (Figure 1). They ate meals family-style with FEMA workers, construction crews, and Red Cross volunteers. They went out into eleven devastated communities and spoke with residents. They stayed up all night before their final presentations and delivered them with passion.

At the end, there was a foot-and-a-half-high stack of reports, codes, maps, renderings, and plans, addressing everything from the regional scale to the architectural scale, from short-term needs like immediate housing to long-term needs like new zoning codes. These tools were offered free of charge to the eleven cities of the coast for use in their rebuilding. They are using many of them now.

As the national team headed home on October 18 (many of us suspecting that we would return again and again) we walked through the Gulfport-Biloxi airport with one of the charrette organizers, John Norquist of the Congress for the New Urbanism. "OK," he said, "let's hold the next charrette in Detroit."

He hit that nail dead on. As devastated as the Mississippi Coast is, the boarded-up and crumbling downtowns do not look all that different from those of countless older American towns and cities reamed out by sixty years of the Long Hurricane of urban disinvestment. And so, the intelligent strategies for rebuilding after disaster found in this book can be applied elsewhere, in or out of the flood zones.

This is not to minimize the experience of our fellow citizens on the Gulf Coast. The hearts of the visiting planners were both broken and captured by their place, after only a week of getting to know it in its newly ravaged condition, and, eventually, in spoken and photographed memories. Mississippi has suffered hugely, and until recently has suffered out of the public eye. When

FIGURE 1.    Xavier Bishop, Mayor of Moss Point, Mississippi (right), works with
HOK's Steve Schukraft at the Mississippi Renewal Forum in Biloxi in October 2005.
Sandy Sorlien.

those of us from up north told our friends last fall that we were working on
post-Katrina planning in Mississippi, they said, "Oh, what's happening with
the Lower Ninth Ward?" As far as the rest of the nation was concerned, the
hurricane only hit New Orleans.

In fact, the eye of Katrina came through Bay St. Louis, Mississippi.
The blow was intense and catastrophic. The hurricane damage statistics from
Mississippi alone would qualify as the worst natural disaster ever to befall the
United States. In Bay St. Louis, Waveland, and Pass Christian, three-quarters
of the buildings were destroyed. The entire 80-mile stretch of the Mississippi
Gulf Coast was scoured by a vicious storm surge that reached 30 feet in some
areas. A FEMA official told us, "The shallow northern Gulf of Mexico is a
storm surge incubator and the Mississippi Coast is the target."

Six months later in Waveland, you could drive through an intact allée of
mature live oaks with nothing left but a dull plain of detritus as far as you
could see on either side. Waveland's main street, Coleman Avenue, was so
wiped out that a first-time visitor cannot even imagine what it might have
been like; there are no clues. Farther east, Biloxi's Point Cadet neighborhood
was also completely destroyed but with more evidence; houses had been reduced by Katrina to piles of sticks, or wrenched into the middle of the street;
the deck of the Bay Bridge had buckled and crumbled (Figure 2), and several

FIGURE 2.   The Biloxi-Ocean Springs Bridge carrying U.S. 90, October 2005.
Sandy Sorlien.

gargantuan casino barges had been heaved up over the beach and six-lane
Highway 90 into residential neighborhoods, crushing antebellum houses and
ancient live oaks. A resident of Pass Christian lamented, "Living on this coast,
you expect that sooner or later you will lose your house to a hurricane. But
you don't expect to lose your whole town. How do you get your arms around
that?"

There are coal towns in West Virginia, and steel towns in Pennsylvania,
and mill towns in New England, where the question of losing the town might
be posed, if only the loss had happened within hours instead of decades.

In Mississippi, it is particularly difficult to contemplate restoring a whole
town when the need for housing is so urgent. Six months after Katrina, 25%
of the state's Gulf Coast residents are living in dispiriting FEMA trailers. The
trailers are meant to be temporary, but experience shows this to be false; some
people in Florida are still living in FEMA-supplied mobile homes thirteen
years after Hurricane Andrew. This situation drove the Renewal Forum architects to design an alternative for immediate housing, the airy and practical
308-square-foot Katrina Cottage. "It's about the same size as the birthplace
of Elvis," claimed a local man quoted in the *Biloxi SunHerald*. Dignified,
permanent, stormworthy housing, the cottage is a far better solution than the
trailer. It can be installed on a homeowner's own lot while he rebuilds, and

later may become a backyard studio, mother-in-law suite, or rental unit (helping with the affordable housing supply), or simply grow to a larger house as the owner's resources recover.

However, for larger parcels it takes time for land acquisition, infrastructure development, permitting, and construction, usually done sequentially. It helps that Mississippi is rebuilding primarily where infrastructure already exists. On the other hand, the process is unusually slowed by delays establishing new flood elevations. Setting these elevations—below which new buildings would be ineligible for insurance or financing—can take as long as eighteen months. The Renewal Forum planners pushed FEMA hard to come out with advisory (unofficial) maps faster than it would have otherwise, but FEMA's explanations of the maps are inconsistent, and property owners understandably feel that they are in limbo. In many cases they will have to raise the house, adding significantly to construction costs.

The impasse is forcing much of the new development out of the cities and into unincorporated areas, which complicates the planning process. It makes it difficult for small developments, which might be quicker to deliver, to integrate into a regional pattern. Small developments need an existing neighborhood context, or a strong vision for regional form, to avoid becoming isolated single-use pods.

In spite of the challenges, the mood on the Coast quickly turned from despair to resolve, but six months later it is turning to panic. Though many areas are still piled with debris, the land is buildable because, unlike New Orleans, there was no lingering flood. Where neighborhoods once stood, the land is dry and the street structure intact. Property owners are chomping at the bit.

Out-of-territory developers are also chomping, and residents are concerned. What comes next, and in what form? What happens when buildings are erected in haste, or when temporary trailers become permanent fixtures, or when condo towers go up too quickly in the wrong place, or in the wrong form? How do planners reconcile immediate needs with long-term planning? How do they connect the building scale to the regional scale?

The answers, we believe, are the rural-to-urban Transect and new zoning and design codes based on it. Transects, first articulated in the late eighteenth century by biogeographer Alexander von Humboldt, are usually seen as continuous cross-sections of natural habitats for plants and animals, ranging (for example) from shores to wetlands to uplands. Species that thrive in one habitat would wither in another. Each habitat is home to a myriad life forms; no habitat is a monoculture.

The specific Transect that New Urbanist codes use is based on the human habitat, ranging from the wilderness to the urban core. It's divided into a range of six Transect Zones, each with its own complex character. None is a monoculture, unlike the conventional suburban development model based on separation of use. The Transect ensures that a community offers a full diversity of building types, thoroughfare types, and civic space types, and that each type strengthens the local character of the zone. The six T-Zones are T-1 Natural, T-2 Rural, T-3 Sub-Urban, T-4 General Urban, T-5 Urban Center, and T-6 Urban Core (Figure 3).

The simplest way to understand the Transect may be to note what is *not* appropriate for any given T-Zone, notwithstanding that the notion "appropriate" is out of fashion among some critics, for fear that it stifles creativity or freedom. But the forces behind sprawl are so powerful, and our default patterns of growth so damaging to the environment, that correctives must be firm. A highway does not belong in a city (T-4 to T-6); a condo tower does not belong in the country (T-2). A parking lot should not enfront a primary urban street. Residences should not be isolated from offices and stores. The poor should not live in segregated enclaves; neither should the rich.

These tenets were common sense and common practice in the first half of the twentieth century, but it has all been lost to separated-use Euclidean zoning, and to design focused on the private realm at the expense of the public. The pattern is self-perpetuating; when there is no public realm worth inhabiting, the private home must hold everything. When you cannot walk to the cinema, each home must have an entertainment center. The complicated many-gabled rooflines of suburban McMansions even mimic an entire village, in a sad paean to what is gone.

What is truly sad is that a traditional village pattern is illegal to build now in most juridictions. New Urbanists and other smart growth proponents want compact, mixed-use development to be legal, and even in areas without zoning codes, to be available and incentivized.

*Without zoning reform, most of our best-loved towns and neighborhoods, from New Orleans to Philadelphia, could not be built again.* In most of this country, with conventional zoning, you can choose to live in *old* walkable, mixed-use, mixed-income neighborhoods, or you can choose new autodependent single-use monocultural subdivisions. You cannot have *new* walkable, mixed-use, mixed-income neighborhoods.

The rural-to-urban Transect was not "invented," it exists. The New Urbanists have simply made it systematic for practical use in zoning and design. Even in America, much of the Transect remains, at least vestigially, in traditional cities, towns, and villages. Places once followed a transect of density and intensity from open country into the city. Civilization required agriculture (T-2) and centralized markets (T-5) with nearby dwellings and other businesses (T-3 and T-4). Now our Transect-based communities have dissolved into sprawl like melted snowballs.

The Transect can be seen from the air, most startlingly in the block

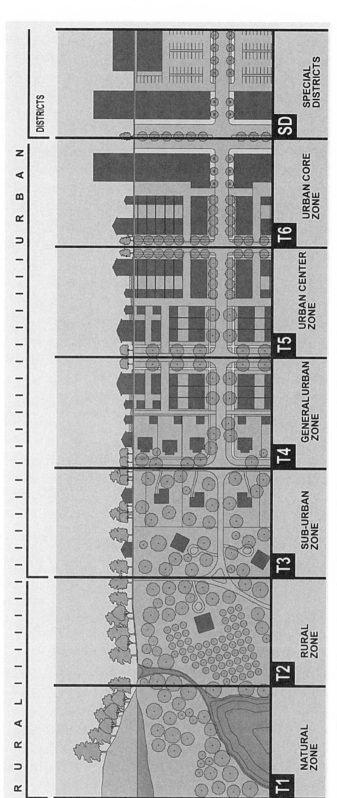

FIGURE 3. Diagram of the rural-to-urban Transect, the framework for the SmartCode and other Transect-based codes and initiatives. Duany Plater-Zyberk and Co.

structure of the ravaged Gulf Coast (Figures 4 and 5). It is this neighborhood structure that the people have said they want back. Repeatedly they have told us that if there was a silver lining to Katrina, it was that the storm took out much of the newer sprawl junk along the beach. "What we do now," said Governor Haley Barbour in October 2005, "will decide what the Coast will look like in ten years, twenty years, and beyond. We must seize this opportunity to do this right."

At the Renewal Forum just after Katrina, most of the 120 New Urbanists in the Isle's damaged ballroom had already worked with, or at least discussed, the Transect. When Andres Duany urged the team heads to consider coordinating all Mississippi plans with the Transect, it became the natural organizing principle for nearly everything produced at the charrette. If you leaf through the thick booklets of Forum plans, maps, and codes, and you will see "T-1" or "T-3" or "T-5" marked on everything from wetlands to thoroughfare types to individual frontages.

Gradually but efficiently, the seemingly intractable scope, multiple scales, and competing timelines of the post-disaster scenario connected into a coherent strategy. Like software into an operating system, zoning codes and other standards (ITE, LEED) may plug into the Transect. Transect-based analysis helps us identify the best parts of the damaged towns, their DNA. We then write prescriptive codes based on that analysis, enabling us to generate those healthy patterns once again.

One of these codes is a unified land use ordinance called the SmartCode, a free-of-charge product of Duany Plater-Zyberk & Co., the Miami-based town planning firm. The three-year-old document has captured the attention of nine of the eleven Mississippi coastal cities. As we write this, well-received SmartCode customization charrettes were just completed for Pass Christian and Gulfport, with others in the works.

The SmartCode folds zoning, subdivision regulations, urban design, and basic architectural standards into one compact document. It is considered a "form-based code" because it strongly addresses the physical form of building and development. Form-based codes oppose conventional Euclidean zoning codes that are based primarily on use and density. Euclidean codes have caused systemic problems over the past sixty years by separating uses, making mixed-use and walkable neighborhoods essentially illegal. The rebuilding of most of the Gulf Coast traditional neighborhoods would be impossible under their current codes, which are separated into Residential, Commercial, and Industrial, and sometimes further separated by building type or use. In the unincorporated coastal Mississippi counties, where there is no zoning, the problem is not that traditional neighborhood development would be illegal, but that sprawl, the default development pattern, is permitted and will con-

FIGURE 4. T-3 Sub-Urban Zone—aerial view of Mississippi Coast with block structure visible, October 11, 2005. Sandy Sorlien.

FIGURE 5. T-5 Urban Center Zone—aerial view of downtown Bay St. Louis, Mississippi, October 11, 2005. Sandy Sorlien.

tinue to gobble up land and require an automobile for every errand. To stop this pattern, a form-based zoning code must be legal and incentivized.

Most form-based codes are applied to the block and building scale only. It becomes very expensive to design a village or city at that scale, and the pattern of development is neither sustainable nor connected if it ignores the larger context of the neighborhood, city, and region. The SmartCode is the only current form-based code based on the Transect at all scales of planning. It also integrates the design protocols of a variety of specialties, including traffic engineering, public works, town planning, architecture, landscape architecture, and ecology.

The SmartCode is a model code, or template, meant to be locally customized by professional planners, architects, and attorneys in collaboration with local stakeholders during a charrette. The recent Gulfport SmartCode charrette was remarkable in that Mayor Brent Warr and City Councilman Brian Carriere were in the studio the entire five days, often with colored pencils in hand helping the designers mark the T-Zones citywide. All stakeholder meetings were open to the public.

The Katrina Cottage is an example of how the different scales of planning can connect. Such a cottage, placed on the lot according to the disposition requirements for its Transect Zone, may become the basis for a coherent block, part of a real neighborhood. A temporary FEMA trailer cannot. The cottage was designed from careful analysis of the housing types of the Gulf region, just as the Transect is used to analyze the neighborhood character, thoroughfare types, and building types of each region for code customizations. Using the Transect, there need not be any disconnect between immediate emergency housing and long-term planning.

Recovery of local character requires an understanding of both the vernacular architecture and the neighborhood patterns that the Transect supports and preserves. The two are related, of course. If a building tradition is stopped in its tracks, as only a force of nature or act of war can do, and we do not attempt to recover it, we guarantee that a living architecture dies. Surely then a revival seems hollow. Instead, New Urbanists support recognizing *living* traditions, letting them evolve with their time. The Renewal Forum included designers who have devoted years, even decades, to the study of the architecture and layout of Southern towns, and the plans show it.

This does not mean modernist buildings cannot work in traditional urbanism. The New Urbanism offers a substantial list of modernist projects, including Aqua in Miami, Prospect in Colorado, and a number of the houses in the renowned resort town of Seaside and its neighbor, Rosemary Beach, Florida. By the same token, there are plenty of examples of New Urbanist projects with mediocre traditional architecture deserving of criticism on the building scale. The most basic tenets of proportion and human scale are abused by designers of all creeds, to the detriment of all who must inhabit the public realm.

Because that is the case, and because so much of the Gulf Coast vernacular has been destroyed (including 350 buildings on the National Register of Historic Places in Mississippi alone) the Renewal Forum architects produced a pattern book with prescriptions and ideas for builders of traditional houses, called "A Pattern Book for Gulf Coast Neighborhoods." It is meant mostly for homeowner-builders; it's being distributed for free at Home Depot stores on the Coast. Modernists hate it, but pattern books are inherently traditional. They are meant to pass on typologies and techniques. They brought patterns from the Old World to the New as America was settled.

The Forum's pattern book, like others produced by Urban Design Associates of Pittsburgh, Pennsylvania, is keyed to the Transect. Some building types are more rural (T2–3) and some are more urban (T4–5). It is doubtful that most modernist styles can be correlated to the Transect without some redefinition, but it would be very interesting to see some movement in that direction.

Meanwhile, the Transect and its associated land use paradigm has taken hold along the Mississippi Coast. If there is anything that illustrates this shift in thinking, it is the unlikely collaboration now underway between the traditional town planning movement and the poster child of sprawl, Wal-Mart. As we write, it has been only two weeks since the Pass Christian Smart-Code customization charrette (February 15–19, 2006). But it appears that Wal-Mart is pursuing seriously the "Wal-Mart Village" ideas proposed by the Renewal Forum's Pass Christian team headed by New Urbanist planners Laura Hall and Lois Fisher.

The situation in Pass Christian was this. A conventional Wal-Mart within the city limits was destroyed along with most of the rest of the town's structures, including the historic town center about five miles from the Wal-Mart site. Wal-Mart provided 15% of the city's tax revenues, and residents depended on it for daily needs. Unlike other Wal-Marts in the region, it had a Gulf view which many shoppers told us they enjoyed, but just like other Wal-Marts the view included a sea of parking. The building was the typical ugly gray box with red and blue stripes. It was isolated from neighborhoods, its vast lot fronting high-speed Highway 90 and nothing else.

Wal-Mart's national Director of Architecture, Bill Correll, and three other Wal-Mart executives attended the SmartCode charrette. All of them stayed in the houses of Pass Christian residents, as did the charrette team. As plans for a walkable, mixed-use, Transect-based Wal-Mart Village were drawn up, Pass Christian residents declared that they wanted a neighborhood form (Figure 6), not the old conventional form. A mixed-use Wal-Mart Vil-

FIGURE 6.    Wal-Mart Village rendering done at the Pass Christian charrette in February 2006. This design allows Wal-Mart to keep its big box and surface parking format, while providing a T-4/T-5 mixed-use center and connections to existing neighborhoods. Eric S. Brown, Brown Design Studio LLC, and Dede Christopher.

lage cannot be built under the old zoning, so the Wal-Mart representatives supported a SmartCode optional overlay on their property to make it possible.

The team began to worry that a successful Wal-Mart Village could act much as conventional isolated Wal-Marts have nationwide, draining the life out of the old downtown five miles west. So during the planning process we discussed coding a different character for the new Village (more density, more intensity of mixed-use, more height coded into the T-5), and a strategy for the historic T-4/T-5 center to pursue retail and entertainment options that Wal-Mart does not do, or does not do well. These might include crafts, cuisine, theater, and marine amenities and supplies for Pass Christian's existing shrimping industry and proposed recreational harbor.

A Wal-Mart Village would be spanking new, a greyfield project on cleared land. But if it is coded to the Transect, it would be well integrated with surrounding neighborhoods that were also Transect-mapped during the SmartCode charrette, and with connecting thoroughfares that respond to the character of the T-Zones through which they pass.

The hope of all involved in the Mississippi Renewal Forum is that on these ravaged shores a regeneration can take place, which in our wilder dreams becomes as beloved in the next century as the memories of the historic towns and serene backbays of this region are now. Some theorists, like mathematician Stephen Wolfram, posit that the evolution of all life started with a simple generative code. Transect-based codes are meant to be generative codes, but they have the advantage of precedent; they have ancestors. Their standards are not arbitrary, they are based on analysis of places like New Orleans, Bay St. Louis, and Boston. You cannot have a walkable town without knowing why people walk and to what; you can't have one without some degree of mixed use in every urban zone, and you can't figure out the metrics and provisions needed for sustainable patterns of development without studying built evidence and extracting its DNA.

A neighborhood wiped out by a sudden storm or a long malaise may seem like a blank slate, but that's not really true. If we want to pick up our traditions in damaged places, we cannot simply start over. It is not only a matter of how places look, but of how they work.

*Note*

1. For more information about the Mississippi Renewal Forum, visit www .mississippirenewal.com

# Afterword
Ronald J. Daniels

A lifetime of information gathering, analysis, and thought earned the British naturalist Charles Darwin the authority to surmise, "In the long history of humankind (and animal kind, too) those who learned to collaborate and improvise most effectively have prevailed." It need not take us a lifetime to understand the pertinence of these words to modern hazard management. And it need not take us a lifetime to learn the benefits of collaboration, either—particularly in periods of crisis and disaster, when our nation requires solidarity most. But in the wake of Hurricane Katrina, a crisis that revealed untenable failing across all American systems—environmental, economic, social, and political—our collaborative efforts at reconstruction will require the kind of innovative wisdom Darwin himself propounded. As scientists, policymakers, scholars, and citizens, we must gather information, we must analyze, and we must think, if we are to effectively—and equitably—prevail.

The compilation of ideas in this book grew out of a conference entitled "Rebuilding Urban Places After Disaster: Lessons from Hurricane Katrina." Held at the University of Pennsylvania in February 2006, it was the second of two Penn-sponsored symposia organized in the wake of Katrina's storm surge, and these pages represent the second of two companion volumes. But while the first book, *On Risk and Disaster*, tried to account for our mistakes in preventing and mitigating last summer's catastrophe on the Gulf Coast, this book asks the question, "What must we do next?" And invariably, "How can we do it better?"

This is the task of the public thinker: witness past mistakes, share information, strategize, do better. The thoughtful, self-conscious, and inclusive process of deliberation Penn President Amy Gutmann encourages in her preface is the cornerstone of effective democratic decision-making and change. As a textual exercise in deliberation, this volume, which harnesses the intellectual resources of the University of Pennsylvania for the benefit of the public good, hopes to pave the way for wise and fair action on the Gulf Coast and beyond.

Many of the ideas in this book may contradict one another. And this should be no surprise to the deliberative thinker. Crises have always elicited conflicts of interest, between community and government leaders, geographic and cultural imperatives, and economic and social necessities. To say nothing of the myriad divergent views held by individual victims, families, and citizens. Democratic action is, in many ways, the process of absorbing all the challenges, hearing all the voices, and then making sound judgments toward a just balance of competing interests and needs.

While as experts, we may generate dozens of different solutions, often, we will agree. It is a testament to the virtues of collaboration that throughout this book, contributors have organically touched upon many of the same themes again and again.

Whether they are discussing natural hazards science or urban transportation, social and cultural stresses or the architecture of place, the experts gathered here have consistently emphasized *bridges*, *linkages*, *connections*, and *networks*. In making New Orleans less vulnerable, we must understand and respect the various linkages between risk assessment and sound public policy. In fortifying a region against future crises, we must plan for cooperation between the public and private sectors, between local and federal authorities, and among families, neighbors, and friends. In responding to the needs of the dispossessed, we must broaden our social networks and expand our safety nets to accommodate the disadvantaged cohorts that are most often overlooked. In recreating a sense of place, we must complement social, economic, and environmental recovery with the preservation of collective cultural values. In building a bridge toward a more resilient future, we must access the knowledge and lessons of crises past: Lisbon 1755, Chicago 1871, San Francisco 1906, Sri Lanka 2004, and others.

Where we observe and enact such bridges, linkages, connections, and networks, we are collaborating beyond the book page and beyond the academy. We are implementing ideas in the world, not merely generating them on paper. The merging of theory and practice has long been a challenge for governments, institutions, and communities, as the failures of Katrina made abundantly clear. But with active, just collaboration among experts, policy makers, community leaders, and citizens, we can work to surmount that challenge. We can produce crisis intervention plans, and then the next time, we can actually intervene. We can outline models for environmental and economic viability, and then we can actually implement them, engendering more sustainable urban centers. We can emphasize cultural preservation in the post-disaster discourse, and then we can actually work to preserve the heritage we cherish.

The post-Katrina world is fully alive to the pressures of "next time." And next time will come, whether it is in five years or one hundred and five. With cooperative thinking and action, we can mitigate disaster, improve response, and save communities, economies, estuaries, and lives.

Darwin noted the dual impact of improvisation and collaboration in the endurance of humankind. And while spontaneous invention can take a species far, nearly a year after Hurricane Katrina made landfall at Buras, Louisiana, the time of its ascendancy has passed. We are now well into the era of collaboration—toward rebuilding, restarting, and alleviating the need to improvise the next time.

With collaboration, we can do better. With collaboration, we will prevail.

# BIBLIOGRAPHY

Abbott, Carl. 1993. *The Metropolitan Frontier: Cities in the Modern American West.* Tucson: University of Arizona Press.

Abrahams, Roger D. with Nick Spitzer, John F. Szwed, and Robert Farris Thompson. 2006. *Blues for New Orleans: Mardi Gras and America's Creole Soul.* Philadelphia: University of Pennsylvania Press.

Ackerman, Frank and Lisa Heinzerling. 2004. *Priceless: On Knowing the Price of Everything and the Value of Nothing.* New York: New Press.

Aguirre, Benigno E. 2002. "'Sustainable Development' as Collective Surge." *Social Science Quarterly* 83 (1) (March).

Alanen, Arnold and Robert Melnick, eds. 2000. *Preserving Cultural Landscapes in America.* Baltimore: Johns Hopkins University Press.

AlSayyad, Nezar, ed. 2001. *Consuming Tradition, Manufacturing Heritage: Global Norms and Urban Forms in the Age of Tourism.* New York: Routledge.

American Scenic and Historic Preservation Society. 1912. 17th Annual Report. New York: Lyons.

Annie E. Casey Foundation. 2005. Kids Count Data Book Online.

Appiah, Kwame Anthony. 2006. "The Case for Contamination." *New York Times Magazine*, January 1.

ARUP. 2006. "From Relief to Future Development." London: ARUP.

Ashraff, Ferial. 2006. Interview with Minister of Housing in Colombo, Sri Lanka. February 7.

Avrami, Erica, Randall Mason, and Marta de la Torre. 2000. *The Values and Benefits of Cultural Heritage Conservation: Research Report.* Los Angeles: Getty Conservation Institute.

Baker, Liva. 1996. *The Second Battle of New Orleans: The Hundred-Year Struggle to Integrate the Schools.* New York: HarperCollins.

Banay, Sophia. 2005. New Orleans' tourism blues. *MSNBC.com*, September 20. <www.msnbc.msn.com/id/9410980>

Bardet, J. P. and M. Kapuskar. 1993. "Liquefaction Sand Boils in San Francisco During the Loma Prieta Earthquake." *Journal of Geotechnical Engineering.*

Barry, John M. 1997. *Rising Tide: The Great Mississippi Flood of 1927 and How It Changed America.* New York: Touchstone Press.

Baumbach, Richard O., Jr., and William E. Borah. 1981. *The Second Battle of New Orleans: A History of the Vieux Carré Riverfront-Expressway Controversy.* Tuscaloosa: University of Alabama Press.

Bernasek, Anna. 2005. "Economic View: Blueprints from Cities That Rose from Their Ashes." *New York Times*, October 9. <http://select.nytimes.com>

Berry, Jason. 2005. "Pompeii on the Mississippi." *Boston Globe*, Op-Ed, December 7.

Berube, Alan and Bruce Katz. 2005. "Katrina's Window: Confronting Concentrated Poverty Across America." *Brookings Institute Policy Brief* 150, March 2006.

Blackford, M.G. 1993. *The Lost Dream: Businessmen and City Planning in the Pacific Coast, 1890–1912.* Columbus: Ohio State University Press.

Blake, Casey Nelson. 1990. *Beloved Community: The Cultural Criticism of Randolph Bourne, Van Wyck Brooks, Waldo Frank & Lewis Mumford.* Chapel Hill: University of North Carolina Press.

Blatt, Harvey, Gerard Middleton, and Raymond Murray. 1980. *Origin of Sedimentary Rocks.* Englewood Cliffs, N.J.: Prentice-Hall.

Boggs, Sam, Jr. 2001. *Principles of Sedimentology and Stratigraphy.* Englewood Cliffs, N.J.: Prentice-Hall.

Botkin, Daniel B. 1990. *Discordant Harmonies: A New Ecology for the Twenty-First Century.* New York: Oxford University Press.

Bourne, Joel K., Jr. 2004. "The Big Uneasy." *National Geographic*, October, 88–105.

Bowean, Lolly. 2005. "In New Orleans, Land Elevation Was a Matter of Race, Experts Say." *Kansas.com*, September 24. <www.kansas.com/mld/kansas/news/nation>

Boze, Jean. 1829. Letter to Henri de St. Gême. October 1. Henri de St. Gême Papers, Manuscripts Division, Historic New Orleans Collection.

Bradford, Gigi, *Michael Gary*, and *Glenn Wallach*, eds. 2000. *The Politics of Culture: Policy Perspectives for Individuals, Institutions, and Communities.* New York: New Press.

Bring New Orleans Back Commission. 2006. *Report of the Cultural Committee, Mayor's Bring New Orleans Back Commission.* <http://www.bringneworleansback.org>

Broad, William J. 2005. "In Europe, High-Tech Flood Control, With Nature's Help." *New York Times*, September 6.

Brooks, David. 2006. "Questions of Culture." *New York Times*, February 19.

Brown, Ben. 2006. "Katrina Cottage Unveiled." Mississippi Renewal Forum. <www.mississippirenewal.com/info/dayJan-11-06.htm>

Brown, Patricia Leigh. 1996. "Higher and Drier, Illinois Town Is Reborn." *New York Times*, May 6.

Brown, Richard. 2005. "Unique Challenges Face FDIC-Insured Institutions After Katrina." *FDIC Outlook*, Winter, 12–18.

Burby, Raymond J. 2006. "Hurricane Katrina and the Paradoxes of Government Disaster Policy: Bringing About Wise Governmental Decisions for Hazardous Areas." *Annals of the American Academy of Political and Social Science* 604 (March): 171–91.

Burby, Raymond J. and Peter J. May. 1998. "Intergovernmental Environmental Planning: Addressing the Commitment Conundrum." *Journal of Environmental Planning and Management* 41 (1).

Burby, Raymond J. and Peter J. May with Philip R. Berke, Linda C. Dalton, Steven P. French, and Edward J. Kaiser. 1997. *Making Governments Plan: State Experiments in Managing Land Use.* Baltimore: Johns Hopkins University Press.

Burby, Raymond J., Arthur C. Nelson, Dennis Parker, and John Handmer. 2001. "Urban Containment Policy and Exposure to Natural Hazards: Is There a Connection?" *Journal of Environmental Planning and Management* 44 (4): 475–90.

Bureau of Economic Analysis. October 2005. "How Are Disasters (Such as Hurri-

canes and Earthquakes) Treated in the National Accounts?" <http://www.bea
.gov/bea/faq/national/disasters.htm>

Bureau of Labor Statistics. "Effects of Hurricane Katrina on BLS Employment and
Unemployment Data Collection and Estimation." September 28. <http://www
.bls.gov/katrina/cpscesquestions.htm>

Burkett, Virginia R., David B. Zilkoski, and David A. Hart. 2003. "Sea-Level Rise
and Subsidence: Implications for Flooding in New Orleans." U.S. Geological
Survey Subsidence Interest Group Conference, Proceedings of the Technical
Meeting, Galveston, Texas, November 27–29, 2001, ed. Keith R. Prince and
Devin L. Galloway. U.S. Geological Survey, Water Resources Division Open
File Report 03–308, pp. 63–70.

Burton, Linda M. 2001. "One Step Forward and Two Steps Back: Neighborhoods,
Adolescent Development, and Unmeasured Variables." In Alan Booth and Ann
C. Crouter, eds., *Does It Take a Village? Community Effects on Children, Adoles-
cents, and Families.* Mahwah, N.J.: Lawrence Erlbaum.

Cass, Julia. 2006. "Some Mardi Gras Traditions Vanish with City's Black Middle
Class." *New Orleans Times-Picayune*, February, 1A, 8A.

CB Richard Ellis. 2005. "Global White Paper: The Hurricanes and Real Estate—
Rebuilding After Devastation." October.

Center for American Progress. 2005. "Who Are Katrina's Victims?" <http://www
.americanprogress.org/site/pp.asp?c=biJRJ8OVFandb=1023681>

Central Intelligence Agency. 2005. *The World Factbook.* Washington, D.C.: CIA.

Chen, Beatrice. 2005. "'Resist the Earthquake and Rescue Ourselves': The Recon-
struction of Tangshan After the 1976 Earthquake." In Lawrence J. Vale and
Thomas J. Campanella, eds., *The Resilient City: How Modern Cities Recover from
Disaster.* New York: Oxford University Press.

City and County of San Francisco. 2005. *Annual Report of the Citizens General Obligation Bond Oversight Committee.*

City and County of San Francisco Department of City Planning. 2005. *Rincon Hill
Plan.* http://sfgov.org/site/planning_index.asp?id=25076

City of New Orleans. 2006. *Situation Report.* April 4. <http://cityofno.com>

City of New Orleans City Planning Commission. 1999. *New Century New Orleans,
1999 Land Use Plan, City of New Orleans.* New Orleans: City Planning Commission, City of New Orleans.

Cohn, Timothy A., Kathleen K. Gohn and William H. Hooke, eds. 2001. *Lessons
from PPP2000: Living with Earth's Extremes.* Report from the PPP2000 Working Group to the Office of Science and Technology Policy, Subcommittee on
Natural Disaster Reduction. Tampa: Institute for Business and Home Safety.

Comerio, Mary C. 1998. *Disaster Hits Home: New Policy for Housing Recovery.* Berkeley: University of California Press.

———. 1993. "Housing Repair and Reconstruction After Loma Prieta." Working
Paper 608. Institute of Urban and Regional Development, University of California, Berkeley.

Comfort, Louise K. 2006. "Cities at Risk: Hurricane Katrina and the Drowning of
New Orleans." *Urban Affairs Review* 41 (4): 501–16.

Coleman, James M. and Sherwood M. Gagliano. 1964. "Cyclic Sedimentation in the Mississippi River Deltaic Plain." *Gulf Coast Association of Geological Societies Transactions* 14: 67–80.

Congressional Budget Office. 2005a. "The Macroeconomic and Budgetary Effects of Hurricane Katrina." Letter to the Honorable William H. Frist, M.D., September 6.

———. 2005b. "The Federal Emergency Management Agency's Disaster Relief Account." September 7.

———. 2005c. "The Macroeconomic and Budgetary Effects of Hurricanes Katrina and Rita." Letter to the Honorable Jim Nussle and the Honorable Judd Gregg, September 29.

———. 2005d. "Testimony on the Macroeconomic and Budgetary Effects of Hurricanes Katrina and Rita." Testimony Before the Committee on the Budget, U.S. House or Representatives, October 6.

Conty, Cathy. 2005. "Keep It Historical, Make It Easy." Letter to the editor, *New Orleans Times-Picayune*, November 2.

Cunningham, Storm. 2002. *The Restoration Economy*. San Francisco: Berrett-Koehler.

Cutter, Susan L., ed. 2001. *American Hazardscapes: The Regionalization of Hazards and Disasters*. Washington, D.C.: Joseph Henry Press.

Da Silva, Jo. 2006. Personal communication, January 26.

Daniels, Ronald J. and Carolyn Clarke-Daniels. 2000. "Transforming Government: The Renewal and Revitalization of the Federal Emergency Management Agency." Arlington, Va.: PricewaterhouseCoopers Endowment for the Business of Government.

Daniels, Ronald J., Donald F. Kettl, and Howard Kunreuther, eds. 2006. *On Risk and Disaster: Lessons from Hurricane Katrina*. Philadelphia: University of Pennsylvania Press.

Daniels, Thomas L. 1999. *When City and Country Collide: Managing Growth on the Metropolitan Fringe*. Washington, D.C.: Island Press.

Dao, James. 2006. "In New Orleans, Smaller May Mean Whiter." *New York Times*, January 22. <www.nytimes.com/2006/01/22/weekinreview/22dao.html>

de Bakker, Liesbeth, 2004. "Delta Works Under Fire." <www.radionetherlands.nl/features/dutchhorizons/weeklyfeature/040623dh. html>

De Grove, John Melvine. 1983. *Land, Growth, and Politics*. Chicago: Planners Press, American Planning Association.

Dewan, Shaila and Janet Roberts. 2005. "Louisiana's Deadly Storm Took Strong as Well as the Helpless." *New York Times*, December 18.

Dinan, Stephen. 2005. "FEMA Allocates $5 Billion for Trailers Yet to Be Built." *Washington Times*, September 13.

Dokka, Roy K. 2006. "Modern Tectonic Subsidence of Southern Louisiana." *Geology*, April.

Domínguez, Virginia R. 1986. *White by Definition: Social Classification in Creole Louisiana*. New Brunswick, N.J.: Rutgers University Press.

Donze, Frank. 2006. "Let Us Decide on Rebuilding, Residents Say." *New Orleans Times-Picayune*, January 15. <www.nola.com>

Douty, Christopher Morris. 1970. "The Economics of Localized Disasters: An Empirical Analysis of the 1906 Earthquake and Fire in San Francisco." Ph.D. Dissertation, Department of Economics, Stanford University.

Dujardin, R. 2006. "Study: Big Easy May Shed Most of Its Poor." *Providence Journal*, January 30.

D'Urzo, Sandra. 2005. "Beyond Survival: The Challenge of Appropriate Reconstruction in Sri Lanka." Paper presented at the Harvard Tsunami Workshop, Cambridge, Massachusetts, November 19.

Earls, F., E. Smith, W. Reich, and K. G. Jung. 1988. "Investigating Psychopathological Consequences of Disaster in Children: A Pilot Study Incorporating a Structured Diagnostic Interview." *Journal of the American Academy of Child and Adolescent Psychiatry* 27: 90–95.

Easley, V. Gail. 1992. *Staying Inside the Lines: Urban Growth Boundaries.* Planning Advisory Service Report 440. Chicago: American Planning Association.

Education Trust. 2003. *The Funding Gap.* <http://www2.edtrust.org/edtrust/product+catalog/main>

Edwards, Jay D. 1994. "The Origins of Creole Architecture." *Winterthur Portfolio* 29, nos. 2–3 (Summer/Autumn): 155–89.

———. 1976–80. "Cultural Syncretism in the Louisiana Creole Cottage." *Louisiana Folklore Miscellany* 4: 9–40.

Edwards, Mark. (forthcoming). "The Evolution of Adequacy as a Basis for Educational Equity Remedies." Ph.D. Dissertation, Policy, Management and Evaluation, University of Pennsylvania.

Eggler, Bruce and Gordon Russell. 2005. "N.O. Considers Bypassing Historic Preservation Law." *New Orleans Times-Picayune*, October 13. <www.nola.com>

Elie, Lolis Eric. 2006. "Restoring Our Heritage Makes Sense." *New Orleans Times-Picayune*, January 11. <www.nola.com>

Elliot, D. O. 1932. *The Improvement of the Lower Mississippi River for Flood Control and Navigation.* Vicksburg, Miss.: Waterways Experiment Station.

Ellison, Ralph. 2002. *Living with Music: Ralph Ellison's Jazz Writings.* Ed. Robert O'Meally. New York: Modern Library.

El Nasser, Haya and Paul Overberg. 2006. "Katrina Evacuees Who Can't Go Home Opt to Hang Close." *USA Today*, February 5.

El Nasser, Haya and Paul Overberg. 2005. "Katrina Victims Settle in Elsewhere." *USA Today*, October 30.

Emanuel, Kerry. 2005. "Increasing Destructiveness of Tropical Cyclones over the Past 30 Years." *Nature* 436 (7051): 686–88.

Energy Information Administration. "Gulf Coast Hurricanes Situation Report." <http://tonto.eia.doe.gov/oog/special/eia1_katrina.html>

Fellowes, Matt and Amy Liu. 2006. "Federal Allocations in Response to Katrina, Rita and Wilma." Metropolitan Policy Program, The Brookings Institution, March 21. <http://www.brookings.edu>

Filosa, Gwen. 2006a. "Urban Pioneer." *New Orleans Times-Picayune*, February 12.

———. 2006b. "True Grit." *New Orleans Times-Picayune*, February 19.

Fischer, Frank. 2005. "Environmental Expertise and Civic Ecology. Linking the University and Its Metropolitan Community." Presented at transForm® the River Farm Conversations for a Sustainable Metropolis. Alexandria, Virginia Tech, National Capital Region, May 4–6.

Fischetti, Mark. 2001. "Drowning New Orleans." *Scientific American*, October, 76–85.

Fisk, Harold N. 1955. "Sand Facies of Recent Mississippi Delta Deposits." Fourth World Petroleum Congress, Rome, Proceedings. Sec. 1/C, 377–98.

Florida, Richard. 2002. *The Rise of the Creative Class: And How It's Transforming Work, Leisure, Community and Everyday Life*. New York: Basic Books.

Forsyth, Ann and Gretchen Nicholls. 2005. "Meeting Metropolitan Housing Needs in Left-Over Places." Presented at transForm® the River Farm Conversations for a Sustainable Metropolis. Alexandria, Virginia Tech, National Capital Region, May 4–6.

Frame, Kristy, Lynne Montgomery, and Christopher Newbury. 2005. "Bank Performance After Natural Disasters: A Historical Perspective." *FDIC Outlook* (Winter): 3–9.

Franks, Jeff. 2006. "New Orleans Mayor Campaigns—In Houston." *Olberlin Times*, March 4.

Frazier, D. E. 1967. "Recent Deltaic Deposits of the Mississippi River: Their Development and Chronology." *Gulf Coast Association of Geological Societies Transactions* 17: 287–318.

Freilich, Robert H. 1999. *From Sprawl to Smart Growth*. Chicago: American Bar Association.

Frey, William H., Jill H. Wilson, Alan Berube, and Audrey Singer. 2004. *Tracking Metropolitan America into the 21st Century: A Field Guide to the New Metropolitan and Micropolitan Definitions*. Washington, D.C.: Brookings Institution.

Friedman, George. 2005. "New Orleans' raison d'être." *Los Angeles Times*, September 11.

Friedman, Gerald M. and John Essington Sanders. 1978. *Principles of Sedimentology*. New York: John Wiley.

Friends of the Cabildo. 1971–97. *New Orleans Architecture*. 8 vols. Gretna, La.: Pelican.

Fullilove, Mindy Thompson. 2004. *Root Shock: How Tearing Up City Neighborhoods Hurts America, and What We Can Do About It*. New York: Ballantine Books.

———. 1996. "Psychiatric Implications of Displacement: Contributions from the Psychology of Place." *American Journal of Psychiatry* 153 (12): 1516–23.

Gadsden, Vivian L. 1995. *The Absence of Father: Effects on Children's Development and Family Functioning*. Report, National Center on Fathers and Families, University of Pennsylvania, Philadelphia.

Garreau, Joel. 2005. "A Sad Truth: Cities Aren't Forever." *Washington Post*, September 11, p. B01.

Gazit, Chana and David Steward. 2001. *Fatal Flood*. Based in part on John M. Barry, *Rising Tide: The Great Mississippi Flood of 1927 and How It Changed America*, made for *American Experience*, WGBH Educational Foundation.

Geertz, Clifford. 1973. "Deep Play: Notes on the Balinese Cockfight," In *The Interpretation of Cultures*. New York: Basic Books.

Gelles, Richard J. and Murray A. Straus. 1988. *Intimate Violence*. New York: Simon and Schuster.

George, P. S. 2006. "Miami: One Hundred Years of History." Miami: Historical Museum of Southern Florida. <http://miami.about.com/gi/dynamic/offsite.htm?site=http%3A%2F%2Fwww.historical-museum.org%2Fhistory%2Fsfhm242.htm> (accessed February 11, 2006).

Getty Conservation Institute. 1998. "The Agora." *GCI Newsletter* 13/2, Summer.

Gladstone, M. Brett. 2006. "Building and Planning Codes Since Loma Prieta." *San Francisco Apartment Magazine*, March. <http://www.sfaa.org.magazine/archives/06/mar/0603.gladstone.html>

Glancy, Jonathan. 2006. "A History of Violence." *The Guardian*, January 12.

Goetzmann, William H. and Glyndwr Williams. 1985. *Atlas of North American Exploration*. Englewood Cliffs, N.J.: Prentice-Hall.

Golden, Olivia. 2006. Young Children After Katrina: A Proposal to Heal the Damage and Create Opportunity in New Orleans. Urban Institute Report. February

Golden, Olivia and Margery Austin Turner. 2005. "Resiliency Is Not Enough: Young Children and the Rebuilding of New Orleans." Urban Institute Report. <http://www.urban.org/publications/900900.html>

Goldenberg, Stanley B., Christopher W. Landsea, Alberto M. Mestas-Nunez, and William M. Gray. 2001. "The Recent Increase in Atlantic Hurricane Activity: Causes and Implications." *Science* 293 (5529) (July 20): 474–79.

Goldman, Jasper. 2005. "Warsaw: Reconstruction as Propaganda." In Lawrence J. Vale and Thomas J. Campanella, eds., *The Resilient City: How Modern Cities Recover from Disaster*. New York: Oxford University Press.

Gordon, Jane. 2005. "A Golden Rule: Enrollment for All; Schools Around the State Are Opening Their Doors to Children Displaced by Hurricane Katrina." *New York Times*, September 18.

Gottmann, Jean. 1961. *Megalopolis: The Urbanized Northeastern Seaboard of the United States*. New York: Twentieth-Century Fund.

Government of Sri Lanka and Development Partners. 2005. *Post-Tsunami Recovery and Reconstruction: Progress, Challenges, Way Forward*. Colombo: Government of Sri Lanka.

Greene, Marjorie R. and Paula A. Schulz. 1993. "Emergency Shelter and Housing Issues Lessons Learned from the Loma Prieta Earthquake." *Proceedings of the 1993 National Earthquake Conference*, 491–500. Memphis.

Grimm, Nancy B. and Charles L. Redman. 2004. "Approaches to the Study of Urban Ecosystems: The Case of Central Arizona Phoenix." *Urban Ecosystems* 7: 199–213.

Groth, Paul Groth and Todd Bressi, eds. 1997. *Understanding Ordinary Landscapes*. New Haven, Conn.: Yale University Press.

Gunderson, Lance, Crawford S. Holling, Lowell Pritchard, Jr., and Garry D. Peterson. 2002. "Resilience." In Ted Munn, editor-in-chief. *Encyclopedia of Global Environmental Change*. Hoboken, N.J.: Wiley, 530–31.

Hahn, A. 2002. "Colleges and Universities as Economic Anchors." Working Paper 3. Baltimore: Annie E. Casey Foundation.

Hall, Peter Geoffrey, H. Gracey, R. Drewett, and R. Thomas. 1973. *The Containment of Urban England*. Vol. 2, *The Planning System: Objectives, Operations, Impacts*. London: Allen & Unwin.

Hankins, John and Steven Maklansky, eds. 2003. *Raised to the Trade: Creole Building Arts of New Orleans*. New Orleans: New Orleans Museum of Art.

Hansen, Gladys. 2006a. "Relocation of Chinatown." Virtual Museum of the City of San Francisco. <http:// www.sfmuseum.net/chin/relocate.htm>

———. 2006b. "A Great Civic Drama." Virtual Museum of the City of San Francisco. <http://www.sfmuseum.org/hist/timeline.htm>

Hatzius, Jan. 2005. "Katrina, Growth, and Rates: Less Now, More Later." *Goldman Sachs Economics Analyst*, September 9.

Healy, Robert G. 1976. *Land Use and the States*. Baltimore: Johns Hopkins University Press.

Heard, Malcolm. 1997. *French Quarter Manual: An Architectural Guide to New Orleans's Vieux Carré*. New Orleans: Tulane School of Architecture.

Henderson, Andrea S. 2005. "Reconstructing Home: Gender, Disaster Relief, and Social Life After the San Francisco Earthquake and Fire, 1906–1915." Ph.D. dissertation, Department of History, Stanford University.

Henry J. Kaiser Family Foundation. 2005. Harvard School of Public Health Survey of Hurricane Katrina Evacuees, Houston, Texas, September 10–12.

Herrick, Thaddeus. 2005. "Teen Tension Trails Hurricane Evacuees into Houston School." *Wall Street Journal*, December 2.

Hess, David. 2005. "The University and Sustainable Regions Industries." Presented at transForm® the River Farm Conversations for a Sustainable Metropolis. Alexandria, Virginia Tech, National Capital Region, May 4–6.

Hill, Jason G. and Frank Johnson. 2005. "Revenues and Expenditures by Public School Districts: School Year 2–2–2003." <http://nces.ed.gov/pubs2006/2006 312.pdf>

Hill, Paul T. and Mary Beth Celio. *Fixing Urban Schools*. Washington, D.C.: Brookings Institution Press, 1998.

Hill, Paul T. and Jane Hannaway. 2006. "The Future of Public Education in New Orleans." <http://www.urban.org/publications/900913.html>

Hirsch, Arnold and Joseph Logsdon. 1992. *Creole New Orleans: Race and Americanization*. Baton Rouge: Louisiana State University Press.

Hoff, David J. 1997a. "Chapter 1 Aid Failed to Close Learning Gap." *Education Week*, April 2.

———. 1997b. "Chapter 1 Study Documents Impact of Poverty." *Education Week*, April 16.

Howe, Deborah A. 1993. "Growth Management in Oregon." In Jay M. Stein, ed., *Growth Management: The Planning Challenge of the 1990's*. Newbury Park, Calif.: Sage.

Hsu, Spencer S. 2006. "Post-Katrina Promises Unfulfilled." *Washington Post*, January 28.

Hurricane City. 2006a. "Miami, Florida's History with Tropical Systems." <http://www.hurricanecity.com/city/miami.htm> (accessed February 11, 2006).

———. 2006b. "New Orleans, Louisiana's History with Tropical Systems." <http://www.hurricanecity.com/city/neworleans.htm> (accessed February 11, 2006).

Initiative for a Competitive Inner City and CEOs for Cities. 2002. *Leveraging Colleges and Universities for Urban Economic Revitalization: An Action Agenda.* Boston: CEOs for Cities.

Jacob, Klaus. 2005. "Time for a Tough Question: Why Rebuild?" *Washington Post,* September 6.

Jagtiani, Sunil. 2006. "Focus on Tsunami Overlooks Sri Lanka's War Refugees." *Christian Science Monitor,* January 4, 10.

Janssen, James S. 1984. *Building New Orleans: The Engineer's Role.* New Orleans: Nelson and Co.

Johnson, David B., 1980. "A Change in the Course of the Lower Mississippi River: Description and Analysis of Some Economic Consequences." Bulletin 12B, Louisiana Water Resources Research Institute, Louisiana State University, Baton Rouge.

Jones, Russell T., Robert Frary, Phillippe Cunningham, J. David Weddle, and Lisa Kaiser. 2001. "The Psychological effects of Hurricane Andrew on Ethnic Minority and Caucasian Children and Adolescents: A Case Study." *Cultural Diversity and Ethnic Minority Psychology* 7: 103–8.

Jonkman, S. N., Marcel J. F. Stive, and J. K. Vrijling. 2005. "New Orleans Is a Lesson to the Dutch." *Journal of Coastal Research* 21 (6).

Jordan, Lara Jakes. 2006. "Katrina Response a 'National Failure.'" Associated Press, February 13.

Judd, Dennis R. and Susan S. Fainstein, eds. 1999. *The Tourist City.* New Haven, Conn.: Yale University Press.

Jumonville, Florence M. 1990. *Guide to the Vieux Carré Survey.* New Orleans: Historic New Orleans Collection.

Kahn, Judd. 1979. *Imperial San Francisco: Politics and Planning in an American City, 1897–1906.* Lincoln: University of Nebraska Press.

Kasman, Bruce. 2005. "Katrina's U.S. Double Edge: A Hurricne and an Oil Shock." *JP Morgan Economic Research Global Data Watch,* September 2.

Katz, Bruce, Matt Fellowes, and Mia Mabanta. 2006. "Katrina Index: Tracking Variables of Post-Katrina Reconstruction." Washington, D.C.: Brookings Institution Metropolitan Policy Program. February.

Katz, Bruce, Amy Liu, Matt Fellowes, and Mia Mabanta. 2005. "Housing Families Displaced by Katrina: A Review of the Federal Response to Date." Washington, D.C.: Brookings Institution.

Kazmann, Raphael G. and David B. Johnson. 1980. "If the Old River Control Structure Fails?" Bulletin 12, Louisiana Water Resources Research Institute, Louisiana State University, Baton Rouge.

Kein, Sybil, ed. 2000. *Creole: The History and Legacy of Louisiana's Free People of Color.* Baton Rouge: Louisiana State University Press.

King, John. 2004. "15 Seconds That Changed San Francisco." *San Francisco Chronicle,* October 17, 18, 19, 20, 21, 22. <http://sfgate.com>

Klein, Naomi. 2005. "Let the People Rebuild New Orleans." *The Nation*, September 26. <www.nation.com/doc/20050926/klein>

Kolbert, Elizabeth. 2006. "Watermark." *New Yorker*, February 27, 46–57.

Konigsmark, Anne Rochell. 2006. "FEMA to Open Apartments to Displaced New Orleanians." *USA Today*, January 31.

Koski, William S. 2003. "Fuzzy Standards and Institutional Constraints: A Re-Examination of the Jurisprudential History of Education Finance Reform Litigation." *Santa Clara Law Review* 43.

Koski, William S. and Henry M. Levin. 2000. "Twenty-Five Years After Rodriguez: What Have We Learned?" *Teachers College Record* 102 (3).

Kreuger, Larry W. and John J. Stretch. 2003. "Identifying and Helping Long Term Child and Adolescent Disaster Victims: Model and Method." *Journal of Social Service Research* 300 (2).

———. 2000. "Long Term PTSD Among Adolescent Disaster Victims: An Empirical Assessment." In Michael J. Zakour, ed., *Disaster and Traumatic Stress Research: Tulane Studies in Social Welfare*. New Orleans: Tulane University Press.

Kucinich, Dennis. 2006. "The Big Fix." *The Nation*, February 6.

Kurlantzick, Joshua. 2005. "The Rebirth of Sri Lanka." *New York Times*, December 25, Sec. 5r, 1, 8, 9.

Landis, John D. 1986. "Land Regulation and the Price of New Housing: Lessons from Three California Cities. *Journal of the American Planning Association* 52 (1).

Landsea, C. W., N. Nicholls, W. M. Gray, and L. A. Avila. 1996. "Downward Trends in the Frequency of Intense Atlantic Hurricanes During the Past Five Decades." *Geophysical Research Letters* 23 (1996): 1697–1700.

Lang, Robert E. and K. A. Danielsen. 2006. "Review Roundtable: Is New Orleans a Resilient City?" *Journal of the American Planning Association* 72 (2).

Lang, Robert E. and Dawn Dhavale. 2005a. "Megapolitan Areas: Exploring a New Trans-Metropolitan Geography." Alexandria: Metropolitan Institute at Virginia Tech Census Report 05:01. July.

———. 2005b. "America's Megapolitan Areas." *LandLines* 17 (3).

———. 2005c. "Beyond Megalopolis: Exploring America's New "Megapolitan' Geography." Metropolitan Institute Census Report Series, Census Report 05:01. Arlington, Metropolitan Institute at Virginia Tech. <http://www.mi.vt.edu/uploads/MegaCensusReport.pdf>

Lang, Robert E., Arthur C. Nelson, and Dawn Dhavale. 2006. "Megapolitans 2.0." Alexandria: Metropolitan Institute at Virginia Tech Census Report 06:01, forthcoming.

LaRock, J. D. and H. Rodriguez-Farrar. 2005. "Katrina and Rita: What Can the United States Learn from International Experiences with Education in Displacement?" *Harvard Educational Review* 75 (4).

Leonard, H. Jeffrey. 1983. *Managing Oregon's Growth: The Politics of Development Planning* Washington, D.C.: Conservation Foundation.

Leopold, Luna B., ed. 1991. *Round River: From the Journals of Aldo Leopold*. Minocqua, Wis.: North Word Press.

———. 1962. "Rivers." *American Scientist* 50: 511–37.

Levy, Clifford J. 2005. "Amid Recovery Efforts, a Rift Threatens to Grow." *New York Times*, December 14. <www.nytimes.com>

Lewis, Peirce F. 2003. *New Orleans: The Making of an Urban landscape*. 2nd ed. Charlottesville: University of Virginia Press.

Logan, John R., Phil Brown, Steven Hamburg, Rachel Morello-Frosch, and John Mustard. 2006. "The Impact of Katrina: Race and Class in Storm Damaged Neighborhoods Preliminary Report." Providence, R.I.: Brown University Center for Spatial Structures in the Social Sciences.

Lomax, Alan. 1950. *Mr. Jelly Roll: The Fortunes of Jelly Roll Morton, New Orleans Creole and "Inventor of Jazz"*. Reprint New York: Pantheon, 1993.

Lonigan, C. Y., M. P. Shannon, A. J. Finch, T. K. Daugherty, and C. M. Taylor. 1991. "Children's Reactions to a Natural Disaster: Symptom Severity and Degree of Exposure." *Advances in Behavior Research and Therapy* 13.

Louisiana Department of Natural Resources. 1998. "Coast 2050:l Toward a sustainable Coastal Louisiana." <www.coast2050.gov/report.pdf>

Louisiana Recovery Authority. 2006."Public Invited to Comment on the Road Home Housing Plan." April 4. <http://lralouisiana.gov>

———. 2005. "Addressing the Challenges of Recovery & Rebuilding from Hurricanes Katrina & Rita, Overview of Comparative Damage from Hurricane Katrina and Rita." December 19. <http://www.lra.louisiana.gov/>

Loyola University Center for Environmental Communications. 2005. "Ecology of the Mississippi River Delta Region." November. <http://www.lloyno.edu/lucec/mrdcontrol.html>

Lubell, Jeffrey. 2006a. "Silent Mortgages—A Critical Tool for Helping Families Rebuild Homes Damaged or Destroyed by Hurricanes Katrina, Rita, or Wilma." Washington, D.C.: Center for Housing Policy and National Housing Conference.

———. 2006b. "Silent Mortgages: Design Issues." Washington, D.C.: Center for Housing Policy and National Housing Conference.

Lynch, Kevin. 1972. *What Time Is This Place?* Cambridge, Mass.: MIT Press.

MacCash, Doug. 2005. "New Urbanism Dominates Rebuilding Chatter." *New Orleans Times-Picayune*, November 14. <www.nola.com>

March, J., L. Amaya-Jackson, L. Murray, and A. Schule. 1998. "Cognitive-Behavioral Psychotherapy for Children and Adolescents with PTSD After a Single-Incident Stressor." *Journal of the Academy of Child and Adolescent Psychiatry* 37 (6).

Mason, Randall. 2006. "Theoretical and Practical Arguments for Values-Centered Preservation." *CRM: The Journal of Heritage Stewardship* (Summer).

———. 2003. "Fixing Historic Preservation: A Constructive Critique of 'Significance'" *Places, a Forum of Environmental Design* 16, 1 (Fall).

———, ed. 1999. *Economics and Heritage Conservation*. Los Angeles: Getty Conservation Institute.

Mason, Randall and Erica Avrami. 2002. "Heritage Values and Challenges of Conservation Planning." In Jeanne Marie Teutonico and Gaetano Palumbo, eds., *Management Planning for Archaeological Sites: An International Workshop Organized by the Getty Conservation Institute and Loyola Marymount University, 19–22 May*

2000, *Corinth, Greece*. Getty Conservation Institute Symposium Proceedings. Los Angeles: Getty Conservation Institute.

Martin, Mike W. and Roland Schinzinger. 2005. *Ethics in Engineering*. 4th ed. New York: McGraw-Hill, 2005.

Mathur, Anuradha and Dilip da Cunha. 2001. *Mississippi Floods: Designing a Shifting Landscape*. New Haven, Conn.: Yale University Press.

"Mayor Moves to Heal New Orleans' Lifeblood Industry." 2005. *CNN.com.*, October 7. <www.cnn.com/2005/US/10/07/neworleans.casinos>

McCarthy, Kevin F., Elizabeth H. Ondaatje, Laura Zakaris, and Arthur Brooks. 2004. *Gifts of the Muse: Reframing the Debate About the Benefits of the Arts*. Santa Monica, Calif.: RAND Corporation.

McCarthy, Kevin, D. J. Peterson, Narayan Sastry, and Michael Pollard. 2006. The Repopulation of New Orleans After Hurricane Katrina. Santa Monica, Calif.: RAND Corporation.

McNatt, Robert and Frank Benassi. 2006. "The Gulf Coast, After the Deluge. *Business Week Online*, March 20.

McPhee, John, 1989. *The Control of Nature*. New York: Farrar, Straus, and Giroux.

Mileti, Dennis S. 1999. *Disasters by Design: A Reassessment of Natural Hazards in the United States*. Washington, D.C.: Joseph Henry Press.

Miller, Ross. 2002. "Out of the Blue: The Great Chicago Fire of 1871." In Joan Ockman, ed., *Out of Ground Zero: Case Studies in Urban Reinvention*. New York: Prestel.

Mississippi Development Authority. 2006. "Homeownership Assistance plan, Partial Action Plan." March 31. <http://www.MSHomeHelp.gov>

Mitchell, Don. 2003. "Cultural Landscapes: Just Landscape or Landscapes of Justice?" *Progress in Human Geography* 27, 6.

Moe, Richard and Carter Wilkie. 1997. *Changing Places: Rebuilding Community in the Age of Sprawl*. New York: Henry Holt.

Moran, Kate, Karen Turni Bazile, and Richard Boyd. 2006. "City, Suburbs Divided on Area's Future." *New Orleans Times-Picayune*, January 22. <www.nola.com>

Morgan, Arthur E. 1951. *The Miami Conservancy District*. New York: McGraw-Hill.

Moses, Jennifer. 2006. "The Catastrophe Is Not Over." *Washington Post*. January 28.

Mt. Auburn Associates. 2005. *Louisiana: Where Culture Means Business*. Baton Rouge: State of Louisiana Department of Culture, Recreation, and Tourism.

Muro, Mark and Bruce Katz (2006). "Raising the Roof in New Orleans." *Urban Land*, March

Musacchio, Laura and Jianguo Wu, invited guest editors. 2004. "Collaborative Research in Landscape-Scale Ecosystem Studies: Emerging Trends in Urban and Regional Ecology." *Urban Ecosystems* 7 (3): 175–314.

National Center for Children in Poverty. 2006. *Child Poverty in States Hit by Hurricane Katrina*. New York: National Center for Children in Poverty.

National Park Service. 2006. "Refuge Cottages, Presidio of San Francisco. <http://www.nps.gov/prsf/history/1906eq/cottages.htm>

———. 2001. *The Secretary of Interior's Standards for the Treatment of Historic Proper-*

*ties, With Guidelines for Preservation, Rehabilitating, Restoring and Reconstructing Historic Buildings.* <http://www.cr.nps.gov/hps/tps/standguide/index.htm>

National Research Council. 1998. *Violence in Families: Assessing Prevention and Treatment Programs.* Washington, D.C.: National Academy Press.

———. 1994. *Practical Experiences from the Loma Prieta Earthquake, Report from a Symposium sponsored by the Geotechnical Board and the Board on Natural Disasters of the National Research Council.* Washington D.C.: NRC.

Nelson, Arthur C. 2004. Toward a New Metropolis: The Opportunity to Rebuild America. Metropolitan Policy Program Survey Series. Washington, D.C.: Brookings Institution. December.

Nelson, Arthur C. 2000. "Smart Growth = Central City Vitality and Higher Quality of Life." In Susan Wachter, R. Leo Penne, and Arthur C. Nelson, eds., *Bridging the Divide: Making Regions Work for Everyone—Shaping the Federal Agenda.* Washington, D.C.: U.S. Department of Housing and Urban Development.

Nelson, Arthur C. and Casey J. Dawkins. 2004. *Urban Containment in the United States: History, Models, and Techniques for Regional and Metropolitan Growth Management.* Chicago: American Planning Association.

———. 1999. "Survey of U.S. Metropolitan Planning Organizations." Manuscript, Graduate Program in Urban Planning, Georgia Institute of Technology.

New Orleans City Council. 1805. New Orleans Municipal Papers, box 2, folder 2 (June 15, 22). New Orleans Municipal Papers, Tulane University Library.

Newsom, Michael. 2006. "A Realistic Plan, Steering Committee Will Have 90-Day Mandate." *Biloxi Sun Herald*, February 24. <http://www.sunherald.com>

*New York Times.* 2005. "The Poor Need Not Apply." Editorial, December 21.

*NOAA Magazine.* 2005. "NOAA Attributes Recent Increase in Hurricane Activity to Naturally Occurring Multi-decadal Climate Variability." November 29. <www.noaa.gov>

Nossiter, Adam. 2006a. "Demolition of Homes Begins in Section of New Orleans." *New York Times*, March 7, A12.

———. 2006b. "Fight Grows in New Orleans on Demolition and Rebuilding." *New York Times*, January 6, A14.

———. 2006c. "Rebuilding New Orleans, One Appeal at a Time." *New York Times*, February 5.

———. 2005. "Thousands of Demolitions Are Likely in New Orleans." *New York Times*, October 23.

Nossiter, Adam and John Schwartz. 2006. "Lenient Rule Set for Rebuilding in New Orleans." *New York Times*, April 13.

Ockman, Joan, ed. 2002. *Out of Ground Zero: Case Studies in Urban Reinvention.* New York: Prestal.

Odell, K. and M. Weidenmier. 2001. "Real Shock, Monetary shock: The 1906 San Francisco Earthquake and the Panic of 1907." Claremont Colleges Working Papers. <http://econpapers.repec.org/paper/clmclmeco/2001–07.htm>

Oliver, Daniel T. 2001. "Charity Done right: How San Francisco Recovered from the 1906 Earthquake and Fire." *The World and I* 16: 1.

Olwig, Kenneth R. 2002. *Landscape, Nature, and the Body Politic: From Britain's Renaissance to America's New World.* Madison: University of Wisconsin Press.

Orfield, Gary and Chungmei Lee. 2005. "Why Segregation Matters: Poverty and Educational Inequality." <http://www.civilrightsproject.harvard.edu/research/deseg/Why_Segreg_Matters.pdf>

Orfield, Myron. 1997. *Metropolitics: A Regional Agenda for Community and Stability.* Washington, D.C: Brookings Institution.

Orr, David W. 2005. "Education and Transformation." Presented at transForm® the River Farm Conversations for a Sustainable Metropolis. Alexandria, Virginia: Virginia Tech, National Capital Region. May 4–6.

————. 2002. *The Nature of Design.* New York: Oxford University Press.

————. 1994. *Earth in Mind.* Washington, D.C.: Island Press.

Ouroussoff, Nicolai. 2005. "Katrina's legacy: theme park or cookie cutter?" *New York Times.* October 18, pp. B1, B8. <query.nytimes.com/gst/fullpage.html>

Page, Susan. 2005. "Evacuees Shun Going Home." *USA Today.* October 13, A1.

Pearce, John. 2006. John Pearce, Partner, Montgomery, Barnett, Brown, Read, Hammond & Mintz. Personal communication, February 17.

Pendall, Rolf, Paula Long, Keith Bonar, Jonathan Martin, and William Fulton. 2001. "Holding the Line: Urban Containment in the United States." Manuscript. Department of City and Regional Planning, Cornell University.

Pendall, Rolf, Jonathan Martin, and William Fulton. 2002. "Holding the Line: Urban Containment in the United States." Discussion paper, Brookings Institution Center on Urban and Metropolitan Policy. Washington, D.C.: Brookings Institution, August.

Percy, Walker. 1961. *The Moviegoer.* New York: Knopf.

Perry, David C. and Wim Wiewel. 2005. *The University as Urban Developer: Case Studies and Analysis.* Armonk, N.Y.: M.E. Sharpe.

Pettijohn, F. J. 1957. *Sedimentary Rocks.* New York: Harper & Brothers.

Phelan, J. 1909. "Rapid Freight Work Done by Southern Pacific Company." *San Francisco Chronicle*, May 7.

————. 1907a. "The Situation in San Francisco." *New York Evening Post*, June 1. <http://www.sfmuseum.org/conflag/phelan2.html>

————. 1907b. "Rejoices at the Fall of Schmitz in 'Frisco, Says Jap Problem Is Only a Labor Question." *Boston Sunday Herald*, June 16. <http://www.sfmuseum.org/conflag/phelan.html>

Pickett, S. T. A., M. L. Cadenasso, and J. M. Grove. 2005. "Biocomplexity in Coupled Natural-Human Ecosystems: A Multidimensional Framework." *Ecosystems* 8: 225–32.

————. 2004. "Resilient Cities: Meaning, Models, and Metaphor for Integrating the Ecological, Socio-Economic, and Planning Realms." *Landscape and Urban Planning* 69 (4): 369–84.

Pielke Roger A. 2005. "Meteorology—Are There Trends in Hurricane Destruction?" *Nature* 438 (7071): E11-E11.

Plunkett, Richard and Brigitte Ellemer. 2003. *Sri Lanka.* Oakland, Calif.: Lonely Planet.

Pope, John. 2006. "Evoking King, Nagin Calls N.O. 'Chocolate' City." *New Orleans Times-Picayune*, January 17. <www.nola.com>

Porter, Douglas R. 1997. *Managing Growth in America's Communities*. Washington, D.C.: Island Press.

Porter, Theodore. 1996. *Trust in Numbers: The Pursuit of Objectivity in Science and Public Life*. Princeton, N.J.: Princeton University Press.

Powell, Donald E. 2006. "Rebuilding Wisely." *Washington Post*, February 2.

Powell, Lawrence N. n.d. "New Orleans: American Pompeii." Manuscript, Department of History, Tulane University.

Price, Willard. 1962. *The Amazing Mississippi*. London: Heinemann.

Prinstein, Mitchell J., Annette M. La Greca, Eric M. Vernbery, and Wendy K. Silverman. 1996. "Children's Coping Assistance: How Parents, Teachers, and Friends Help Children Cope After a Natural Disaster." *Journal of Child Psychiatry* 25 (4).

Ratnayke, L. L. 2006. Interview with Vice-Chairman of the University Grants Commission, Colombo, Sri Lanka, February 9.

Regional Plan Association and Lincoln Institute of Land Policy. 2006. *America 2050*. New York: Regional Plan Association.

Regis, A. Helen. 2001. "Blackness and the Politics of Memory in the New Orleans Second Line." *American Ethnologist* 28 (4): 752–77.

———. 1999. "Second Lines, Minstrelsy, and the Contested Landscapes of New Orleans Afro-Creole Festivals." *Cultural Anthropology* 14 (4): 472–504.

Riad, Jasmin K. and Fran H. Norris. 1996. "The Influence of Relocation on Environmental, Social, and Psychological Stress Experienced by Disaster Victims." *Environment and Behavior* 28 (2).

Rittel, Horst W. J. and Melvin M. Weber. 1973. "Dilemmas in a General Theory of Planning." *Policy Sciences* 4: 155–69.

Rivlin, Gary. 2006. "Patchy Recovery in New Orleans." *New York Times*. April 5, C1, C6.

Roberts, Deon. 2006a. "Fallen Landmarks: Most Historic Losses Were Neglected Even Before Katrina." *New Orleans City Business*, January 16. <www.neworleans citybusiness.com>

———. 2006b. "Modern Homes Could Replace Historic Ones." *New Orleans City Business*, January 16. <www.neworleanscitybusiness.com>

Rodin, Judith. 2005. "The 21st Century Urban University: New Roles for Practice and Research." *Journal of the American Planning Association* 71 (3): 1–11.

Rogers, Kim Lacy. 1993. *Righteous Lives: Narratives of the New Orleans Civil Rights Movement*. New York: New York University Press, 1993.

Rosenberg, M. 2005. "Displaced by Katrina, Coping in a New School." *New York Times*, December 18.

Rossi, Peter Henry, James D. Wright, and Eleanor Weber-Burdin. 1982. *Natural Hazards and Public Choice: The State and Local Politics of Hazard Mitigation*. New York: Academic Press.

Rozario, Kevin. 1996. "Nature's Evil Dreams: Disaster and America, 1871–1906." Ph.D. dissertation, Yale University.

Russell, Gordon, Frank Donze, and Laura Maggi. 2006. "Buyout in Works." *New Orleans Times-Picayune*, February 13.

Rutter, Michael. 1987. "Psychosocial Resilience and Protective Mechanisms." *American Journal of Orthopsychiatry* 57 (3).

Rybczynski, Witold. 2006. "Rebuilding NOLA." *Wharton Real Estate Review* 10 (1): 1 92–102.

Sakakeeny, Matt. 2006. "Resounding Silence in the Streets of a Musical City." *Space and Culture* 9 (1): 41–44.

San Francisco Fire Department. 1989. "Water Supply System Review." <http://www.sfmuseum.net/quake/revawss.html>

San Francisco Redevelopment Agency. 2006. Transbay redevelopment project area. <http://sfgov.org/site/sfra_page.asp?id = 5583>

Sard, Barbara and Douglas Rice. 2005. "Changes Needed in Katrina Transitional Housing Plan to Meet Families' Needs." Washington, D.C.: Center on Budget and Policy Priorities.

Sauer, Carl. 1963. "The Morphology of Landscape." In Sauer, *Land and Life: A Selection from the Writings of Carl Ortwin Sauer*, ed. John Leighly. Berkeley: University of California Press.

Sawislak, Karen. 1995. *Smoldering City: Chicagoans and the Great Fire, 1871–1874*. Chicago: University of Chicago Press.

Schach, Janice Cervelli. 2005. "Metropolitan Transformation through Restoration." Presented at transForm ® the River Farm Conversations for a Sustainable Metropolis. Alexandria, Virginia Tech, National Capital Region. May 4–6.

Schwartz, John, 2006a. "Concern over Soil Content as Levee Repairs Continue." *New York Times*, February 9.

———. 2006b. "Levee Plans Fall Short of FEMA Standards." *New York Times*, March 31, A14.

———. 2005. "Full Flood Safety in New Orleans Could Take Billions and Decades." *New York Times*, November 19.

Scott, Mel. 1969. *American City Planning Since 1890*. Berkeley: University of California Press.

Sen, Amartya. 1999. *Development as Freedom*. New York: Knopf.

———. 1998. "How Does Culture Matter?" In Vijayendra Rao and Michael Walton, eds., *Culture and Public Action*. Stanford, Calif.: Stanford University Press.

Sengupta, Somini. 2005. "Battered by War, Sri Lankans Elect Hawkish President." *New York Times*, November 18.

Sepic, Matt. 2005. "Post-Disaster Rebuilding, Away from Danger Zones." *National Public Radio's Day to Day*, November 10. <http://www.npr.org/templates/story/story.php?storyId = 5007249> (accessed February 17, 2006).

Shenkel, J. Richard, Robert Sauder, and Edward R. Chatelain. 1980. *Archaeology of the Jazz Complex and Beauregard (Congo) Square, Louis Armstrong Park, New Orleans, Louisiana*. Research Report. 2. New Orleans: University of New Orleans, Archaeological and Cultural Research Program.

Shinkle, Kurt D. and Roy K. Dokka. 2004. "Rates of Vertical Displacement at Benchmarks in the Lower Mississippi Valley and the Northern Gulf Coast." NOAA Technical Report NOS/NGS 50.

Shklar, Judith N. 1992. *The Faces of Injustice*. New Haven, Conn.: Yale University Press.

Shutkin, William A. *The Land That Could Be: Environmentalism and Democracy in the Twenty-First Century*. Cambridge, Mass.: MIT Press, 2000.

Simerman, John, Dwight Ott, and Ted Mellinik. 2005. "Facts Challenge Assumptions: Katrina Victims Diverse. White, Non-Poor People Died Along with Black, Poor." Knight Ridder Newspapers, December 30.

Smith, Carl S.. 1995. *Urban Disorder and the Shape of Belief: The Great Chicago Fire, the Haymarket Bomb, and the Model Town of Pullman*. Chicago: University of Chicago Press.

Smith, Gavin. 2006. "Prepared Statement of Gavin Smith to Senate Committee on Homeland Security and Governmental Affairs," January 17. <http://www.msplanning/gulf_coast_renewal.htm>

Soss, Neal et al. 2005. "Disentangling Katrina and Energy." *Credit Suisse First Boston U.S. Economics Digest*, September 9.

Speed, Leland. 2006. Director, Mississippi Development Authority. Personal communication, February 19.

Spitzer, Nick. 2005. "Rebuilding the 'Land of Dreams.'" In notes to *Our New Orleans: A Benefit Album*. Nonesuch Records: New York.

———. 2003. "Monde Créole: The Cultural World of French Louisiana: Creoles and the Creolization of World Cultures." *Journal of American Folklore* 116, 459 (Winter): 57–72.

———. 2002. "The Aesthetics of Work and Play in Creole New Orleans." In Stephen Maklansky and Jonn Hankins, eds., *"Raised to the Trade": Creole Building Arts of New Orleans*. New Orleans: New Orleans Museum of Art.

Steinberg, Michele and Raymand J. Burby. 2002. "Growing Safe." *Planning, the Magazine of the American Planning Association* 68 (4).

Steinhauer, Jennifer. 2005. "Smaller Towns Bore the Brunt of Rita's Force." *New York Times*, October 1, A1, A10.

Steinitz, Carl, Héctor M. Arias, Scott D. Bassett, Michael Flaxman, T. Goode, Thomas Maddock, III, David A. Mouat, R. Peiser, and Allan Shearer. 2003. *Alternative Futures for Changing Landscapes: The Upper San Pedro River Basin in Arizona and Sonora*. Washington, D.C.: Island Press.

Stipe, Robert, ed. 2003. *A Richer Heritage: Historic Preservation in the Twenty-First Century*. Chapel Hill: University of North Carolina Press.

Stohr, Kate. 2005. "San Fran's Lessons for New Orleans." *Business Week*, September 12. <http://businessweek.com>

Stotz, Dietrich. 2006. Site visit and interview in Batticaloa District, February 12.

Straus, Murray A., Richard J. Gelles, and Suzanne K. Steinmetz. 1980. *Behind Closed Doors: Violence in the American Family*. New York: Doubleday/Anchor.

Suhayda, Joseph N. and Nedra Korevec. 2001. "Community Haven: Building Resilience to Hurricane Flooding." Paper presented at the National Hurricane Conference,

Washington, D.C., April 12. <http://www.lwrri.lsu.edu/1998_2002WEB/down loads/NHC_JNS.ppt>

Taylor, Peter J. and R. E. Lang. 2006. "U.S. Cities in the World City Network," in Peter J. Taylor, Ben Derudder, Piet Saey, and Frank Witlox, eds., *Cities in Globalization: Practices, Policies, and Theories*. London: Cambridge University Press.

———. 2005. "U.S. Cities in the World City Network." Center on Urban and Metropolitan Policy Survey Series. Washington, D.C.: Brookings Institution, February.

Tedeschi, Bob. 2006. "City Hall Gets More Efficient, Despite a Hurricane (or Two)." *New York Times*, April 5, G5.

Thevenot, Brian. 2005. "Race, Class on Everyone's Mind." *New Orleans Times-Picayune*, October 2. <www.nola.com>

Thomas, Greg. "Panel: Rebuilding Must Be Visionary; Plan Should Focus on 'New Urbanism'." *New Orleans Times-Picayune*, November 13. <www.nola.com>

Throsby, David. 2001. *Economics and Culture*. New York: Cambridge University Press.

Tierney, Kathleen. 2006. "Social Inequality, Hazards, and Disasters." In Ronald J. Daniels, Donald F. Kettl, and Howard Kunreuther, eds., *On Risk and Disaster: Lessons from Hurricane Katrina*. Philadelphia: University of Pennsylvania Press.

Toole, John Kennedy. 1980. *A Confederacy of Dunces*. Baton Rouge: Louisiana State University Press.

Tourism Concern. 2005. *Post-Tsunami Reconstruction and Tourism: A Second Disaster?* London: Tourism Concern. January 25. <www.tourismconcern.org.uk>

Turner, M. A. 2006. "Building Opportunity and Equity into the New New Orleans: A Framework for Policy and Action." <http://www.urban.org/publications/900 930.html>

Twain, Mark, 1883. *Life on the Mississippi*. Boston: James R. Osgood.

UNESCO. 2000. *World Culture Report 2000: Cultural Diversity, Conflict, and Pluralism*. Paris: UNESCO.

UN Development Programme. 2003. Sustainable Sri Lankan Cities Programme, "Tools to Support Participatory Urban Decision Making." Paris: UNDP.

UN High Commission for Refugees. 2005. November 22. <www.unhcr.org> Vicksburg, Miss.: Waterways Experiment Station.

U.S. Army Corps of Engineers. 2006. Atchafalaya River Navigation Book. <www .mvn.usace.army.mil/atchafalaya/hydro.html>

———. 2000. *Design and Construction of Levees*. Washington, D.C.: USACE.

———. 1984. *Lake Pontchartrain, Louisiana, and Vicinity Hurricane Protection Project: Reevaluation Study*. New Orleans: USACE, July.

———. No date. *The Mississippi Basin Model*.

U.S. Department of Health and Human Services, Administration on Children, Youth and Families. 2005a. *Child Maltreatment: 2003*. Washington, D.C.: U.S. Government Printing Office.

U.S. Department of Health and Human Services, Office of Inspector General. 2005b. *State Standards and Practices for Content of Caseworker Visits with Children in Foster Care*. Washington, D.C.: U.S. Government Printing Office.

U.S. Department of Housing and Urban Development (HUD) and U.S. Bureau of the Census. 2005. *American Housing Survey for the New Orleans Metropolitan Area: 2004: Current Housing Reports*. Washington, D.C.

U.S. General Accounting Office. 1996. "Disaster Assistance, Improvements Needed in Determining Eligibility for Public assistance." Washington, D.C.

———. 1992. "Earthquake Recovery Staffing and Other Improvements Following the Loma Prieta Earthquake." Washington, D.C.

———. 1991. "Disaster Assistance Federal State and Local Responses to Natural Disasters Need Improvement." Washington, D.C.

———. 1990. "Loma Prieta Earthquake Collapse of the Bay Bridge and Cypress Viaduct." Washington, D.C.

———.1976. *Cost, Schedule, and Performance Problems of the Lake Pontchartrain and Vicinity, Louisiana, Hurricane Protection Project*. PSAD-76–161. Washington, D.C.: U.S. GAO, August 31.

U.S. House of Representatives. 2006. *A Failure of Initiative: Final Report of the Select Bipartisan Committee to Investigate the Preparation for and Response to Hurricane Katrina*. Washington, D.C.: U.S. Government Printing Office.

———. 1965. Lake Pontchartrain and Vicinity, Louisiana. House Document 231. Washington, D.C.: U.S. Government Printing Office, July 6.

U.S. House of Representatives, Committee on Ways and Means. 2004. *2004 Green Book: Background Material and Data on the Programs Within the Jurisdiction of the Committee on Ways and Means*. Washington, D.C.: U.S. House of Representatives, Committee on Ways and Means.

U.S. House of Representatives. 2005. Louisiana Recovery Corporation Act. H.R. 4100. Sponsored by Rep. Baker.

University of Pennsylvania School of Design. 2004. *Toward an American Spatial Development Perspective*. Philadelphia: Department of City and Regional Planning, University of Pennsylvania. <http://www.rpa.org/pdf/TowardASDfinal.pdf>

Upton, Dell. 1995. "New Orleans: Domestic Social Space." In Mark P. Leone and Neil Asher Silberman, eds., *Invisible America: Unearthing our Hidden History*. New York: Henry Holt.

Urban Development Authority. 2005. "Proposed Housing Projects for the Affected Families, Hambantota District." Colombo: UDA.

Urban Land Institute. 2006. "Report of the ULI Advisory Workshop on New Orleans Housing Policy." Working Draft, February 17.

Vale, Lawrence J. 2005. "New Orleans Will Rise Again." Op-ed, *Boston Globe*, September 25.

Vale, Lawrence J. and Thomas J. Campanella. 2005a. "The City Shall Rise Again: Urban Resilience in the Wake of Disaster." *Chronicle of Higher Education*, January 14, B6-B9.

———. 2005b. *The Resilient City: How Modern Cities Recover from Disaster*. New York: Oxford University Press.

Vlach, John Michael. 2002. *Raised to the Trade: Creole Building Arts of New Orleans: Teachers Manual*. New Orleans: New Orleans Museum of Art.

———. 1986. "The Shotgun House: An African Architectural Legacy." In Dell

Upton and John Michael Vlach, eds., *Common Places: Readings in American Vernacular Architecture.* Athens: University of Georgia Press.

Vlahos, Kelley Beaucar. 2006. "FEMA Defends Trailer Purchase." FoxNews.Com (February 20). <http://www.foxnews.com/story/0,2933,185369,00.html> (accessed February 20, 2006).

Von Winterfeldt, Detlof. 2006. "Using Risk and Decision Analysis to Protect New Orleans Against Future Hurricanes." In Ronald J. Daniels, Donald F. Kettl, and Howard Kunreuther, eds., *On Risk and Disaster: Lessons from Hurrican Katrina.* Philadelphia: University of Pennsylvania Press.

Walsh, Bill. 2006."New Orleans Public Housing Still in Limbo." *New Orleans Times-Picayune,* March 28. <http://www.nola.com>

Webster P. J., G. J. Holland, J. A. Curry, and H. R. Chang. 2005. "Changes in Tropical Cyclone Number, Duration, and Intensity in a Warming Environment." *Science* 309 (5742): 1844–46.

Weitz, Jerry. 1999. *Sprawl Busting: State Programs to Guide Growth.* Chicago: American Planning Association.

Wells, H. G. 1920. *The Outline of History, Being a Plain History of Life and Mankind.* New York: Macmillan.

White, Michael. 2004. *Dancing in the Sky* Basin Street Records: New Orleans.

Whitelaw, W. E. 1980. "Measuring the Effects of Public Policy on the Price of Urban Land." In J. Thomas Black and James E. Hoben, eds., *Urban Land Markets: Price Indices, Supply Measures, and Public Policy Effects.* ULI Research Report 30. Washington, D.C.: Urban Land Institute.

Williams, Raymond. 1985. *Keywords* Rev. ed. New York: Oxford University Press.

Winchester, S. 2005. "Before the Flood." *New York Times,* September 8. <http://select.nytimes.com>

Wolshon, Brian. 2002. "Planning for the Evacuation of New Orleans." *ITE Journal* 72 (2): 44–49.

World Bank. 2005. "Tsunami Recovery in Sri Lanka: An Enormous Task But Signs of Progress." October 21. <http://web.worldbank.org/WBSITE/EXTERNAL/NEWSOctober 21>

Zandi, Mark. 2005. "Hurricane Katrina: The Economic Fallout." *Regional Financial Review,* August–September. <economy.com>

# ACKNOWLEDGMENTS

*Rebuilding Urban Places After Disaster: Lessons from Hurricane Katrina* is the second of two books by the University of Pennsylvania Press that address the key challenges posed by Hurricane Katrina. While the first volume, *On Risk and Disaster*, sought to identify lessons from Katrina about how to best prevent and manage risks from future disasters, this volume focuses on what must be done now and how we can do better next time. Both volumes drew their inspiration from University of Pennsylvania President Gutmann's issuance of the Penn Compact—an urgent call for societal engagement at the University. This work is the result of a timely and exceptional scholarly collaboration between policy makers, scientists, and academicians across multiple disciplines and is the outgrowth of "Rebuilding Urban Places After Disaster: Lessons from Hurricane Katrina," convened by the University of Pennsylvania on February 2–3, 2006. Participants explored the complex process of rebuilding urban communities in the wake of disaster. More than 300 academics and students, many from the Penn community, as well as policy makers, advocates, and Gulf Coast residents, joined in the symposium.

We are delighted to have this volume as part of The City in the Twenty-First Century book series of Penn's Institute for Urban Research (IUR), and we are deeply grateful for the effort it took to make it happen. We thank those who contributed to the symposium and who connected it to on-the-ground rebuilding, such as the "Penn on the Front Lines" panel, who shared with the audience the extraordinary work of the Penn community in disaster response. Likewise, a special thanks to native New Orleanians Eddie Bo, craftsman and musician, and Earl Barthè, traditional plasterer, who expressed the importance of building upon the unique cultural strengths of New Orleans and the Gulf Coast throughout the rebuilding process. Also, thank you to Provost Lester Lefton of Tulane who brought a sensational group from Tulane— Yvette Jones, Paul Barron, and Reed Kroloff—and Tom Bonner from Xavier to the symposium to share the experiences of two universities trying to rebuild their campus and their city.

The Institute is grateful for the continual support of its Advisory Board. We extend special thanks to members of the board who contributed to the symposium: Paul Farmer, Executive Director, American Planning Association; Marc Morial, President and CEO of the National Urban League; Chief John F. Timoney, Miami Police Department; and Marilyn Jordan Taylor, Chairman of the Urban Land Institute. We also thank the U.S. Geological Survey for its support of the symposium and Penn's Science Impact Lab for Urban Systems (SILUS).

There are so many individuals and organizations that have helped produce this volume. To the authors, who labored under extraordinarily tight timelines to produce thought-provoking, timely material, we are incredibly grateful for your contributions. It was a privilege and a pleasure to work with you all. And without Amy Montgomery, program consultant for IUR, none of this would have been possible.

The Institute for Urban Research is indebted to Provost Ronald Daniels and Lois Chiang, Executive Director of the Provost's Office. Your enduring support was invaluable to the completion of this volume and the overwhelming success of the symposium. We also thank Jelani Newton from IUR for his assistance with the symposium.

We would also like to thank the many individuals from across the University who provided for both the symposium and the volume: the deans of all twelve schools, who supported this endeavor from the start, advising the Provost as to the wealth of talent that existed within the Penn community; Assistant to the President, Stephen Steinberg; Director of Media Relations, Ron Ozio, and News Officers, Julie McWilliams and Jacquie Posey; *Almanac* editor, Marguerite Miller; and the University of Pennsylvania Press Publicity and Public Relations Manager, Ellen Trachtenberg.

To the leadership and staff and Penn Press, particularly Eric Halpern and Peter Agree, we simply could not have produced this manuscript without your expertise and guidance. Their assistant Laura Miller has been indispensable, and to Edward J. Blum, our development editor: you outdid yourself once again. Your thoroughness and thoughtfulness are evident on every page of this volume.

The views expressed in this volume are those of the individual authors and not those of our sponsor organizations.

# CONTRIBUTORS

ELIJAH ANDERSON is Charles and William L. Day Distinguished Professor of the Social Sciences and Professor of Sociology at the University of Pennsylvania. He is the author of the classic work, *A Place on the Corner: A Study of Black Street Corner Men*, *Streetwise: Race, Class, and Change in an Urban Community*, for which he was honored by the American Sociological Association with the Robert E. Park Award for the best published book in the area of Urban Sociology, and *Code of the Street: Decency, Violence, and the Moral Life of the Inner City*, winner of the Komarovsky Award of the Eastern Sociological Society. He also has made appearances on the *Jim Lehrer Newshour* and has written for the *New York Times Book Review* and the *Atlantic Monthly*, among other publications. He is director of the Philadelphia Ethnography Project, and his current work concerns how Philadelphians live "diversity" in everyday life.

JONATHAN BARNETT, Professor of Practice in City and Regional Planning and Director of the Urban Design Program at the University of Pennsylvania, also practices urban design as a professional in charge at Wallace Roberts & Todd, LLC in Philadelphia. He was part of the WRT team retained to prepare the initial reconstruction plan for New Orleans. He has been an advisor to many cities on urban design, has written well-known books and articles about the history, theory, and practice of urban design, and is a fellow of both the American Institute of Certified Planners and the American Institute of Architects.

JOHN BECKMAN, AICP, is a principal at Wallace Roberts & Todd, LLC. He is responsible for a variety of large-scale planning work including neighborhoods, cities, and the institutions that support them. He has completed major planning projects in most of the ten largest cities in the United States and many smaller towns and communities. He was Principal-in-Charge of the Action Plan for Rebuilding New Orleans, prepared for the Bring New Orleans Back Commission.

EUGENIE L. BIRCH, co-Director, Penn Institute for Urban Research, is Lawrence C. Nussdorf Professor in Urban Research and Education and Chair of the Department of City and Regional Planning at the University of Pennsylvania School of Design. Professor Birch has published widely in two fields: history of planning, and contemporary planning and housing. She is currently engaged in a longitudinal study of downtown living, with her most recent work in this area published by the Brookings Institution Metropolitan Policy Center. Other articles have appeared the *Journal of Urban History*, *Journal of Planning Education and Research*, *Journal of the American Planning Association*, and *Planning* magazine. She was President of the Association of Collegiate Schools of Planning, coedited the *Journal of the American Planning Association*, and is currently chair of the Planning Accreditation Board. From 1990 through 1995, she was a member of the New York City Planning Commission. In 2002, she served on the jury to select the designers of the World Trade Center site. Elected to the American Institute of Certified Planners College of Fellows, she is also a Fellow, Urban Land Institute and a member of the board of New York's Municipal Art Society.

RAYMOND J. BURBY is Professor of City and Regional Planning at the University of North Carolina at Chapel Hill, associate editor of *Natural Hazards Review*, and former coeditor of the *Journal of the American Planning Association*. From 1992 to 2000 he was a Distinguished Professor of City and Regional Planning and held the John M. DeBlois Chair in Urban and Public Affairs at the University of New Orleans. His research focuses on issues related to land use, natural hazards, and environmental quality.

STEVEN COCHRANE is managing director at Moody's Economy.com, where he directs the firm's regional economics service. He manages a large-scale econometric system of regional models which are used to provide projections of economic, demographic, real estate, and financial indicators. He is editor of *Regional Financial Review*, the Moody's Economy.com monthly publication that analyzes current macro, regional, industry, and international economic trends. He is also a frequent contributor to economy.com's Dismal Scientist website, where he comments on a variety of macroeconomic and regional economic issues. Dr. Cochrane received his Ph.D. in regional science from the University of Pennsylvania, his master's degree from the University of Colorado, and his bachelor's degree from the University of California at Davis.

DILIP DA CUNHA is an architect and city planner. He is on the faculty at Parsons School of Design, New York, and visiting faculty at University of Pennsylvania. He received a Ph.D. from the University of California at Berkeley and master's degrees from Massachusetts Institute of Technology and School of Planning and Architecture, New Delhi. He is principal in the practice, Mathur/da Cunha and author with Anuradha Mathur of *Mississippi Floods: Designing a Shifting Landscape* and *Deccan Traverses: The Making of Bangalore's Terrain*.

RONALD J. DANIELS, Provost of the University of Pennsylvania, is the author of numerous scholarly articles and books. His scholarly interests lie in the law and economics of the corporation and the regulatory state. His current scholarship focuses on the challenges of building strong laws and legal institutions on developing states. His most recent publications include, as coauthor, *Rethinking the Welfare: Government by Voucher* and *The Political Economy of Rule of Law Reform in Developing Countries*. He is active in public policy formulation and has contributed to several Canadian public task forces.

THOMAS L. DANIELS is a Professor in the Department of City and Regional Planning at the University of Pennsylvania. He teaches land use planning and environmental planning, and is the coauthor of *The Environmental Planning Handbook*, published by the American Planning Association.

BARBARA FAGA, FASLA, is Chair of the Board of EDAW—environmental, economic, planning, and design consultants with 1200 employees and 28 offices worldwide. Projects include the Tax Allocation District (TAD) Feasibility Study and Redevelopment Plan for the Atlanta BeltLine; Diagonal Mar Parc, Barcelona; Schuykill River master plan, Philadelphia; and the Wharf District Park Plan of the Rose Fitzgerald Kennedy Greenway, the park over the $15-billion Big-Dig in Boston. She was named one of the top 15 women changing the world of architecture by DesignIntelligence in 2005. She is author of *Designing Public Consensus: The Civic Theater of Community Participation for Architects, Planners, and Urban Designers*. She attended Michigan State University and Georgia Institute of Technology.

KENNETH R. FOSTER is Professor of Bioengineering at the University of Pennsylvania. He has written extensively about risk assessment, and teaches a course on engineering ethics. He is a registered professional engineer, and Past President of the Society on Social Implications of Technology of the Institute of Electrical and Electronics Engineers.

VIVIAN L. GADSDEN is Associate Professor of Education and Director of the National Center on Fathers and Families at the University of Pennsylvania. She also has chaired the Penn Symposia on Equity, Access, and Race. She studies intergenerational learning and life-course development among vulnerable children and families in school, home, and community contexts. Her scholarly work includes a forthcoming volume on incarcerated parents and their children as well as numerous articles and edited volumes on literacy and learning; schooling; parent-child and father-child engagement in low-income and minority families; and issues of race, gender, and class.

RICHARD J. GELLES is Dean of the School of Social Policy & Practice at the University of Pennsylvania and holds the Joanne and Raymond Welsh Chair of Child Welfare and Family Violence in the School of Social Work at the University of Pennsylvania. He is Director of the Center for the Research on Youth and Social Policy, co-Director of the Field Center for Children's Policy, Practice, and Research, and Director of the Ortner-Unity Program on Family Violence. His book *The Violent Home* was the first systematic empirical investigation of family violence and continues to be highly influential. He is author or coauthor of 25 books and more than 100 articles and chapters on family violence. His recent books include *The Book of David: How Preserving Families Can Cost Children's Lives*, *Intimate Violence in Families*, and *Current Controversies on Family Violence*.

ROBERT GIEGENGACK is currently Davidson Kennedy Professor in the College, and Professor of Earth & Environmental Science in the School of Arts and Sciences at the University of Pennsylvania. He studies the long-term history of variation in climate to extend our observational baseline deeper into the past than is accessible from the instrumental record of atmospheric variables. He teaches undergraduate and graduate courses in environmental science, geology, palaeoclimatology, and environmental geology. He has been a member of the faculty at Penn for 38 years.

AMY GUTMANN took office in July 2004 as the eighth president of the University of Pennsylvania, where she also holds faculty appointments in Political Science, Communication, Philosophy, and Education. She came to Penn from Princeton University, where she served as Provost (2001–2004), Laurance S. Rockefeller University Professor of Politics (1990–2004), Academic Advisor to the President (1997–98), Dean of the Faculty (1995–97), and was Founding Director of the University Center for Human Values. She is a former President of the American Society of Political and Legal Philosophy, a Fellow of the American Academy of Arts and Sciences, W. E. B. Du Bois Fellow of the American Academy of Political and Social Science, a Member of the American Philosophical Society, and a Fellow of the National Academy of Education. She serves on the Board of Directors of the Carnegie Corporation and in 2005 was appointed to the National Security Higher Education Advisory Board, a committee that advises the FBI on national security issues relating to academia. In 2003, she was awarded the Centennial Medal by Harvard University for "graduate alumni who have made exceptional contributions to society." She has published more than 100 articles and essays and edited books in political philosophy, practical ethics, and education that have been translated into many languages. Her most recent books include *Why Deliberative Democracy?* (with Dennis Thompson), *Identity in Democracy*,

*Democratic Education*, *Democracy and Disagreement* (with Dennis Thompson), and *Color Conscious* (with K. Anthony Appiah). Her reviews have appeared in the *New York Times Book Review*, *Times Literary Supplement*, *Washington Post*, and other general publications.

GARY HACK is Dean and Paley Professor of the School of Design of the University of Pennsylvania, a multidisciplinary school that includes architecture, city and regional planning, landscape architecture, historic preservation, and fine arts. He teaches, practices, and writes about urban design internationally. He has recently stepped down from chairing the Philadelphia City Planning Commission, and has served on numerous boards and commissions over his 40-year career.

YVETTE M. JONES is Chief Operating Officer and Senior Vice President for External Affairs at Tulane University, where she is responsible for all day-to-day administrative functions and externally related activities at the University. She is the senior officer responsible for institutional advancement and the University's $700 million campaign; federal, state, and local government relations; public relations and university communications; technology transfer and business development; institutional research; and strategic and campus planning.

FILLIP KSIAZKIEWICZ is an Associate Economist with Moody's Economy.com. He has a B.A. in Economics from the University of Alberta, and has completed all but the thesis requirement for a Master's Degree in Economics. He has previously worked as an Economic Analyst for Alberta Finance and as a Researcher for the Department of Justice in Canada.

ROBERT E. LANG is Director of the Metropolitan Institute at Virginia Tech and Associate Professor in the Tech School of Planning and International Affairs. He is currently a Distinguished Visiting Professor in Arizona State University's School of Public Affairs and Fellow of the Urban Land Institute. He is also coeditor of *Opolis*, the first academic journal focused on suburban studies, associate editor of *Housing Policy Debate*, and book review editor for the *Journal of the American Planning Association*.

P. PATRICK LEAHY was appointed Acting Director of the U.S. Geological Survey, U.S. Department of the Interior, on June 20, 2005. He previously served as the USGS Associate Director for Geology, where he was responsible for basic earth science programs, including worldwide earthquake hazard monitoring and research, geologic mapping of land and seafloor resources, volcano and landslide hazards, and assessments of energy and mineral resources. He holds undergraduate and graduate degrees in geology and geophysics from Boston College, and a doctorate in geology from Rensselaer Polytechnic Institute.

LESTER A. LEFTON is Senior Vice President for Academic Affairs and Provost of Tulane University. He is responsible for overseeing the University's 10 deans and more than 550 faculty members on its uptown campus, as well as the graduate school, libraries, and international programs. Noted for his energetic teaching style and his widely used introductory psychology textbook in its eighth edition, he is known for his active involvement with undergraduate students and his interest in higher education issues.

JEFFREY LUBELL is Executive Director of the Center for Housing Policy. Prior to coming to the Center, he served as Director of the Policy Development Division in the Office of Policy Development and Research at the U.S. Department of Housing and Urban Development, as a housing policy analyst at the Center on Budget and Policy Priorities, and as a consultant working on housing and asset-building issues. He is a graduate of Harvard Law School and Harvard College.

RANDALL MASON is Associate Professor at the University of Pennsylvania School of Design, where he teaches in the Graduate Program in Historic Preservation. He worked previously at the Getty Conservation Institute and the University of Maryland, and holds a doctorate from Columbia University. His research and practice focuses on urban history, economic and social issues surrounding contemporary historic preservation, and vernacular memorials. He is currently completing a book about the origins of historic preservation in New York City, entitled *Memory Infrastructure*.

ANURADHA MATHUR is an architect and landscape architect and Associate Professor at the School of Design, University of Pennsylvania. She is coauthor with Dilip da Cunha of *Mississippi Floods: Designing a Shifting Landscape* and *Deccan Traverses: The Making of Bangalore's Terrain*.

ARTHUR C. NELSON is Professor and Director of Urban Affairs and Planning at Virginia Tech's Alexandria Center, associate director of the Metropolitan Institute, and associate editor of the *Journal of the American Planning Association*. His research focuses on issues related to land use, urban containment, public finance, and metropolitan governance.

THOMAS W. SANCHEZ is an Associate Professor of Urban Affairs and Planning at Virginia Tech's Alexandria Center, research fellow with the Metropolitan Institute at Virginia Tech, and nonresident senior fellow at the Brookings Institution in Washington, D.C. He holds a Ph.D. in City Planning from the Georgia Institute of Technology. His research is in the areas of transportation, land use, and questions of social equity in planning.

JAMES SIPES is an award-winning landscape architect with more than twenty-five years of experience encompassing a wide range of planning, design, research, and communication projects. His work is broad-based and multi-faceted and includes environmental planning and design, watershed management, park and recreation design, urban design, natural and cultural resource management, and community-based design. Jim has received national recognition for his writing, has written more than 200 articles for a variety of publications, and recently received the Bradford Williams Medal award for outstanding writing. He is currently a Senior Associate with EDAW.

SANDY SORLIEN, a Philadelphia native, teaches a course called "The Photography of Urban Place" at PennDesign and is the author of the photographic book *Fifty Houses: Images from the American Road*. In a parallel career as a code writer and photographer for the New Urbanists, she was head of the Coding Team at the Mississippi Renewal Forum, a massive post-Katrina planning charrette for eleven devastated cities. Since then she has returned to the Gulf Coast three times to give SmartCode follow-up seminars and will return twice more this month, for charrettes in Gulfport and Pass Christian, Mississippi.

LELAND R. SPEED is Executive Director of the Mississippi Development Authority. He is involved in the recovery and rebuilding efforts in Mississippi. Prior to his association with the Development Authority, he founded East-Group Properties and Parkway Properties; both publicly traded Real Estate Investment Trusts.

NICK SPITZER is Professor of Folklore and Cultural Conservation at the University of New Orleans. He is also a documentary media producer and creator of *American Routes*, the nationally syndicated public radio program devoted to music and culture of New Orleans and the Gulf South. Spitzer, who has worked in Afro-Creole communities of rural French Louisiana and urban New Orleans for three decades, has written extensively, produced ethnographic films, made sound recordings, and curated museum exhibits on the topic of cultural creolization and music, including jazz and zydeco. Spitzer is known for his work in cultural policy and with Afro-Creole community-based traditions in music, Mardi Gras, and the building arts.

HARRIS STEINBERG is Executive Director of PennPraxis, the clinical practice arm of the School of Design of the University of Pennsylvania. Steinberg is an adjunct assistant professor of architecture at Penn, a member of the Philadelphia Historical Commission and a fellow of the American Institute of Architects.

FREDERICK STEINER is Dean of the School of Architecture and Henry M. Rockwell Chair in Architecture, University of Texas at Austin. Previously, he was director of the School of Planning and Landscape Architecture, College of Architecture and Environmental Design, Arizona State University (ASU) and taught planning, landscape architecture, and environmental science at Washington State University, University of Colorado-Denver, and the University of Pennsylvania. In 1998 he was the National Endowment for the Arts Rome Prize Fellow in Historic Preservation and Conservation at the American Academy in Rome. He received his Ph.D. and M.A. degrees in city and regional planning and a Master of Regional Planning from the University of Pennsylvania. He earned a Master of Community Planning and a B.S. in Design from the University of Cincinnati.

RYAN SWEET is an Assistant Economist with Moody's Economy.com. He received a M.A. in Economics from the University of Delaware and a B.A. in Economics from Washington College.

DELL UPTON is David A. Harrison III Professor of Architectural History and Anthropology at the University of Virginia, where he has taught since 2002. For twenty years before that he was professor of architectural history at the University of California, Berkeley. Upton's most recent book is *Architecture in the United States*. He is currently completing a study of urban space and citizenship in early nineteenth-century Philadelphia, New York, and New Orleans.

LAWRENCE J. VALE is Professor of Urban Design and Planning, and Head of the Department of Urban Studies and Planning at MIT. He is the author of three prize-winning books about urban design and public housing: *Architecture, Power, and National Identity*, *From the Puritans to the Projects*, and *Reclaiming Public Housing* Most recently he is coeditor, with Thomas J. Campanella, of *The Resilient City: How Modern Cities Recover from Disaster*.

SUSAN M. WACHTER is co-Director, Penn Institute for Urban Research and Richard B. Worley Professor of Financial Management and Professor of Real Estate and Finance at the Wharton School of the University of Pennsylvania. She has taught at Wharton since 1972 and served as chair of its Real Estate Department from 1997 to 1999. She studies real estate economics, urban economics, and housing finance. She served as Assistant Secretary for

Policy Development and Research at the U.S. Department of Housing and Urban Development from 1999 to 2001. As director of the Wharton GIS Lab, she is a national expert in housing analysis and the first woman to head the American Real Estate Urban Economics Association. She is currently researching default and delinquency models, tenure choice and homeownership affordability, real estate price index methodologies, and the modeling of neighborhood change.

RACHEL WEINBERGER is Assistant Professor of City and Regional Planning at the University of Pennsylvania. A planning practitioner for over 15 years, she has only recently joined academia. Her areas of interest and expertise revolve around transportation and economic development, transportation, and equity and the use of transportation infrastructure as a tool with which to shape urban places, at both regional and local scales. She has written on the effects of transportation infrastructure on local property values, gender differences in commute times, and transportation and location choice. Her primary current research seeks to understand how transportation fund distribution policies affect transportation outcomes.

ROBERT YARO is the President of Regional Plan Association. Headquartered in Manhattan and founded in 1922, RPA is America's oldest and most respected independent metropolitan research and advocacy group. He is also Practice Professor in City and Regional Planning at the University of Pennsylvania. He chairs the Civic Alliance to Rebuild Downtown New York, a broad-based coalition of civic groups formed to guide redevelopment in Lower Manhattan in the aftermath of September 11. He is coauthor of *A Region at Risk* and *Dealing with Change in the Connecticut River Valley*.

MARK ZANDI is Chief Economist and cofounder of Moody's Economy .com, Inc., where he directs the company's research and consulting activities. Moody's Economy.com, an independent subsidiary of the Moody's Corporation, provides economic research and consulting services to businesses, governments, and other institutions. He was educated at the University of Pennsylvania, where he did his Ph.D. research with Nobel laureate Lawrence Klein and Gerard Adams.